MAKERS
of the United States
AIR FORCE

John L. Frisbee

AIR
FORCE
History
Museums
PROGRAM

1996

Library of Congress Cataloging-In-Publication Data

Makers of the United States Air Force.

    (USAF warrior studies)
    Bibliography: P.
    Includes index.
    1. Aeronautics, Military—Unites States—Biography.   2. United
States Air Force—Biography. I. Frisbee, John L., 1916-   . II. Series.
UG626.M35 1987   358.4'0092'2 [B]   87-600206
ISBN 0-912799-41-2 (pbk.)

Reprinted 1996. Originally published by the Office of Air Force History, United States Air Force, Washington, D.C., 1987

On cover (*from left to right, top to bottom*): Bernard A. Schriever, Nathan F. Twining, Frank M. Andrews, George C. Kenney, Hugh J. Knerr, Hoyt S. Vandenberg, Benjamin D. Foulois, Robinson Risner, William E. Kepner, Harold L. George, Benjamin O. Davis, Elwood R. Quesada.

For sale by the U.S. Government Printing Office
Superintendent of Documents, Mail Stop: SSOP, Washington, DC 20402-9328
ISBN 0-16-048757-9

Foreword

The fiftieth anniversary of the United States Air Force offers us an opportunity to recognize and appreciate the role that a number of gifted military and aviation pioneers played in shaping the world's only global air and space force.

This book, a joint product of the Air Force History and Museums Program and the Air Force Historical Foundation, was first published in 1987. It has proven an indispensable reference work for anyone interested in the history of the service and, particularly, in the role that key individuals have played in its evolution. Many of the individuals profiled in this book are well-known to students of air and space power. Most had notable combat careers. Others were organizers, men who shaped the service according to far-seeing vision. They are a diverse bunch of over-achievers, many of whom were strongly opinionated, even about each other. But all of them were dedicated to an ideal: to produce a new form of military force, a force that would achieve victory in war by exploitation and dominance of the third dimension. In this, they were totally and uncompromisingly unified, a band of brothers who took this vision from the ground and brought it, with devastating force, to the skies of America's enemies. On this, the Air Force's Golden Anniversary, all Americans owe them our grateful appreciation.

Richard P. Hallion
Air Force Historian

Preface

Almost a decade ago, a military history book program was started under the auspices of the Air Force Historical Foundation to identify and recognize those general officers who helped shape the United States Air Force into a separate service and those who played a major role in making it the great aerospace power that it is today. Two outstanding books by the noted author DeWitt S. Copp were published in 1980 and 1982. The first, *A Few Great Captains*, described the key roles played by such daring and dedicated men as Hap Arnold, Frank Andrews, Tooey Spaatz, Ira Eaker, Billy Mitchell, and Benny Foulois in the turbulent years of the 1920s and 1930s. A second, *Forged In Fire*, dealt with World War II politics, the military strategies developed during that conflict, and the problems associated with developing an independent Air Force. Again Arnold, Spaatz, Eaker, and Andrews were the major players.

Spurred on by the critical acclaim that was given to these books, the Air Force Historical Foundation recently sponsored three major biographies on Generals Eaker, LeMay, and Spaatz. Thomas M. Coffey's *Iron Eagle* provides a revealing and sensitive insight into the outstanding career of one of the Air Force's greatest air commanders, General Curtis E. LeMay, covering his outstanding leadership during World War II and later as Chief of Staff, United States Air Force. James Parton, who was General Ira C. Eaker's aide in England during World War II, has written *Air Force Spoken Here*, a full-scale biography that describes General Eaker's role in building the mighty Eighth Air Force and his successful crusade for a strong national defense and a separate Air Force. The biography of General Carl A. Spaatz, "Ike's Eagle," by David Mets is scheduled for publication in 1987.

Realizing that it takes more than a handful of leaders to ensure the creation, growth, and continuing success of the Air Force, the Foundation decided to produce an anthology in which it identified twelve unique individuals whose careers provide penetrating and valuable insights into those major elements that give new meaning to the definition of leadership. After much reflection, twelve outstanding leaders—Hoyt Vandenberg, Nathan Twining,

George Kenney, Bernard Schriever, Frank Andrews, Benjamin Davis, Harold George, William Kepner, Elwood Quesada, Benjamin Foulois, Hugh Knerr, and Robbie Risner—were selected for inclusion in this anthology. While it was recognized that many other individuals also merit special note for their distinguished Air Force accomplishments, it was decided that the careers of the above-mentioned twelve general officers best represented a cross-section of Air Force leadership and the unique problems they faced during the last half century. In both peace and war they faced challenges that brought out the best in each of them, and their accomplishments, encompassing everything from combat operations to high command, have produced some of the major milestones in the history of military aviation.

After reading the stories of these distinguished officers whose lives and careers are briefly captured in this book, it will be apparent that each one reflected, at one time or another, many of those important traits to be found in most successful leaders and general officers. These included ability, charisma, confidence, courage, dedication, experience, and initiative, as well as intelligence, integrity, knowledge, loyalty, managerial capability, personality, pride, sensitivity to the welfare of subordinates, and willingness to accept responsibility. Such traits provided the framework for developing leaders their country could depend upon and trust.

The Air Force Historical Foundation is deeply grateful to the United States Air Force, and particularly to the Office of Air Force History, for publishing this anthology as one of its Warrior Studies. The Foundation also wishes to express its gratitude and thanks to the Aerospace Educational Foundation for its strong support and major financial contribution toward the successful research, writing, and publication of this anthology. The Air Force Historical Foundation believes that it is essential reading for each officer, noncommissioned officer, and airman aspiring to a place of leadership in the Air Force.

Brian S. Gunderson
Brig. Gen., USAF, Ret.
President
Air Force Historical Foundation

Acknowledgments

The preparation of this book was supported by grants from the Air Force Historical Foundation and the Aerospace Education Foundation, a non-profit affiliate of the Air Force Association. Publication was sponsored and administered by the Office of Air Force History.

Special thanks are due to retired Lt. Gen. John B. McPherson, who conceived the idea of short biographies of Air Force leaders on whom full-length biographies have not been published, at least recently. At the time, General McPherson was President of the Air Force Historical Foundation. He has provided constant encouragement and advice throughout the preparation of the manuscript, as have his successor, Brig. Gen. Brian S. Gunderson, USAF (Ret.), and retired Col. Louis H. Cummings, Executive Director of the Foundation.

Gen. Russell E. Dougherty, USAF (Ret.), formerly Executive Director of both the Air Force Association and the Aerospace Education Foundation, and his former deputy, Lt. Gen. Andrew B. Anderson, USAF (Ret.), have been enthusiastic supporters of the project, generously contributing both substantive and managerial advice.

Special recognition also goes to Dr. Richard H. Kohn, Chief, Office of Air Force History, for advice, painstaking review of the manuscript, and its final editing. Three members of his professional staff, Col. John F. Shiner, Deputy Chief; Herman Wolk, Chief, General Histories Branch; and Jacob Neufeld, Chief, Air Staff Branch, read the entire manuscript with the discriminating eye of experienced airpower historians, contributing their special insights and detailed knowledge of the men and events described here. Dr. Alfred M. Beck and Ms. Laura L. Hutchinson of the Editorial Branch guided the manuscript through the publication process, and the administrative staff prepared the typescript. Photographs appearing in this volume are primarily from collections at the Department of Defense Still Media Records Center, the National Air and Space Museum, the Library of Congress, and the National Archives. Those sources of illustrations outside official government repositories are noted.

Retired Air Force officers who read all or parts of the manuscript and offered invaluable suggestions are Generals Bryce Poe II and James H. Doolittle, Lt. Gen. Devol Brett, and Maj. Gen. Haywood S. Hansell, all of whom were friends or close associates of many of the men whose careers and contributions to the evolution of the United States Air Force are recounted in the pages that follow.

John L. Frisbee

Contents

Photographs

MAKERS
of the United States
AIR FORCE

1

Introduction:
Men with a Mission

John L. Frisbee

An airplane flying at forty miles an hour could not possibly drop a bomb within half a mile of its target. That was the opinion of Brig. Gen. James Allen, head of the U.S. Army's Signal Corps, which had just added an Aeronautical Division on August 2, 1907. It was not exactly an informed opinion. The Army had no airplanes, and so far as General Allen knew, no one had tried dropping bombs from one of the flying machines then in existence. In fact, some of the Army's staff officers doubted that there really was such a thing as an airplane. The Army did have experience with balloons, however, and dirigibles seemed a better bet for aerial reconnaissance or even bombing.

After some prodding from President Theodore Roosevelt, the Army, with scant enthusiasm, accepted 3 bids in February 1908 for an airplane that would carry 2 people at 40 miles an hour for 125 miles. The Wright brothers were the only ones to show up with a flying machine. They began a series of demonstration flights at Fort Myer, across the Potomac from Washington, in September 1908. On September 17, the plane crashed, severely injuring Orville Wright and killing his passenger, Lt. Thomas Selfridge—the first of many officers who would lose their lives in the long passage from an airplane to an air force.

In June of the following year, the Wrights were back at Fort Myer with an improved machine. On July 30, 1909, the last of a series of demonstrations took place, Lt. Benjamin D. "Benny" Foulois riding along with Orville. The Wright plane was accepted by the Army on August 2, amidst considerable local fanfare but little national attention. The Army's lone plane and the few others that occasionally sputtered into the air were curiosities. Not even the most ardent supporters of aviation foresaw that the descendents of these frail, unreliable machines would transform the nature of warfare more rapidly and more drastically than any other invention in the long history of military affairs.

From the point of view of the Army's handful of aviation enthusiasts, progress in military aviation was painfully slow. In 1910, Benny Foulois, who had taught himself to fly through correspondence with the Wrights, was the Army's only active pilot, flying its only airplane, at Fort Sam Houston, Texas. Neither Congress nor the Army was much interested in what still was regarded as an invention of dubious military worth. Between 1908 and 1913, only $430,000 was appropriated for Army aviation, while Germany and France spent fifty times that amount, and Russia nearly thirty times as much.

In a relative sense, however, compared to the several thousand years of evolution in ground and sea warfare, air power developed very rapidly. When Benny Foulois retired from his post as Chief of the Air Corps at the close of 1935, the B–17 Flying Fortress of World War II fame had completed its test flights and in January 1936, a contract for the first 13 Fortresses was signed by the Army. General Foulois died in 1967, just 6 decades after the Army's Aeronautical Division was formed. At the time of his death, the United States Air Force, which he had helped to create, was equipped with supersonic fighters, bombers with a range of 8,000 miles or more, intercontinental ballistic missiles, and thermonuclear weapons.

But an air force is more than an agglomeration of aircraft, bombs, and bullets. It needs several other elements: a clear understanding of its purpose, or mission; a body of ideas (concepts and doctrine) governing in broad terms how it will carry out its mission; strategy and tactics for the efficient use of its equipment; a system for supplying its material and human needs; a research and development organization to keep ahead of potential enemies; experienced leaders; and sound organization to coordinate and direct its activities. These elements were lacking when the Army's only aviation unit first took to the field on March 15, 1916, commanded by Capt. Benny Foulois. The 1st Aero Squadron was ordered to help Brig. Gen. John J. Pershing scout out the bandit, Pancho Villa, and bring him back from Mexico, dead or alive. The squadron's unarmed, underpowered Curtiss JN–2 biplanes could not make it over the mountains or cope with the strong winds of northern Mexico. By April 20, only two of its eight planes were in commission.

In August 1916, Congress, dismayed by the demonstrated inadequacy of its military aviation in contrast to European air forces that had been in combat for two years, appropriated $13.2 million for the Army's air arm. That act may be regarded as the take-off point for what, thirty-one years later, was to become the United States Air Force. It also was one of several times when the Air Force—and its predecessors—was rescued from financial or organizational doldrums by a poor showing in tasks for which it was not equipped, by the approach of a war for which it was unprepared, or by a clear threat to the country's security.

The men whose stories are told in this book played important roles in developing the elements of air power that were lacking when Benny Foulois led his feeble force on the Mexican border. They were men with a mission—pioneers who earned a place in the history of the Air Force and of this country. Their individual contributions to the making of the United States Air Force are told in the chapters that follow, but first we should look at the constantly changing military-political climate in which they operated and at some of the obstacles that had to be overcome between 1914 and American involvement in the Vietnam War.

During the 4 years of World War I, military aviation grew from infancy to puberty. When the guns of August sounded in 1914, none of the European combatants had an airplane that had been designed for combat use. Their unarmed aircraft had a top speed of about 65 miles an hour and were used initially only for reconnaissance. By the spring of 1918, both sides had armed pursuit planes that flew at 130 miles an hour, and multi-engine bombers with a wing span of 100 feet.

In April 1917 when the United States entered the war, the U.S. Army's air arm numbered about 100 pilots and no combat aircraft. Wildly optimistic plans for darkening the skies of Europe with American-built airplanes fell far short of realization. Of the 740 planes in U.S. front-line units when the war ended, fewer than 200 were made in this country, and those were British-designed DH–4s. Despite a late and inauspicious start, the United States did train about 10,000 pilots during the war, and those who reached the front shot down 781 enemy planes and participated in 150 bombing raids between April 3 and November 11, 1918.

The Army Air Service emerged from the war with a nucleus of experienced airmen, including several whose careers are described in this book. Brig. Gen. Benny Foulois served for a time as Chief of the Air Service, American Expeditionary Force. Harold George, Hugh Knerr, and George Kenney were war-trained pilots—George and Kenney with combat experience. Frank Andrews commanded wartime flying schools. William Kepner, a combat Infantry officer who watched the air battles over France from the ground, decided then that his future lay with the Air Service. These men became key figures in a thirty-year postwar campaign for the separate and independent Air Force that was brought to full maturity by those airmen who appear in the latter part of the book.

The stage for that campaign was set during the war. Before the fighting stopped, a majority of ground officers agreed that air superiority over the battlefield was important, though not decisive. They considered observation

3

to be the primary function of aviation, pursuits the most important type of aircraft (since they could protect friendly observation planes), and bombers merely an extension of artillery. As late as 1928, the General Staff of the Army still gave observation planes priority over bombers at budget time. The Army view of air power was essentially auxiliary; aviation was, and should remain, an extension of ground forces to be controlled by ground officers at division, corps, or field army level.

Many airmen, led by Brig. Gen. Billy Mitchell who was influenced by the ideas of Italian Colonel Giulio Douhet and Britain's Maj. Gen. Hugh Trenchard, saw air power in quite a different light. While not denying the usefulness of observation, pursuit, and short-range bombardment, they believed military aviation's greatest potential lay in its offensive capability: the outcome of a war could be decided by long-range bombers, flying deep into enemy territory to attack airfields, war-supporting industry, and transportation nets in a strategic campaign. That idea was largely theoretical. Only a few strategic bombing missions were flown, and those late in the war. The mobility of aircraft, used either strategically or tactically, and their ability to mass firepower at a decisive point could be exploited, the airmen believed, only if all armed aircraft were centrally controlled by an aviator who understood how to use this new weapon of war effectively.

Battlelines between the Army General Staff and the aviators, who were part of the Army and thus under the General Staff, were drawn by the early 1920s. The major issues of organization, command, doctrine, strategy, and priorities would not be settled completely for many years.

In the early postwar years, several bills for establishment of a separate air force were introduced in Congress. Two of the more vociferous supporters of separation from the Army were the flamboyant Billy Mitchell and the five-foot-seven-inch Benny Foulois, who had been reduced to his permanent rank of major after the war, as had most other officers. Mitchell took his case to the public, while Foulois repeatedly told Congress that a hide-bound, myopic General Staff was thwarting the development of a new and potentially decisive means of national defense. Neither man endeared himself to the General Staff.

Except for his court-martial, Billy Mitchell probably is best remembered for sinking the "unsinkable" German battleship *Ostfriesland* off Cape Hatteras in 1921, to demonstrate the effectiveness of bombers in coastal defense. Harold George was one of the hand-picked pilots of Mitchell's Provisional Brigade. Mitchell and his supporters believed the future of the Air Service lay in strategic air power. In an increasingly isolationist America, the only mission that would justify building a bomber force was coastal defense. The bomber men had something more in mind, but realized that their vision of a long-range strategic force had to await the development of aircraft and engines that were up to that task.

It would be more than a decade before ideas and technology began to mesh. The pitifully small defense budgets of the twenties and thirties provided little support for research; and new airplanes, when there was money for them, came in penny packets. The airmen themselves fared no better. George Kenney, an MIT-trained engineer and a graduate of the Air Service Engineering School, remained a captain for seventeen years—not unusual at that time. Like other competent officers, he could have left the service for a better-paying job with industry or one of the infant airlines, but building a radically new kind of military force was a compelling challenge that held many of the best officers.

There were some mildly encouraging signs of progress toward an independent air force in the two decades following World War I. Several boards and committees recommended establishing a general headquarters (GHQ) air force that would contain all combat aircraft as a compromise between the General Staff's determination to keep control of its air arm, and the airmen who wanted a separate air force. All of those proposals were shelved, while the frustrated airmen turned to some backstairs maneuvering in an attempt to spur congressional action. The issue was finally brought to a head by the Air Corps' poor showing at carrying the mail when President Franklin Roosevelt canceled commercial contracts in 1934. It was obvious that something had to be done to improve the effectiveness of an Air Corps that suffered from underfunding, a lack of standardization, and skewed priorities.

In July 1934, a board headed by former Secretary of War Newton Baker recommended that a GHQ air force be set up immediately, in time of peace rather than as a wartime measure, which previous boards and committees had favored. The General Staff accepted that recommendation, not entirely on its merits but in part to curb further clamor for independence by the Air Corps and its supporters on Capitol Hill. After some delay, the new GHQ Air Force opened its doors at Langley Field, Virginia, on March 1, 1935, under veteran airman Brig. Gen. Frank Andrews. It was a command within the Air Corps, and thus remained part of the Army, but its creation was the single most important step thus far toward independence.

Before the GHQ Air Force, all combat planes were parceled out to the Army's corps area commanders, who were responsible for administering their squadrons and training them according to their personal notions of how air power should be used. By and large, those commanders still held the Army's World War I view of air power as an auxiliary of the ground forces. They were little interested in the ideas of an independent strategic mission for long-range bombers. Now, all operational units would be consolidated in the GHQ Air Force under an experienced airman who was responsible directly to the Army Chief of Staff in peacetime and to a combat theater commander in time of war. Andrews could train his men as they would fight, and develop the strategy, tactics, and organization that soon would be needed in World War II.

The new arrangement was not without shortcomings. While the GHQ Air Force Commander controlled all combat units, the Chief of the Air Corps was responsible only for the flying training schools, procurement of supplies and aircraft, and developing doctrine. This division of responsibility, designed to prevent the Air Corps from gaining too much power, created internal friction until Army Chief of Staff Gen. George C. Marshall gave Air Corps Chief Maj. Gen. Henry H. "Hap" Arnold authority over both the Air Corps and its combat arm in November 1940.

While the GHQ Air Force issue was being threshed out in the early 1930s, two essential building blocks of an effective air force fell into place. First, the vision of a long-range, four-engine bomber, for which Foulois, Andrews, Hugh Knerr, Harold George, and George Kenney had risked their careers, became a reality when the first B–17 completed its test flights in 1935. When Andrews's tenure as Commander of the GHQ Air Force ended in 1939, he was reduced in rank to colonel and banished to a backwater post in Texas, later to be rescued from oblivion by George Marshall. Lt. Col. Hugh Knerr and Maj. George Kenney, both members of Andrews's GHQ Air Force staff, received similar treatment. Fighting for a principle—for a new concept of warfare that challenged traditional Army doctrine—was not the route to rapid promotion or good assignments.

The second building block was carved out at the Air Corps Tactical School, Maxwell Field, Alabama. Between 1934 and 1936, a group of officers headed by Harold George, formalized a comprehensive doctrine of air warfare—or at least of strategic air warfare. A then-novel method of analysis, described in the chapter on Harold George, supported a conclusion that high-altitude, daylight bombing of an enemy's war-supporting industry and transportation systems could win a war. Their conclusions were anathema to all but a few of the Army's ground officers, however. This was offensive warfare, and in the 1930s, military people were discouraged from even discussing such an idea. It took faith and moral courage for Hal George and his colleagues to buck the system. Their heretical ideas were not widely accepted until six months before Pearl Harbor, and then largely because of General Marshall's blessing.

Although most airmen considered the General Staff to be a principal obstacle, all was not harmony within the Air Corps itself. During the 1920s, the pursuit plane had held sway as the supreme instrument of aerial warfare. In the thirties, the pursuit men, led by Claire Chennault and his supporters—among them Hoyt Vandenberg, who was the Tactical School's chief instructor in pursuit tactics, and Bill Kepner—fought a rear-guard action against the bomber advocates and their much-improved B–10s and B–17s. Then there were the impatient, who wanted a completely independent air force immediately, as opposed to the less-impatient, who supported a gradual, step-by-step progress toward separation from the Army. The former group centered around Frank Andrews; the latter around Hap Arnold. Intrigue and infighting over which of these men should lead the Air Corps is recounted in the chapter on Hugh Knerr.

By the eve of World War II, the Air Corps, which became the Army Air Forces on June 20, 1941, had achieved in whole or in part most of the elements of an independent force. All these elements were to undergo evolutionary—in some cases, revolutionary—changes during and after the war. For example, in the first year of combat over Europe, it became apparent that both the Tactical School theorists and the GHQ Air Force practitioners had been less than omniscient. Harold George's Tactical School group, unaware of the potential of radar in air defense, had believed that large formations of heavily armed strategic bombers could defend themselves against enemy fighters. That proved not to be the case. In its preoccupation with big bombers, the Air Corps had neglected to develop long-range fighters to go along with the bombers and protect them. One of the men responsible for solving the fighter escort problem and saving the strategic bombing campaign was Bill Kepner, fighter tactician and earlier the Air Corps' premier airship expert during its brief flirtation with lighter-than-air craft.

Both the Tactical School and GHQ Air Force had paid too little attention to developing tactical aviation for support of ground forces, as the North Africa campaign of late 1942 and early 1943 showed. Tactics, techniques, and organization for air-ground cooperation had to be worked out almost from scratch, based to a large extent on experience of the Royal Air Force and Germany's Luftwaffe. Two of the men most deeply involved in correcting that oversight were Hoyt Vandenberg, who later was to be the first full-term Chief of Staff of the United States Air Force, and Elwood "Pete" Quesada, one of the most colorful and innovative air commanders of the war. If Quesada had an equal in dash and inventiveness, it was George Kenney, the AAF's air commander in the Southwest Pacific and first chief of the postwar Strategic Air Command.

World War II ended with two nuclear explosions over Hiroshima and Nagasaki in August 1945, signaling the demise of thousand-plane bomber raids and much of the doctrine of strategic warfare that had been devised at the old Air Corps Tactical School. Six months later, General Arnold, who led the Army Air Forces through the war, was succeeded by Gen. Carl "Tooey" Spaatz, the last commander of the AAF who would become the first Chief of Staff of the United States Air Force. On April 29, 1948, General Spaatz retired, passing leadership of the newly independent Air Force to Hoyt Vandenberg.

The problems facing the youthful-looking Vandenberg, once described as the handsomest man in Washington, were monumental. They included completing the establishment of an organization adapted to air operations; beginning a transition from propeller-driven to jet aircraft; modifying doctrine, strategy, and tactics to accommodate nuclear weapons; starting development of ballistic missiles, which Germany had introduced in the last year of the war; and arranging for the supporting services that the Army had provided before Air Force independence. These problems were compounded by explosive postwar demobilization, by clear evidence that our wartime Soviet ally had become a potential enemy, and by the Korean War which began in June 1950. When Vandenberg became Chief of Staff, Air Force strength had plummeted from a wartime high of nearly 2.4 million men and women to 387,000. There were not enough people with the right skills to man the few operational squadrons and groups remaining. That particular problem was complicated by racial segregation, which prevented transferring skilled people among units. The Air Force, under Vandenberg and Air Force Secretary Stuart Symington, took the lead among U.S. military services in desegregation. Confidence that it would work was based on the wartime performance of the AAF's only all-black fighter group, led by Benjamin O. Davis, Jr. Davis, the first black to graduate from West Point in the twentieth century, the first to command a flying outfit, and the first to become an Air Force general, had proved that not just he, but many blacks, could perform as well as whites in aerial combat and in the highly technical job of maintaining and supporting first-line aircraft.

General Vandenberg was forced by terminal illness to retire in June 1953. He was succeeded by Gen. Nathan F. Twining, a World War II air commander in the Pacific and the Mediterranean, and a man of great common sense. Nate Twining served for ten tumultuous years in Washington as Vandenberg's Vice Chief of Staff, then as Chief of Staff, and finally as the first airman to be appointed Chairman of the Joint Chiefs of Staff. As Air Force Chief, Twining, like his predecessor, fought some acrimonious battles with the Army and Navy over control of tactical air forces, nuclear strategy, the division of responsibility for air defense, and the adequacy of airlift. During his tenure as chief, the Strategic Air Command was built up as a deterrent to a nuclear-armed and aggressive Soviet Union. The Air Force assumed a permanent, peacetime state of combat readiness, and became an aerospace force with the addition of intercontinental ballistic missiles.

The man directly responsible for developing a missile force was Bernard Schriever who later, as head of the Air Force Systems Command, was in charge of all Air Force research and development, and the procurement of air weapons and equipment. Bennie Schriever's pioneering management techniques won for this country the early missile race against the Soviet Union and established new standards for managing multi-billion dollar programs.

The last man whose story is told here is Robinson Risner, who symbolizes the professional competence, dedication, and moral and physical courage that are the indispensable ingredients of a military force. Robbie Risner was a jet ace in Korea, a combat commander in Vietnam, and an indomitable leader of American prisoners of war through his seven and a half years of imprisonment and torture in Hanoi.

In the years covered by the careers of these men, the Air Force grew from a tiny organization with the one simple mission of observation to a technically complex force of global range. There was, especially from the mid-1930s on, a constant interplay of ideas and technology. At times, ideas about air warfare spurred the development of technology; at other times, technology forced the modification of ideas and sometimes fostered new thinking about the capabilities and uses of air and space weapons.

The men whose stories are told in the chapters that follow are but a few of the many who were major contributors to the development of doctrine, strategy, tactics, equipment, and supporting services that moved the Air Force from seat-of-the-pants simplicity to its present technical and professional sophistication. Why, then, were these twelve selected? Why were Brig. Gen. Billy Mitchell, Gens. Henry H. Arnold, Carl Spaatz, and Curtis LeMay, and Lt. Gen. Ira Eaker—five men whose names come to mind immediately—not included?

The purpose of this volume, and others that may follow, is to acquaint readers with airmen of the United States Air Force and its predecessor organizations who significantly affected the development of the Air Force, but whose legacy may have been dimmed by the passage of time. Full-length biographies of Mitchell, Arnold, Spaatz, Eaker, and LeMay either have been published recently or are in preparation; hence they were not considered for this book.

A list of some seventy air officers was submitted to the Governing Trustees of the Air Force Historical Foundation and to the Air Force Association, the book's initial sponsors. Recipients were asked to select twelve men whose careers spanned the life of the Air Force and who filled with distinction a variety of roles in its evolution. Responses were by no means unanimous, as one would expect. But a consensus formed around these twelve. They are a vital part of the Air Force heritage, and their contributions to an important element of American security should not be forgotten.

2

Benjamin D. Foulois:
In the Beginning

John F. Shiner

Benjamin Delahauf Foulois, better known to history and to his contemporaries as "Benny" Foulois, was one of military aviation's pioneers—in 1910 the Army's only active pilot. Foulois was slight of stature, combative, outspoken, often impetuous, and seldom diplomatic. Despite a stormy career, centered on the fight for an independent air force, he was appointed Chief of the Air Corps in 1931. Along the way, especially as chief, Foulois's crusading zeal and intemperance earned him the enmity of President Franklin Roosevelt, some powerful members of Congress, and most of the War Department General Staff. When he retired in December 1935, there was no ceremony, no medal, for the pioneer who had done so much for military aviation.

An event that took place twenty-nine years later typifies the characteristics that endeared Benny Foulois to Army flyers and to the public, but not always to his civilian and military superiors. President Lyndon Johnson, who was running against Senator Barry Goldwater in the 1964 presidential campaign, was persuaded that a special medal should be struck for the eighty-five-year-old warrior. A ceremony was held in the East Room of the White House, complete with distinguished guests, speeches honoring Foulois, and presentation of the medal by President Johnson. Foulois responded with a few remarks on the state of the nation and the world, then pointing to the paneled entrance said: "I hope to see President Barry Goldwater walk through that door next year." There were no late departures from the ceremony.

Foulois was born in the country village of Washington, Connecticut, on December 9, 1879. Benny completed eleven years of school and in 1896, at age sixteen, went to work in his father's plumbing business. Two years later, the sinking of the battleship *Maine* and the possibility of war with Spain filled the newspapers. Foulois ran off to New York City to join the military. The Navy would have nothing to do with this short, rather slight young man. The Army was less choosy. Fifteen minutes after entering a recruiting station, he emerged as a private in the 1st U.S. Volunteer Engineers.

Foulois's early military experiences took him to Puerto Rico and the Philippines. He served with the Engineers in Puerto Rico during the war with Spain and was mustered out of service as a sergeant in January 1899. He immediately sought an appointment to West Point, but was turned down because of his weak academic background. Benny thereupon enlisted as a private in Company G, 19th Infantry, which soon was sent to the Philippines to help put down the native insurrection. Young Foulois faced more than his share of close combat during the next several months. Cool under fire and a natural leader, he was promoted to company first sergeant in 1901 and to second lieutenant a few months later. Foulois at first balked at the order from his superiors to take the commissioning exam. Years later he said, "I didn't win my commission on the basis of the answers on the test. Whatever value they attached to my two years of field service must have outweighed my ignorance."

The new lieutenant soon set to work solving a major problem for his troops—the high incidence of venereal disease. The pragmatic Foulois concluded that the only way to check this scourge was to establish an official bordello, with medical inspection of the working girls. Opening the house in an old Spanish convent did not earn universal approval for the project.

After a second tour of duty in the Philippines in 1905, Foulois entered the Army's professional education program—his avenue to eventual involvement in aeronautics. He compiled an unimpressive record at the Infantry and Cavalry School at Fort Leavenworth, Kansas, graduating near the bottom of his class. Foulois claimed this was due to eye trouble. The post surgeon had told him that either he would have to stop studying or wear glasses. Foulois made his decision: "I stopped studying."

His lack of academic talent did not, however, prevent his assignment to the Army Signal School upon graduation. The Signal Corps was responsible for all balloon activity; only recently, in 1907, it had established an aeronautical division. Foulois became interested in the potential of aviation, and wrote his school thesis on "The Tactical and Strategical Value of Dirigible Balloons and Aeronautical Flying Machines." This must have impressed his superiors, for in July 1908 the Army ordered him to Washington, D.C., for aviation duty in the Office of the Chief Signal Officer.

For the next year and a half Lieutenant Foulois was intimately connected with the Army's first real flying experience. He was one of three officers to check out in the War Department's first airship. The experience left him unenthusiastic about airships. As a member of the newly created Aeronautical

Board, he also took part in the Army's initial evaluation of a heavier-than-air machine. This strange new contraption fascinated Foulois. Between dirigible flights he watched the Wright brothers assemble their "aeroplane" on the Fort Myer, Virginia, parade field across the Potomac from Washington. He wondered how "such a combination of cloth, wire, pulleys, chains, and wood could ever carry two people aloft for an hour at the fantastic speed of forty miles an hour"—the War Department's minimum requirements—yet he was anxious to give the machine a try. Instead, Lt. Thomas E. Selfridge got the nod as passenger on the September 17, 1908, test flight—a flight that ended in disaster when the wooden propeller broke and the aircraft plummeted to earth. Selfridge died almost immediately and Orville Wright was badly injured. The Wrights built a new plane and continued the evaluation flights in 1909.

Foulois finally got his chance. After laying out the trial course between Fort Myer and Alexandria, Virginia, he flew as the "navigator-observer" during the final test flight. "I would like to think that I was chosen on the basis of my intellectual and technical ability," he said, "but I found out later that it was my short stature, light weight, and map-reading experience that had tipped the decision in my favor."

The Army bought the Wright aircraft; the agreement required the inventors to teach two officers to fly the machine. Benny was slated to be one of the trainees until he made disparaging remarks about the worth of dirigibles that were contrary to the official War Department view. The Army brass decided to put this outspoken little lieutenant in his place. A shocked Foulois received orders to proceed at once to an aeronautical meeting in France. Upon his return, his superior allowed him to join the temporary flying school the Wrights had set up at College Park, Maryland. Soon after his arrival in October 1909, the first two trainees, Lts. Frank P. Lahm and Frederic E. Humphreys, badly damaged the airplane. Since Orville and Wilbur had technically fulfilled the terms of their contract by soloing these two men after a little more than three hours instruction, the Wrights repaired the plane and departed for home. A disappointed Foulois had a few minutes of dual instruction before the mishap but had not soloed.

The War Department sent both Lahm and Humphreys back to their regular assignments, leaving Benny and the Wright aircraft as the Army's entire heavier-than-air flying force. Foulois was eager to get on with his aviation training and was sure the Army would hire the Wrights back. Instead, in December the War Department ordered him to take the plane to Fort Sam Houston, Texas, where the weather was better. Brig. Gen. James Allen, Chief Signal Officer, told Foulois: "Your orders are simple, Lieutenant. You are to evaluate the airplane. Just take plenty of spare parts and teach yourself to fly."

Lt. Benjamin Foulois in Wright Type B aircraft, taken at Ft. Sam Houston, Texas, 1911.

Benny Foulois and his crew of nine enlisted men set up operations at Fort Sam Houston in early 1910, guided by the Wrights' instructions that came by mail from Dayton. On March 2, the plane was ready to go and so was the young aviator, who exhibited at least outward calm as he steered the plane down the launching rail and into the air. On that day Foulois made four flights, the longest of twenty-one minutes. He also established three personal firsts: his first solo takeoff, first solo landing, and first crack-up. The only man ever to learn to fly by mail, he kept up a lively correspondence with the Wrights over the next several months, asking their advice in the aftermath of crashes and various airborne difficulties.

This was a heady time for the thirty-year-old lieutenant. He began modifying the plane and experimenting with ways to use it to support ground forces. He substituted wheels for the original skids and installed the first airplane seat belt after nearly being thrown out of the machine while attempting to land in gusty winds. Foulois also demonstrated the airplane's practical use in military operations by doing aerial mapping, photography, and observation of troop movements. When trouble erupted along the Mexican border, he set a cross-country distance record of 106 miles on March 3, 1911, while on a reconnaissance flight. The same year he designed the first air-to-ground wireless system and demonstrated its practicality. The Army, however, remained unimpressed with military aviation. Its fragile plane spent more time in the repair shop than in the air.

14

During 1910–11, Foulois flew occasional indoctrination missions for the benefit of unappreciative Army officers at Fort Sam Houston. On one dawn sortie he buzzed "the tents occupied by sleeping officers of the division head-quarters staff at about ten feet" and ended the day's airpower display with "a power dive over the headquarters latrine." These demonstrations did not noticeably improve the ground officers' opinion of military aviation.

By 1912, Foulois had spent more than four years on detached service with the Signal Corps. Federal law required him to rejoin his own branch, the Infantry. Since the Army had finally decided a year earlier to expand its

Right: Orville and Wilbur Wright with Foulois at Ft. Myer, Virginia; *below:* Army's first airplane, Wright Type B, accepted at Ft. Myer in 1909.

National Archives

15

air fleet and pilot force, American military aviation would continue to develop for a time without him. But Lieutenant Foulois's love of flying was not dampened. He soon began working his way back into a flying job. In December 1913, he wangled an assignment as troubleshooter for the commandant of the Army's new aviation school at San Diego, where accidents had been all too frequent. (Twelve of the first forty-eight Army officers assigned to flying duty were killed in accidents.) Never afraid to get his hands dirty, Foulois organized and personally instructed a course in engine repair for flying students. He also insisted that flyers wear helmets and other protective equipment on all flights. The school's casualty rate dropped almost to zero.

*   *   *   *   *

A year later Foulois organized the Army's first tactical air unit, the 1st Aero Squadron, at San Diego. In 1916 he took his force of eight Curtiss JN–2s to Mexico as part of the punitive expedition, led by Brig. Gen. John J. Pershing, against the bandit, Pancho Villa. The squadron's pilots tried gallantly to carry out reconnaissance and liaison missions, but operating at relatively high altitudes (about 10,000 feet) over the mountainous terrain of northern Mexico was too much for their underpowered planes. By the end of the sixth week all eight aircraft either were worn out, needed major repair, or were wrecked in crashes. All the while Captain Foulois bombarded the War Department with fruitless requests for better planes.

The 1st Aero Squadron's accomplishments were extremely meager. Its military usefulness, according to Foulois, "could be summed up in one successful scouting mission: they had once found a lost and thirsty cavalry column. " The dearth of suitable American flying equipment during the Mexican expedition demonstrated how far the United States lagged behind Europe in military aviation. With World War I nearly two years old, the Army had only one tactical squadron in 1916, and it was equipped with underpowered training planes. A year later, the United States still did not have a single aircraft comparable to those being used in Europe.

After the punitive expedition and a brief tour of duty as aeronautical officer for the Army's Southern Department, Foulois was posted, in March 1917, to the Aviation Section, Office of the Chief Signal Officer, in Washington. With the American declaration of war in April, he was promoted to temporary major and put to work drafting a program to expand the air arm. Two months later he was made a temporary brigadier general. He had no time to celebrate, for he was busy putting the finishing touches on a plan for an air organization adequate to support an army of three million men. Foulois's proposal called for appropriations of $640 million and included a draft of the legislation needed to carry out the program. When the Army General Staff disapproved of the plan because of its high cost, the wiry little aviator boldly testified before the House Military Affairs Committee in behalf of enabling legislation. Foulois was delighted when Congress passed his bill on July 24, 1917. In his view, it would lay the foundation for an effective air arm both during the war and in the more distant future. He had bucked the system and gotten away with it. He would attempt to do this many times in the years ahead to advance the cause of military aviation.

Foulois was sent to France in November to become Chief of the Air Service, American Expeditionary Force (AEF). According to his memoirs, General Pershing had personally requested him for this important job, believing Foulois could end the chaos within the fledgling Air Service in France. The arrival of Foulois and his staff did not bring order. Instead, it produced more friction and confusion. The air officers already in France were for the most part Regulars and rated aviators. They resented having Foulois's staff, fresh from the States with many recently commissioned nonflying officers, imposed on them. Foulois believed his staff brought logistical and administrative skills that were essential to operational success, but others saw things differently.

Gen. John Pershing (right) calls Foulois to France to be Chief of the Air Service, American Expeditionary Force (AEF).

Brig. Gen. William "Billy" Mitchell, Air Service Commander for the Zone of Advance, was Foulois's bitterest critic. Mitchell referred to the new arrivals as "carpetbaggers," charging that "a more incompetent lot of air warriors have never arrived in the zone of active military operations since the war began." Pershing, the AEF Commander in Chief, called his new air staff "a lot of good men running around in circles." Foulois, whose only previous command had been a squadron of fewer than ten planes, had not measured up to the difficult task of creating, from scratch, an effective wartime organization.

In May 1918, Pershing reorganized the AEF Air Service and brought in as its new chief, Brig. Gen. Mason M. Patrick, a ground officer and West Point classmate. Foulois was appointed Chief of the Air Service, First Army— the only American field army thus far formed. He soon requested that he be made Patrick's assistant and that Mitchell be given the First Army job. This change took place on August 1.

Although Foulois recommended Mitchell for the post he himself had held, the two men harbored an intense and lasting dislike for each other. Mitchell, who was senior in rank before the war, had bitterly resented Foulois's elevation to Chief of the Air Service, AEF, and complained to Pershing about the feisty aviation pioneer's alleged inefficiency. For his part, Foulois considered Mitchell one of his biggest headaches, both insubordinate and ill-informed on logistics. Still, Foulois recognized Mitchell's leadership ability and was honest enough to recommend him for the prestigious job of leading the combat air operations of the First Army.

Foulois's and Mitchell's backgrounds and personalities were so different that they probably would not have been friends even if they had not clashed

Gen. William Mitchell leads public campaign for a separate air arm.

over issues of command in France. Mitchell was flamboyant and relatively wealthy. Foulois, the ex-enlisted man, came from humbler origins. He preferred a pair of overalls to a neatly tailored uniform and felt at home amidst the grime and hubbub of an aircraft repair shop. Mitchell had important family connections reaching all the way to the U.S. Senate and was at home in Washington society; the rough-hewn Foulois enjoyed a good drinking party and a game of poker with his fellow officers. He had a wealth of practical knowledge about aviation, while the more publicity-oriented Mitchell was a relative newcomer to the flying game. Their differences in style carried over into the methods each adopted in the postwar struggle to free military aviation from the control of ground officers. Mitchell directed much of his campaign toward swaying public opinion. Foulois believed that officers should keep controversy within the government. He fought his battles for an independent air force in testimony before Congress and other official investigative bodies.

*   *   *   *   *

The question of a separate air force was raised almost immediately after the war. Swift demobilization of American forces and radically reduced defense spending hit the Air Service particularly hard. Air officers, knowing the General Staff did not appreciate the combat potential of military aviation, feared the Army's leaders would reduce the Air Service to its meager prewar size in order to free more funds for the ground forces. When the air arm's officer strength fell from a wartime high of 20,000 to 200 in 1919, the aviators were ready to fight. They were assisted by a rash of bills introduced in Congress during 1919–20 to create an independent air force. As expected, ranking Army and Navy officers testified against all such proposals. They regarded military flyers as upstarts, denied that air power would ever be able independently to affect the outcome of war, and argued powerfully against removing a useful auxiliary from the control of the existing services.

Foulois did not immediately join the fray. He remained in Europe until July 1919, working with General Patrick on the air provisions of the Versailles Treaty. However, when he did return he became the leading Air Service advocate for independence. Now head of the Liquidation Division in the Office of the Chief of the Air Service, Foulois made many appearances before congressional committees that were considering bills to establish a separate air force. Neither postwar reduction to the rank of major nor his five-foot-seven-inch stature diminished the biting character of his remarks.

19

During each visit to the congressional hearing room he defiantly attacked the General Staff as ill-suited to administer, control, and provide for the future development of military aviation. On October 7, 1919, he told the House Committee on Military Affairs:

> The General Staff of the Army is the policymaking body of the Army and, either through lack of vision, lack of practical knowledge, or deliberate intention to subordinate the Air Service needs to the needs of the other combat arms, has utterly failed to appreciate the full military value of this new military weapon and, in my opinion, has utterly failed to accord it its just place in our military family.

He went on to damn the General Staff's prewar lack of concern for aviation that had resulted in the gross weakness of the Army's air arm in 1917.

Foulois repeated his criticism of the War Department later before the Senate Military Affairs Committee. He could get vitriolic when he was mad, and that day he was hopping mad. He condemned the General Staff for its inability to understand the full value of military aviation. During the World War, flyers had used the airplane for rudimentary strategic bombing, interdiction, counterair operations, and close air support. Yet, the Army was now seeking to use it almost exclusively in what he considered the "defensive" roles of reconnaissance and artillery spotting. Foulois believed, like other knowledgeable flyers, that air power's real value lay in concentrated, offensive employment—a concept unappreciated by the ground officers who ran the Army. He asserted that, "based on practical experience in Army aviation, ever since its birth in 1908, I can frankly state that the War Department has earned no right or title to claim further control over aviation." Let the Army have observation planes, but the rest of the air arm should operate as a separate service. In subsequent years he never wavered from this view.

Billy Mitchell, Maj. Henry H. "Hap" Arnold, and others joined Foulois in the 1919–20 campaign. Each took his turn before the congressional committees, but Army and Navy opposition, together with the Air Service's unimpressive record as an offensive force in the Great War, were more persuasive. The Army Reorganization Act of 1920 gave the air arm neither independence nor autonomy. The result was a growing cleavage between the aviators and the Army ground officers who controlled the General Staff.

The aviation branch of the Army remained poorly funded and firmly under General Staff control throughout the 1920s. Although the rest of the Army also suffered a lack of funds during this period, and the General Staff was gradually coming to appreciate the offensive potential of tactical aviation by the end of the decade, the aviators never abandoned their goal of independence. In Benny Foulois's opinion, and that of most other Army flyers, a separate air force was essential if military aviation was ever to reach its potential and effectively serve the nation.

Foulois soon realized that his congressional campaign for independence had not endeared him to the Army's leadership. It seemed a good idea to leave town until the dust settled, so in the spring of 1920 he volunteered to serve as the military attaché to Germany. He arrived in Berlin in May 1920, traveled freely in Germany during his four-year tour, and became a drinking friend of Hermann Goering and Ernst Udet—men who would lead the Luftwaffe a decade later.

One's place on the Army's promotion list, not the ratings on one's officer effectiveness reports, determined advancement in the 1920s. In February 1923, there were enough vacancies in the grade of lieutenant colonel for Foulois and others who had the same number of years' service to be promoted. The new "light colonel" returned to the United States fifteen months later to attend the one-year course at the Army's Command and General Staff School, Fort Leavenworth, Kansas. Foulois remained an uninspired student, but he realized that completing the course was a prerequisite for important positions in the Army.

Halfway through the school year Foulois's ambition got the best of him. When news circulated through the Air Service grapevine in early 1925 that Mitchell was about to lose his job as Assistant Chief of the Air Service, Foulois saw this as his big chance. He temporarily let his studies at the Command and General Staff School slide in favor of a letter-writing campaign to senior Army officers and politicians asking them to support him as Mitchell's replacement. Perhaps the War Department had not yet forgotten his congressional testimony of five years earlier. In any event, Lt. Col. James E. Fechet got the job. Foulois received an assignment in mid-1925 that tempered his disappointment—command of a major flying unit. He was put in charge of the showplace of Army aviation: Mitchel Field, Long Island.

Foulois recalled years later being "as eager to get my hands on the controls of our new planes as a teenager approaching the driving age." During the next 2 years he worked to whip his 9th Observation Group into a combat-ready force. This was a little difficult, for his people were frequently called on to assist in public relations activities. Typical of these was a stunt in which Babe Ruth was to catch a baseball dropped from an Army plane circling at 250 feet while media representatives and an eager crowd looked on. Ruth was knocked flat during the first 2 attempts. Undaunted, he tried again and this time held on. Reported Foulois, "The last I saw of the Babe he was slowly flexing his burning hand and trying to smile about it as he left in a big limousine."

Foulois went to Washington infrequently during his tenure at Mitchel Field. However, he willingly made the trip to testify before the Morrow Board, which was investigating military aviation in the autumn of 1925 at the behest of President Coolidge. Dwight Morrow's group, fully aware that Coolidge opposed creating a separate air force, fell under the General Staff's influence from the outset. Despite that formidable opposition, Chief of the Air

Service General Patrick, Billy Mitchell, Benny Foulois, and others tried their best to win the board's support for independence. Foulois repeated the arguments that he had used in 1919–20: "Based on my knowledge of the past seventeen years I am fully convinced that aviation will never reach its proper place in the scheme of national defense so long as it remains in the control of the War Department General Staff." Maj. Horace M. Hickam gave perhaps the best summary of the situation: "I am confident that no general thinks he can command the Navy, and no admiral thinks he can operate an army, but some of both believe they can operate an air force." The airmen again were bitterly disappointed.

The 1926 Air Corps Act resulting from the Morrow investigation granted the air arm a five-year expansion program, gave it some representation on the General Staff and established an Assistant Secretary of War for Air, but left Army aviation under General Staff control. Army generals and Navy admirals would go on supervising their respective air organizations.

Although failing to win Air Corps independence, Foulois was not stymied in his determination to gain a greater role in the future development of military aviation. When it was announced in mid-1927 that Patrick would soon retire and Fechet would replace him as Chief of the Air Corps, Foulois left few stones unturned in his quest for the assistant chief's job. He wrote to everyone he thought could help, including the governor of his home state, Connecticut. His persistence paid off: on December 20, 1927, he became Assistant Chief of the Air Corps with the temporary rank of brigadier general.

Brig. Gen. Foulois (left) with Chief of the Air Corps Maj. Gen. Jim Fechet.

Foulois spent the next three and a half years preparing for the day when he might succeed Fechet. At first he concentrated on gaining experience in the Washington office of the Chief of the Air Corps, where he was responsible for everything from training to war planning. After eighteen months, he arranged a one-year exchange of duties with the Chief of the Air Corps Materiel Division in order to become more familiar with the air arm's research and procurement activities, for which the Dayton-based division was responsible. Back in Washington in July 1930, Foulois again took charge of planning and policy matters.

He got his big chance to put into practice all he had learned when Fechet selected him to command the Air Corps' 1931 maneuvers. This was to be by far the largest U.S. Army air exercise ever attempted. The Chief of the Air Corps had decided to form a provisional air division of roughly 670 planes and use them in a series of aerial demonstrations over major cities in the Great Lakes region and the eastern United States. The number of aircraft taking part would severely tax the small air arm, but the exercise would be a good test of Air Corps mobility.

Foulois was an excellent choice to organize and command the maneuvers. A doer rather than a deep thinker, he performed best when dealing with the real and the tangible. He was not afraid to make decisions or to experiment. And he led by example. All units were to be in place in the Dayton area by May 18. Foulois and his staff left by air from Washington on May 12, but the first flight of three single-seat aircraft, which he led, ran into bad weather over Cumberland, Maryland. The general pressed on, while his much younger fellow aviators headed back to Bolling Field and clearer skies. A second flight of three also turned back. Foulois had some good-natured comments on the piloting ability of his Washington cohorts when they finally arrived later in the day. He believed in flying safely, but he also believed in realistic training.

The air maneuvers, which Foulois supervised much of the time from his own plane, were an unqualified success. His force flew nearly 38,000 hours, sometimes in close formation for up to 4 hours at a stretch with more than 600 aircraft in the sky at once, but not one serious accident occurred. This was a remarkable record and a tribute to Foulois's planning and leadership, for which the National Aeronautic Association awarded him the Mackay Trophy "for the most meritorious flight of the year."

Foulois's exceptional performance as commander of the provisional air division probably was a major factor in his selection to succeed Jim Fechet as Chief of the Air Corps. Shortly after the conclusion of the maneuvers Fechet announced that he would retire in December. By the end of the first week in June many eastern papers ran stories praising Foulois's fine record and claiming the popular assistant chief had already been tapped to replace Fechet. The War Department leadership was irritated, since President Hoover

Above: a flight of B–2 Condors over Ocean City, New Jersey, during the 1931 maneuvers; *left:* presentation of the Mackay Trophy to Foulois for his leadership during the maneuvers. Assistant Secretary of War for Air F. Trubee Davison looks on.

apparently had not yet reached a decision. Assistant Secretary of War for Air F. Trubee Davison wanted to know the source of the news stories: Foulois claimed he had no idea where they came from. Whether Foulois or some of his friends were the culprits remains a mystery. He did have newspaper friends, and he was not about to discourage their speculation. Nevertheless, on July 13, 1931, the Army's Adjutant General informed a jubilant Benny Foulois that he would become Chief of the Air Corps upon General Fechet's retirement. The rank and file of the Air Corps seemed genuinely happy with Hoover's choice.

Jim Fechet was granted three months terminal leave, effective September 8, and Foulois took over as acting chief at that time. On December 21, 1931, he formally assumed command and pinned on his second star. Over the next four years he would lead the Air Corps through one of its periods of greatest transition.

*   *   *   *   *

For several years there had been a running debate between the services over who was responsible for the nation's territorial defense. Until the arrival of the airplane, there was a clear line of division to which all agreed—the coastline. Aircraft created a new avenue of attack on the United States as well as a new weapon for defense. Unlike ships and foot soldiers, planes were not forced to stop at the shoreline. During the 1920s, Billy Mitchell and Mason Patrick campaigned vigorously to gain for the Army air arm full responsibility for coastal defense. They argued that only aircraft could defeat both airborne and seaborne attacks. Benny Foulois and virtually all other military aviators agreed; coast defense was the Air Corps' rightful mission. The Navy, however, adamantly maintained that all aircraft flying over the open seas must be Navy planes.

Foulois and his fellow flyers were delighted when Army Chief of Staff Maj. Gen. Douglas MacArthur apparently put an end to the debate by reaching an agreement on January 7, 1931, with the Chief of Naval Operations, Rear Adm. William Pratt. The Air Corps was to defend the coast, while naval aircraft would be carried out to sea to assist the fleet. The MacArthur-Pratt agreement failed to specify how far offshore Air Corps planes could operate when seeking out an enemy force, and the agreement did not have complete support within the Navy. Naval aviators contained their anger until Pratt retired in 1933; they believed over-water coast defense was their business, and theirs alone.

25

As acting air chief, Foulois went to work at once to ensure that aerial coast defense would remain exclusively an Air Corps responsibility. Aware that the Army air arm had neither the training nor the equipment to carry out the newly won mission effectively, he immediately established a school at Bolling Field to develop coast defense navigation and plotting equipment and tactics. The school did some useful research between 1932 and 1934, but for reasons largely beyond its control, the Air Corps continued to lack suitable aircraft and equipment as well as realistic coast defense training during most of the 1930s.

Foulois also began a campaign to force the General Staff to adopt a realistic strategy and combat organization for the aerial coast defense mission. Results were slow in coming. Foulois began carping at the General Staff as soon as he took over as acting chief. He eventually spoke directly to General MacArthur about the Army's lack of aerial coast defense planning and in the spring of 1932 proposed a strategy for air defense employment. He maintained the Air Corps' coast defense mission should be broken into three phases. During the first phase the air arm would operate reconnaissance and strike aircraft to locate and attack an invasion force out to the limit of aircraft range. This action would be independent of local ground force control. In the second phase—when the enemy was within range of Army shore guns—the Air Corps would spot targets for the Coast Artillery and make air strikes on the invasion fleet. Should the enemy get ashore, the conflict would enter its third phase, with the Air Corps directly aiding the ground forces in repelling the enemy from the beaches. Throughout the coast defense campaign the air arm would operate as a consolidated air strike force, taking its orders directly from Army General Headquarters (GHQ). This GHQ air force would have to be ready in peacetime so it could concentrate in the proper location and begin overwater reconnaissance well in advance of hostilities.

After a long and bitter struggle in which Foulois antagonized important General Staff senior officers, the bulk of his plan was accepted. Chief of Staff MacArthur's January 3, 1933 policy letter, "Employment of Army Aviation in Coast Defense," adopted Foulois's three phases of employment and endorsed long-range, overwater reconnaissance to locate an enemy force. However, it also provided that ground commanders in the zone of operations could, in some circumstances, control the GHQ air force.

Foulois and his Air Corps subordinates were pleased with the policy and began at once to carry out more detailed planning, to include developing a list of additional aircraft required. Since the Air Corps had not yet been given funds to complete the 1926 five-year expansion that would bring it up to 1,800 serviceable planes, the General Staff was livid over Foulois's 1933 request for 4,459 aircraft to support the coast defense mission. The nation was in the midst of the Great Depression, and the War Department was not about to starve further the rest of the underfunded Army to expand the Air Corps. Foulois had to make do throughout his tenure with between 1,400 and 1,650 planes. Nevertheless, he had moved the Air Corps forward on two fronts with his coast defense plan. He had won for the air arm a firmer claim to an important air mission, and he had forced the Army to recognize that a consolidated air strike force—a GHQ air force—was needed.

After Admiral Pratt's retirement in 1933, the new Chief of Naval Operations, Rear Adm. William H. Stanley, ignored the agreement with MacArthur and reopened the interservice struggle over aerial coast defense. To Foulois's chagrin, the Army and Navy worked out a fuzzily worded compromise in 1935 that confused the issue of air defense responsibility. The Air Corps and the Navy each continued to act as if it, alone, was responsible. But Foulois had won a long-sought and important victory—Army approval for developing long-range reconnaissance bombers, culminating in production of the B–17 prototype in 1935. The Navy, however, continued to deny the Air Corps' right to operate distant, overwater patrols. Confusion over aerial coast defense responsibilities, and the resulting lack of cooperation between Army aviators and the Navy, paved the way for the 1941 disaster at Pearl Harbor.

*   *   *   *   *

Throughout the nearly three-year struggle to resolve the coast defense impasse, Foulois had not neglected his campaign for the air arm's independence. During his first two years as air chief, he pursued a dual course—arguing before Congress for a separate air organization, while at the same time working within the War Department for permission to establish a GHQ air force, a centrally controlled aviation strike force. His coast defense plan was a step toward that latter, and lesser, goal. Bills to create a separate air force, or to reorganize the defense establishment, cropped up on a recurring basis in the early 1930s, usually introduced as depression-era economy measures. Presidents Hoover and Roosevelt joined the Army and Navy in opposing all such changes, but this did not deter Foulois.

In February 1932, after serving only two months as Chief of the Air Corps, a slightly less outspoken Benjamin Foulois was back on Capitol Hill telling members of Congress that they should thoroughly study the nation's defense organization and ultimately create an air force coequal with the Army and Navy. He quickly developed a good working relationship with Congressman John J. McSwain of South Carolina, the new Chairman of the House Military Affairs Committee. McSwain shared Foulois's views on the need for an independent air force, and over the next two years encouraged the air chief to persist in his campaign.

Foulois testified before the congressman's committee on March 31, 1933, supporting a bill to establish a separate air force. Senior General Staff officers were again angry over the air chief's unwillingness to support the War Department line, but there was little they could do for the present to prevent him from speaking his mind when called upon to do so by Congress. The bill got nowhere, while Foulois further antagonized his superiors.

The Chief of the Air Corps made better headway on the GHQ air force issue. He began a running dialogue with the General Staff in 1932 and eventually beat down Army resistance. The struggle was not easy. The General Staff was reluctant to establish a consolidated air organization in peacetime. It liked the existing arrangement that gave senior ground commanders throughout the U.S. control over the air resources in their geographic areas. The General Staff feared that establishing a GHQ air force would take the Air Corps a step closer to independence and encourage the aviators to concentrate on strategic bombing rather than direct Army support.

Foulois, like other aviators, believed in the importance of strategic bombing, but this was not the issue as far as he was concerned. Concentrated, offensive employment of air power was the proper method no matter if the mission was coast defense, ground support, or long-range strategic bombardment. By the late 1920s the General Staff had agreed in principle to establish a GHQ air force in time of war. Foulois wanted the War Department to take the next step—create the new organization in peacetime so the Air Corps could train as it would fight. He even hinted in a December 1932 letter to MacArthur that the aviators might become less persistent in their campaign for independence if a GHQ air force were soon brought to life. He also made it clear that the Chief of the Air Corps should command the new organization.

Foulois's office kept up a steady stream of correspondence with the General Staff on the GHQ air force issue. Through the air chief's efforts the Army eventually came to see the value of a centrally controlled combat air organization for peacetime coast defense, and as an effective air support organization for the ground forces at the onset of war. The Army's senior leadership realized, too, that Foulois was right that establishing the new combat command would moderate the move for air independence. In October 1933, the War Department officially endorsed the conclusions of a board headed by Deputy Chief of Staff Maj. Gen. Hugh A. Drum that a GHQ air force should be organized in peacetime. Foulois's campaign had paid off, but his persistence created such resentment toward him that there was virtually no chance the Army would allow the Chief of the Air Corps to command the new organization when it was brought to life.

Foulois and his staff were pleased with the Drum Board decision, but

Maj. Gen. Hugh Drum

when the Army took no immediate steps to implement it, the aviation pioneer stepped up his efforts to win complete independence for the air arm. In early February 1934, he secretly slipped a bill to Congressman McSwain designed to achieve that end. McSwain immediately introduced it as his own and called Foulois to testify in its behalf. The air chief obliged, resorting to his old tactic of damning the Army's inept handling of the Air Corps. He branded the General Staff the "main obstacle" to proper development of aviation. What was needed, he said, was an "independent organization that can function without a lot of obstruction" from the red-tape bound ground leadership.

Senior General Staff officers were angered by Foulois's testimony. That anger turned to bitterness when they learned months later that his staff had written the bill. In their eyes Foulois was clearly a self-serving renegade who no longer deserved their trust. Nevertheless, the General Staff moved to establish the GHQ Air Force, hoping to undercut this renewed threat of air independence. Implementing action was held up in the spring of 1934 only because the Air Corps was heavily involved in carrying the nation's airmail.

* * * * *

The 1934 airmail episode was not a happy experience for the Air Corps, or for its chief. On February 9, President Roosevelt canceled government mail contracts with the commercial airlines, which he believed had been arranged through collusion and fraud. Before doing so he had representatives of the Post Office Department check with Foulois to determine if the Air Corps could temporarily take over airmail operations. Foulois looked on the request from the President as tantamount to an order. Besides, he was not the kind of man to give up on anything without a try. A good job carrying the mail might persuade Congress to purchase much needed replacement aircraft and gain public support for independence. The mail operations also would provide a good readiness test for the Air Corps.

After three hours' discussion with members of his staff, Foulois told the Post Office people he could see "no reason why the Army could not handle the mails and handle them satisfactorily." Asked when the Air Corps could take over this task, Foulois shot from the hip: "I think we can be ready in about a week or ten days." Roosevelt had his answer. Later that day he announced the contract cancellations and ordered the Air Corps to begin hauling the mail on February 19.

The Chief of the Air Corps had erred on two counts. Because of the hastily arranged discussions with the Post Office Department officials, he did not consult Army Chief of Staff Douglas MacArthur until after he had volunteered the Air Corps' services. MacArthur was caught off guard. Believing the Army's reputation was on the line, he told a press conference: "I have the utmost confidence the Army will handle the airmail in a magnificent way." MacArthur did not like surprises; Foulois's stock no doubt dropped another notch in the War Department.

The second error was Foulois's failure to consider that the airmail assignment required proficiency in night and instrument flying—skills his aviators lacked. Imbued with the "can do" spirit that we prize in our leaders, he charged ahead without giving the issue serious thought. He told himself that flying the mail could be no more hazardous than normal peacetime training. Perhaps that was true, but the public had never been concerned with the Air Corps' large number of flying accidents. Flying the mail was another story.

The Air Corps also was poorly equipped for mail service. Army planes normally did not have the "blind flying" instruments or radios that were absolutely essential for their new task. The majority of Air Corps planes were light and maneuverable. Pilots were trained primarily for combat operations in good weather during daylight hours, when the enemy could be located and engaged. As one combat veteran pointed out: "In war we must see our objective." Flying the mail was essentially a nighttime job that involved navigating across long stretches of country in all kinds of weather. Foulois was not totally insensitive to this. He ordered each mail plane equipped with a directional gyro, artificial horizon, and at least a radio receiver. Mechanics hastily installed this equipment, frequently in hard-to-see locations.

Loading Route 12 mail into plane at Denver, Colorado, as part of the Army
Air Corps airmail operations during 1934.

Foulois also ordered a quick instrument refresher course for his airmail
pilots, but it was too little and too late. Army aviators, with only limited bad-
weather flying experience, were not about to trust their fate to some new-
fangled gauges. Instead, they tended to rely on the seat of their pants when
they encountered bad weather, or they tried to go low, beneath the clouds.
To compound the situation, as operations started on February 19, the nation
was hit by some of the worst winter weather in its history. Snow, rain, dense
fog, and icy gales prevailed throughout the month of February across much
of the country.

Air Corps pilots struggled valiantly against the elements in their open
cockpit machines, and Foulois did everything possible to ensure his aviators
complied with strict flying safety rules. Still, the first weeks of the operation
were marked by crash after crash, which took the lives of six Air Corps flyers.
Roosevelt and the congressional Democrats were embarrassed. Clearly the
Air Corps was not up to the task. Just as clearly—in FDR's view—Foulois
had put him in a difficult spot.

In late March, Roosevelt authorized new contracts with the commercial
airlines, which would take over all airmail routes by June 1. With the arrival
of better weather in mid-March, increased instrument proficiency, and the
assignment of some larger transport planes to the operation, the Army aviators
did a much improved job during the last months of the operation. The Air
Corps' overall record, however, was not good: twelve deaths, sixty-six crashes,
and a completion rate for scheduled flights of only 65.83 percent.

The airmail episode did produce some positive results. Military flyers received valuable training and instrument-flying experience, and the Air Corps awakened to the need for an extensive instrument training program. This new appreciation for an all-weather capability would pay great dividends during World War II. Also, the airmail affair was the final stimulus that brought the GHQ Air Force into being. Secretary of War George Dern appointed a special committee to analyze Air Corps deficiencies. That body, influenced by the General Staff, called for the immediate creation of a centrally controlled, consolidated air strike force in its July 1934 report.

Foulois was a member of this special committee chaired by former Secretary of War Newton Baker. However, the Air Corps chief kept a low profile during the Baker Board's deliberations. The other uniformed members of this group were senior ground officers who held no love for Foulois. Only recently the origin of Congressman McSwain's latest bill to create a separate air force had come to light. Then there was the Army's embarrassment over the Air Corps showing in the airmail fiasco. Foulois, well aware in the spring of 1934 that some members of Congress were after his scalp, decided this was the time to show his fellow board members what a cooperative person he really was. He refused to comment when Army aviators appeared before Baker's group to argue the case for an independent air arm. Instead, he asked the board's endorsement only for a GHQ air force and for completing the Air Corps' aircraft expansion program begun in 1926. The aviation pioneer

Newton Baker chairs 1934 board recommending creation of a GHQ air force.

was ready to put aside, for the time being, his dreams of a separate air organization in order immediately to gain these objectives. Other members of the Air Corps were soon to take the same view.

The Baker Board's mid-July report was quickly acted upon by the General Staff. On March 1, 1935, the GHQ Air Force finally came into being as the Army consolidated all Air Corps attack, bombardment, and pursuit aircraft under the command of veteran aviator Lt. Col. Frank M. Andrews. Those air combat units previously had been controlled by the Army corps area commanders in whose regions they were stationed. Andrews, promoted to the temporary rank of brigadier general, was to report directly to the Army Chief of Staff in peacetime and the theater commander in time of war. Foulois's persistence had finally secured a centrally controlled air strike force for the Air Corps. The GHQ Air Force, capable of offensive, concentrated operations unhindered by the whims of local ground commanders, would serve as the model for America's World War II air organization.

For Benjamin Foulois it was less than a complete victory. The Chief of the Air Corps had no control over this force. His responsibilities remained as they were before—to organize, train, and equip the Army's air arm and to develop employment doctrine. This division of responsibility between Air Corps Headquarters and the GHQ Air Force (later called the Air Force Combat Command) would not end until the eve of U.S. entry into World War II, years after Benny Foulois had retired. Furthermore, the Army's corps area commanders retained administrative responsibility for air installations in their areas. Essentially the GHQ Air Force was a compromise between those airmen who advocated independence and those in the War Department who thought the Air Corps' primary responsibility was to support ground forces.

The new GHQ Air Force not only gave the Air Corps a more sensible arrangement for carrying out its coast defense responsibilities; it also gave it the kind of organization that could best carry out strategic bombardment. While Foulois was not a doctrinal innovator, he fully agreed with the views of his subordinates: coast defense might be the Air Corps' most important immediate mission in wartime, but once the enemy's invasion forces had been driven off, it was the air arm's strategic air campaign against the hostile nation that would win the war. Since the War Department adamantly denied the decisiveness of strategic bombardment, and since the American public was opposed to even considering offensive military operations, Foulois and his subordinates had to walk a fine line.

During his four-year tenure as chief, Foulois encouraged the Air Corps Tactical School at Maxwell Field, Alabama, to continue refining strategic bombardment doctrine, while he worked rather quietly within the War Department to win greater acceptance of the usefulness of long-range bombers. Foulois never made strategic bombing a major issue in his somewhat

33

antagonistic relationship with the General Staff. Yet some senior Army officers like MacArthur and his War Plans Division Chief, Brig. Gen. Charles E. Kilbourne, came to the conclusion by 1934 that in some circumstances, air activity beyond the immediate theater of ground operations might be useful. They believed that bombing rear areas, while not decisive in its own right, could assist the army indirectly.

Foulois realized the current state of aviation technology did not support the claims of Air Corps Tactical School strategic bombing advocates. Nor could planes of limited range and load carrying capacity be shifted quickly from coast to coast to attack an enemy's invasion fleet. It was obvious to him that the Air Corps could not ignore aircraft research and development, even in the Depression years, if it hoped to serve the nation effectively in time of war. He agreed with others in the Air Corps; bombers were the most important planes because they could protect the American homeland and then go on to destroy an enemy's warmaking capabilities in a strategic air campaign.

In March 1933, Foulois submitted to the General Staff a request to develop an experimental bomber with a 5,000-mile range and a speed of 200 miles an hour. He pointed out that the aircraft could move rapidly to defend either coast as well as Panama, Hawaii, or Alaska, but he astutely avoided mentioning that it also would be an ideal plane to carry out a long-range strategic air campaign against an enemy's heartland. In May 1934, much to his surprise, a less than enthusiastic General Staff gave grudging approval to the project. Foulois had only recently implied in congressional testimony that the Army had hindered aircraft development. Because of that and the air arm's poor showing in the airmail operation, MacArthur probably felt he had no choice but to approve what the Air Corps called "Project A." The Boeing-built XB–15 did not fly until 1937, and subsequent flight tests showed that it was too large for engines available at the time. Nevertheless, Project A and later research and development started by Foulois advanced the state of aeronautical technology and led to the unparalleled U.S. heavy bomber forces of World War II.

The air chief was not satisfied to merely provide for the future. When the Air Corps finally received more money for aircraft procurement in mid-1934, Foulois directed his staff to seek bids for new bombers. He was elated over the Boeing entry in the August 1935 prototype flyoff. The XB–17 cruised 2,100 miles from the company's Seattle plant to Dayton, Ohio, at an average speed of 232 miles an hour. Here was an aircraft to make strategic bombardment possible. Technology had finally caught up with doctrine.

*   *   *   *   *

The Air Corps had made great progress under Foulois, but his last two years as chief were not happy ones. Senior Army officers were angered by his open advocacy of a separate air force and his uncooperative attitude whenever Air Corps interests were involved. They also complained that he spent too much time out flying and visiting air units across the country to discharge his duties in Washington properly. But Foulois's greatest headaches in 1934–35 came from Congress rather than from the General Staff.

The problems started in February 1934 when the House Military Affairs Committee decided to investigate military aircraft procurement. Foulois and previous Chiefs of the Air Corps had played somewhat loose with procurement statutes, using negotiated contracts rather than competitive bidding to buy new planes. The aviators believed they could better control quality and prices by arranging contracts with proven producers. Applicable laws and Army regulations contained enough loopholes to allow this practice, and, indeed, the Judge Advocate General of the Army had consistently endorsed such contracts as acceptable under the law. Air Corps procurement officers were careful to ensure aircraft manufacturers did not make exhorbitant profits.

When Congressman McSwain and his colleagues learned in early 1934 that the Air Corps had been using negotiated contracting, they were dismayed. The procurement provisions of the 1926 Air Corps Act had been written specifically to foster competitive buying practices. Members of the House Military Affairs Committee, stunned by fatalities during the early weeks of the airmail operation, suspected the Army air arm was buying inferior planes under an illegal procurement system. They wanted to ferret out the guilty parties; a full investigation was in order.

Representative William Rogers's subcommittee of the House Military Affairs Committee opened hearings on March 7. Rogers was clearly on a witch-hunt. His subcommittee did not stop to determine if Air Corps aircraft were, in fact, inferior. Instead, it charged ahead looking for the corruption the members were sure they would uncover, only to find there had been none. The subcommittee realized investigations that reveal no misdeeds soon lose the publicity on which politicians flourish. It needed to find a guilty party. Rogers and his colleagues decided that Foulois, a leading advocate of negotiated contracts, might be a suitable candidate. He had defended negotiated purchasing during testimony before the subcommittee on March 7. When some of the lawmakers argued that such contracts violated Army regulations (which they did not), Foulois became riled. Without considering his words, he shot back: "That is perfectly all right. I have overlooked the Army regulations and broken them hundreds of times in the interest of the Government, and I will break them again." This angry outburst helped the subcommittee to focus on him as its target.

So, too, did the airmail episode set Foulois up for attack by the subcommittee. Not only had he assured the President that his aviators could do the job; on March 1, without really looking into the situation, he had told the Rogers subcommittee that the Air Corps was properly trained and equipped for the operation. Congressmen Rogers and Lister Hill believed Foulois and defended the Air Corps against charges to the contrary on the House floor, arguing that bad weather, not deficiencies, was the cause of early difficulties. When accidents continued, the subcommittee members concluded that Foulois had intentionally misled them, and they began a review of his earlier testimony in search of more equivocations. Their attention was quickly drawn to his February 1 testimony before McSwain's committee, supporting the bill to create a separate air force.

Foulois had appeared before the Military Affairs Committee on the short-notice request of McSwain and had used his customary approach of campaigning for Air Corps independence by damning the General Staff's purportedly inept handling of military aviation. Foulois had prefaced his remarks by saying he was only expressing his personal opinion. Then, at his vitriolic best, he lashed out in an unguarded manner, mixing opinion with fact. To McSwain's delight, Foulois told the committee that "the main obstacle" to military aviation progress over the past twenty years "has been the War Department General Staff." These remarks, replete with overgeneralizations, now became a wellspring of trouble for him as the Rogers subcommittee checked them for accuracy. Foulois had not deliberately lied to McSwain's committee. He had simply followed his usual approach of stating the case against the General Staff in the worst possible terms.

Concern over the air chief's deceptiveness, rather than his involvement in negotiated contracting, became the driving force behind the Rogers subcommittee's continued investigation. The congressmen latched onto every inconsistency and every biased opinion in Foulois's February 1 testimony in an attempt to prove his duplicity. During May and early June 1934, Rogers called senior Army officers to testify in closed session on the accuracy of Foulois's remarks and his fitness to serve as Chief of the Air Corps.

As might be expected, the ground officers were pre-disposed to describe Foulois in unfavorable terms. General Kilbourne, who had butted heads repeatedly with him over the past two years, objected strongly to Foulois's contention that the General Staff knew nothing about military aviation and was unresponsive to Air Corps needs. Other senior officers joined in rebutting the assertions made by the air chief. Committee members asked Kilbourne for his appraisal of Foulois. "For a man to come up here and make such statements as he had made to you, which are easily capable of being refuted, it looks like he is crazy," volunteered the Chief of the War Plans Division. Deputy Chief of Staff General Drum went even further: "My personal opinion is that he is not a fit officer to be Chief of the Air Corps."

The subcommittee now had the views of several ranking officers with which to refute Foulois's February 1 statements. Never mind that all parties to the issue were expressing their personal opinions. Rogers and his fellow congressmen now had additional "evidence" to support their preconceived position. From their prospective, the investigation had been a success; an individual had been found who was responsible for both illegal contracting and the air-mail debacle. Further, that same individual had lied to the members of Congress. The Rogers subcommittee charged Foulois with all three offenses in its June 15, 1934, final report and demanded that he be removed immediately from his position as Chief of the Air Corps.

His rage nearly out of control, Foulois reacted at once to the congressmen's final report. In a bitter statement to reporters on June 17, he damned the subcommittee's use of secret sessions, argued his innocence, and challenged Rogers and his colleagues: "I am ready and willing at any time to meet my accusers in an open court." The frustrated air chief demanded the subcommittee provide him a transcript of the hearings, a necessary step if he was to refute the charges against him. He renewed this plea throughout the summer, but Rogers would not budge.

Public opinion quickly sided with Foulois as newspapers throughout the country protested both the subcommittee's findings and its secret methods. A *Washington Evening Star* editorial summed up the press criticism:

> The House Subcommittee on Military Affairs did not content itself with merely making to the Secretary of War a report of its findings. It tried—if you can call it a trial—General Foulois, found him guilty, and acting as judge and jury, sentenced him to be dismissed, and called upon Mr. Dern to carry out the sentence. This appears, at best, to be a high-handed proceeding on the part of the subcommittee. . . . A trial conducted behind closed doors, with the prosecutors acting as both judge and jury, is certainly repugnant to all ideals of American justice.

Secretary of War George Dern, no friend of Foulois's, took a similar view. When Rogers demanded that Dern remove the Air Corps Chief immediately, the Secretary replied that the subcommittee would first have to give Foulois a complete transcript of the testimony so that he could respond to the charges. The impasse lasted into December 1934, while the distraught Foulois spent considerable time worrying about his fate. The press continued to support him. The media was not about to see the general railroaded by a few members of Congress.

In December, Dern and Rogers finally reached a compromise. The War Department would have the Army's Inspector General (IG) investigate the charges against Foulois, and the subcommittee would provide the IG a transcript of the secret hearings. Foulois was displeased by this turn of events; he had little confidence that the investigation would be impartial, especially with Congressman Rogers and other lawmakers taking such an active interest in the case. During April 1935, the House Military Affairs Committee became impatient with the slow pace of the Army's inquiry and implied that it would

Secretary of War George Dern

sit on all pending War Department legislation to encourage the speedy conclusion of the investigation.

Secretary Dern released the IG's findings on June 14, findings that pleased Foulois and angered the subcommittee. The Inspector General exonerated the Chief of the Air Corps on all charges save one: "General Foulois did depart from the ethics and standards of the service by making exaggerated, unfair, and misleading statements to a Congressional committee." For this minor misdeed Dern sent Foulois a letter of reprimand. Both the Chief of the Air Corps and the Rogers subcommittee considered the IG's conclusions tantamount to an acquittal.

Benny Foulois knew he had spent too much time over the past year defending himself rather than running the Air Corps. He thought his ordeal now was over. Rogers was livid. On June 15, on the House floor, he blasted what he called "a slap on the wrist administered to a liar and perjurer." The subcommittee's vindictive chairman would not give up his campaign to oust Foulois.

Rogers's attacks and the continuing hostility of the Military Affairs Committee persuaded Foulois to reach a difficult decision in August 1935. He concluded that the committee members' feelings toward him might adversely affect subsequent Air Corps legislation. Frustrated and disheartened by the continued pressure for his removal and wanting to spare his beloved Air Corps further problems, Foulois announced that he would retire at the end of December and would begin terminal leave on September 25.

At the end of September, General Foulois slipped quietly out of Washington, sick at heart. He returned just as quietly on Christmas Day, going out to Bolling Field for his last flight as an Air Corps pilot. As his O–38F lifted into the sky, he again experienced that special elation known only to aviators. That evening Foulois partied with members of his staff and reminisced about old times. Six days later, on New Year's Eve, he stopped by his office to clean out his desk. He still was *persona non grata* in the War Department; no one from the General Staff dropped in to say goodbye. Foulois signed out at five o'clock. At the age of fifty-six his career as a military officer was over.

General Foulois remained a strong advocate of air power throughout the remainder of his life. He settled in Ventnor, New Jersey, but was frequently on the road during the years leading up to World War II, speaking on the need for preparedness and the importance of military aviation. Few people were interested in what he had to say until Hitler's forces conquered Poland and Western Europe in 1939 and 1940.

During the Second World War, Foulois ran New Jersey's civil defense program; afterward he returned to private life. When his wife became terminally ill in 1959 and was confined to the Andrews Air Force Base Hospital near Washington, Foulois moved into base guest quarters to be near her. After she passed away, Air Force Chief of Staff General Thomas D. White invited him to continue living at Andrews and to undertake a speaking tour on behalf

Gen. Benjamin D. Foulois

Air Force Magazine

39

of military aviation. Foulois accepted both offers. After twenty-five years, he was once again part of the Air Force he had helped to create. Over the next several years he traveled more than a million miles to tell the story of military aviation and stress the importance of air power.

In his last years, General Foulois lost neither his keen understanding of air power nor his earthy sense of humor. In an autobiography, completed shortly before his death in 1967, he argued convincingly for an air campaign against North Vietnam that included virtually all elements found some five years later in the Air Force's and Navy's extremely successful Operation Linebacker and Operation Linebacker II. While he was deadly serious about air power, he was the kind of man who loved a good laugh with his friends. On one occasion he showed up for a luncheon with a note hung around his neck: "This is General Benjamin Foulois. He requires two martinis before lunch." It was signed by the Surgeon General.

The man who had first flown with the Wright brothers and had been a driving force in the development of U.S. military aviation died on April 25, 1967, at the age of eighty-seven—loved and honored in retirement as he had not been that sad New Year's Eve of 1935 when he had closed a distinguished military career.

Sources

Only two books treat General Benjamin Foulois's life in detail. Benjamin D. Foulois and Carroll V. Glines, *From the Wright Brothers to the Astronauts: The Memoirs of Major General Benjamin D. Foulois* (McGraw-Hill, 1968) provides highly readable and interesting, but somewhat uncritical, coverage of Foulois's military career. John F. Shiner, *Foulois and the Army Air Corps* (Office of Air Force History/GPO, 1983) is a detailed study of Foulois during his years as Chief of the Air Corps (1931–35). Primary source material on Foulois's career is plentiful. The bulk of it is located in the Library of Congress Manuscripts Division. However, some excellent material on his experiences through World War I can be found in the Air Force Academy Library's Special Collections Division.

There is a small number of good books treating the Air Service/Air Corps during Foulois's active duty career. DeWitt S. Copp, *A Few Great Captains* (Doubleday, 1980), while focusing on other pre-World War II U.S. military aviation figures, captures well the flavor of the Army air arm during its first thirty years. Alfred Goldberg (Editor), *A History of the United States Air Force, 1907–1957* (D. Van Nostrand, 1957) is the best-known general survey of the development of American air power. While it emphasizes the post-1941 years, it contains a good overview of U.S. military aviation down to World War II. Robert Frank Futrell, *Ideas, Concepts, Doctrine: A History of Basic Thinking in the United States Air Force* (Air University, Maxwell AFB, Alabama, 1971) has two good chapters on the evolution of air missions, doctrine, and strategy within the Army air arm between 1907 and 1941. Carroll V. Glines, *The Saga of the Air Mail* (D. Van Nostrand, 1968) and Paul Tillett, *The Army Flies the Mails* (University of Alabama Press, 1955) both are readable and generally accurate accounts of the 1934 air mail episode. Edwin H. Rutkowski, *The Politics of Military Aviation Procurement, 1926–1934* (Ohio State University Press, 1966) is the best volume on the procurement problems faced by Foulois.

Articles dealing with Foulois and/or the Army air arm during his career are not plentiful. John F. Shiner provides a brief overview of the aviation pioneer in his "Benjamin D. Foulois," *Air Force Magazine* (April 1979). Three sequential articles written by General Foulois about his pre-World War I aviation experiences are invaluable for capturing the essence of the man. Titled "Early Flying Experiences," they appeared in *Air Power Historian* (April and July 1955 and April 1956). John F. Shiner's "General Benjamin Foulois and the 1934 Air Mail Disaster," *Aerospace Historian* (Winter 1978), and Eldon W. Downs, "The Army and the Air Mail," Air Power Historian (January 1962), provide good, brief coverage of one of the most difficult episodes during Foulois's tenure as Chief of the Air Corps. Shiner's "Birth of the GHQ Air Force," *Military Affairs* (October 1978), describes the aviators' struggle to win a centrally controlled air strike force during the interwar years and focuses on Foulois's part in that effort. Shiner's "The Air Corps, the Navy, and Coast Defense, 1919–1941," *Military Affairs* (October 1981), provides balanced coverage of the struggle between the Navy and the Army air arm for control of the coast defense mission, in which Foulois was a key participant.

3

Frank M. Andrews:
Marshall's Airman

DeWitt S. Copp

In war nothing is so commonplace as sudden death. But when the victim is a high-ranking officer of recognized brilliance, his loss can be shattering and the ironies of what could have been linger amidst the engulfing emptiness of unfulfilled promise. So it was on the afternoon of May 3, 1943, when the B–24 Liberator in which Lt. Gen. Frank M. Andrews was flying crashed against a fog-shrouded promontory while making a landing approach to Meeks Field near Keflavik, Iceland. Andrews was commanding general of all U.S. forces in the newly formed European Theater of Operations (ETO). He had held his post for just three months, having arrived in England on February 4, the day after his fifty-ninth birthday. The decision to transfer him from his command of U.S. Middle East Forces had been approved by President Roosevelt, Prime Minister Churchill, and the Combined Chiefs of Staff at the Casablanca Conference in January.

It was U.S. Army Chief of Staff Gen. George C. Marshall who had summoned Andrews to the conference from Andrews's headquarters in Cairo, Egypt. Privately, however, Marshall had previously informed Andrews of what was afoot, for between them lay a tacit bond of understanding and mutual appreciation that dated back to their first meeting in August 1938. At that time, Andrews was a temporary major general in his third year as Commander of General Headquarters (GHQ) Air Force, the combat arm of the Army Air Corps that had been established in 1935. Marshall, a permanent brigadier general who had once served as chief of staff to Andrews's father-in-law, Maj. Gen. Henry T. Allen, had just been appointed head of the Army General Staff's War Plans Division (WPD).

43

Andrews, in that last summer of European peace, was having a difficult struggle, trying to prevail on Secretary of War Harry H. Woodring and War Department leaders to build up the country's air strength. In confidence, Andrews had told Eugene Meyer, publisher of *The Washington Post*, that every major country in the world was better prepared than the United States to defend itself. Helping to prove the point, Secretary Woodring had decided to cancel any further production of the Flying Fortress, the Boeing B–17, around which Andrews was determined to establish U.S. air supremacy.

What Andrews confined to Meyer, he told Marshall in far greater detail when the new Chief of WPD spent a day with him at Langley Field, Virginia, GHQ Air Force headquarters. Following their initial get-together, Marshall wrote his host: "I think I learned quite a bit about the problem and will look forward to some further meetings when I have better coordinated my thoughts with the information available. . . . " The further meetings quickly followed. Andrews invited Marshall to accompany him on a comprehensive nine-day inspection of the GHQ Air Force and aircraft production facilities. No ground officer in such a high level and important post had ever been given a more complete tour, and no airman was better equipped to play host than Andrews.

They traveled aboard Andrews's Douglas DC–2, with Andrews often at the controls and Marshall riding in the copilot's seat. What Andrews introduced Marshall to in their coast-to-coast sweep was an eye-opener for the fifty-eight-year-old War Plans Chief. The production, servicing, training, and quality of an air force could not be achieved with the same equations that were used for ground forces. It was an axiom few ground officers had ever understood. As Andrews put it:

Gen. George C. Marshall (left) and Lt. Gen. Frank M. Andrews

> If it takes three months to train an artilleryman and ten months to build a cannon, then you have got to have a reserve of cannon. But when it takes a year to build an airplane and up to three years to train the crews to operate and maintain that airplane, then there is not quite such a big argument for a reserve of airplanes, particularly where aeronautical advancement in types is as rapid as it is today. We cannot afford to equip the air force of tomorrow with the airplanes of yesterday.

What Andrews had to say about air power and the potential of its strategic use with the B-17, his position on the need for air independence from War Department control, and what he believed must be done in all these areas, was also of prime interest to Marshall. He listened, he observed, he asked questions. The journey and its impact—air maneuvers to air depots, experimental aircraft design to outdated operational models—was a unique experience for Marshall. In retrospect, there is little doubt that Andrews's career was to be directly affected by it while Marshall's understanding and appreciation of air power was strongly influenced.

An astute judge of character, Marshall obviously came away impressed by the clarity of Andrews's thought and the genial yet firm assurance of the airman's manner. Both came from southern backgrounds. Andrews was born in Nashville, Tennessee, on February 3, 1884, and though Marshall was born in Uniontown, Pennsylvania, on December 31, 1880, he had graduated from Virginia Military Institute in 1901. Marshall was reserved and outwardly cool by nature, his sense of humor well concealed; Andrews's warmth was nicely balanced by his directness and the quality of his intellect. Both men shared an inbred, old-world courtesy. Andrews's deft touch in seeing to it that his guest, wearing one less star than Andrews, was shown the deference and respect of a senior at all their stops could not have been lost on Marshall.

When the tour was over, Marshall wrote to his old mentor, Gen. John J. Pershing, expressing his enthusiasm, describing the itinerary, and remarking: "Altogether I had a most interesting trip professionally and a most magnificent one personally." To Andrews he declared: "I want to thank you again . . . for the splendid trip you gave me, and especially for your personal efforts to make it a pleasant one and highly instructive. I enjoyed every minute of the trip and my association with you, and I really think I acquired a fair picture of military air activities in general. A little study will help me to digest something of all I saw. . . . With warm regards."

What Marshall was looking for was an orderly plan by which the country's defenses could be built, with the focus on production and training. No such plan existed, and he appreciated having the benefit of Andrews's thoughts, particularly as they applied to the lack of a realistic program for building U.S. air power.

Three and a half years earlier, in December 1934, another Army officer of equal stature had directly influenced Andrews's career. The officer was Chief of Staff Maj. Gen. Douglas MacArthur. The two had not flown

45

Lt. Gen. Frank Andrews in cockpit of B–17.

anywhere together, but MacArthur selected Andrews to command the airmen's long-sought GHQ Air Force. MacArthur never offered a public explanation for his choice of Andrews for this most important of air commands. But a quick look at some of Andrews's previous activities offers insight into the forward reach of his thinking at a time when the military was economically and strategically constrained, locked into the rigidity of the status quo.

*   *   *   *   *

Shortly after MacArthur was appointed Army Chief of Staff in November 1930, Andrews developed an intense interest in instrument flying. It had been aroused by the *Mount Shasta* affair of 1931, in which he had been a principal planner and organizer while serving as Chief of Training and Operations (G–3) in Air Corps Chief Maj. Gen. James Fechet's office. This was a Billy Mitchell-type test in which bombers of the 2d Group, led by Maj. Herbert A. Dargue, would fly out to sea from their base at Langley Field and sink the *Mount Shasta*, an old freighter. After two days of searching in bad weather, the bombers finally located the ship and scored one hit out of forty-two bombs dropped. Navy guns sank the target, much to the chagrin of the airmen. The claim that the Air Corps was capable of defending U.S. coastal waters took a beating. Andrews, not looking for excuses, weighed the causes of failure and arranged to take the three-week instrument training course, inadequate at best, at the Advanced Flight School, Kelly Field, Texas.

A year later he got permission from Air Corps Chief Maj. Gen. Benjamin D. Foulois to publicize air mobility by making an epic journey. He led a flight of five aircraft from San Antonio, Texas, to France Field in the Panama Canal Zone. Previously, Andrews had flown coast to coast numerous times in everything from DH–4s to the new all-metal Northrop Alpha, but the long operation of shepherding antiquated Keystone bombers and a pair of Douglas amphibians on a 2,200-mile jaunt down through Central America stimulated ideas on all-weather flying.

In June 1933, Andrews graduated from the Army War College and was assigned to command the 1st Pursuit Group at Selfridge Field near Detroit, Michigan. He was resolved to eradicate the belief of most pursuit pilots that when the weather was bad you did not fly if you could avoid it. At Selfridge, he found there was not a single gyro compass or gyro horizon—standard equipment on commercial aircraft—amongst the planes of his three squadrons. His letters to the chief's office brought no direct response. Close friends in the Materiel Division at Wright Field told him that orders from above were to not parcel out the gyros because they were in such short supply and must be held against the far distant day when new aircraft would be coming off the line.

Although Andrews made very little progress in establishing an instrument program at Selfridge, Foulois did set up two small "avigation" schools at Langley and at Rockwell Field, California, in the fall of 1933. Brig. Gen. Oscar Westover, Assistant Chief of the Air Corps, was a prime mover in that development. He and Andrews had been classmates at West Point, and through him, Andrews's letters may have had an effect. Andrews knew only too well that inadequate instrument training was dictated as much by the War Department attitude as by lack of funds.

Immediately after Andrews arrived at Selfridge, an event occurred that strongly reinforced his thinking about instrument flying, logistics, and navigation. He became host at an internationally publicized aviation venture. In July 1933, Italian Air Marshal Italo Balbo led a flight of twenty-four twin-engine Savoia Marchetti torpedo bombers on a 6,000-mile flight from Orbetello, Italy, to North American cities. Andrews led two squadrons of the 1st Pursuit Group to greet the Italian flyers in the air as they crossed the U.S.-Canadian border near Detroit and to escort them to a landing at Chicago's World Fair.

The colorful Italian air marshal went on to a presidential welcome at the White House, completing the longest mass flight in aviation history. The War Department classed the undertaking as an aerial stunt with little military meaning, but Andrews, and most airmen, recognized the obvious significance of the mission. Balbo and his men had clearly demonstrated that with proper aeronautical equipment and training, airmen soon would be able to fly long distances in adverse weather to reach any adversary's industrial heartland. If the War Department failed to recognize what military leaders of other countries foresaw, U.S. air power could not keep pace. Andrews was determined to see that this did not happen.

It was several months after the Balbo flight, in October 1933, that the Drum Board, appointed by MacArthur and named for its chairman, Maj. Gen. Hugh A. Drum, endorsed creating a consolidated combat air arm, the GHQ Air Force. While reaffirming the Air Corps' mandate of coastal defense, this fell short of Air Corps' aspirations for greater independence from War Department control. The only airman on the five-man board was Foulois. The others were ground-bound General Staff officers whose view of air power and its potential was fixed not so much on the sky as on the trench. Further, the Drum Board scoffed at the meaning of the Balbo epic, and to Andrews and other like-minded airmen the message was clear. The Air Corps would never realize its potential until it gained independence.

There was nothing new in the belief, nor in the concept of a combat arm for the Air Corps. It had been forced into being by political circumstances rather than War Department willingness to accept a long-sought military necessity. The plan for an air force with its own command and staff within the Army Air Corps had first been proposed in 1923 by the Lassiter Board (named for its chief, Brig. Gen. William Lassiter), that examined the role of U.S. military aviation. The board recommended that while the main purpose of an air arm was to directly support the ground forces, some units not so engaged could be used against other targets as a separate strike force. The idea had originated with Col. Edgar S. Gorrell during World War I and was tried out with considerable success by Billy Mitchell against the Germans in the St. Mihiel and Meuse-Argonne campaigns in 1918. Five years later, the Lassiter Board approved assembling such a peacetime force, but it took more than a decade and a gaggle of additional boards before MacArthur gave his blessing. This was not so much a blessing as a recognition that the War Department was caught between fractious congressional demands supporting a separate air force and the War Department securing a coastal defense mission for the Air Corps over Navy objections.

When, by the end of the year, nothing had been done to implement the Drum Board's recommendations establishing a GHQ Air Force, the impatience of those who believed that a separate air force was imperative grew, and with it a determination to make a new bid for independence. Such a bid must come through congressional action, and Selfridge Field in Michigan was somewhat far afield to exert political influence. Yet Andrews did. His ability to do so was fostered by his good friend, Lt. Col. Walter H. Weaver, who was serving on Foulois's staff as G-2, Chief of Information. Their friendship dated back to West Point days. They corresponded frequently, and Weaver's letters reflected the general spirit of insurrection within the chief's office. Associates such as Maj. Carl "Tooey" Spaatz and Capts. George C. Kenney and Robert Olds had had their fill of what they saw as War Department stultification and were determined to risk whatever was necessary to get free of it.

Weaver sent an advisory to this effect not only to Andrews but also to Lt. Col. Henry H. "Hap" Arnold, commanding at March Field; to Maj. Hugh J. Knerr, Chief of the Field Service Section in the Engineering Branch at Wright Field; and to Lt. Col. Horace M. Hickam, commanding the 3d Attack Group at Fort Crockett, Texas. Weaver declared that the Air Corps was "in a rather crucial position. I don't know if anyone is going to help it unless we do something for ourselves."

The "doing something" would be to draft a bill for independence and put it in the hands of a congressman powerful and persuasive enough to hold open hearings. At the hearings, a host of airmen would testify and support the bill's passage. In the midst of a shattering depression and an unsympathetic administration, it hardly seemed likely that many congressmen or much of the public would be interested in creating a new branch of the service. But the airmen had a champion in Congressman John J. McSwain of South Carolina, Chairman of the House Armed Services Committee. The War Department saw him as a threat; Benny Foulois's conspirators regarded him as a friend.

Weaver was welcome in the upper social circles of the military hierarchy, his father having risen to command the Coast Artillery. Through such association, he had come to know McSwain. Since the congressman had never met Andrews, but suddenly made a special flight to Selfridge Field in January 1934 to spend a weekend at the Andrews's home, there is little doubt that the meeting had been arranged by Weaver.

The first thing McSwain did upon arriving back at the Capital was to write Andrews a letter of appreciation and thanks. On February 2, 1934, directly after his visit to Selfridge, McSwain threw the War Department into a tailspin by offering a bill to his committee that embodied everything separate air force proponents were seeking. Just the day before, the War Department had placed before McSwain its long overdue recommendation that incorporated the creation of a GHQ air force. But it failed to include any of the burning wants of the airmen, such as a separate promotion list. Some could see in the McSwain bill a counter-demand aimed at forcing more concessions from the General Staff, knowing full well the bill itself would never pass. MacArthur, who referred privately to the Military Affairs Chairman as "McSwine," was not inclined to offer anything further, and it appeared that a battle royal was in the making. At that moment the entire issue was over-shadowed and held in check by an unexpected event.

On February 9, 1934, through a piece of political misjudgment, President Roosevelt stripped the commercial air carriers of their franchises to carry the mail and assigned the task to the Air Corps. Air Corps Chief Foulois had agreed that in ten days' time he could have his planes equipped and ready to take on the specialized task of maintaining a major share of the nation's airmail routes. There were three factors militating against the success of the Air Corps mission, which used the acronym AACMO—Army Air Corps Mail Operation: its ill-equipped aircraft, its pilots who were ill-trained for instrument flying, and the worst nationwide winter weather on record.

In the ten days between Roosevelt's decision and the start of AACMO, Foulois, who had given considerable lip service to the need for instrument training but had been prevented by lack of funds from doing much about it, launched a frantic campaign to equip his planes with radios and rudimentary flight instruments, and to give the pilots some instrument training. It was too late. In March, Roosevelt was forced by a series of weather-related crashes to ground the operation for ten days.

As the winter weather abated and pilots gained experience in weather and night flying, the Air Corps' performance improved. Nevertheless, the public generally, and the War Department and certain congressmen specifically, considered the 78-day AACMO a dismal failure. In truth, despite the loss of a dozen pilots and crewmen and 66 accidents, crews delivered more than 770,000 pounds of mail without losing a single letter and completed more than 65 percent of all scheduled flights.

During the airmail operation, Andrews continued to push for instrument equipment, but with little success. Thirty-eight of his sixty-two pilots were assigned to AACMO, among them Lts. Curtis E. Lemay, Earle E. Partridge, and Mark Bradley. The 1st Pursuit Group was so stripped of men and equipment that it no longer could be considered operational, but Andrews could take heart in the fact that during AACMO the Air Corps established its first blind flying school at Wright Field. Capt. Albert F. Hegenberger, a pioneer along with Jimmy Doolittle in the development of military instrument flying, was the school's first director.

The Air Corps' improving performance after AACMO's disastrous beginning did not dispel the outcry within the War Department and Congress for investigation of air preparedness. A new board was formed—the fifteenth in sixteen years—to be chaired by and named for former Secretary of War Newton D. Baker. It served the same old purpose: on the surface, to chart a course for the Air Corps, and beneath it, to assure that the course was not directed toward independence. It, like the Drum Board, whose members were a part of the Baker Board, was in favor of a GHQ air force.

On May 23, 1934, even before the Baker Board had made known its recommendations, Andrews was ordered to report to the War Department to chair a committee that was, he told his father, "to make recommendations on organization of the Air Corps for greater mobility." Serving with him were such keen thinkers as Spaatz, Hickam, Knerr, and Kenney. Their work was completed by mid-June. What they had created was the organizational structure for a combat air arm.

Andrews learned in October that he was to return to Washington to serve in the War Department Operations and Training Section, G–3, charged with working out the tables of organization for a GHQ air force he and his committee had put together in June. In the two months that followed, he realized that his duties might well come to naught. Congressional hearings and board recommendations notwithstanding, the formation of a GHQ air force was in no way assured, since General MacArthur's continuance as Army Chief of Staff was in doubt. Andrews saw that, without MacArthur's determination, powerful elements within the faceless General Staff would see to it that the concept of an air force remained just that, smothered in words and grounded by committees. Fortunately, President Roosevelt stopped playing coy and let it be known that he wanted Douglas MacArthur to remain as Chief for another year.

Thereupon, the biggest question in town was who would command the nascent air force. Benny Foulois was out, in political trouble on all fronts. His assistant chief, General Westover, who had been AACMO's titular

Gen. Douglas MacArthur

51

commander, was considered a contender. So were some seventy other officers, many of them senior to Andrews. It was MacArthur alone who made the final decision to name Frank Andrews Commander of the GHQ Air Force with a two-grade promotion to brigadier general. That Andrews, a "heretofore obscure field officer," as *Time* magazine put it, was selected was a tribute to his demonstrated ability as a commander and staff officer. It was also, to some degree, a result of fortuitous circumstances.

Following graduation from West Point in 1906, Frank Andrews had served eleven years as a cavalry officer in the Philippines, Hawaii, and the States. In 1917, he transferred to the Signal Corps for duty with the Aviation Division. Three years earlier, Andrews had married Josephine "Johnny" Allen, daughter of General Henry Allen, and had moved into the all-important social inner circle of the War Department, where his father-in-law was a power. Both Andrews and his wife also were champion polo players.

From August 1920 to February 1923, Andrews commanded the U.S. Army Air Service's European air force of thirteen DH-4s under his highly popular father-in-law, who was in charge of all U.S. occupation forces in Germany. On his return to the States, Andrews spent four years at Kelly Field, Texas, in flight training assignments, followed by attendance at the Air Corps Tactical School, then at Langley Field, Virginia, and the Command and General Staff School at Fort Leavenworth, Kansas. Since he was not in Washington when Billy Mitchell was fighting his battles of the 1920s, Andrews had never been considered one of "Mitchell's Boys," although he was a confidant of Mitchell after the latter's resignation in 1926.

Deputy Chief of Staff Hugh Drum, in a letter to Newton Baker, explained the reasoning behind Andrews's selection to head the GHQ Air Force: "We all feel he [Andrews] will be able to meet the situation and develop the force along the lines contemplated. Furthermore, in addition to being an efficient flyer, he has been in harmony with all the War Department has been trying to do."

*　　*　　*　　*　　*

On March 1, 1935, Andrews officially assumed command of GHQ Air Force at Langley Field. Permitted to name his own principal staff, Andrews chose Majs. Hugh Knerr as his chief of staff; Harvey B. S. Burwell as G-1; Follett Bradley as G-2; Capt. George Kenney as G-3; and Maj. Joseph E. McNarney as G-4. All were vintage airmen; Bradley, Kenney, and McNarney combat veterans. Knerr, Bradley, and Kenney had long been strong

Brig. Gen. Frank Andrews and staff being honored with an aerial view at the newly created GHQ Air Force headquarters, Langley Field, Virginia.

independence advocates. Knerr was a bomber-first zealot, a stubborn visionary who not only foresaw but also played a direct role in developing the long-range bomber. Kenney's three years at MIT helped to stimulate ideas that encompassed everything from aeronautical experimentation to correcting the translation from French to English the strategic bombardment theories of Giulio Douhet. Bradley, like Knerr, was a graduate of Annapolis. He had taken his first airplane ride as an observer with pilot Lt. Hap Arnold in 1911. Most recently, he had hand-carried an air independence petition coast to coast getting the signatures of airmen who were in favor of a separate air force. Burwell had flown with the 1st Aero Squadron on the Mexican border in 1916. Later he served as operations officer for Andrews in Germany. McNarney, who commanded observation squadrons in France during the war, had written a book on air tactics and was well regarded in the War Department. Noted for the caliber of his intellect and the dourness of his manner, McNarney kept his own counsel on the issue of independence.

At the outset, independence became a moot question for Andrews. Calling the sixty-seven officers of his staff together, he said, in effect: This is the best we can get. Separation from the Army will come some day, but for now we have a five-year mandate to build a combat air force, and we are going to do that. We have three wings—the 1st at March Field, commanded by Brig. Gen. Hap Arnold; the 2d here at Langley, commanded by Brig. Gen. H. Conger Pratt; and the 3d at Barksdale, Louisiana, commanded by Col. Gerald Brant. We have a service test to prepare for in December. Let us get to it.

What they had to work with was considerably less than what had been recommended by the Drum and Baker Boards and approved by MacArthur. Instead of a force of 980 aircraft, Andrews had 446, with only 176 classed as modern. Instead of 1,245 pilots, he had less than half that number, and his enlisted strength was equally inadequate. But if the numbers did not add up, the spirit and professionalism to make the combat air force fly was fully there. There was enormous enthusiasm throughout the Air Corps for Andrews and for the new organization.

In those first few months of shakedown and preparation there was only one sour note, and it was sounded privately between Andrews and MacArthur. Prior to taking command, Andrews had testified in executive session before McSwain and his Military Affairs Committee. He had been asked questions concerning U.S. response to the very remote possibility of an attack by Canada, Great Britain, or France. He used as the basis of his answers War Department contingency plans for such an eventuality. Several weeks later, through not untypical carelessness, his testimony and that of War Plans Division Chief Brig. Gen. Charles E. Kilbourne were released to the press. The headline results embarrassed Roosevelt, who demanded of McSwain and Secretary of War George H. Dern that something be done to prevent such leaks. Dern agreed, and replied that the officers had given their private opinions, supposedly in secrecy.

Andrews explained that his testimony "represented views on an abstract military study with no concrete political thoughts or reference. " He believed that would be the end of it, in spite of outcries by peace groups calling for his and Kilbourne's dismissal. Instead, he was stunned by a harsh letter of admonition from MacArthur. Certainly the Chief of Staff was fully aware of the circumstances surrounding the incident and knew that Andrews's statements before the committee were given on the basis of War Department policy.

Andrews called on MacArthur, seeking an answer to what he believed to have been a mistake, and with the knowledge that the letter would become a part of his official record. He came away from the meeting angry and disappointed. MacArthur had brushed the admonition aside, telling Andrews to forget it. Andrews never would. Loyalty up-and-down was an inviolate principle. The fact that MacArthur had selected him as GHQ Air Force Commander made no difference.

Between the time of Andrews's falling out with General MacArthur and his getting to know George Marshall some three years later, profound political and military changes were in progress on a global scale. There had been Italian aggression against Ethiopia, Japanese aggression against China, and a border war between Russia and Japan. There was civil war in Spain in which the Fascist and Communist dictators were testing their weaponry. And in Europe, Hitler was expanding the boundaries of the Third Reich, annexing the Rhineland and Austria, with the Sundetenland and then all of Czechoslovakia threatened next. In all these moves the importance of air power had grown, particularly among the aggressors, and was recognized as a critical weapon in their military-political planning.

Such recognition was much slower within the Roosevelt administration. The reasons are well known: the President's belief in the fleet, a policy of isolationism which the public supported in the belief that Europe and Asia should be left to fight their own wars, the geography of oceans protecting the hemisphere from attack, and at root, a continuing failure within the War Department to understand fully or to accept the meaning of strategic air power.

Only in retrospect and with the above in mind is it possible to realize the towering importance of Andrews in his role as GHQ Air Force Commander. It was not so much a matter of the size of his command as it was his view on how the forces must be employed. Any air officer who had passed through the doors of the Air Corps Tactical School knew the doctrine of offensive strategic air power: defeat of an enemy by destroying his industrial capacity to wage war through long-range, high-altitude, precision daylight bombing. Andrews was in a position to translate doctrine into strategy and tactics, no matter the lack of understanding or the opposition in the War Department.

At Selfridge, Andrews had not been able to put through his plan for instrument flight training. At Langley the word went out that all pilots in the GHQ Air Force were to be instrument rated. And soon they were. *Mobility* was the action word. Instrument flying enlarged mobility as did ever-extending aircraft range, altitude, and speed. Somewhat providentially they coalesced in October 1935 with the production of the first long-range bomber worthy of the name—the four-engine Boeing B-17 Flying Fortress. And then with so much hanging in the balance, when the long-awaited aircraft was ready for competitive judging, it crashed on its maiden test flight at Wright Field. The result was that the Douglas B-18, a mediocre twin-engine plane with far less mobility, was selected to form the backbone of U.S. bomber power for the next five years.

Andrews, recognizing the severity of the loss, acted swiftly. With the support of Brig. Gen. Augustine W. Robins, Chief of the Materiel Division, and the approval of the new Air Corps Chief, Maj. Gen. Oscar Westover, he was able to gain reluctant War Department agreement to purchase thirteen of the big Boeings on an experimental basis.

Above: Boeing B-17 Flying Fortress; *left:* Maj. Barney Giles (right), pilot of the first B-17 to land at Langley Field, is greeted by Andrews.

The first of the B-17s was flown into Langley Field from Seattle, piloted by Maj. Barney Giles and a proud crew, on March 1, 1937. She was a sleek and majestic beauty in the eyes of the beholders. But by then Andrews realized that a modern air force worthy of the name could not be built within the existing command mold—a mold that placed GHQ Air Force and the Air Corps in a competitive, often acrimonious association, controlled by a War Department whose antiquated organizational structure acted as a ponderously held bridle on the need for change.

Secretly, with Hugh Knerr, Andrews had drafted a new bill for Congressman J. Mark Wilcox of Florida, a member of the House Military Affairs

Committee who had long championed the concept of a separate air force. The Wilcox bill proposed "to create an Air Corps under the Secretary of War, to be known as the United States Air Corps." As Andrews put it, "The bill would recognize air power as being on an equal footing with military and naval power. . . .The Chief of Aviation . . .would be placed on an equal status under the Secretary of War with the Chief of Staff of the Army. . . ."

When Army Chief of Staff Malin Craig sent Andrews a copy of the bill and asked for his comments, Andrews, with a perfectly straight face, wrote a detailed critique in support. Later, when Craig called him to talk about the bill, the Chief of Staff, with an equally straight face, admitted he had not taken the time to read it. Craig already knew that the President and powerful congressmen, not to mention the Secretary of War, were against even holding hearings on H.R. 3151. Voices crying out in the wilderness of fixed concepts are quickly silenced. If nothing else, Andrews's attempt illustrated the change in his thinking. His desire and determination to seek mobility was horizontal as well as vertical.

Since the political and military emphasis was on *defense*, it was not possible to speak in terms of *offense*. But a bomber like the B–17 with a cruising speed of 230 miles an hour, a service ceiling of 25,000 feet, and a range of 2,200 miles, was obviously a defensive-offensive weapon of great promise. And while Secretary of War Woodring was calling, in 1938, for a balanced air arm with a promised 2,320 planes by June 1940, based on the belief that two or three smaller planes could be bought for the price of one large one, Andrews concentrated on building a strategic air force around the power and promise of the B–17. What he hoped to do was convince Westover and the War Department that over the next three years ninety-eight of the Boeings should be purchased, enough to equip his Air Force with two groups.

He demonstrated the B–17's promise time and time again, in maneuvers and long-distance flights. For example, in August 1937, during war games with the Navy, the 2d Bomb Group's B–17s, operating under almost impossible ground rules, sought out and soaked the USS *Utah* with water bombs 285 miles off the California coast. The Navy insisted that the outcome of these games be kept from the public. It was not.

Matters dealing with the promise of aircraft came to a head in May 1938. Conducting the largest aerial maneuvers on record, Andrews sent three of his B–17s out to sea some 700 miles in very stormy weather to intercept the Italian liner *Rex*, which represented an attacking task force. The photograph of two of the B–17s flying past the *Rex*, taken by Capt. George W. Goddard in the third bomber, made the front page of newspapers around the world. It sent a message to friends and to potential adversaries alike. The message bounced off the War Department, and Craig, instead of praising Andrews for the performance, informed him that henceforth his planes were not to

Two B-17s flying past the liner *Rex*, May 1938.

venture more than a hundred miles off the coasts. When Andrews passed this order to Colonel Robert Olds, Commander of the 2d Bomb Group, Olds informed his crews that from now on all practice missions over open water would remain within the hundred-mile limit but courses would be plotted north and south.

The continuing effort by Andrews to augment the strength of his B-17s fell on deaf ears; cost and necessity were the principal barriers. When he let it be known that ultimately he wished to build his bomber strength to 244 B-17s, or one-quarter of his promised total while phasing out the inferior B-18, opponents began to refer jokingly to the Boeing as "Andrews's folly."

In a letter to Hugh Knerr, who had been transferred to Fort Sam Houston, Andrews wrote: "The situation with reference to our strategic mission and the proper equipment with which to perform it, seems to be getting progressively worse, and we have no court of appeal that I can think of. . . ." Then came the August 1938 meeting with Marshall. The War Plans Division Chief, upon returning from his nine days of air power indoctrination, found that, indeed, the airmen had no real representation on the General Staff. He was to become Andrews's court of appeal.

On October 18, 1938, Andrews sent Marshall congratulations on his becoming Deputy Chief of Staff. He enclosed a copy of a talk he had recently given at the War College, saying it expressed the views of practically the entire operating personnel of the Air Corps . . . [who] believe in a larger percentage of high performance, large capacity bombers. . . . In every test or exercise we have ever had . . . this plane stands out head and shoulders above any other type; yet for 1940 and 1941 our estimates do not include a single one. For the support of the Monroe Doctrine on the American Continent such a plane would be of inestimable value. In the control of three important defiles of the world, Singapore, the Mediterranean, and Panama . . . the large capacity plane is easily the outstanding weapon.

He continued in considerable detail: ". . . any program of increasing our air power that does not provide us with an increase of equipment, a practical personnel plan concurred in by the men who, in peace and war, are responsible for the operations, is a half-baked plan and will prove a disappointment when the emergency arises."

Andrews then confessed with characteristic frankness,

I have only a few months [left] in this job of mine, and I will be glad to get out of it for, as it works out, I carry the responsibility and very little authority. I don't even know who my principal assistants are to be until their selection is announced. There is no future in it, and it is like sitting all the time on a powder keg. But in these few remaining months I hope to be included in the discussions and conferences on future plans and policies for the development of our air force. . . .

He was not included, possibly as a result of the meeting he had been invited to attend the previous month. On September 21, 1938, Air Corps Chief General Westover was killed in a crash at Burbank. The next day Andrews was asked by Army Chief of Staff Malin Craig to report to him in Washington. He found himself in a meeting with Craig and all the assistant chiefs. Craig informed him they were prepared to recommend to the President that Andrews succeed Westover on the condition that he stop trying to promote the B–17. Andrews politely refused to accept the condition, and a few days later it was announced that General Hap Arnold was to be the new Air Corps Chief, a choice Andrews and many other airmen hailed as an excellent one.

In view of his position, Andrews knew that when his tour of duty as GHQ Air Force Commander was up on March 1, 1939, his tenure would not be extended. He hoped that he would be assigned to head the Training Command, and if not that, the Air Corps Tactical School. Instead, with no prior warning, he was given the Billy Mitchell treatment: reduction in rank to his permanent grade of colonel and exile to Fort Sam Houston as District Air Officer. There can be no doubt that Secretary of War Woodring approved the action whether he originated it or not. The last straw for Woodring had been a public declaration by Andrews at the National Aeronautic Association convention on January 16, 1939, that the U.S. was a sixth-rate air power. This made headlines across the country, just at the time Woodring was assuring the public of the nation's aerial strength.

When Andy Andrews, wearing mufti, was given a farewell review at Langley, there were few dry eyes. The mail that flooded in, reflecting sorrow, anger, frustration, and praise for him, came from admirers high and low, military and civilian. Truth be known, Andrews was not all that downcast

Gen. George Marshall

by the vindictive action. He was confident that his isolation would be of short duration, partly because he could see the direction of world events and partly, perhaps, because he knew that Marshall would not let him go to seed.

* * * * *

On July 1, 1939, George Marshall became Acting Chief of Staff of the U.S. Army. His first move was a formidable one. He appointed as his new Assistant Chief of Staff for Training and Operations (G–3), Frank W. Andrews, promoting him to a brigadier general of the line. Later Marshall was to say that when he submitted his choice to Woodring, Assistant Secretary of War Louis Johnson, and outgoing Chief of Staff Malin Craig, he knew he had a fight on his hands. He added it was probably the only time in the trio's association they had ever been in full agreement on anything. Nevertheless, Marshall prevailed and the appointment was announced. It was the first time in U.S. military history that an airman had been appointed one of the four assistant chiefs of staff on the Army General Staff.

Andrews received word of it while on leave. The telegram recalling him was followed by a sustained roar of approval from airmen everywhere. Not since F. Trubee Davison had been Assistant Secretary of War for Air (1926–33)

60

had an air officer felt there was anyone "up there" who knew what they were all about. As Andrews had said to Marshall in a previous letter: "Under our present scheme of organization the operating personnel have very little contact with the powers that be. We know our stuff, but we cannot get it across." Now, thanks to the new Chief of Staff, the "stuff" was going to get across. With Marshall's encouragement, Andrews would bring other air officers into G–3 with him. The point was not lost on anyone.

The fifteen months Andrews served as Army G–3 was a period of turmoil. In Europe the Allied and Axis powers went to war, and relations between the U.S. and Japan grew increasingly tense. Trying to build U.S. defenses in a strongly isolationist atmosphere produced political conflict and made increases in military strength difficult and slow. Andrews's job of developing the method and policies of buildup covered all the component parts of the Army, not just the air, and measured against these demands were the military needs of England and France. It was a time of great effort and greater shortages.

Overall U.S. policy went under the heading of Hemispheric Defense, and nowhere was this defense seen as more vulnerable than in the Panama Canal Zone. Military and naval shortages in the Zone were endemic. The President of Panama, Arnulfo Arias, was pro-Nazi. So were numerous military and political leaders of other Latin American countries; still others were on the fence. South America was webbed with 20,000 miles of German-run airlines, some flying Junkers aircraft that could be converted quickly to bombers. There were large populations of German, Italian, and Japanese residents throughout Central and South America. French Guiana as well as the islands of Guadeloupe and Martinique were viewed as critical danger points following the fall of France. To further heighten White House concerns, British intelligence was working round-the-clock, anxious to create in Washington the fear of Nazi action in the hemisphere. Toward that end, the British sent Roosevelt a supposedly authentic secret German map, showing the Third Reich's partitioning of South America.

The fall of France shook U.S. political and military leaders hard. In September 1940, the President revealed that fifty World War I destroyers had been turned over to the desperate British in return for permission to build bases on their Caribbean islands. In October, it was announced that Andrews would be going to Panama to command the newly established Panama Canal Air Force (PCAF).

When Andrews, now a major general, arrived in the Canal Zone in early December, just a year before Pearl Harbor, he saw air power as the backbone of both Canal and U.S. coastal defense. He thought he had a fairly good picture of the Zone's existing air strength, but four months later he was writing Marshall,

... you probably know that we do not have a modern combat airplane in the entire area. . . . Fifty fighter airplanes, with an effective warning service and complete communications, could accomplish far more in the Canal defense than could five hundred such fighters, operating under present conditions. The warning service planned, with its communications, fails to meet our needs as does also the inter-airdrome communications.

This last involved a fundamental problem of which Marshall was acutely aware. The Commander of the Panama Canal Department, Lt. Gen. Daniel Van Voorhis, was a sixty-two-year-old artillery officer who believed an air force should be used as an adjunct to his artillery and not much else. It was Andrews's job to convince him otherwise and to present a plan of air defense that would encompass the Canal Zone and the Caribbean basin, aiming toward what would eventually become a Caribbean Defense Command. Marshall knew this. Andrews knew this. But somehow Van Voorhis failed to get the message. He was senior in grade to Marshall. His view from Quarry Heights was fixed. Andrews's plan was ignored. What Andrews had in mind was to divide the Caribbean into three regional commands—Panama, Trinidad, and Puerto Rico—each having its own bomber and interceptor forces, each commander having considerable freedom of action, with a central headquarters at Howard Field on the west side of the Isthmus.

The principal defense in Van Voorhis's mind was to be built around coast artillery and antiaircraft units. In April 1941, Andrews was to write Marshall: "Drawing upon all the tact and diplomacy that I possess I feel that I have failed to gain Van Voorhis's complete confidence, consequently, I have made slow progress in selling him my ideas on the organization and operating of the Air Forces in the Caribbean. . . . Things seem to move so slowly and time is now a precious commodity." Marshall knew how precious, and shortly thereafter Von Voorhis received direct orders from the War Department which jarred him into action. The PCAF became the Caribbean Air Force (CAF), and implementation of Andrews's plan was begun in earnest.

That same month, Brig. Gen. Follett Bradley, who was in overall command of Andrews's skimpy air units in Puerto Rico, was threatening to resign. Andrews flew to Puerto Rico to investigate the problem. The problem was Maj. Gen. Edmund L. "Mick" Daley, in command of the Puerto Rican Department. Daley, an engineer, had been a classmate of Andrews at West Point. Daley's policy was that he commanded all CAF troops while they were on the ground, and Bradley and his staff had control only when the planes were airborne. This was not often, as Daley used the airmen for duties that had nothing to do with building air power. Andrews heard this from Bradley and several squadron commanders and then paid a call on Daley, accompanied by his aide, Lt. Hiette S. Williams, Jr. They were ushered into Daley's vast office, which was furnished with a huge bare desk, a chair, and nothing else. When its owner made no effort to have chairs brought in for his guests, Williams left the room to find one for his CO.

Once Andrews was seated, he inquired mildly, "Mick, where is your paper work?"

"I don't need any, Andy. I make all the decisions myself," Daley said.

"How do you keep your staff informed?" Andrews asked.

"I don't need a staff. I don't trust them anyway."

"What happened to the letter I wrote you? I never received an answer." Andrews sounded matter-of-fact.

Daley opened a drawer in his desk, pawed around, and came up with the unanswered correspondence. After a few more questions and equally blasé responses, Andrews signaled Williams to follow him out of the office. In the hall he instructed his aide: "Send this message to General Marshall. 'Am relieving Daley this date. Future assignment immaterial.'" He then told Williams to transmit the message outside the normal traffic flow via a direct frequency from San Juan to the War Department.

The significance of Andrews's unique summary action was twofold. Both men were major generals but Daley ranked Andrews on the permanent list. Although Andrews was Chief of the Caribbean Air Force, Daley was not under his command but took his orders from Van Voorhis. Yet Andrews relieved him. He could not have done so without authority from Marshall that outflanked the normal military chain of command. In a letter to Lt. Col. Thomas R. Philips, the Assistant Chief of Staff for Military Intelligence of the Puerto Rican Department, Andrews later wrote: "There is no question but that we have too many congealed minds in responsible positions and that one of our biggest problems is how to correct the existing situation and prevent recurrence in the future." He added that General Marshall was both aware of and worried about the same problem.

During an important diplomatic venture in mid-July 1941, Andrews represented Marshall in making delicate state visits to Latin American capitals, principally Buenos Aires and Rio de Janeiro. While Andrews was in Rio, Marshall informed him he was to succeed Van Voorhis as Caribbean Defense Commander. With the appointment would come promotion to lieutenant general, the first airman to attain such a rank and the first airman to head a joint command. Amid a deluge of congratulatory messages came one from his wife, Johnny: "You're the brightest star of them all," she cabled. "What took you so long?"

In the last three months before Pearl Harbor, Andrews continued to convert the Caribbean into an "American lake." From the time of his arrival in the Canal Zone Andrews had adopted the belief that war could come at any time, and he impressed the same awareness on all who served with him. He knew that in time, if there was time, all the shortages would be filled; that his organizational structure for the Caribbean was sound and workable.

His most serious doubt was the role of the Navy in an area that was largely water but where his own land and air forces, slim as they were, dominated. It all came down to the issue of unity of command and the old sore point of who was in charge beyond land's end. The point was never really resolved before the war came.

In December 1941, Andrews was sent the same alerts from the War Department as commanders in Hawaii and the Philippines, but his airmen had their planes camouflaged and dispersed on outlying jungle strips. When war did come, Andrews's forces were as prepared as they could be under circumstances that left much to be desired: one radar station on the western side of the Canal, a half-dozen B–17s his total heavy bomber strength.

With Pearl Harbor, all attention in Washington was focused on the Pacific. But until the Battle of Midway in June 1942, the Caribbean, generally, and the Canal, particularly, were considered a critical theater of operations where enemy action was anticipated momentarily.

Following the Battle of Midway, Secretary of War Henry L. Stimson visited Andrews and returned to Washington tremendously impressed with the Caribbean defenses and their commander. Shortly thereafter, Andrews was summoned by Marshall to report to the War Department for a talk. Part of what the talk was about jolted Andrews; in fact, angered him. MacArthur had informed the War Department and Hap Arnold that he was not satisfied with the performance of his principal airman, Maj. Gen. George H. Brett, and wanted a replacement. He suggested Andrews for the job. Ordinarily such a request would have brought a quick rejection because Andrews, like MacArthur, was a theater commander, and to come under MacArthur in any guise would be a step down the ladder of command. But these were not ordinary times. The war was in a swirling state of flux, Axis power at its high tide mark, Allied strategy not fully formulated or agreed upon and still badly lacking in necessary forces and equipment. Even so, it does not seem likely that Marshall would have wanted to shift Andrews to the Pacific unless he felt Andrews might be willing to accept the challenge to develop MacArthur's air power against Japan. Andrews said no to the offer and shortly thereafter returned to his Caribbean Command.

*   *   *   *   *

When Andrews came again to Washington on October 20, 1942, he knew the purpose was for reassignment. But this time he arrived with a purpose of his own. Through his longtime friend and confidant, Hugh Knerr, who had retired from the Army and was working for Sperry Gyroscope, he had learned that a move was afoot to make the Army Air Forces that had been formed in June 1941 into a separate air force. He was disturbed by what he judged to be the mismanagement of air power at a crucial moment. Through Walter Weaver, he had been trying to get his opinions put before Roosevelt. The point of contact at the White House was the President's military aide, Maj. Gen. Edwin "Pa" Watson. Watson, however, warned Andrews that he was in danger of ruining his career if he persisted. FDR was dead set against any moves that did not come as a united recommendation from the top. Andrews was too astute to gamble on such a contentious position at such a time. He backed off, willing to accept the present arrangement because of Marshall.

The Chief of Staff had more immediate considerations on his mind, and he had again chosen Andrews to play a major role in them. Operation Torch, the invasion of North Africa, was to be carried out principally by U.S. forces, its purpose to secure Tunisia and the Magreb while the British, driving westward out of Egypt, attacked Rommel's Afrika Korps. Egypt was to be the eastward anchor in the nutcracker operation. U.S. units in the area, which encompassed the Levant, the Nile Delta, Eritrea, and Iran, were largely air and included four heavy bomb groups and a scattering of service commands. The idea was to combine them all under one command—U.S. Army Forces in the Middle East, USAFIME. Marshall, with the Joint Chiefs' approval, wanted Andrews to take over the disparate organizations, which were suffering from a lack of cooperation, unify them to support the British Eighth Army, and then use the bombers against Italian and Balkan targets. Additionally, he was to assist in improving the flow of U.S. equipment to the Russians via the Persian Gulf.

On October 30, two days after Gen. Bernard Montgomery launched his attack against Rommel and a week before U.S. forces went ashore in North Africa, Andrews took off for the last time from his Caribbean headquarters and for the first time in a B-24, heading for Cairo, Egypt. The plane was a B-24D, specially equipped with BTO, a newly developed radar device for bombing through the overcast at low level.

While he had served in the Caribbean for nearly two years, Andrews's command of USAFIME was extremely brief, lasting only three months. In that short time he brought cohesion to the widely spaced service units under his control. Two weeks after his arrival he wrote Marshall a detailed account of his progress: no unity of command amongst the British but fine cooperation nonetheless. As to the future: "I am working now on some plans for the use of our bombardment when we get the Axis out of Africa. Now, of course, everything is devoted to that objective. I hope soon to be able to make contact with Eisenhower's forces in West Africa with a view to some joint planning in the North African area. . . ." He hoped, he told Hap Arnold, to be able to use his bombers of the Ninth Air Force, under the command of Maj. Gen. Lewis Brereton, against strategic targets. He was anxious to have Brereton's B–24s employed on night raids against Italian shipping and port facilities, using BTO. The problem was that Brereton had only two crews trained to operate the radar equipment, and the British were dead against its use lest it fall into enemy hands. If nothing else, Andrews's desire to use his bombers for low-level bombing by night through the overcast indicated his openness and flexibility in the method of attack. Like George Kenney, Andrews was not married to a single concept of bombardment but was willing to use any technique that would get the job done. He was impatient to get the enemy out of Africa, he told Arnold. "We must have the whole north coast of Africa as one air theater. . . . "

To Marshall, Andrews sent a two-page memo, titled: *Thoughts on Allied Nations European Strategy in 1943*. He began: "It is assumed that we have as yet no definite overall plan for combined Allied military action for 1943. I feel free, therefore, to advance my own ideas with, however, no claim of originality for them." He foresaw "two main practical lines of action." One was "to build up a force in England to invade . . . the Continent of Europe as soon in 1943 as possible." The other was to "implement an all-out air offensive against the Axis." To this he added corollaries that included a Middle East offensive against the Aegean, hoping to bring Turkey into the war, an invasion of Italy, the establishment of air bases there to attack Germany, and the possibility of operations against Norway to protect the northern shipping route to Russia. Of the two plans, he came down on the side of the second.

At Casablanca, two weeks later, the Combined Chiefs of Staff would, in the course of their historic ten-day conference, adopt much of what was in the second option proposed by Andrews. Andrews's thoughts on future strategy combined viewpoints from both sides of the conference table, where the U.S. chiefs felt they were being mousetrapped by the more carefully prepared and unified British. Agreement was finally reached on all major issues, including the mounting of a combined USAAF-RAF bomber offensive against the Third Reich.

In this regard, until the meeting at Casablanca on January 15, 1943, Eisenhower, Arnold, and Spaatz had taken the oft-repeated position that the bombing efforts of the Eighth Air Force in England and the operations of the U.S. Army and Air Forces in North Africa were all a part of one theater and the same command. At the meeting on the 15th, Marshall announced that he felt the time had come to establish a separate European theater of operations in the United Kingdom. He was proposing that Frank Andrews command it. Eisenhower arrived at Casablanca that same day, was informed by Marshall of his wishes, and agreed to the change.

Army and Navy officials at the Casablanca Conference, January 1943.

Aside from considerations of geography and an as yet unresolved military campaign, Marshall's motivation for the change is clear enough. The British were dragging their feet on agreement for an invasion of Normandy. Marshall wanted a commander in London who had the qualities of leadership and administrative ability necessary to direct a buildup toward that end. He also wanted an airman on a high enough level to keep the bomber offensive on track—someone who could cooperate with the British but not be swayed by their adroitness and charm. Perhaps the most intriguing point in the sudden shift was that Andrews knew it was coming even before he received a message from Marshall asking him to be in Casablanca within forty-eight hours.

At Casablanca, Andrews received official word of his new assignment and found he had an immediate problem. The continuance of daylight bombardment was in grave jeopardy. Prime Minister Winston Churchill had decided to convince FDR that the strategy was not working and should be dropped for RAF-type night operations. Arnold, learning of the danger, had sent for Maj. Gen. Ira C. Eaker, Eighth Air Force Commander, and Spaatz to support him in what he saw as a very real threat to a doctrine that had been twenty years in the making. Now Andy Andrews had arrived. The four airmen could join forces to fight for a belief that was the warp and woof of U.S. air power.

67

Advocates of continued daylight bombing included *above*: Ira Eaker, and at *right*: Carl Spaatz (left) and Hap Arnold

Eaker spent a critical half-hour of debate with the Prime Minister. Arnold took a twilight stroll with him, dined with him, and stressed the need to continue daylight operations. Spaatz, who wanted to return to England to resume command of the Eighth Air Force, reiterated the U.S. position in a talk with Churchill. Present also were Churchill's air leaders and Arnold.

Andrews met with the British leader and Air Chief Marshal Charles "Peter" Portal to discuss the directive under which he would be taking command in the ETO. He told the Prime Minister flatly that he felt the main issue before them was daylight versus night bombing, and that it would be a mistake to create a command organization that would force U.S. bombers into night operations. Churchill brought up his earlier talk with Eaker. Later he was to write that Eaker had "almost" convinced him, but there can be little doubt that the convincing was also done by Andrews, Arnold, and Spaatz, not to mention Churchill's Air Marshals Portal and Slessor. Had it been otherwise, there is no telling how profoundly the war in Europe would have been affected. What can be said is that a crucial U.S. air victory was won at Casablanca, not against the enemy but against an Allied leader.

In the three months remaining to Andrews, he established himself in London and began the organizational and logistical buildup for what in sixteen months would become Operation Overlord, the Allied invasion of occupied Europe. His most immediate concern, however, was Ira Eaker's Eighth Air Force. The Eighth had been practically disembowled by the demands of air

Lt. Gen. Frank M. Andrews

power for the invasion of North Africa. Due to the needs of seven other theaters and to shipping losses to U-boats, promised replacements of crews and aircraft were not forthcoming. Arnold's endemic impatience was making life miserable for Eaker, whose bombers were few and whose losses were mounting. Andrews provided a bulwark and a calm, steady influence. He knew that in time the promised men and equipment would arrive. His letters to Marshall show that the problems in England were a repeat of those he had faced in the Caribbean and the Middle East: shortages of equipment and trained personnel and the uncertain exigencies of combined leadership.

In late April, Andrews dispatched Eaker to Washington to resell the Combined Bomber Offensive that had been agreed upon at Casablanca but was in trouble due to War Department critics and demands by the Navy. This was Andrews's final action in the long battle to use air power as the principal strategic weapon in the Allied arsenal.

Andrews's most distant command was in Iceland and he decided to go there to inspect the troops and evaluate the men in command. Just before he took off on May 3 with key members of his staff, he wrote a letter to his son, Lt. Allen Andrews. In it he said,

> Our air buildup is coming along nicely now but we continue to have a tough time with our daylight bombing. It is quite evident that we have not yet found just exactly the right combination. We should grow better at a faster clip. I am looking for the answers, our losses are running too high. Leadership and experience are two of the troubles. We will work it out.

Tragically, there was no more time for him to work it out.

*   *   *   *   *

There are those who believe that Andrews's flight to Iceland was the intended first stop on a secret summons to Washington by Marshall. In view of the relationship between the two and the circumstances of the moment, the belief does not seem illogical. The Trident Conference was about to begin in Washington. Hap Arnold had suffered a heart attack and would not be able to attend. Many issues thought resolved at Casablanca were coming unstuck, not the least of which was the Combined Bomber Offensive. That Marshall would want Andrews present for matters dealing with the invasion buildup and the British refusal to be tied down to it, makes sense. Yet, there is no official record of such a recall, even though Andrews's widow was left by Marshall with the impression that such was the case.

Andrews's failure to land, as instructed by air traffic control at Prestwick, Scotland, before proceeding to Iceland, is seen by some as an indication of his haste to reach Washington, but by others as simply Andy Andrews, an instrument pilot who reveled in bad weather and who would use the prerogatives of his rank to override what he considered an unnecessary delay. It is known that had he lived he was soon to receive his fourth star. And so, at the end, a degree of mystery hangs over his departure. He had said that when the end came he hoped it would be in the cockpit, and he got his wish. Everyone else who knew him or served under him deeply mourned his loss.

Marshall, who delivered the eulogy at the memorial service for Andrews in Washington, said of him that he was one of the Army's few great captains. To Johnny Andrews, Marshall had written: "He was a great leader and in his post abroad was on his way to rendering a tremendous service to the Allied cause."

History does not reveal its alternatives, and Andrews's sudden death leaves some haunting questions. Had he lived, would he have commanded the Normandy invasion, as so many of his contemporaries believed? Certainly Marshall had placed him in the position to oversee the buildup for that then-unresolved strategy. And what then? Whatever his future might have been, Andrews's star was in swift ascendancy when it was snuffed out, and all the bright promise of tomorrow became reflections on the ordeals of yesterday, the yesterday of a military leader whose name will ever by joined with strategic air power and the fight for air independence.

Sources

The papers of Lt. Gen. Frank M. Andrews are located in the Manuscript Division, Library of Congress, Washington, D.C.; Tennessee State Archives, Nashville, Tennessee; and the Archives of the USAF Academy, Colorado Springs, Colorado. Other papers and additional information are provided by Allen Andrews, son of General Andrews, and Col. Hiette S. Williams, Jr., USAF (Ret.), General Andrews's aide from 1936–39 and 1940–41. Documents and correspondence to and from Andrews during his command of USAFIME and of the European theater are located in the ETOUSA files, RG 338, Modern History Field Branch of the National Archives at Suitland, Maryland.

The author's books, *A Few Great Captains* (Doubleday, 1980) and *Forged in Fire* (Doubleday, 1982) provide a general reference. Both books contain extensive bibliographies and notes.

4

Harold L. George:
Apostle of Air Power

Haywood S. Hansell, Jr.

Among the architects of American air power, few rank higher than Harold George. He was a farsighted and courageous prophet, a creator of strategic air concepts, doctrine, and plans, and commander of the World War II Air Transport Command, which added to air power a new element of global, strategic mobility.

Harold Lee George was born in West Somerville, Massachusetts, on July 19, 1893. After completing high school, where he excelled in hockey, he expected to enter Massachusetts Institute of Technology, but his plans were thwarted by family misfortunes. In 1914, he found a civil service job with the Treasury Department in Washington, D.C., so he also could enroll at George Washington University Law School. During this period he became a Reserve second lieutenant of Cavalry.

When the United States declared war on Germany in April 1917, George had completed three years toward his degree. He immediately reported for active duty at Fort Myer, Virginia, applied for flying training and resigned his commission in the Cavalry to become a Flying Cadet. He received his wings and a commission as a second lieutenant in the Aviation Section of the Signal Corps at Love Field, Dallas, Texas, on March 29, 1918, and was

---

This first-person account is based on General Hansell's association with General George during their service as instructors at the Air Corps Tactical School at Maxwell Field, Alabama, before World War II. They also served together in the Air War Plans Division, the Air Staff, where they helped draft the air war plan that governed Army Air Forces operations during that war.

sent to France for combat indoctrination and training at Clermont. Two months later, he joined the 163d Bomb Squadron of the 2d Day Bombardment Group at Ourches-sur-Meuse, on the Meuse-Argonne Front, where he flew combat missions until the Armistice on November 11, 1918.

After the war, Hal George left the Army, reported back to the Treasury Department, and resumed his law studies at George Washington University. He worked part-time as law clerk for James McReynolds, Associate Justice of the U.S. Supreme Court, until he received his law degree in 1920. George's training in law was to stand him in good stead during his military career. To an unusually bright mind, that training added a talent for logical thought and persuasive presentation. These talents proved invaluable, not only to him, but to the Army Air Forces as well.

John Williams, his boss at Treasury, urged Hal to become a national bank examiner, an occupation that could lead to lucrative positions in industry. But George had been infected with the flying bug. On September 20, 1920, he again was commissioned a second lieutenant, this time in the Regular Army, and was promoted to first lieutenant on April 14, 1921, while assigned to the 49th Bomb Squadron, at Kelly Field, San Antonio, Texas. In June 1921 George

Capt. Harold L. George

74

Brig. Gen. William Mitchell

was among the carefully selected few to become members of the 14th Bombardment Squadron in Brig. Gen. William Mitchell's brigade that conducted the bombing tests against German warships off the Virginia capes. Hal participated in sinking the "unsinkable" German battleship, *Ostfriesland*. It was then that he fell under the personal magnetism and embraced the vision of Billy Mitchell—a legacy that never dimmed. George testified for General Mitchell in his court-martial, carried Billy Mitchell's torch for the rest of his military career, and contributed enormously toward bringing Mitchell's dream of air power to fruition in World War II.

From the battleship tests, George went to Aberdeen Proving Ground in Maryland for four years of testing bombardment weapons and techniques. Next, he was assigned to head the Bombardment Branch of the Operations Division in the Office, Chief of the Air Corps in Washington, where he was associated with such future air leaders as Maj. Carl "Tooey" Spaatz and Capt. Robert Olds. His next assignment was with the 5th Composite Group in Hawaii, which he joined in July 1929. Two years later, he was selected to attend the Air Corps Tactical School at Maxwell Field, Alabama.

*   *   *   *   *

Harold George reported to the Tactical School as a student in the class of 1931–32. He and Lt. Kenneth N. Walker, instructor in bombardment, established a warm friendship. Hal's fine record as a student prompted Walker to urge that he remain at the school as an instructor. Walker departed for the Army's Command and General Staff School at Fort Leavenworth, Kansas, and Hal became Chief of the Bombardment Section, a position he held for the next two years.

At the conclusion of the 1933–34 school year, Col. John F. Curry, the commandant, organized the academic program into three departments: Air Tactics, Ground Tactics, and Basic and Special Instruction. The Department of Flying completed the organization. Under the Department of Air Tactics were grouped the Air Force, Attack, Bombardment, Pursuit, and Observation Sections. With the new organization, the Air Force Section taught air strategy and coordinated employment of bombardment, attack, and pursuit. There also was a course in naval operations, taught by the assistant commandant, Lt. Col. Herbert Dargue, a graduate of the Naval War College.

Before this reorganization, each section chief had been king in his own area. There was no coordination among them, no governing concept for the development and application of the several air components, no concerted philosophy of air power. The new Department of Air Tactics, renamed the Department of Air Tactics and Strategy in October 1935, provided a core around which such a philosophy could be molded. It was an important step. Even more important was the selection of the department's director.

Air Corps Tactical School Building, Maxwell Field, Alabama.

The senior Air Corps officer among the instructors in the department was Maj. Frederick I. Eglin. The director was to have the temporary rank of lieutenant colonel. In 1934, Commandant John Curry made a difficult decision: he picked Capt. Harold George to become the new director. That decision proved to be a milestone in the evolution of American air power. To the everlasting credit of Freddy Eglin, he gave Hal George his enthusiastic and loyal support. Under George's tenure as Director of the Department of Air Tactics and Strategy, the American concept of strategic air warfare took form, with coherent principles and doctrines of air employment.

That strategic concept was based on the work of such pioneers as the Italians, Count Gianni Caproni and Gen. Giulio Douhet; South African Gen. Jan Smuts; Britain's Lord Hugh Trenchard and Capt. Basil Liddell Hart; and Billy Mitchell. They in turn were followed by Air Service and Air Corps leaders Maj. Gens. Mason Patrick and James E. Fechet and by more junior officers, among them Frank Andrews, Hugh Knerr, Carl Spaatz, and "Tony" Frank. But these leaders dealt only in broad generalities. The Tactical School translated air power potential into a specific strategic concept: great powers can be fatally weakened by bombing carefully selected targets whose destruction will collapse vital industrial systems. Donald Wilson, as Chief of the Air Force Section, had begun a study of the industrial organs and services of a developed nation, and their vulnerability to air attack. Harold George built on that foundation a complete strategic concept of air warfare. As his assistant instructor in the Air Force Section, I followed his leadership with enthusiasm and admiration.

Hal George's views were clearly and boldly expressed when he was given the opportunity, in 1934, to testify before the President's Commission on Aviation, headed by Clark Howell. George said:

> The object of war is now and always has been the overcoming of the hostile will to resist. The defeat of the enemy's armed forces is not the ultimate object of war; the occupation of his territory as a military operation is not necessarily the object of war. Each of these is merely a means to an end; and the end is overcoming his will to resist. When that will is broken down, when that will disintegrates, then capitulation follows.
>
> Before the advent of air power there was no means whereby pressure could be applied directly to break down the hostile will without first defeating or containing the hostile surface forces.
>
> Now, gentlemen, the question of moment to us is this: Has air power brought into existence a means which enables the application of pressure directly against those establishments and institutions which are vitally essential for the very existence of a modern civilized nation and, through the application of that pressure, the overcoming of the hostile will? My answer, or rather the answer of those who believe in the potentialities of air power, of those who have made the study of air power their life's work, is decidedly in the affirmative.

The strategic objective outlined by George was later expanded to include not only the enemy *will* to resist, but also his capability to persist in battle, or in support of his social structure, or both. The operative expression in

George's testimony has been: "those establishments and institutions which are vitally essential to the very existence of a modern civilized nation." This was the key to the American philosophy of strategic air warfare. What were those essential institutions? What would be the effect of their destruction?

Before his departure for Leavenworth in the summer of 1934, Don Wilson, Chief of the Air Force Section, had looked for the specific structures that supported the will and capability of an industrialized nation to wage war, but there were serious obstacles to his inquiry. The Tactical School lacked strategic air intelligence on potential enemy nations, and the War Department, responding to the national mood, prohibited any study of offensive military operations against foreign nations. Wilson therefore adopted an ingenious ploy. Analyzing the importance and vulnerability of our own industrial and social fabric would reveal the systems most vital to our power and most vulnerable to air attack. The lessons could then be applied to other industrialized nations. Furthermore, they would indicate the areas and facilities on which defense should be concentrated. This fell within War Department restrictions.

The Department of Air Tactics and Strategy expanded Don Wilson's inquiry. Harold George and his assistant, Capt. Bob Webster, made some detailed analyses of rail and inland-waterway transportation systems, electric power generating and switching stations, and factories that produced essential components of machinery and munitions. They found the number of critical targets to be relatively small, and vulnerable to large, accurately delivered bombs. They then turned to the most politically and morally sensitive target system of all—cities. Using New York as an example, they estimated that if seventeen targets within the city's transportation, water, and electric systems were destroyed, the city no longer would be habitable. With very precise bombing, this could be done without vast destruction or mass casualties.

But could attacking air forces get through enemy defenses to reach vital enemy targets? This question of "counter air force strategy" generated a lot of heat at the Tactical School. The proponents of strategic offensive air power contended that they could. The air defense advocates, led by Capt. Claire Chennault, claimed they could not. That argument raged in a period when the new bombers, the B-10 and B-17, were almost as fast at altitude as the current crop of fighters, and when radar was in an experimental stage. Under these circumstances the defending fighters were at a tremendous disadvantage. If they waited on the ground until the bombers crossed the frontier and then tried to overtake them, the chase was practically hopeless. If they patrolled in the air until the bombers appeared, only a fraction of the fighters could be kept aloft and the bombers had the advantage of the initiative in selecting time, place of attack, and mass.

The argument leaned toward the bombers. But Harold George recognized

Claire Chennault, a strong air defense advocate at the Tactical School.

the danger to the air offensive posed by enemy fighters. He and the Bombardment Section supported the development of long-range escort fighters, a position vehemently opposed by Chennault as Chief of the Pursuit Section, who favored short-range, high-performance interceptors.

These questions were debated heatedly in an atmosphere of intellectual ferment that may be hard to imagine today. For the first time an integrated doctrine for the use of air power was emerging, and the technology to support it seemed to be within reach. Strategic concepts and principles of employment were put in writing. Texts were written, revised, and written again. George's leadership resulted in a philosophy of air employment that was uniquely American.

The substance of that philosophy as defined at the Tactical School was that "the will and capability of a modern industrialized nation to wage war can be undermined and caused to collapse by destruction of carefully selected targets in the industrial and service systems on which the enemy people, their industries, and the armed forces are dependent; and this method of waging strategic air warfare is, in general, preferable to area attack of cities or industrial areas." Carrying out that strategic doctrine called for a clear definition of national purpose and strategic objectives, collecting strategic intelligence in order to select critical targets, providing air offensive forces that could reach their targets with acceptable losses, improving bombing accuracy, and developing bombs capable of destroying the selected targets. Harold George believed that these requirements could be met.

It should be remembered that the Air Corps was still part of the Army and that the air power doctrine developed at the Tactical School was not accepted by the War Department. Its General Staff was dominated by ground officers, many of whom believed that the mission of the Air Corps was coastal defense and support of ground force operations. An independent strategic mission for air power was not universally accepted, even after it was tacitly acknowledged through establishment of the General Headquarters Air Force in 1935. Under those conditions, it took a considerable amount of faith, vision, and courage to advocate publicly heretical ideas that threatened the long-established missions of one's parent service. Those were qualities that Harold George possessed in abundance.

But it was not all work and no play at the Tactical School. We formed warm and lasting friendships. When Harold George was about to leave Maxwell for the Army's Command and General Staff School at Fort Leavenworth, several of us who had worked with him and for him decided to commemorate the occasion. We took a gallon of Alabama moonshine, which had been aged in a charred keg for over six weeks, and some vittles of various kinds, picked up Harold, and went to a picnic ground in the woods. We talked and sometimes listened and sang and drank while the hours slipped away. Finally we noticed the burgeoning of dawn. To paraphrase an old Irish ballad:

> T'was a fine time we had at the party
>   The five of us slept not a wink.
> The laughter was boistrous and hearty
>   With plenty of toddy to drink.
> Sure the whiskey was free as the air is
>   And we managed to store it away.
> We chattered and sang like canaries,
>   And settled affairs of the day.
> It was early daylight in the morning
>   When the party for Harold broke up.
> The cock in the yard crowed a warning
>   And we all took a turn at the cup.
> But the best of good friends must be parted
>   And all of us then went our way,
> The five of us all happy hearted.
>   And where did we go, did you say?

We went to Hal's quarters for breakfast, at his insistence. We paused at the front door, four of us vaguely apprehensive about this predawn invasion of the George household. But Hal put our fears at rest. "This is my home," he said firmly, "and in my home I am King."

The door opened softly and a dulcet voice said, "Good morning gentlemen. I'll take care of the King."

Hal was gone, and in rapid order, so were we.

Reverting to his regular rank, Captain George arrived at the Army's Command and General Staff School in the fall of 1936. On completing the course in June 1937, he was ordered to Langley Field, Virginia, to command the 49th Squadron, 2d Bombardment Group of the GHQ Air Force. It was a choice assignment—one of the most favored in the Army Air Corps. That group was the only outfit equipped with the new Boeing B-17C Flying Fortress. Not only was it the first outfit to be so equipped; it seemed likely to be the last. The War Department decided, over the protests of Maj. Gen. "Hap" Arnold, Chief of the Air Corps, and Maj. Gen. Frank Andrews, Commanding General GHQ Air Force, that the B-17 was not needed in the Army mission. Less expensive, two-engined bombers would do. No funds for buying B-17s were in the 1940 budget. The dozen B-17Cs in the 2d Bombardment Group were very precious indeed, and their crews were selected with great care.

George was with the group for four years, ending up as its commander. During that time the group never lost a B-17, in spite of the fact that it carried out some record-breaking and pioneering flights. They included good-will flights to Buenos Aires, Rio de Janeiro, and Bogota carried out on instructions from the White House.

George took part in another flight, less publicized but very important. Brig. Gen. George C. Marshall, then Chief of the War Plans Division of the General Staff, decided to make an inspection tour of the Caribbean area and Panama. George flew him in a B-17. Immediately after General Marshall boarded, engines were started, chocks removed, and the airplane taxied out for takeoff. General Marshall was shown the flight plan and the navigation checkpoints, and his attention was called to each checkpoint as it was reached—precisely on time. On the flight to Point Borinquen, Puerto Rico, one engine lost oil pressure. It was gently shut down, the propellor feathered, and power of the other engines increased. General Marshall had not noticed

Lineup of 6 Boeing B-17s before a goodwill flight to Buenos Aires, Argentina.

the change. George brought him up to the cockpit and pointed to the stationary propellor. He explained that there was no reason to be concerned. With a four-engine bomber the loss of one engine could easily be compensated with the other three. The mission would proceed as scheduled and the airplane could reach base as planned. This was not so with a two-engine bomber. General Marshall was noncommittal, as usual, but he had not missed the point. The Air Corps gained a staunch supporter of four-engine bombers.

*   *   *   *   *

On September 1, 1939, Hitler launched his attack on Poland. The Luftwaffe's first objective was to defeat the Polish Air Force, which proved to be an easy task. There were some disturbing implications, however. Bombers of both sides were shot down by fighters. General Arnold was far from happy. On November 14, 1939, he said the widely held Air Corps belief that large bombardment formations could defend themselves against fighters was open to question. General Arnold blamed acceptance of bomber invulnerability on teachings of the Air Corps Tactical School, and called on Maj. Gen. Delos Emmons, Commander of the Air Combat Command (successor to the GHQ Air Force) to submit a study of the bomber-versus-fighter problem.

Harold George was called upon to testify. In what was surely one of the most wrenching decisions of his career, he told General Emmons: "There is no question in my mind but that American bombardment units could not today defend themselves against American pursuit units." That forthright statement must have tried him sorely; it ran counter to all he wanted to believe. But it was a courageous and honest assessment that produced favorable results. The Air Combat Command found that "aerial operations of the present European conflict confirm the results of World War I: that is that the present bombardment airplane cannot defend itself adequately against pursuit attack."

Drastic action was called for. Unless bomber formations could penetrate enemy air defenses, the American concept of daylight, precision, strategic air warfare would have to be abandoned in favor of night area bombing, or alternatively, the air force might be reorganized as no more than a supporting arm of the ground forces. To avoid these alternatives, the B–17C was almost completely redesigned with more powerful engines, a greater bomb load, power-operated gun turrets and hand-operated waist guns, protective armor, and self-sealing fuel tanks.

The Battle of Britain added further discouragement to the proponents of the air offensive. In September 1940, General Arnold said that if we became involved in Europe, the Air Corps might have to conduct the bulk of its bombardment operations at night. Radar and fighter control systems had increased enormously the effectiveness of defensive fighters. But the outcome of the Battle of Britain had been much closer than the British wished to acknowledge. The supreme effort of RAF Fighter Command on September 15, 1940, had left the defenses totally exhausted. If the Luftwaffe had resumed daylight attacks on September 16, it would have found the skies over Britain almost clear of defenders. The Luftwaffe did not come back. The will of the German High Command had wilted.

It still was not clear that the air offensive would be unable to reach its targets. The German bombers were low-performance, ill-armed medium types; their escorting fighters were of very limited range. Tooey Spaatz, an observer on the scene, believed large formations of heavily armed, high-performance B–17Es could succeed, but a serious effort should be made to develop escort fighters. No fighter was developed for that specific purpose, but the range of the P–38, P–47, and P–51 was extended with external fuel tanks. By early 1944, P–51s were escorting the bombers to Berlin and beyond.

*   *   *   *   *

On June 20, 1941, Secretary of War Henry Stimson approved a reorganization of the Army Air Corps on the recommendation of General Marshall. The Air Combat Command, which had reported directly to the Army Chief of Staff, would be under General Arnold, who became Chief of the Army Air Forces (AAF) and Deputy Chief of Staff, U.S. Army, for Air. The air arm was unified within the War Department. General Arnold was authorized a staff, organized along the lines of the War Department General Staff, though the whole air organization was still under the General Staff. The new staff became known as "The Air Staff." General Arnold appointed Brig. Gen. Carl Spaatz as his Chief of Staff and named Lt. Col. Harold George Assistant Chief of Air Staff for War Plans.

Hal arrived in Washington on July 10. He organized his division in two groups: The War Plans Group with Lt. Col. Ken Walker as chief; and the Projects Group, headed by Lt. Col. Howard "Pinkie" Craig. A few days earlier, I had returned from England, where I had been sent as an observer and where, as chief of General Arnold's Strategic Air Intelligence Branch, I had been consulting with RAF Intelligence. I was transferred to the Air War Plans Division as chief of the European Branch of the Air War Plans Group. Lots of chiefs but no Indians.

On July 9, 1941, the day before Harold George arrived in Washington

National Archives

Secretary of War Henry Stimson

to set up the Air War Plans Division, the President had sent a secret letter to the Secretaries of War and Navy, asking them to prepare an estimate of "overall production requirements required to defeat our potential enemies." He wanted a prompt reply. The Secretary of War forwarded the request to the Chief of Staff of the Army. The deadline for a reply was one month later, August 11. The request went, naturally, to the War Plans Division of the War Department General Staff, with authority to call on any agency of the War Department for assistance.

The Joint Army-Navy Board met to work out a scheme of approach, including a joint grand strategy. The Army and Navy were unable to agree on a specific strategy, and each set about preparing its own requirements under general guidance of Joint War Plan Rainbow-5. That plan recognized the Atlantic theater as the primary area of operations, including "a sustained and unrelenting air offensive against Germany" (the words of the American-British Conversations #1, ABC-1, agreed upon in March and incorporated into Rainbow-5 in July), defense of the Western Hemisphere, and a strategic defense in the Pacific area.

The task facing the War Plans Division (WPD) was enormous. Some idea of the magnitude of forces required was needed as a basis for industrial mobilization. The War Plans Division took a traditional approach. Since the primary task of the combined British-American armies would be to defeat the German Army, the U.S. Army in Europe, with British assistance, would have to be superior to German ground forces in Western Europe. WPD came up with a rough figure of some 4 million men in U.S. combat organizations, and a total of about 5 million men in Europe. Allowing for a "division slice" of approximately 30,000 men, that would call for 133 divisions. Logistics support for 5 million men in Europe would require a fleet of a thousand ships, which would have to be built. The Maritime Commission estimated that would take about 2 years.

The War Plans Division was about to estimate air requirements on a similar basis, relating the size of our air force to the size of the enemy air and ground forces, and to our own ground forces. The division had some air officers assigned to it. One of them, Lt. Col. Clayton Bissell, proposed to Brig. Gen. Leonard Gerow, Chief of WPD, that he ask Gen. Arnold for temporary assignment of additional AAF officers. Presumably the air requirements would be computed on the basis of official War Department doctrine as expressed in TR 440-15:

> Air operations, like any other operations, are governed by the same fundamental principles that have governed warfare in the past. Air Forces constitute a highly mobile and powerful element which conducts the air operations required for carrying out the Army Mission.

Maj. Gen. Hap Arnold checks map with his staff, *l. to r.*: Lt. Col. Edgar Sorenson, Lt. Col. Harold George, Brig. Gen. Carl Spaatz, Maj. Gen. Arnold, Maj. Haywood Hansell, Jr., Brig. Gen. Martin Scanlon, and Lt. Col. Arthur Vanaman.

Harold George got wind of Bissell's intentions and went directly to Tooey Spaatz. George feared that the War Plans Division would provide only an air support force for the Army. He pointed out that the Air War Plans Division of the Air Staff had been created for just such a task as this and should be given responsibility for it. Together they urged General Arnold to intervene. General Arnold blandly proposed to General Gerow that the newly created Air War Plans Division prepare the air part of the report, which would be known as AWPD-1.

General Gerow accepted this proposal, and on August 4 that responsibility was passed to the Air War Plans Division. General Gerow stipulated only that the general provisions of ABC-1 and Rainbow-5 would govern the approach. George realized that air requirements would have to be based on a strategic air plan. Thus the Air War Plans Division, now officially twenty-four days old, undertook the preparation of an air war plan on an unprecedented scale, with a due date seven days ahead. The plan would have to provide for four principal air tasks: air operations to defend the Western Hemisphere, an air offensive against Germany and lands occupied by German forces, supporting air operations for a land invasion and subsequent campaigns on the European continent, and air operations for strategic defense in the Pacific. Within this guidance, the latitude was unlimited.

There was no guidance for national and military objectives, the strategy of the air offensive, specific objectives in that offensive, targets to be attacked, the size and composition of the air forces, or the timing of various major strategic operations, including planning dates for mobilization, the outbreak of war, the phased buildup of all forces, and the final surface offensive in Europe. Yet these were the factors that determined the air requirements.

General Arnold was called away to join General Marshall, Adm. Ernest King, and President Roosevelt at the Atlantic Conference with Mr. Churchill and the British Chiefs of Staff in Placentia Bay, Newfoundland. He did not return until after AWPD-1 was completed, so Harold George had no further opportunity to seek guidance or support in laying out the plan that was to determine the future of the Army Air Forces. If the task was staggering, so too was the opportunity. At George's request, Maj. Laurence Kuter, on duty in the Operations Division of the General Staff (G-3), was loaned to the planning team.

Harold George directed the project himself. He received assistance from a number of offices, but the "task force" that prepared and presented the plan included only George, Lt. Col. Kenneth N. Walker, Major Kuter, and myself. We had all been together in the Department of Air Tactics and Strategy at the Tactical School. "Air War Plans Division-Plan No. 1," or AWPD-1, was straight American air power doctrine, as evolved primarily at the Air Corps Tactical School under Harold George.

AWPD–1 preparers (shown here as general officers), *clockwise from upper left*: Laurence Kuter, Haywood Hansell, Harold George, and Kenneth Walker

Air Force Magazine

In tracing the development of AWPD-1, it is relevant to review the world situation as it existed in the first week of August 1941. The United States was not at war in either Europe or the Pacific. In the Far East, Japan had been at war with China for nine years and had occupied Manchuria, most of the coast of China, Formosa, and French Indo-China, and was at the borders of Burma. Japanese forces were moving toward the Netherlands East Indies with its wealth of oil and natural resources. U.S. relations with Japan were nearing a breaking point. In the Mediterranean, the Germans had come to the rescue of the Italians in North Africa. Field Marshal Erwin Rommel was operating along the African coast with great success. French North Africa was under the authority of the German-dominated Vichy government of Marshal Petain, whose forces controlled Tunisia, Algeria, Morocco, and the west coast of Africa south to Dakar, the nearest point in Africa to South America. In Western and Northern Europe, Hitler held uncontested control. Only the United Kingdom remained free, but it was losing shipping at a frightening rate to the German U-boat campaign.

In Eastern Europe, the greatest drama of all was unfolding. On June 22, Hitler had attacked Russia by surprise with a force of 163 divisions. By the latter part of August, the Germans were within 200 miles of Moscow and had captured almost a million prisoners at a cost of 441,000 casualties. Materiel losses had been heavy, and the strain on the German logistics system was acute. Nevertheless, it seemed likely that the Soviets would be knocked out of the war before winter.

This was the general situation around which the size, composition, and deployment of air forces and the selection of targets was worked out. The lack of a prescribed national objective under which military requirements could be calculated was a troublesome first obstacle. But by agreement of all military and administration officials, Germany, Italy, and Japan constituted a military menace to the future security and prosperity of the United States. If the President should find it necessary to declare war, it was the business of the military to remove those threats and establish conditions in which peace would not be dominated by foreign military power. This must be done with the least loss of American life that was consistent with military success. In the absence of political advice on U.S. objectives, George accepted that as the end-purpose of war against the Axis powers. It did not necessarily entail conquest of territory.

Harold George really had two basic problems and had to make two strategic decisions on which the plan could be based. One related to the most effective use of air forces, particularly in strategic air war against the European Axis powers. The other concerned the content of a plan that would be acceptable to the War Department. Official War Department doctrine did not recognize the potential decisiveness of strategic air warfare, but geared air operations to supporting the ground forces in carrying out the Army mission—defeat of the Nazi army in battle and reconquest of territory in Europe. The Army was unquestionably in the seat of authority. Army Air Forces officers were still a part of the United States Army. If the air plan were rejected by the War Department General Staff and by the Secretary of War, there was not the ghost of a chance that the President would ever hear of it.

Defining the basic concept of the strategic air plan for a "sustained air offensive against Germany" was, properly, the first order of business for the planning team. Three options were considered: (1) A plan based on victory over Germany *primarily* through strategic air warfare, followed by similar air strategy against Japan; (2) A plan based on an initial massive strategic air offensive against Axis Europe in the hope that it would be decisive, but with preparation for air support of an invasion if necessary, plus combined operations if needed; (3) A plan based on victory through invasion and combined operations, with no prospect of decisive strategic air warfare, followed by air-sea-land offensives in the Pacific.

There were a number of factors pertinent to Harold George's first decision: (1) Initial operations could not be a combination of surface and air campaigns in the European-Atlantic area. The Army would need about two years after mobilization day to muster, equip, train, and transport the necessary ground forces. The Army Air Forces, on the other hand, could move much more quickly. They were well along in mobilization as a result of President Roosevelt's decision to expand American aviation. (2) A successful air war to defeat the German *Air Force* was necessary *before* an invasion could be undertaken, even if ground forces were ready for such a venture. (3) As long as Britain held out, there were base areas available at once for an air offensive against Germany. (4) The German state was supporting one of the greatest military operations in all time against Russia. The German economy and industry, presumably drawn taut by these demands, were at their maximum vulnerability to disruption from the air. If we waited, and Russia collapsed, this vulnerability would be vastly reduced. (5) If Russia were defeated, long-range air warfare would be the *only* feasible method of waging war for a very long time. (6) In the Pacific, where grand strategy contemplated initial defensive operations, the main burden would fall on the U.S. Navy.

A second factor affected George's decision on strategy: any Air Staff plan had to have very strong substantiation and logical support to be accepted by higher authority. It would have to run the gauntlet of the War Department General Staff and the Joint Army-Navy Board, if it were to reach the Secretaries of War and Navy, to say nothing of the President. It could hardly be expected that the United States would voluntarily pin its future exclusively on an untried theory of victory through air power.

George thought a reasonable case could be made for an all-out strategic air offensive, if it was clearly stated that the strategy was backed up by concurrent preparation for a subsequent combined invasion. If the strategic air war succeeded in bringing about capitulation, so much the better. In any event, a preliminary and successful air offensive was necessary before a surface invasion could be undertaken.

Harold George decided to adopt a strategic air approach, stated in these terms: "To conduct a sustained and unremitting air offensive against Germany/ Italy to destroy the will and capability of those countries to continue the war and to make an invasion either unnecessary or feasible without excessive cost." Air forces to support and operate in coordination with the ground forces in case invasion of Europe should be required would also be provided.

Since the principal objective was an unlimited air offensive against Germany, the first problem was to select the main economic and industrial targets whose elimination would contribute most to destroying Germany's ability to wage war. Fortunately, much analysis of German targets had been done by the Strategic Air Intelligence Section over the past year.

The target systems and specific targets selected were:

Primary Air Objectives (to undermine the German will and capacity for war).

1. *Electrical Power.* The majority of German civil and military industry operated on electric power. Targets in this system were small, but easily distinguishable in daytime and vulnerable to large bombs. It was estimated that destroying fifty power plants would reduce German electric power capacity by about sixty percent. The remaining capacity would be inadequate to maintain voltage and keep the system operating. Knocking out selected switching stations would further reduce the system's capacity, which already was sharply rationed, to a level below minimum requirements for German industry.

2. *Transportation.* In planning for a major war, Germany had dispersed critical components of its industry, thus increasing demands on its transportation system. About seventy-two percent of tonnage was carried by railroads, twenty-five percent by waterways, and three percent by trucks. The rail system was working at near-capacity, with the great majority of traffic centered on the Ruhr Valley—the heart of German heavy industry. Repeated bombing of fifteen marshaling yards would seriously disrupt traffic throughout the entire system. Bridges across major rivers would be difficult to hit from high altitude, but if destroyed they could not be replaced quickly. German canals, it was believed, could be neutralized by destroying fourteen targets—three ship elevators, nine sets of locks, and the inland harbors at Manheim and Duisburg.

3. *Synthetic oil and petroleum.* It was estimated that German domestic production and importation of petroleum, the latter principally up the Danube from Romania, plus the manufacture of synthetic oil from coal, would meet

wartime requirements. About 60 percent of aviation gasoline was thought to come from domestic synthetic production (postwar investigation showed that actually the figure was close to 90 percent), and 80 percent of that production was concentrated in 27 plants, located from 400 to 1,000 miles from air bases in England.

Intermediate Air Objective: (to neutralize the German Air Force).

As long as the German Air Force was free to operate over Europe, the effectiveness of U.S. Army Air Forces and Royal Air Force bombers would be seriously constrained. Furthermore, invasion of the Continent by Allied armies, if required, would not be possible. The German Air Force could be defeated or controlled by crippling aircraft, engine, and aluminum manufacturing facilities either through direct attack, or by disrupting the electric power system; by depriving it of aviation fuel; and by fighting in the air. This was considered an intermediate objective since defeat of the Luftwaffe, by itself, would not destroy the will and capability of Germany to continue the war. It simply opened the way to effective operations against primary objectives, whose destruction would assure victory.

Hal George and his team concluded that 154 targets, if destroyed or disrupted and kept out of operation continuously for 6 months, would paralyze the German war-making machinery and produce economic chaos. It also would vastly reduce the operational effectiveness of the German Army if invasion of the Continent should be necessary after the devastation caused by the air offensive. The number of targets by system were: electric—50; transportation (rail, canal, highway)—47; synthetic petroleum facilities—27; aircraft assembly plants—18; aluminum plants—6; magnesium plants—6.

The majority of the targets might be rebuilt or repaired within two to four weeks. Heavy electric generating equipment, where destruction was more or less permanent, was the exception to the rule. Most of the other targets would have to be bombed twelve times. The entire complex of industrial systems should be subjected to this massive demolition for a period of six months prior to D-day, if an invasion was necessary.

The method used in preparing the plan and estimating the required force was logical. (1) Each type target was analyzed to determine the proper size bomb and the number of hits that would be required. (2) The number of bomb drops needed to achieve a 90 percent probability to obtaining that number of hits was computed, using peacetime bombing range experience multiplied by a factor of 2.25 to represent the estimated influence of enemy fighter attacks, antiaircraft artillery fire, weather, and other combat conditions. This resulted in a circular error probability (CEP—the radius of a circle in which one half of the bombs dropped would strike) of about 1,250 feet, which proved quite accurate for the initial operations in 1943. Later experience reduced the CEP to 820 feet. (3) Based on British meteorological forecasts, the rate of operations was set at 5 daylight operations per month. This turned out to be substantially correct. (4) The number of aircraft "aborts" due to mechanical failure and the number of aircraft lost to enemy action on the way to the target was estimated. (5) Finally, the total number of bombers (primarily B–17s and B–24s) needed to knock out all the targets was computed, based on an intensive campaign of 6 months *after the force had reached full size*. The attrition rate for aircraft and crews would require *replacement of the entire combat force every 5 months*.

The plan called for a large number of B–36-type aircraft (which were under study) with a 4,000-mile radius of action in case the British Isles should be untenable. Twelve groups of B–29s (then under development) were planned for deployment in the vicinity of Cairo, to be used against targets in Eastern and Southern Germany and the oil facilities near Ploesti, Romania. Twelve more were scheduled for Northern Ireland. The B–36s would operate from the Western Hemisphere. The bulk of the bombers, based in England, would be B–17s and B–24s.

At the conclusion of the sustained air offensive, if an invasion was still necessary, the majority of the strategic air force would be temporarily directed against targets of immediate importance to the amphibious assault, but would return to the primary strategic targets as soon as possible, as a part of "combined operations on the continent." The strategic air forces would continue to operate from bases in England.

In addition to these strategic forces, the plan called for tactical air forces aggregating 10 groups of medium bombers, 13 groups of light bombers (A–20), and 13 groups of dive-bombers, together with 2 photo reconnaissance squadrons, 198 observation squadrons, and 19 transport groups. Ten pursuit groups were scheduled for England and 6 for Cairo as part of the strategic air forces. In addition, 5 pursuit groups would be set up as a strategic reserve. A similar approach based on missions to be performed was adopted to determine the number of planes required to defend the Western Hemisphere and provide strategic defense in the Pacific. The planners also had to determine the number of fighter aircraft needed to achieve and maintain air supremacy in every potential theater of war. And they had to determine the size and composition of the tactical air forces to support the ground forces during their operations against the German Army.

The total number of organized combat air units required came to 207 groups (21,008 first-line aircraft) without the B–36-type bombers; 251 groups (24,748 aircraft) with them, plus 37,051 trainers for a total of 58,059 aircraft of all types excluding the B–36s and 61,799 operational aircraft with them. These figures included an average of 128 percent of combat aircraft in depot reserve. The entire force was to be manned by 179,398 officers and 1,985,518 enlisted men, (including those in B–36 units) in the following categories:

135,526 pilots, navigators, bombardiers, observers, and gunners; 862,439 technicians, 60,153 nonflying officers; and 1,106,798 nontechnical personnel, for a total of 2,164,916.

In AWPD-1 the planners recommended an air force of 251 combat groups (including transports and B-36s). In August of 1945, 4 years later, there were *243*, a difference of 3 percent. AWPD-1 recommended 64 groups of B-29s at a time when that plane had not yet flown. On the day of Japan's surrender in August 1945, 60 groups of B-29s were operating in the far Pacific. They were bombing the mainland of Japan, and 2 B-29s had dropped the 2 atomic bombs that ushered in the nuclear era.

The completed plan was mimeographed, and the whole package deposited with the War Department General Staff at midnight of the August 11 deadline. But delivering the Air Annex, AWPD-1, to the War Plans Division was hardly the end of the affair. If the plan was to produce anything beyond mental exercise, the General Staff, and especially its chief, had to be convinced of its worth.

The prospect facing Harold George was not encouraging. The Army Air Forces was proposing that the War Department abandon its doctrine on the proper employment of Army aviation and accept the thesis that the primary instrument of warfare against Axis powers in Europe should be a vastly expanded air force. Only after a successful air offensive against Germany would the Army play a significant role, and then it would be against a German state whose back had been broken by air warfare. The proposal, coming from one of the subordinate elements of the Army, was nothing if not brash.

Presenting this proposal to the War Department hierarchy was a hazardous venture. The formal presentation was made by the 4 officers who had done most of the work of preparing the plan: Harold George, Kenneth Walker, Laurence Kuter, and me. The General Staff was confronted with a staggering array of nearly 25,000 combat aircraft: roughly 4,000 heavy bombers (B-17 and B-24), 2,000 very heavy bombers (B-29 and B-32), 3,740 very long-range bombers (B-36), 1,050 medium bombers, 8,800 fighters, 950 light bombers, 1,250 dive bombers, 1,050 transports, and 1,900 observation planes, plus a large number of training planes. This expansion was from a force that had boasted 12 B-17s 3 years earlier. And this force would have to be replaced every 5 months of combat. But Hal George never faltered in his presentation. To one objector he said, quite calmly: "This is what it takes. If we are unwilling to provide it, we had better stay out of the war."

The most crucial presentation—for Gen. George Marshall, Chief of Staff of the Army—was on August 30. Averell Harriman, the President's representative to Russia, was also present as were General Arnold, Gen. Muir Fairchild, Gen. Leonard Gerow, and Colonel Bundy of WPD. Marshall was the one man in the War Department who could, with a gesture, dismiss the entire effort. The plan had to have his endorsement, else it would have no chance whatsoever of acceptance by the Joint Board, by the Secretary of War, or by the President, if it ever got that far. When the presentation ended, General Marshall simply said, "Gentlemen, I think the plan has merit. I would like for the Secretary and the Assistant Secretaries to hear it." In my opinion this was one of the major milestones in the evolution of American air power. It was not the first time nor was it the last that General Marshall showed himself a man of vision, wisdom, and courage. And the Army Air Forces benefited immensely from his support and understanding.

General Marshall decided to take the plan directly to Secretary of War Henry L. Stimson, bypassing the Joint Board, where it assuredly would have been vetoed by the Navy. On September 11, the Secretary was briefed in his own office. Only General Marshall and Harold George were present with him. George summed up the meeting in these words: "Without a question being asked, they listened to the end. Secretary Stimson said, 'General Marshall and I like the plan. I want you gentlemen to be prepared to present it to the President. I will speak to him about the date. Thank you for coming to my office.' "

On September 25, the "Victory Program" in its printed and bound form was forwarded by the Secretary of War to the President. Included in it was AWPD–1. It is one of the misfortunes of our time that the presentation to the President never took place. If it had, it is reasonable to believe that Franklin Roosevelt would have grasped the scheme as rapidly as had Mr. Stimson, and it would probably have appealed to his broad imagination. An understanding by the President might have saved some of the diversions of strategic air power that later occurred in Europe, and that ruled out the possibility of Germany's capitulation without an invasion. Mr. Roosevelt never really understood the strategy of air power, though he endorsed its creation.

AWPD–1 was a pioneering effort. No air operations on that scale and with those objectives had been envisioned before. The plan was written before the computer era and at a time when operations analysis was in its infancy. It could not have been completed in the short space of seven days save for the fact that all senior participants had been thoroughly imbued at the Air Corps Tactical School with Hal George's ideas on the proper use of air power.

*   *   *   *   *

After Pearl Harbor, Harold George served briefly as Air Member of the Joint Plans Committee, while retaining his position as Chief of the Air Staff's

Gen. Hap Arnold, Chief of the Army
Air Forces

Air War Plans Division. Then one day in March 1942, General Arnold sent
for him. "Harold, " he said, "I want you to take over the Ferrying Command.
Bob Olds is sick, though he won't admit it, and the Chief Flight Surgeon
recommends that he be hospitalized. " Hal protested vigorously that he was
a heavy bombardment specialist, that he knew nothing about air transports,
and that with a war on he wanted a bomber command.
General Arnold replied,

> Harold, I know all that. But what you don't know is that this is one of the finest oppor-
> tunities you could possibly hope for. You're not leaving the strategic air business—
> you're entering it. This is an opportunity to establish the world's greatest air transpor-
> tation system, reaching literally everywhere in the free world. This is strategic air move-
> ment and supply as it has never been dreamed of. You take this job and make the most
> of it. Come back a year from now and if you still feel this way I'll get you a bomber
> command.

General Arnold immediately recommended George's promotion to brigadier
general, which took effect the following month.

General Arnold was right. The Ferrying Command, which became the
Air Transport Command (ATC) in June 1942, was a challenge to Harold
George's innovative strategic talent. Air mobility became the third leg of air
strategy, taking its place with the air offensive and air defense. Global air
transport added a new dimension to strategic warfare. George's command participated in every major strategic campaign. He and his staff were involved
in strategic plans, not just in terms of air movement, but as a creative element in arriving at basic strategy itself. It was not only a case of providing
air transportation; it was injection of a new dimension of mobility in selecting a strategic plan of operations.

When Operation Torch, the plan for the invasion of North Africa in November 1942, was being considered, ATC was in at its birth. Bombers and fighters were actually moving on the 10,000-mile trek down the coast of South America, across the South Atlantic into central Africa, and across the Sahara Desert to Oran well before the assault echelons hit the beaches. Aircraft arrived in the combat zone under ATC control only days after the landings. That air movement was one of the key factors in weighing the feasibility of the operations plan for Torch. Combat forces were moved, under ATC control, to MacArthur in the Pacific. When the B–29 depot destined for Guam was lost at sea, the XXI Bomber Command was supported for several months directly out of Sacramento, California, 8,000 miles away, by ATC. The air support of China, over the forbidding "Hump," was a strategic venture of the first magnitude by itself. Finally, as the ultimate gesture of victory, the ATC flew the 11th Airborne Division, the 27th Infantry Division, advanced echelons of General MacArthur's headquarters and Gen. George Kenney's headquarters, and the initial detachment of ATC into Tokyo, the capital of a once triumphant Japan.

Initially Harold George had in his command about 11,000 people and 130 transports, but only a handful of them were flown by military crews. By the end of the war George commanded more than 300,000 people and 3,090 transport aircraft, 90 percent of which were flown by military crews. He was assisted by one of the most gifted and dynamic leaders in aviation—Cyrus R. Smith, who left the presidency of American Airlines to become Deputy Commander of ATC and eventually a major general in the Army Air Forces.

Harold George retired in 1947 as a lieutenant general. Perhaps the greatest accolade came from an old associate and companion in arms, General Tooey Spaatz, the first Chief of Staff of the United States Air Force. General Spaatz wrote:

> As Chief of the War Plans Division of the Air Staff, your progressiveness and imagination led to the development of a plan for the air war in Germany which was so sound that it was utilized as the basic plan on which modifications were made to meet changing conditions. . . . Your masterful, diplomatic, and successful operation of the Air Transport Command gained not only for you but the Army Air Forces an international reputation for ability to accomplish the seemingly impossible.

The air power that grew out of Harold George's plan fatally weakened the ability of Hitler's Third Reich to support the Nazi armed forces, and brought economic chaos to the German state itself. In the words of the U.S. Strategic Bombing Survey, "it was decisive." Air power was also the decisive element in bringing Hirohito's Japanese empire to unconditional surrender without a costly invasion of the Japanese home islands. After the war, that air power became the primary military instrument for the furtherance of U.S. policy, an American policy dedicated to peace and justice.

Sources

The development of American concepts, principles, and doctrines of air warfare at the Air Corps Tactical School, in which Harold George played a leading part, is well told by historian Robert Frank Futrell in *Ideas, Concepts, Doctrine: A History of Basic Thinking in the United States Air Force 1907–1964* (Air University, Maxwell AFB, Alabama, 1971). George's leadership in the creation and "selling" of AWPD–1 is described in detail in H.S. Hansell, *The Air Plan That Defeated Hitler* (Arno Press, 1980) and in Vol I of *The Army Air Forces in World War II: Plans and Early Operations*, edited by W.F. Craven and J. L. Cate (University of Chicago Press 1951; Reprint, Office of Air Force History, 1983). The story of AWPD–1 also is told by DeWitt S. Copp in "The Pioneer Plan for Air War," *Air Force Magazine*, October 1982. The real appraisal of AWPD–1 comes from consideration of the effects of air warfare as prescribed by the plan. Those effects are described in general in the *Summary Report of the U.S. Strategic Bombing Survey* (Government Printing Office, 1946), and in detail in the separate reports of working committees, especially the reports on oil and transportation. An excellent digest and comment on the USSBS (except for electric power) is provided by David MacIssac in the first of ten volumes of the *Survey*, published by Garland Press in 1976. But perhaps the most telling testimony is presented by Albert Speer, Minister of Munitions in Hitler's Third Reich, in his *Inside the Third Reich* (MacMillan, 1970). George's experience with the Air Transport Command is described in the May 17, 1943, issue of *Time* magazine, and in Vol. VII of *The Army Air Forces in World War II: Services Around the World*.

5

Hugh J. Knerr:
The Pen and the Sword

Murray Green

Our first meeting in August 1969 still comes vividly to mind. The door to his apartment in a comfortable, but not expensive, address in Coral Gables, Florida, swung open and I looked into the deepest blue eyes I had ever seen. Not frosty blue, but sparkling with faint amusement, the eyes were deep-set under bushy brows that twitched when he spoke with feeling. The frame was lean, spare, and erect; the voice not harsh, but slightly cracked. His warm handshake was somewhat assuring. I was aware that the subject that brought us together—his recollections of Gen. Henry H. "Hap" Arnold—had caused Hugh Knerr discomfort. Relations during their active careers were strained on several occasions. If his manner was initially hesitant, Knerr's words were not minced: "Hap Arnold was smart; Frank Andrews was intelligent." Chipping away at that distinction, I uncovered a lode of reminiscence about Lt. Gen. Frank Andrews, man and leader, worshipped by Knerr. That affection and respect was wholly reciprocated. Andrews seldom made an important decision between 1935 and 1943, the last eight years of his life, without consulting Hugh Knerr.

Their close association began in March 1935, when Andrews, promoted to brigadier general and given command of the newly established GHQ Air Force with headquarters at Langley Field, Virginia, plucked Knerr from a

The author conducted numerous interviews and an extensive correspondence with General Knerr during the period 1969 to 1971.

supply job in Dayton, Ohio, to be his chief of staff, and second in command. Under GHQ Air Force were consolidated all air combat units located in the Army's corps areas, while the Chief of the Air Corps, in Washington, retained control of supply and training. GHQ Air Force was the War Department's first organizational recognition of the concept of unified air striking power—a compromise that would satisfy proponents of evolutionary progress to a separate air force and, it was hoped, quiet the zealots who wanted an independent air force immediately.

For the next three years under Andrews, Knerr helped build an embryo strategic air organization, the trained crews, and the bases that were to serve America so well in World War II. But in the view of Andrews and Knerr, GHQ Air Force was not given the proper tools to do the job. They wanted more than one hundred B–17 Flying Fortresses in two combat groups, but by mid-1937, had gotten only thirteen in the guise of "experimental" bombers. The Army General Staff did not accept the strategic air mission, but rather conceived of the GHQ Air Force as an element of continental defense—hence the preference for two-engine bombers. Mainly, the General Staff viewed the Army's air arm in a support role, to aid the ground forces in securing their next objective.

Maj. Hugh J. Knerr

Maj. Gen. Frank Andrews, Commander of the GHQ Air Force, was held in great esteem by Knerr.

Hap Arnold, as Assistant Chief of the Air Corps in 1936, and two years later as Chief when Gen. Oscar Westover was killed in a plane crash, was cast as a compromiser and obstructionist by Andrews and Knerr. That view was shared by many of their contemporaries who believed that air power independence was essential immediately for national security. But Arnold had learned his own lesson in military politics in the decade following the Mitchell court-martial. He had been exiled to a cavalry post at Fort Riley, Kansas, and served his penance. Now, as Assistant Chief, he counseled a gradual approach in the matter of procuring B-17s and of seeking a separate air force.

*   *   *   *   *

Gradualism was not part of Hugh Knerr's personality, though his outspoken manner frequently deceived others as to his intensity of purpose. This determination first showed as a youngster when Wilbur Wright, another impatient man, would chase young Knerr out of the Wrights' cycle shop on Third Street in Dayton, Ohio. Hugh Knerr, then age ten or eleven, would come back and earn a few cents sweeping out the shop under the tolerant eye of the other Wright. "Orville was more patient," Knerr recalled years later,

101

"even to letting me help him with kites at about the time of the Spanish-American War. "

Actually, the Knerr family home was in Atchison, Kansas, where Dr. Ellsworth Knerr, Hugh's father, accepted an appointment at Midland College as Professor of Sciences. With degrees in chemistry and physics, Dr. Knerr had left a lower paying teaching job at Parsons College, a small Presbyterian institution in Fairfield, Iowa, where Hugh was born in May 1887.

Each summer, the Knerr family would visit in Dayton, Ohio, where Hugh's grandfather owned a paper mill. Family transportation around town was mostly by bicycle. Among the half-dozen two-wheelers in the barn, one or more might need adjustment or repair. Generally, they awaited Hugh's summer visit to be taken down to the Wrights' shop where he found occasional employment—when Wilbur was not around.

Young Hugh was fascinated with things military. He told of riding out West Third Street to the Soldiers' Home in Dayton, "where the veterans of the Civil War, in their faded blue uniforms with the peaked forage caps, would tell me lurid tales of the war. " He also showed interest in flying. When the family returned to Kansas, he remembered, "my father built a large boxkite for me. With the help of neighbor kids, I succeeded in giving our cat a bouncing ride in a strong wind that frightened it into taking off for the hills. "

Hugh Knerr, just turned seventeen, won an appointment to the U.S. Naval Academy in June 1904. In his memoir, he tells of midshipmen cruises aboard the USS *Hartford*, a square-rigger that had been Admiral Farragut's flagship in the battle of Mobile Bay during the Civil War. Manpower for working the ship as it cruised up the Atlantic coast was furnished by midshipmen under the watchful eyes of veteran officers. Midshipman Knerr's station was on the main royal, the topmost sail, 100 feet above deck. The first night out, the *Hartford* ran into a squall with too much sail on. At the call, "All Hands, " the crew tumbled out of hammocks onto the slanting deck and rushed topside into a dark confusion of shouted orders and cold, wind-driven rain. Knerr and his mates scrambled up the rigging in bare feet and spread out on the yardarms, struggling to control the heavy sails—one hand for the ship and one for personal safety—while the ship pitched in heavy seas. Morning muster revealed no absentees, but Knerr never forgot the harrowing and, to him, needless danger aboard the ancient square-rigger.

Ensign Knerr, youngest to graduate in the class of June 1908, read every account he could get his hands on about aerial flight which, for him, had a greater fascination than the romance of the sea. His repeated inquiries into the Navy's fledgling air program caused him to be ordered abruptly to Panama. He spent the next three and a half frustrating years at sea, all the time hoping for assignment to some aviation-related job. Late in 1911, he was allowed to transfer to the Army's Coast Artillery, not his first choice, but a step toward subsequent assignment to the Signal Corps Aviation Section. He managed that in 1916, when it appeared the United States would soon be involved in the war. In December 1917, Knerr won his pilot's wings at the San Diego Aviation School, but was sent overseas in the wrong direction, to his keen disappointment. Posted to Hawaii, Captain Knerr served as Department Air Officer and Commander of the Ford Island Air Base at Pearl Harbor.

At war's end, Knerr was sent to Dayton, Ohio, a bustling aviation base, but soon ran into trouble by challenging authority. He was inclined to cut corners when Army regulations conflicted with what he thought was right, a characteristic that would haunt his career until retirement. Captain Knerr received a letter ordering him to Washington to explain to a penny-pinching War Department his unauthorized use of aviation gasoline in private automobiles. The hearing was conducted by an unsympathetic Maj. Gen. Charles T. Menoher, non-flying Chief of the Army Air Service, whose qualifications for the job included a willingness to keep a skeptical eye on the shenanigans of Assistant Chief of Air Service Billy Mitchell and other air zealots.

Knerr tried to explain that he had authorized a small gasoline allowance for the base medical officer to make calls on patients scattered about the city of Dayton, after Knerr's request for an ambulance had been turned down. When General Menoher expressed disbelief, a defiant Captain Knerr said he would do the same thing again in like circumstances. All the while, Billy Mitchell, standing in the doorway, was shaking his head, trying to warn Knerr to stop before he completed the damning sentence.

"I was promptly bounced out of the air," Knerr later recalled, and sent to the Coast Artillery in Florida. His exile lasted almost two years. In 1922, a new Air Service regime under Maj. Gen. Mason Patrick recalled Knerr to Air Service duty. After a refresher flying course, Captain Knerr returned to Dayton and was given his first command, the 88th Observation Squadron. It was a homecoming of sorts. His tour brought back memories of a decade before when the Wrights' flying machines, built for the Signal Corps, rose unsteadily over Huffman Prairie where his grandfather's factory once stood.

In 1925, at the Air Service Tactical School at Langley Field, Virginia, Knerr silently stewed over Billy Mitchell's court-martial in Washington. He had become convinced that the Air Service's future would be best fulfilled by developing bombardment aviation. His frustration mounted at the Command and General Staff School at Fort Leavenworth, Kansas, the next step up the military ladder. "I chased Generals Grant and Lee up and down and across the country as if there had been no World War," he recalled. One reason for his discomfiture emerged from his final tactical assignment. Knerr threw observation aircraft into a classroom reconnaissance exercise, whereupon "a fog would suddenly be ordered by the school." Upon graduation, Knerr was marked down as a man to be watched, not so much for his command potential, but as a future troublemaker.

In 1927, Knerr was back at Langley Field discharging his responsibilities aggressively as Commander of the 2d Bombardment Group. His crews were taking considerable punishment flying Keystone and Martin bombers with open cockpits and gun stations. Convinced that "we could not survive in combat," he submitted a letter in October of that year to Air Corps Headquarters in Washington—the Air Service had become the Air Corps in July 1926—urging the development of an enclosed cockpit bomber capable of carrying a 1,000-pound bomb to a service ceiling of 10,000 feet at a speed of not less than 150 miles an hour. Months later, in 1928, Knerr sent forward additional recommendations for two new monoplane, multi-engined bombers: one with high speed, substantial firepower, and short range; the other, a long-range bomber with heavy load capacity.

In the summer of 1929, Major Knerr tried out some of his ideas. He decided to burn up the 2d Group's entire year's allotment of fuel on a mass flight from Virginia to the Pacific coast. Its purpose was to bring to public attention the ability of air units to defend both coasts on short notice. The 2d Group stretched its capability to the limit. The flight took off on August 7, 1929, at dawn and reached San Diego at sunset on the 8th, refueling as necessary en route. With only basic navigation aids, the ninety-mile-per-hour craft had to be flown every second to maintain control while dodging thunderstorms over the Rockies. Although the crews were exhausted, Major Knerr detailed Lt. Leonard "Jake" Harman to fly out beyond land's end, symbolically to bomb Bishop's Rock Buoy. Several good press notices were balanced somewhat by a decidedly negative reaction in nearby Navy headquarters.

As Commander of the 2d Bomb Group, Knerr experimented with two types of bomber formations that were to be adopted by American air units in war fifteen years later. First, there was an "attack" column made up of three-plane elements, in tight formation and stacked down so top gunners could see clearly to fend off pursuit attacks from the rear. His javelin became a standard formation used in the European and Pacific theaters. Maj. Gen. Haywood S. "Possum" Hansell, later a wartime bomber commander, wrote fifty years later of the training he received as a lieutenant in the 2d Bombardment Group. Knerr's "idea of leadership was to lead," General Hansell observed. Knerr's techniques and tactics "proved invaluable when modern bombers made possible the attainment of his vision."

In 1930, Hugh Knerr moved on to the Materiel Division, Wright Field, Ohio, to head the Field Service unit. Basically, his was a supply job, but Knerr worked with Maj. Clinton "Jan" Howard and other resident aircraft engineers to help organize a design competition. Out of that collaboration emerged requirements for advanced bombers: first the all-metal monoplane, the Martin B-10; then, the Boeing B-17 Flying Fortress.

Early in 1934, Major Knerr and his crews were heavily occupied trying to patch up a motley assortment of airmail planes in order to keep the Central Air Mail Zone operational. President Roosevelt had canceled the commercial carriers' contracts in a political dispute. The Army Air Corps was ordered to carry the mail, and between February and May 1934 suffered sixty-six crashes and twelve fatalities. Initially, it was a stumbling performance, due to unsuitable aircraft, primitive navigation equipment, pilot inexperience, and the worst late-winter weather in decades. While the record improved during the last weeks of Air Corps service, the President was angered. The public perception was a black eye for the Army Air Corps. Speaker Henry T. Rainey rose on the floor of the House of Representatives to exclaim that, if the Air Corps was "not equal to carrying the mails, I would like to know how it would do carrying bombs."

To redeem the Air Corps' tarnished reputation, the War Department General Staff authorized a flight by ten spanking new Martin B-10 bombers to Alaska. They were to be made ready for the long flight in Dayton, Ohio. Major Knerr was charged with the task of modifying and testing those bombers. At the last minute, Lt. Col. Hap Arnold, who had burnished his own reputation at March Field, was named to command the flight. Knerr was assigned as executive officer, second in command.

One of the 10 Martin B-10s on U.S. Army Air Corps Alaska flight in 1934.

Assistant Secretary of War Harry Woodring (left) and Maj. Gen. Foulois greet Lt. Col. Hap Arnold upon his return from Alaska flight.

Ten B-10s took off from Washington in mid-July 1934, flew to Alaska, then came back to participate in Army maneuvers on the east coast. By early September, each bomber had flown 18,000 miles without major mishap. The bombers had overflown the rugged arctic terrain and exposed for the first time, photographically, via the perceptive cameras of Capt. George W. Goddard, the frigid fastnesses of Alaska and the vast strategic and economic potential of that distant land.

On one leg back, the bombers flew southeastward from Juneau, Alaska, 980 miles nonstop, and most of it over water, to Seattle, Washington, a feat never before accomplished by a single plane, much less by 10 bombers in formation. While the flight was publicly acclaimed, unknown to Arnold and Knerr, it caused consternation at senior War and Navy Department policy levels. The flight had intruded upon the U.S. Navy's mission of defense against seaborne attack on the United States. In fact, the Navy, without prior announcement, restaked its claim to that mission. Six seaplanes flew up the Pacific coast headed for Alaska the very same day the B-10s left Washington. Both flights shared the day's headlines, especially in west coast newspapers. The seaplanes were accompanied by a large supply ship and 3 aircraft tenders stationed at intervals along the Canadian and Alaskan coasts to provide fuel and engine overhaul as necessary. The Navy planes took 28 days to reach southeastern Alaska, and 18 days to make the return trip. That was nothing to boast about publicly, which probably added to the acerbity of comments on the Air Corps flight by Capt. Ernest J. King, USN, featured speaker at the Athletic Club on the very evening the B-10s returned to the "forty-eight." Their spectacular flight, which won the Mackay Trophy as the greatest aviation achievement of 1934, started a chain of circumstances that soured Knerr's relationship with Hap Arnold, who was awarded the Distinguished Flying Cross for leadership of the flight, while other members went unrewarded.

*   *   *   *   *

Though the Alaskan Flight somewhat redeemed the Army Air Corps in public esteem, serious questions about its fighting qualities remained. President Roosevelt had already set up the Newton D. Baker Board, which began its deliberations while the Alaskan Flight was in progress. The Baker Board's principal recommendation, like that of an earlier Army board, led to the establishment of the GHQ Air Force and brought about a conjunction of the careers of Frank Andrews and Hugh Knerr. Their collaboration as Commander and Chief of Staff, respectively, to make the GHQ Air Force a real fighting organization with strategic offensive as well as defensive missions brought them onto a collision course with the War Department General Staff and with Gens. Oscar Westover and Hap Arnold, Chief and Assistant Chief of the Air Corps.

That clash was no accident, but rather a classic example of "divide and conquer." The GHQ Air Force was given operational responsibility to protect our shores from air attack and to provide tactical air support for the ground forces, while the Office of the Chief of Air Corps was made responsible for supply, individual training, key air personnel assignments, and internal control of air budget strings, as noted in the chapter on Maj. Gen. Benjamin Foulois. This contrived setup pitted Andrews-Knerr in an adversary relationship vs. Westover-Arnold, when all four air leaders were essentially striving towards identical goals.

Differences in their immediate objectives were apparent at military budget hearings in Washington between 1936 and 1938. The War Department General Staff was then rutted in an approved program for 2,320 planes with a stringent budget ceiling. As the General Staff did not accept an Air Corps role of long-range strategic air bombardment, its preference was for two-engine Douglas B-18s over the Boeing B-17. Moreover, almost three B-18s could be purchased for the cost of one B-17. Unfortunately, the B-18 did not have the "legs" to fly 2,400 miles from California to Hawaii. It had to be disassembled and

Formation of two-engine Douglas B–18s, aircraft that the War Department
General Staff wanted to procure over the Boeing B–17.

deck-loaded aboard a ship, requiring almost a month in transit to reach and
thus to reinforce the Philippines. That fact rendered absurd the official GHQ
Air Force mission to help defend America's distant Pacific possessions. Hugh
Knerr scornfully referred to the B–18 as "a converted passenger airplane with
machineguns."

Knerr accompanied Andrews to those War Department Budget Committee hearings at which they advanced a proposal to buy more than one hundred B–17s to equip two combat groups. Knerr fumed: "Arnold was sitting
at the table . . . as an observer and the argument I was carrying on got pretty
hot and heavy. I looked toward Arnold for a little support but I got none."

The built-up frustrations among senior staff down at Langley Field provoked Col. Walter H. "Tony" Frank, Lt. Col. Walter Weaver, and Col. Knerr
to exchange notes in a conspiratorial vein. "Dear Lenin," "Dear Trotsky," and
"Dear Stalin," respectively, they would write one another. Underneath their
gallows humor ran a serious thread of concern that America was unprepared
in the air. The Japanese were gobbling up East Asia after invading Manchuria
in 1931. Hitler came to power two years later, and now he and Mussolini posed
a clear danger to the European democracies. Unless they were stopped, another
world war was likely. If America became involved, the air advocates, rebelling
against the military status quo, did not want another American Expeditionary
Force bogged down overseas in the carnage of static trench warfare. They

envisioned the long-range strategic bomber as *the* technological breakthrough that could win such a war in less time, with fewer casualties.

The Langley Field rebels were not about to accept the status quo by default. One of their schemes to demonstrate publicly the B–17's capability, hopefully to build a congressional backfire against the War Department's opposition, succeeded beyond their best expectations. On May 12, 1938, three B–17s, led by Maj. Caleb V. Haynes and navigated by Lt. Curtis E. LeMay, flew over 700 miles out over the Atlantic Ocean, guided in equal parts by dead reckoning and Lady Luck, radar being a few years away from operational status. The formation broke out of dense cloud cover to confront the Italian liner *Rex*, their simulated enemy attacker, at masthead height. Two bombers banked by the stacks while dozens of excited passengers waved from the decks at the friendly intruders. The dramatic scene was captured on film by Air Corps photographer George Goddard in the third B–17, which stayed back. A sensational photo was carried on the front pages of *The New York Herald Tribune* and many other newspapers.

In Washington, at the Munitions Building where Maj. Gen. Malin Craig presided as Army Chief of Staff, and in the adjacent Navy Building on Constitution Avenue, the *Rex* affair was greeted with anger and repudiation which, for those military officials, blotted out the implied significance of the feat. According to then Maj. Ira Eaker, who happened to be in General Andrews's office the day after the *Rex* incident when General Craig phoned to administer a "Dutch Uncle" lecture, all GHQ Air Force flights would thereafter be limited to 100 miles out to sea, for safety reasons. To this day, the 100-mile restriction is shrouded in mystery and controversy. In 1946, Hanson W. Baldwin, military editor of *The New York Times*, an Annapolis graduate and a strong supporter of naval causes, challenged air advocates to produce documentary evidence that such an order was ever issued. An intensive search of Air Staff files proved unsuccessful. Years later, Lt. Gen. Ira Eaker recalled a conversation with Frank Andrews in London that he said took place in April 1943. Andrews said he had a copy of the restriction order and promised to produce it. A month later, he was killed in a plane crash in Iceland. A search of his files failed to produce the document.

Yet, evidence exists that airmen felt bound by the restriction, written or oral. Months later, in October 1938, Andrews offered written congratulations to Brig. Gen. George C. Marshall, just designated to succeed General Craig as Army Chief of Staff. His felicitations included a plea. No operating airman could understand the handicap "imposed upon us by restricting GHQ Air Force training limits at sea to a distance of 100 miles," Andrews wrote. Ten months later, after taking office, Marshall ordered a change. Air Corps Circular 60–1, of August 24, 1939, subject: "Flights To Sea," permitted Army land-based multi-engined aircraft to operate anywhere to their maximum range. It was none too soon, as World War II started just a week later with Hitler's attack on Poland.

For the War Department General Staff, the *Rex* mission was probably the last straw. Over the next few months the wasp nest at GHQ Air Force, Langley Field, was broken up and scattered. Col. Follett Bradley, G-2, was shipped off to Puerto Rico. Lt. Col. Joe McNarney, G-4, was assigned to the War Department in Washington. Hugh Knerr was reduced to his permanent rank of lieutenant colonel and sent to San Antonio. His command, the air component of the VIII Army Corps Area, did not lack for irony: "I was . . . to occupy the same dingy office vacated by . . . Billy Mitchell thirteen years before," he mused.

Frank Andrews himself suffered a similar fate when his tour as GHQ Air Force Commander ended in March 1939. He was reduced to his permanent rank of colonel, then shipped to San Antonio to occupy the seat lately warmed by Knerr who, with nearly thirty-one years of service, chose to retire on disability. An old back injury incurred in a De Havilland plane crash years back, no doubt aggravated by recent frustrations, helped convince Knerr that a brighter future might be found out of uniform. The humiliation of Frank Andrews, "the image of an ideal leader of strong men," was for Knerr the last blow.

If there was a sense of relief in higher military precincts that Knerr was out of the way, such elation was premature. He was hired by Sperry Gyroscope. He also established contacts with aircraft designer and writer Alexander de Seversky, another airpower zealot, and later began a literary collaboration with William Bradford Huie, a prolific writer with access to first-class literary markets.

* * * * *

Germany's pulverization of Poland in September 1939 marked the start of World War II. The Luftwaffe provided the sledgehammer. General Marshall, now Army Chief of Staff, looked to Frank Andrews, son-in-law of Brig. Gen. Henry T. Allen, who served with Marshall in the First World War, for advice on the employment of air power. Marshall brought Andrews back to Washington and assigned him to the War Department General Staff. As G-3, Operations, Brig. Gen. Andrews was the first airman to hold so high a post in the General Staff.

Andrews, in turn, campaigned to have Knerr restored to active duty. In late 1940, Andrews was named Commander of the new Panama Canal Air

Force and began to pressure General Arnold, Chief of the Air Corps, to authorize Knerr's assignment to Andrews's staff in Panama. Despite Arnold's assurances, each request seemed to get lost in the War Department paper mill. One negative response hinged on Knerr's retirement disability. At Walter Reed Hospital, he took another physical examination, got a satisfactory bill of health, and still nothing happened.

By spring 1941, Knerr's ardor to return to uniform cooled, primarily because his personal cause had been superseded by a larger one. Legislation for a separate air force was gaining political momentum. The Luftwaffe was successful all over Europe except during the Battle of Britain, when it was stopped by another independent air force. Fresh interest stirred Capitol Hill to take another look at the state of U.S. air power. In May, the House of Representatives had formed still another investigating committee. Hearings were announced, and commitee chairman Rep. Jack Nichols requested an audience with President Roosevelt for himself and Col. Bob Olds, a leading air advocate. The FDR Library files at Hyde Park, New York, show that the request was blocked by Brig. Gen. Edwin "Pa" Watson, military aide to the President.

Those files also show another urgent memorandum from Rep. Jack Cochran, Chairman of the House Select Committee on Government Reorganization, and a loyal administration supporter. Matters were getting out of hand in the chamber, Cochran told the President. Rumors abounded in Capitol cloakrooms that the White House was about to recommend a "United Air Corps." Such a White House intention would publicly embarrass Chairman Cochran. "For many years, I have been sitting on all the bills calling for a Department of Defense as well as others providing for a United Air Corps," he reminded the President. Attached to his complaint was a pleading cover note from Stephen Early, presidential press secretary: "What, if anything, can I tell Jack, please? S.T.E."

The President's reply was to the point: "Will you tell Jack definitely that every Army, Navy, and Marine Corps officer recommends against it, even officers in the air service, except a minority of the latter? From all the information we have been getting in this war, this would be no time for the United States to set up a separate air corps. F.D.R."

The presidential attitude of June 19, 1941, was not known to Knerr. He had been busy working with sympathetic congressmen, particularly Rep. Mark Wilcox, of Florida. Knerr's letter to Andrews, reflecting those efforts, was written one day earlier: "Dear Andy: In order that you may not be taken by surprise . . . the old ghost of a separate air arm is walking again. I have been carrying on a quiet campaign for the past year . . . and the thing is rapidly coming to a head." Hearings would start on June 23 on a new bill introduced by Wilcox based on an earlier one drafted by Knerr "as a starter."

111

"This time," Knerr wrote hopefully, "I am trying to get a close personal friend of FDR behind it with the idea that he will be made the new Secretary of Air. That is where we fell down before. Dirty business, and I hate it," he confessed, "but I have found that it is by such means that things are accomplished now." Knerr identified Paul Scott, a Miami attorney, as the President's friend. "The biggest problem left," assuming a separate air arm could become law, was to devise a means of ensuring that FMA (Andrews), not HHA (Arnold) would become the first air marshal. "Frankly, I am stumped," Knerr's letter continued. "Looks like the only way to do it would be to discredit the leadership of HHA while FMA was fighting for the things that the present war has proven to be essential to victory."

Having written that, Knerr was smitten by remorse mixed with caution. To act vindictively might undo all they had planned for so long. Utterly frank about Arnold, he wrote: "Although he lifted no finger to help me when I needed it, I can't quite come around to smearing him. Besides, it might discredit the whole movement if someone picked up the idea. I could be accused of personal motive. So, it looks like the old slicker is sitting pretty again."

One day later, on June 20, 1941, the Army Air Forces came into being with Arnold as Chief. The concept was based on a plan, largely the work of Brig. Gen. Carl "Tooey" Spaatz, Arnold's Chief of Staff, and implemented as soon as the President gave the green light for an alternative to a separate air force. Within the Army, Arnold was moved up the ladder to become a Deputy Chief of Staff for Air. The AAF was going to be allowed to have its own planning staff, subordinate to the War Department General Staff, which retained control of budget and senior staffing. The AAF had achieved a status comparable to the Marine Corps' semiautonomy within the U.S. Navy, according to Brig. Gen. Leonard T. Gerow, War Department General Staff officer.

In his new position, Arnold walked a tightrope. With the possible exception of Spaatz, Eaker, and his immediate office staff, a large majority of "early bird" fliers was unenthusiastic about the Army Air Forces. Most supported—and many worshipped—Andrews as the Moses who would lead them out of the War Department wilderness. All along, Andrews had been senior rank to Arnold. More important, Andrews had held key combat-type command jobs for the past decade. Arnold, on the other hand, had achieved his reputation through a masterful public and congressional relations job at March Field, California. His monthly air shows attracted Hollywood stars by the dozen. His quick response to aid victims of the 1933 earthquake that shook nearby Long Beach, his handling of the Civilian Conservation Corps in the state, along with his command of the Western Air Mail Zone and the Alaskan flight—all these activities had garnered favorable attention. More important, his astute management had won for him the patronage of Malin Craig, IX

Maj. Gen. Malin Craig (left) becomes Army Chief of Staff in 1935 and insures Hap Arnold's (right) appointment to Assistant Chief of the Air Corps in 1936.

Army Corps Area Commander at the Presidio in San Francisco, who succeeded Douglas MacArthur as Army Chief of Staff late in 1935. It was Craig who brought Arnold to Washington in January 1936 as Assistant Chief of the Air Corps.

When General Westover was killed, Arnold, with a major assist from General Craig, won the reluctant favor of President Roosevelt to be named Chief of the Air Corps. Nearly three years later, in 1941, Arnold gained General Marshall's support for the post of Chief and subsequently Commanding General, AAF, in part, because he was willing to live with Marshall's strongly-held belief, expressed at the American Legion Convention in 1941, that a separate air force—"a great error"—would disrupt the War Department's "splendid organization." Marshall added "that nothing has developed as a result of the present war which indicates that a change should be made in the present setup."

The air advocates in no way accepted the Army Air Forces as the final solution to the defense problem they foresaw, if America was drawn into World War II. Some of them shared Knerr's view that Arnold had positioned himself to gain the top post. It remained for Andrews to exercise a calming effect on his most devoted disciple, urging in his June 23, 1941 letter that Knerr acknowledge the *fait accompli*, and not allow "your dilemma about HHA"

113

to trigger an overreaction: "Arnold is capable, all right. He is probably the best man available to head it up," Andrews wrote. Arnold "is a much better politician than you or I, as he very clearly demonstrated when he sat back and let us butt our heads against the stone wall and kept himself in the background," a wry reference to the frustrations of the B–17 budget hearings of several years before.

Having said that, Andrews revealed his own dilemma over continuing the separate air force struggle. He praised Knerr for his devotion to the cause, yet he owed a debt to General Marshall for restoring him to favor. Then, tilting a bit away from that obligation, Andrews wrote: "Even with a man as broadminded and as farseeing as Marshall at the head of the Army, no matter how progressive Marshall may be himself, the rank and file of the Army has not changed materially."

In this climate of uncertainty within the air community, it took every bit of Arnold's acknowledged political skills to coax or cajole disgruntled airmen to face reality and get on with the tremendous air expansion program being set in motion. Quite aware that his old friend, "Andy" Andrews was less than fully committed to the compromise, Arnold prodded Andrews in the guise of congratulating him for having been named, in July 1941, to head the Caribbean Defense Command, the first time a U.S. airman had been given command of joint air-ground forces in a theater. "We are no longer the fifth wheel of the wagon," Arnold wrote. If the Air (i.e., Andrews) failed in that job, airmen could not very well fault the General Staff. Some day, Arnold predicted, there would be a separate air force. "I have always said that it is bound to come, but I also say that right now, is not the time for it."

Their strained relationship carried into August 1941, when Arnold visited the Caribbean Defense Command and promised Andrews more planes. Andrews's letter to Knerr dismissed the promise as just talk, since the Caribbean had a low priority compared to Europe and the Pacific. He also expressed disbelief in Arnold's "claim that he had done all he could" to restore Knerr to active duty, "leaving me with the impression that there is a snag somewhere else." Andrews wanted Knerr to head his planning staff and promised: "I will eventually get to the bottom of it."

*   *   *   *   *

Very likely there was more than one snag at senior policy levels as Knerr's by-lines or his literary footprints were visible across the spectrum of major publications. In August 1941, *Time* did a favorable cover story on Andrews, prominently mentioning Knerr. Hugh Knerr's by-lines advocating expanding strategic air power while questioning the U.S. Navy's intrusion into land-based aviation appeared in four successive issues of *American Mercury*, starting in August 1941. In October of that year, *Fortune* carried two main stories, one a detailed history of the heavy bomber's development, called "A Tool For Mr. Churchill." The other gave credit to "a little group of tenacious air-corps officers who risked their careers for the bomber." The list included Arnold, George Kenney, Ken Walker, Bob Olds, Harold George, and Hugh Knerr. "But, most of all," the text read, all praise "must go to Frank Andrews who . . . framed the specifications for the Boeing B-17." Andrews's exile, his recall by General Marshall, and his promotion to head the first unified ground and air theater in the Caribbean were recounted. For Andrews, *Fortune* said, "how sweet must the vindication be."

Knerr sent the advance text of the *Fortune* articles to Andrews along with a background letter confessing to having supplied much of the material. From the galleys the editors had sent him, Knerr said he had "scratched several names that they had inserted, including mine, and put Arnold's in. No need of getting him mad while we are keeping your name before the public." When his contributor's copy arrived, Knerr learned "they did not have my name scratched." He wrote Andrews in another letter, "I find you can accomplish a lot more when you are not identified."

September and October 1941 passed, and still no official word on Knerr's pending application for return to active duty. In November, Andrews, tired of waiting, persuaded Sperry Gyroscope to send Knerr down to Panama to inspect Sperry gunsights and other equipment in use there. "General Andrews gave me a desk in his headquarters and a list of problems confronting him," Knerr wrote in his memoir. "As in former times, I gave him an uninhibited report on each item." That advice appeared to be well received. "An occasional chuckle from his office next door indicated we were in tune again," Knerr wrote.

In the frantic weeks that followed Pearl Harbor, Andrews, now strongly supported by Arnold and Assistant Secretary of War for Air Robert A. Lovett, stepped up the campaign to have Knerr recalled. Their collective efforts were still unavailing. In February 1942, "when it became evident that powerful influences were against my return," Knerr recalled, Andrews again requested that Sperry Gyroscope send Knerr back down to Panama. Andrews assured Sperry's president, Reginald E. Gillmor, that Knerr had been of more help on his previous visit than the Army or Navy.

But Knerr detected with renewed hope more than a flicker of life in the separate air force body. Knerr could serve that cause better by remaining a civilian. The time seemed right. In the weeks after Pearl Harbor, bewilderment, then anger seized many Americans, not accustomed to defeat.

Suddenly, Hugh Knerr was a man in considerable public demand. Out of his typewriter rolled one smoking article after another. In its issue of February 9, 1942, *Time* said that unless the AAF received more autonomy, "the hue and cry for a separate air arm . . . will go up again." In his work for *American Mercury*, Knerr had come in contact with a first-rate polemicist, William Bradford Huie, who attacked all those he believed had blocked the development of strategic air power. Huie and Knerr later would collaborate on a book.

Meanwhile, Sperry had approved another visit to Panama, and Knerr spent a couple of weeks in February 1942 focusing on two projects, one military, the other political. He completed a five-point memorandum recommending improvements in the air defense of the Panama Canal, feared to be the next target for either German U-boats or Japanese carrier air attacks. Andrews signed and sent it off to Washington. In the political sphere, Knerr worked on proposed legislation to reorganize the AAF with a concurrent shuffling of senior personnel. He would have had Arnold sent off to Africa to command U.S. air forces bolstering the British effort to keep Rommel out of the Middle East, while Andrews was to return to Washington to command the new "Air Army." Maj. Gen. Walter "Tony" Frank was his choice to succeed Andrews in the Caribbean. Frank, one of the GHQ Air Force rebels and a very senior officer, was then mouldering in a supply job in Dayton, and yearned for a combat command.

At the Munitions Building, General Marshall set up a committee under Maj. Gen. Joseph McNarney, recalled from his London observation post. The

Joseph McNarney (shown here as Lt. Gen.) was appointed to head committee that would stem idea of a separate air force.

McNarney Committee's goal was to head off the snowballing separate air force idea, whose time Knerr thought had finally arrived. General Arnold assigned Brig. Gen. Laurence Kuter, one of his brightest young assistants, to the task force. Cols. Bill Harrison (Cavalry) and Otto Nelson completed the working group. Kuter's diary recalls that his "sole duty" for many weeks was to produce a reorganization of the War Department that, once and for all, would stifle the separate air force gang, and last out the war.

* * * * *

On March 9, 1942, the McNarney Plan took effect. The reorganization elevated the Army Air Forces under Arnold to equality with the Army Ground Forces under Lt. Gen. Lesley J. McNair, and the Army Services of Supply, led by Lt. Gen. Brehon B. Somervell. By General Marshall's order, Arnold achieved somewhat more equality than McNair and Somervell. He sat with the Joint Chiefs and the Combined (US/UK) Chiefs of Staff, a major step ahead, though neither Marshall nor Admiral King treated him fully as an equal. It was "Dear General" and "Dear Arnold" when Arnold and Marshall exchanged official views. Admiral King consistently refused to deal directly with Arnold on air matters of mutual concern. He went through Marshall, his perceived equal.

When the smoke cleared from this latest skirmish, Knerr had achieved none of his principal goals: no separate air force, no orders for Andrews to return to Washington, and no recall of Knerr to active service. Hugh Knerr went back to his typewriter to wait for a more opportune time. His article in the June 1942 *American Mercury* applauded the partial unification of ground and air forces in the Caribbean while the Navy's Sea Frontier operating out of Puerto Rico ran its own show. There was one victory of sorts. Publicity that Knerr and others generated nipped in an early stage a Navy-sponsored plan to gain authorization for construction of wider Panama Canal locks to accommodate the *Montana*-class battleship, although the Navy began to lose interest in building such behemoths after Pearl Harbor and switched its emphasis to aircraft carriers.

The Navy Department by this time had had its fill of Hugh Knerr, a Sperry Gyroscope employee who appeared to spend most of his time pounding out articles criticizing the naval service. By virtue of its own contracts with Sperry, the U.S. Navy had some leverage. In July 1942, Knerr was called into Sperry's front office by President Gillmor and admonished. He was fired a few weeks later, "at the insistence of the Navy Department," Knerr believed.

117

He said he accepted dismissal "with good grace," assuring a disconsolate Tom Morgan, the Sperry official who handed him the pink slip, that he had just begun to fight for the principles he believed in.

In addition to his writing, Knerr signed on with the Getts Lecture Agency for a series of public appearances. On October 10, a peremptory telephone call to his home in Epping Forest, near Annapolis, ordered Knerr to report at once to Secretary of War Stimson's office. Walking in, Knerr was surprised to see Joe McNarney, his G-4 at Langley Field where they both served the GHQ Air Force just five years before. McNarney had "a smile on his face as he greeted me," Knerr remembered. "At last, I thought, I was to be returned to active duty."

It was nothing of the sort. McNarney now had a higher loyalty and a solemn duty. He reprimanded Knerr for having embarrassed the War and Navy Departments with his writing and speaking. McNarney wanted Knerr's word that he would forthwith cease such activities, to which Knerr replied: "I will not!" Whereupon McNarney rose from his chair, looked across the desk at Knerr, and began to read from a piece of paper. Knerr was "directed to refrain from all public written and oral comment on the conduct of the war." He was forbidden to discuss in public "tactical use and organizational relationships of the armed forces of the United States and its Allies."

Knerr flushed as these words were read. Though the words "court-martial" were not mentioned, the threat seemed clear. He would be recalled to duty, all right, for the sole purpose of being court-martialed. Should he defy authority as Mitchell did? A lot of people had begun to pay attention to him.

Hugh and Hazel Knerr gave serious thought in the next few days to the direction he should take. They decided he should stand down from a public performance of the martyr's role. First, he was not suited to it by temperament or experience. Billy Mitchell had been flamboyant, charismatic; Knerr was a reflective and somewhat retiring person. He functioned best in small groups, often behind the scenes, where ideas rather than forensics counted. Second, and not least in Knerr's calculation, was concern for their son, Navy Lt. Hugh S. Knerr, an Annapolis graduate like his father, and, in a sense, hostage to his father's good behavior.

Hugh Knerr took a step back. He requested the Getts Agency to let him pull out of his commitments. Several engagements were canceled, but the Milwaukee, Wisconsin, Town Hall sponsors had sold a lot of tickets and demanded that Knerr fulfill his contract. He gave that speech, and another at White Sulphur Springs, West Virginia. His theme was America's mortal danger for having neglected air power, but he turned it around as if he were delivering his remarks from Hitler's viewpoint. Upon his return to Epping Forest, Hazel met him at the door, wide-eyed with worry. There had been another phone call. He was to report once more to Secretary Stimson's office. As he drove into Washington on October 21, 1942, Hugh Knerr ran through his mind names of judge advocates he had known through the years. Would he have to retain a lawyer? Would they really court-martial him?

* * * * *

The Secretary's office in the brand new Pentagon building was big, and it had a river view. Otherwise, the meeting started as a *reprise* of the first one, with McNarney seated at the desk. This time, Joe spoke softly. Secretary Stimson, after considerable discussion with others, had decided that Knerr's expertise was too valuable to be lost to the war effort. Knerr was to be brought back on duty as a lieutenant colonel.

It was a moment of rich satisfaction, though tinged with bitterness. The Army could not lick Hugh Knerr, so it was asking him to rejoin it. Suppose he refused McNarney? What could they do? That he was being silenced through a recall the Army did not want to make angered him, but the prospect of rejoining forces with Frank Andrews, just selected to head the U.S. Army Forces in the Middle East, was irresistible. Knerr could have, and upon reflection should have, held out for restoration of his eagles, the rank he held at Langley Field five years before. But he did not.

Luckily for the Army and for the nation, bringing Knerr back on duty turned out to be more than just a move to control what he said and did. As McNarney stated with accuracy, Knerr had a proven record of accomplishment in logistics. The war, up to that time, was not going well. Knerr was really needed. And so, after a hesitant acceptance, he was led to an adjoining office where Hap Arnold awaited him with a friendly greeting and words of praise for his stand on principle. Arnold, however, did not offer Knerr an assignment with Andrews. As a starter, Hap complained that logistics at the Gravelly Point depot, near Washington National Airport, had gotten out of hand. Knerr was to report to Brig. Gen. Clements McMullen, the Air Service Command facility chief. He was to observe and report directly to Arnold, but was given no specific deadline.

Had Arnold soft-soaped him? Was he to be shelved for the duration? If that was their intention, they had the wrong patsy. Knerr took the assignment, fulfilled it in record time, and waited for the next one. Arnold was pleasantly surprised to find Knerr's detailed and candid report on his desk. Whatever his original motivations, Arnold was always in a hurry to get a job done, and Knerr's report put a finger on a key weakness. Half of the AAF

119

aircraft dependent upon the Gravelly Point facility were grounded for lack of parts, while the authority to obtain them was not clearly defined.

To Knerr's surprise, Arnold accepted the report at face value, forthwith closed down the materiel office at Gravelly Point, and ordered logistics control centered in the Air Service Command (ASC) headquarters in Dayton, Ohio. More than that, Knerr was transferred to ASC under Maj. Gen. Tony Frank, a change that pleased and benefited all parties concerned. Knerr soon busied himself reorganizing ASC into three divisions—supply, maintenance, and personnel—each headed by a general officer. Coordinating staff was reduced to a minimum. In a letter to Andrews expressing pleasure that he was back in harness in a productive capacity, Knerr wrote: "No more buck-passing" at ASC.

Most pleased with his new assistant, General Frank put in papers for Knerr's promotion to brigadier general. Secretary Stimson blocked that promotion personally, though Knerr won his eagles, in his words, as "the result of a fluke." An order sent through by Maj. Gen. George Stratemeyer, chief of staff to General Arnold, appointing Knerr a colonel in the Regular Army was published in the *Army Register* before it had made all the bureaucratic stops. "Secretary Stimson was furious," Knerr's diary recorded, but Stimson did not contest the promotion.

Stimson and other high officials were angered by publication of William Bradford Huie's, *The Fight for Air Power*, in time to catch the Christmas 1942 book trade. Although evidence of Knerr's collaboration had been hastily removed, the Navy was hardly mollified by the nasty attack upon its middle-aged "battleship admirals" who, Huie charged, made the trek to the Navy's aviation school at Pensacola, Florida, went through the motions, and acquired gold wings, while most of the AAF leadership had been tested in combat against German Fokkers in 1917–18.

*   *   *   *   *

In the spring of 1943, Arnold ordered Maj. Gen. Ira Eaker, now commanding the Eighth Air Force in the United Kingdom, to undertake an immediate study of what logistics would be needed to supply a force of seventy bomber groups and twenty-five fighter groups, manned by half a million men. The mission: a massive daylight bombardment of Germany to start as soon as possible. Maj. Gen. Follet Bradley (once G–2, GHQ Air Force) was selected to organize the study and formulate the plan which bore his name. His request that Hugh Knerr be assigned as his deputy was granted.

Maj. Gen. Follet Bradley (at right, talking with Brig. Gen. Haywood Hansell) was selected to organize plan for daylight bombardment of Germany.

On May 4, 1943, Bradley and Knerr flew to Prestwick, Scotland, to choose key staff members and to start the organization rolling. Knerr looked forward to this assignment. He would be working, if indirectly at first, for General Frank Andrews who, at Casablanca in January 1943, was appointed Commanding General of the European Theater of Operations. Knerr's hopes and dreams finally seemed to be coming to fruition. Although Knerr speculated that General Marshall was grooming Andrews to lead the invasion of continental Europe, more likely Marshall had in mind commanding the cross-Channel invasion himself, and wanted Andrews for his top air commander.

On the long transatlantic flight, excitement grew in Hugh Knerr. As the plane taxied to the Prestwick ramp, Knerr casually looked out the window at the assembled dignitaries, then peered intently, for he had failed to spot the chiseled features of Frank Andrews in the waiting group. Moments later, Knerr received the greatest shock of his life. Andrews's plane had crashed into a mountain in Iceland the day before. Only the tail gunner survived, miraculously.

In June, a month later, came another traumatic experience. Follett Bradley was laid low by a sudden, severe heart attack during an inspection trip to North Africa. That left the whole Bradley plan in limbo. The next senior supply man was Maj. Gen. H.J.F. Miller, incumbent Eighth Air Force Service Commander. However, Bradley sent back to Arnold a frank assessment, dictated while he was flat on his back. It was quite remarkable for its total candor:

> I am certainly sorry to play out like this, but I think the work for which I was sent to England and Africa is in pretty good shape for others to carry along.
>
> The Service Command was really a mess, but it was not by any means the sole fault of the Service Command or its Commander. Ably assisted by Hugh Knerr and his Colonel McDonald, we went through that setup with a fine-toothed comb and made

many recommendations. None of these recommendations is gravy. They must all be acted upon, and promptly, for if this is not done, the heavy bomber offensive from U.K. will fall flat on its face, and the ground forces will have to fight their way into Germany.

In view of the above, you may wonder why I do not recommend Miller's relief and reduction at the present time. It is simply that there is no one better at the present time who is available. He has a background of experience, and although he is too kind-hearted, I believe that with the setup we have proposed for him, he can make a go of it. Of course, the best man for the job is Hugh Knerr, but I am afraid the powers that be would pass out at the mere suggestion of giving him the necessary rank and authority to swing the job.

I do hope, though, that whatever influences are still potent enough to keep Knerr's promotion from him have died out. He really doesn't give a damn whether or not he is made a Brig. General, but there is no question but that his work and usefulness would be facilitated, if he were promoted.

One thing would have interested you very much in England. Several luncheons and cocktail parties, etc., were given for me by the big shots in the R.A.F., and in every instance, Hugh Knerr was accorded the official place and cordiality of a two-star General, not that of a Colonel. I thought this treatment from the British, who are quite rank conscious, quite significant.

Whatever lingering resentment Arnold may have held against Knerr was washed away by Bradley's words. Arnold, an impatient man, accused by some of his peers of riding roughshod over his contemporaries to complete the job, refused to accept the "kindhearted" Miller who Bradley thought could make a go of the job. With General Marshall's approval, Arnold swept aside the accumulated animosities, and bulldozed through the War Department Knerr's promotion to brigadier general. Assistant Secretary Lovett hand-carried the paper work into Stimson's office, requesting that he be notified immediately if there was adverse action. Stimson went off on a short vacation. It was July 1943. Hugh Knerr had won his star!

That chore done, Arnold hustled Knerr, his new Eighth Air Force Service Commander, into the job. At the key Burtonwood Depot, General Knerr supplanted traditional British maintenance and service procedures by assembly-line maintenance. Damaged aircraft and overhauls came in at one end of an immense building and were flown back to their squadrons from the other.

Two months later, Arnold was impressed by the progress when he visited the U.K. There were areas that could be improved further. Arnold's original plan to send whole depot units overseas was not working. Knerr claimed better results could be obtained if replacements were sent over, then trained on the job. Arnold agreed to abandon the depot-unit concept, one of his pet projects, when he saw the transformation Knerr had already effected in so short a time.

Knerr got along splendidly with Ira Eaker, who was transferred from command of the Eighth Air Force in December 1943 and sent to the Mediterranean theater. He stood in equally well with General Tooey Spaatz, who came up from North Africa with General Eisenhower and was appointed

Top-ranking officers of WW II, shown here in 1947, from l. to r. : Gen. of the Army Dwight D. Eisenhower, AAF Deputy Commander Lt. Gen. Ira C. Eaker, and AAF Commanding Gen. Carl Spaatz

Commander of U.S. Strategic Air Forces in Europe (USSTAF). In General Order No. 1, USSTAF, Spaatz designated Knerr as his Deputy Commander for Administration, raising him to a coequal level with Maj. Gen. Fred L. Anderson, Deputy Commander for Operations. It was a first in any U.S. air organization. Knerr wore two stars three months later as he accepted an added responsibility for logistics support of the Fifteenth Air Force, operating out of Italy.

Afforded a better overall vantage point on interservice operations, Hugh Knerr—who never thought he could—actually mellowed towards the sister service that gave him his first uniform and training. The tempering process took place during periods of worry over the safety of precious aircraft and other AAF cargo deck-loaded aboard tankers zig-zagging across the North Atlantic to avoid the hungry U-boat packs, and mostly getting through. The Navy, he wrote, did "a magnificent job . . . in getting the convoys across." When his friend from Annapolis days, Commodore Philip V. H. Weems, brought in one more convoy, Knerr was down at the London docks to shake his hand. "I felt contrite over having been too rough on the Navy at times," he confessed in his memoir.

The last year of the air war in Europe was mostly a succession of triumphs for Allied forces. That success, in fairness, was due as much to the outpouring from America's cornucopia as it was to the bravery of its flyers, the planning of its leaders, or the logistical genius of Hugh Knerr and his associates. Knerr, of course, was now in a position to receive major credit for that accomplishment. Only days after General Spaatz announced the end of the strategic air war in Europe on April 17, 1945, Knerr was summoned to Rheims for a meeting with Spaatz and Eaker. They told him that Arnold wanted him to head the Air Technical Service Command (ATSC), the senior logistical job in the Army Air Forces. Knerr took over the three-star job from retiring Lt. Gen. William S. Knudsen, but did not remain long enough to have a major impact on the command's operation. His Pacific Air Logistics Plan was never activated, as hostilities ended in August 1945.

Two months later, Knerr received two communications of diametrically opposite thrust. One, a letter of commendation from General Arnold, said in part, "The contributions of your Command represent one of the greatest ever to be made in the history of aviation." The other was a telegram from Spaatz, getting ready to step into Arnold's shoes as Commanding General, AAF. A list of senior personnel had been compiled in the Pentagon. Those who made it would be offered senior rank and choice assignments in the postwar air force. Those who did not would mark time until they retired. Spaatz's wire read: "It is a great personal disappointment your name was not among those given a General Officer rank. "

Knerr once again felt victimized by ancient animosities. He would retire for the second time a colonel, but the wheel of fortune had a couple of turns left for him. War Department Order #308 of December 27, 1945, detailed Knerr to a three-star slot on the Joint Strategic Planning Committee (JSPC) of the Joint Chiefs of Staff. But Knerr never sat down with the committee, as that wheel, on its next turn, came up "lemons. " General Eisenhower, succeeding General Marshall as Army Chief of Staff, informed Spaatz that Admiral Nimitz, succeeding Admiral King as Chief of Naval Operations, strongly objected to Knerr's assignment to a joint staff planning job. Knerr would not have an open mind about large capital ships in postwar planning, Nimitz charged.

Nimitz's opposition was not without validity, though Knerr had for several years shown signs of mellowing with age and war experience. He seemed quite ready to let old wounds be bound up and healed. But William Bradford Huie, his erstwhile collaborator, was not. Huie had one last polemic in his arsenal. *The Case Against The Admirals*, published at that very time, finished off Knerr's chances of appealing Nimitz's allegation. Knerr was embarrassed by the fulsome praise tossed in his direction: "In all the Army and Navy disputes since the first World War—disputes in which the safety of the nation was involved, I know of only two officers who have dared to go to the people with blunt facts, " Huie wrote. "These two were General Mitchell, who was

National Archives

Admiral Chester Nimitz

cashiered for it, and Gen. Hugh Knerr, who was persecuted in a manner which I shall describe. . . . You may never have heard of him, yet on his record, he is America's ablest planner of aerial warfare. . . ."

The JSPC appointment was not pursued despite Eisenhower's expressed resentment to Spaatz over the Navy's intrusion into an internal War Department matter. Knerr accepted another post as Assistant to the Commanding General, AAF, to reorganize the Air Board. This agency was comprised of the top-level military leadership and made recommendations on crucial policy issues.

In October 1947, soon after the National Security Act of 1947 became law, Knerr was named the first Air Inspector of the United States Air Force. Although he set up the services' initial watchdog system, he seemed weary now and retired for the second time in 1949, forty-five years after entering the U.S. Naval Academy. He was a man of courage, vision, and organizational genius whose contributions to the establishment and shaping of the United States Air Force are a legacy to be treasured by those who have followed after him.

Sources

There is no published biography of Maj. Gen. Hugh J. Knerr, but he is mentioned frequently in such standard works as *The Army Air Forces in World War II*, Vols. I–III (University of Chicago Press, 1951; Reprint, Office of Air Force History, 1983); *A History of the United States Air Force 1907–1957*, edited by Alfred Goldberg (D. Van Nostrand, 1957); and Robert Frank Futrell's *Ideas, Concepts, Doctrine: A History of Basic Thinking in the United States Air Force 1907–1964* (Air University, Maxwell AFB, Alabama, 1971). Knerr also figures prominently in DeWitt S. Copp's popularized history of the Air Service/Air Corps/AAF through World War II, *A Few Great Captains* and *Forged in Fire* (Doubleday, 1980 and 1982).

A principal source for this essay is the author's interviews with General Knerr from 1969 to 1971, extensive correspondence with him throughout that period, and subsequent correspondence with his widow, Hazel Knerr, until 1977. Other valuable interviews were with Generals George C. Kenney, Ira C. Eaker, and Curtis E. LeMay.

The author supervised endowment of the Knerr papers to the U.S. Air Force Academy, Colorado Springs, Colorado, in 1972. Among the papers is an unpublished memoir, *The Vital Era, 1887–1971*, which includes frank insights into relationships with military contemporaries, especially Frank Andrews and Henry H. Arnold.

In the Library of Congress Manuscript Division, the Arnold papers (especially boxes 9 and 201) contain material pertinent to Knerr as do the Andrews papers, boxes 4 and 5. The National Archives, Military Division, War Department, AGO File 210.52 documents in detail the aborted DFC recommendation for the Alaska flyers.

General Knerr's views on American military preparedness immediately before World War II and the role of air power in defense are expressed in the *American Mercury* and *Fortune* articles mentioned in the text.

6

George C. Kenney:
The Great Innovator

Herman S. Wolk

George Churchill Kenney was the antithesis of a general officer as sometimes caricatured in Western literature. He was short, crewcut, voluble, and completely lacking in pomposity. Kenney had an earthy sense of humor, a mastery of colorful though not always quotable language, and a fine sense of the dramatic. He was not impressed with rank—his own or anyone else's—and he did not intend to fight his war with the weapons and ideas of the last one. George Kenney was an innovator; his motto, "Hell, let's try it."

When Kenney was sent to the Southwest Pacific to command allied air forces in that area, it was with the prediction that he would not last under the imperious Gen. Douglas MacArthur. But MacArthur thought he needed a rebel, and he got one. He characterized Kenney as born to be a pirate, and when the fighting was over, said that no air commander of World War II surpassed George Kenney as a combat leader.

Kenney's particular brand of leadership was a melding of personality and experience going back to his introduction to flying in 1910. He was born on August 6, 1889, at Yarmouth, Nova Scotia, where his parents were visiting, grew up in Brookline, Massachusetts, and in 1907 enrolled at Massachusetts Institute of Technology. The restless Kenney, who became "kind of bored with MIT," left its campus in 1911, before graduating, to take a railroad surveyor's job in Quebec. He next worked in Boston as a civil engineer helping to construct buildings for MIT, moved to the New York, New Haven and Hartford Railroad as a hydraulic engineer, then went into general contracting as head of a small engineering corporation.

Kenney had become excited about flying while at MIT. Taking leave of his classes one day in 1910, he convinced a well-known flyer, Claude Graham White, to give him a ride in a Farman pusher. Kenney recalled: "From then on, I knew that was what I was going to do. I never got such a kick in my life as this terrific speed. " He and two friends built a copy of a monoplane that Louis Bleriot had flown across the English Channel in 1909. It reached an altitude of four feet, and fortunately, was demolished after a few flights.

In the summer of 1917, Kenney enlisted in the Army and took flying training at Mineola, Long Island, under one of the early flyers, Bert Acosta. George Kenney's first three landings were "dead-stick. " After the first one, Acosta was appalled. Kenney retorted, "any damned fool can land it if the motor is running. I just wanted to see what would happen in case the motor quit. "

In November 1917, after less than twenty hours in the air, he went to Issoudun, France, as a first lieutenant in the 91st Aero Squadron. Before the war ended, he had become commanding officer of the 91st, had flown seventy-five missions in French two-seater Salmsons, downed two German planes, and earned the Distinguished Service Cross and Silver Star. Kenney was promoted to captain and remained in Germany until June 1919. He decided to stay in Army aviation. After serving on Mexican border patrol, he was assigned to an aviation detachment at Fort Knox, Kentucky, where he worked to develop "spotting, " with the field artillery.

In France Kenney met Brig. Gen. William "Billy" Mitchell. According to Kenney, Mitchell directed him to fly "special missions. " These were flights to find American troops, sometimes in large numbers, that had become lost. Kenney recalled that Mitchell would say, "George, go find this outfit. The last I heard of them they were in such and such a place. " Kenney and his cohorts would fly at almost treetop level, looking for American uniforms. From that experience, according to Kenney, the idea of "attack aviation" came to him. It was safer to fly at low altitude where aircraft were less exposed to ground fire.

After the Armistice, Air Service strength fell precipitously from a wartime high of 195,000 officers and men to an average of about 10,000 throughout the 1920s. Nevertheless, that decade saw significant pioneering in concepts of air warfare and in military aviation technology despite pitifully small defense budgets. George Kenney, who remained a captain for seventeen years after the war (except for one year when he reverted to first lieutenant), established a reputation as both a technical and conceptual innovator.

In 1921, Kenney graduated from the Air Service Engineering School at McCook Field, Ohio. Although he found the school just as tough as MIT, he graduated first in his class and was named Air Service representative and test pilot at the Curtiss Aircraft factory, Garden City, Long Island. Curtiss

Capt. George C. Kenney

had contracted to build the MB–1 bomber, originally produced by the Martin company.

From 1923 to 1925, Kenney was assigned to the Inspection and Contract Sections of Production Engineering at the Air Service Engineering Division back at McCook Field. Energetic and restless as ever, he conceived the idea of mounting machineguns on a plane's wings instead of on the engine cowling where they had to be synchronized to fire, at a much slower rate, through the propellor arc. He demonstrated its feasibility by attaching two .30-caliber machineguns to the wings of a considerably modified DH–4. It was an idea ahead of its time, a significant though rejected breakthrough in the development of aircraft armament. In 1941, the Curtiss P–40 fighter still had two .50-caliber machineguns on the cowling, in addition to two .30-caliber guns mounted in the wings.

Kenney next attended the Air Corps Tactical School, then at Langley Field, Virginia, graduating in 1926. The Air Service became the Army Air Corps in July of that year. The following year, he graduated from the Command and General Staff School at Fort Leavenworth, Kansas. During 1927–29, he returned to the Tactical School as an instructor.

The Tactical School was the Air Corps' leading laboratory for developing doctrine and tactics. In the early years of Army aviation, the so-called "air force" part of combat flying, as opposed to observation aviation, consisted of pursuit, bombardment, and attack. The mission of pursuit was to destroy an enemy's air force, primarily through aerial combat, while bombers hit military objectives on the ground and water, and attack aviation struck opposing surface forces with machinegun fire. During the mid–1920s, pursuit and attack were considered the major classes of Army aviation. The bomber advocates were not far behind. The argument subsequently to be considered was whether bombers could defend themselves against pursuit aircraft and break through to their target.

It was at the Tactical School that Capt. George Kenney came to know Maj. Frank M. Andrews. Andrews was a student, while Kenney was an instructor. Kenney impressed Andrews with his quick wit and imaginative mind and with his ability to grasp the crux of a technical problem and drive through to the solution. Kenney made attack aviation one of his specialities. He taught the subject and revised the basic textbook.

During the late 1920s and early 1930s, the doctrine and tactics of pursuit aviation were being challenged by the proponents of bombardment aviation. Italian Gen. Giulio Douhet's writings, espousing the primacy of mass bombardment as the way to cripple the enemy's industry and his will to fight, were beginning to be debated in the Army Air Corps. While at the Tactical School, George Kenney corrected Dorothy Benedict's translation of Douhet from French to English.

From 1933 to 1935, Kenney served in Washington in the Plans Division, Office of the Chief of the Air Corps. Under Maj. Gen. Benjamin D. Foulois, Chief of the Air Corps, Kenney became an increasingly strong advocate of an independent air force. In March 1935, the Air Corps made a significant stride in the development of air power by establishing the General Headquarters (GHQ) Air Force, described in the chapters on Generals Foulois and Andrews. Brig. Gen. Frank M. Andrews was named its commander.

Andrews now called on Captain Kenney, making him Chief of Operations and Training, Headquarters, GHQ Air Force, at Langley Field. Others on Andrews's staff were Maj. Hugh J. Knerr, Chief of Staff; Maj. Follett Bradley, G–2; and Maj. Joseph T. McNarney, G–4. Although establishment of GHQ Air Force was far short of the independence championed by Kenney and his colleagues, it was beyond doubt an important step forward.

Andrews was determined to make the GHQ Air Force combat ready. He and Kenney emphasized instrument and night flying. They wanted a mobile, effective force. As G–3, Kenney wrote the tables of organization and planned maneuvers. Forces were trained to repel enemy ships approaching U.S. coasts and to strike enemy ground forces. Tactics were planned. Maneuvers matched pursuit against bombardment planes. The results were weighed. Kenney, now a temporary lieutenant colonel, recalled that, "during the first year, I was home at Langley Field something like thirty-nine days; the rest of the time I was all over the country."

Andrews and Kenney wanted B–17s, the new four-engine, long-range bombers. Andrews sent Kenney to convince the War Department General Staff. According to Kenney: "They said there was no sense in having an airplane as big as that. . . . They didn't like some of the remarks I made because I was a temporary lieutenant colonel and a permanent captain, and these were all major generals." He was also caught in the middle of the argument between Andrews and Maj. Gen. Oscar Westover, who succeeded Foulois as

Right: Maj. Gen. Oscar Westover; *below:* Kenney (as a Lt. Gen.) in cockpit of a Boeing B-17, an aircraft that he and Brig. Gen. Frank Andrews tried to promote.

131

Chief of the Air Corps, over Andrews's advocacy of more planes, especially long-range bombers, and greater autonomy.

As a result of his support for Andrews's position and perhaps of his participation in the *Rex* affair, where he had flown in the lead B-17 with Caleb Haynes (see chapter on Knerr), Westover's staff ordered Kenney to Fort Benning, Georgia, as an instructor in the Infantry School. This was a blow to both Kenney and Andrews. During 1936–38, Kenney taught liaison between air and ground forces, defense and attack of river lines, and machinegun drill. Fed up with the routine, he went to see Army Chief of Staff Maj. Gen. Malin Craig about another assignment. Craig told Kenney to take it up with Brig. Gen. Henry H. "Hap" Arnold, Assistant Chief of the Air Corps. Arnold told him to see Westover. General Westover suggested that Kenney might take over an observation squadron at Mitchell Field, Long Island. Although this was a first lieutenant's command, Kenney did not care as long as he left Fort Benning. As it turned out, Kenney spent much of his time in Washington on special assignments for Arnold, while one of his junior officers ran the squadron.

Westover was killed in an air crash in 1938. He was succeeded as Chief of the Air Corps by Arnold, who assigned Kenney to a trouble spot as Chief of the Production Engineering Section of the Air Corps Materiel Division at Wright Field, Ohio. In Kenney's opinion, from this point through the rest of his career, Arnold viewed him as a troubleshooter. "Everytime he got something going wrong," noted Kenney, "he would say, 'send George Kenney out there; he is a lucky SOB. He will straighten it out.' I never was supposed to have any brains; I was just lucky."

*   *   *   *   *

Meanwhile, the Nazi attacks on Poland, France, and the Low Countries had infused President Franklin D. Roosevelt's military plans with a sense of urgency. The President had provided the Air Corps with what General Arnold later called its "Magna Carta." Aircraft production was to be given a high priority. Roosevelt, appreciative of air power's potential, wanted planes, and he wanted them quickly.

Kenney was in the middle of the European maelstrom, having been ordered in February 1940 to the American embassy in Paris as Assistant Military Attaché for Air. He left in May, just before the Germans broke through the French defenses. Characteristically, he brought back ideas for several important aircraft modifications, including bullet proof glass to protect the pilots, installation of power turrets in bombers, and plans for an efficient oxygen system, similar to that used by the Luftwaffe.

Kenney's badgering for these vital improvements led Arnold to send his troubleshooter back to Wright Field to see the modificiations through development and production. However, in December 1941, the Japanese attacked Pearl Harbor, decimating the Pacific fleet, and catching Army airplanes on the ground. The United States was at war. Kenney requested Arnold to assign him to an operational command. According to Kenney, Arnold approved, but only after production output reached 4,000 planes a month. When that goal was reached, in March 1942, Arnold sent him, with the temporary rank of major general, to take over the Fourth Air Force in San Francisco, from Maj. Gen. Jacob Fickel. The Fourth's missions were air defense of California, Oregon, and Washington, and training units for overseas assignments.

Kenney again assumed the role of fixer. The Fourth Air Force was in trouble. Pilots were cracking up P–38s and A–29 Lockheed Hudson attack bombers. Kenney straightened things out, instructing the pilots how to fly the P–38 on one engine and how properly to land the A–29 so it didn't ground-loop. This was Kenney's judgement on Fickel: "He was a nice guy, but he belonged in supply. . . . a damned good supply man, but he didn't belong in the combat show." Subsequently, the two-engine P–38 became one of Kenney's favorite fighter planes.

Two-engine P–38

*   *   *   *   *

George Kenney's tenure as Commander of the Fourth Air Force was short-lived. The Philippines had been lost to the Japanese. On orders from President Roosevelt, Army Commander General Douglas MacArthur had evacuated Luzon and gone to Australia in March 1942 to organize the defense of that country. His air commander, Lt. Gen. George H. Brett, was already in Australia. There was not much American air power left in the Southwest Pacific.

The Japanese advance rolled through the southern Phillipines, most of New Guinea, and many islands northeast of Australia. Japan was in control of everything in the Pacific west of Midway. Invasion of the Australian continent itself seemed a possibility.

However, in May and June 1942, the battle of the Coral Sea and Midway showed the Japanese that they had a fight on their hands. The Japanese lost heavy warships, including carriers, and several hundred planes in those actions. In the battle of Midway, a turning point, they lost four attack carriers, leaving them only three heavy carriers. They failed to occupy Midway, about 1,200 miles west of Pearl Harbor.

Meantime, Japanese troops secured a foothold on Guadalcanal, occupied points in the southern Solomons, and were pushing forward from the north coast of New Guinea across the Owen Stanley mountains towards Port Moresby. On July 12, 1942, Kenney, in Washington, was informed by Arnold and Gen. George C. Marshall, Army Chief of Staff, that MacArthur had approved Kenney as his air commander, replacing Brett. Apparently MacArthur had been offered Maj. Gen. James H. Doolittle, but had turned him down. Evidence also indicates that Marshall and Arnold wanted Lt. Gen. Frank Andrews to replace Brett as MacArthur's airman. Andrews, whose antipathy toward MacArthur went back to the early 1930s, was furious at Arnold for making this recommendation.

For Kenney, the assignment would be much tougher than running the Fourth Air Force from San Francisco. He did not know MacArthur well, and had never served directly under him. Kenney knew Brett and respected him. However, in Kenney's opinion, Brett was another commander who did not "belong in the combat show. " He was a good supply man. Brett and MacArthur's Chief of Staff, Maj. Gen. Richard K. Sutherland, seldom agreed about anything. Brett's staff, and his organizational structure, left a great deal to be desired. Kenney had heard that MacArthur did not like airmen.

Another negative factor confronted Kenney. Marshall and Arnold had made it quite clear that defeat of Germany was the first priority of the Allies. A major effort in the Pacific would have to wait until Hitler was defeated.

Nonetheless, as he headed to his new post, Kenney counted the plusses. He would have Brig. Gens. Ennis Whitehead and Kenneth Walker under him. He had known them for years.

On the operational side, Kenney would have the P–38, a fighter he liked, even though Arnold and others did not. It had two engines and long range in a theater where distance counted. Also, he would have 3,000 parachute fragmentation bombs shipped to Australia. In 1928, Kenney had thought of the idea of putting parachutes on bombs for low-level attack, to prevent bomb fragments from hitting the plane. He had other ideas. He thought about the concept of "skip bombing." This was low-altitude bombing, from fifty feet, releasing the bomb several hundred feet from an enemy ship. The bomb would skip along the water until it hit the vessel. Kenney's assistant, Maj. William G. Benn, was enthusiastic about the idea. Kenney directed Benn to put this tactic into practice after arrival in Australia.

MacArthur's Chief of Staff, General Sutherland, though judged by Kenney to be brillant and conscientious, was also egotistical and protective of MacArthur to a fault. MacArthur himself had little confidence in the ability of the air forces. He believed they had contributed almost nothing. He had thought little of Brett. As for Brett himself, he confided to Kenney that MacArthur made all decisions, relying only on Sutherland and his staff. The Southwest Pacific Area under MacArthur was supposed to be a unified command, but advice from its air element had been totally neglected. Brett told Kenney: "I have seen General MacArthur just seven times. Every endeavor I have made to explain what I was trying to do has been lost among lengthy

Lt. Gen. George Kenney as Commander of the 5th Air Force meets Gen. Douglas MacArthur (center) and party in Australia.

dissertations which I would not take the time to deliver to a second lieutenant. . . . He is . . . absolutely bound up in himself. " Brett considered Sutherland a bully, and thought that he had blocked ideas which MacArthur would otherwise have approved.

The fifty-three-year-old Kenney recognized that he had to make his own role clear immediately. Many years after the war, he recounted his first meeting with MacArthur for John F. Loosbrock, then editor of *Air Force Magazine*, and Dr. Murray Green. Allowing for a certain amount of embroidery worked by the passage of time and General Kenney's flare for the dramatic, the outcome of the meeting, though perhaps not the details, seem to be as General Kenney described them.

After a lengthy oration on war in general and the Southwest Pacific war in particular, General MacArthur told Kenney that he wanted an air commander who would be loyal to him. Kenney, who grew restive and "madder than hell" as the lecture proceeded, got off the sofa and said to MacArthur: "General, I didn't ask to come out here. You asked for me. I think it's one of the smartest things you ever did, because I am the best goddamn air force commander in the world today." MacArthur started to say something, but Kenney kept right on talking. He said that his airmen would be loyal to MacArthur "because my gang is always loyal to me, and through me they will be loyal to you. You be loyal to me and my gang and make this thing fifty-fifty, or I'll be calling you from San Francisco and telling you that I have quit. "

Kenney figured he would be on his way back to Washington the next day. "But the Old Man looked at me kind of funny. He walked over and put his arm around my shoulder and said, 'You know, George, I think you and I are going to get along with each other just fine.' "

Kenney realized many things would have to be corrected. In a confrontation with Sutherland over who was to issue air orders, Kenney told MacArthur's chief of staff that he would make the decisions as to air objectives and units to be committed to action. Sutherland backed down. Kenney would deal directly with MacArthur.

A great deal of work had to be done immediately if the Japanese were to be checked and ultimately defeated. Kenney had confidence in Brig. Gen. Ennis Whitehead, his Deputy Commander, and in Brig. Gen. Kenneth Walker, Fifth Air Force Bomber Commander. He liked Lt. Col. Paul B. Wurtsmith, whom he would put in charge of the Fifth's newly formed fighter command in November. Kenney was convinced that he could work with the Australians and the other Allied forces. His own Fifth Air Force had 245 fighters, mostly P–40s; 53 light bombers, mostly A–20s; 70 medium bombers, the majority Martin B–26s; 62 B–17 heavy bombers; and 36 transports. Kenney was determined to get more planes, including P–38s with wing fuel tanks, range being a severe problem in the Southwest Pacific.

Right: Lt. Gen. Kenney with Brig. Gen. Paul B. Wurtsmith in New Guinea; *below:* Lt. Gen. William S. Knudsen (left) discusses strategy with Maj. Gen. Ennis C. Whitehead (center), and Lt. Gen. Kenney.

Among his major difficulties were personnel, organization, maintenance, and supply. He moved fast to put in charge men in whom he had confidence. He wanted "operators." Within the first week, Kenney noted, "I got rid of a couple of major generals and a couple of brigadiers and about forty colonels and lieutenant colonels and one captain." He also needed crew replacements. And too many people were issuing instructions, with or without the approval of commanders. He tore up the existing, convoluted, almost incomprehensible organizations of headquarters and the commands and told his commanders to establish clear lines of authority.

The maintenance and supply systems were almost at a standstill. The supply network was centered in Australia, 1,500 miles from the war in New Guinea. According to Kenney:

> The rear area, which was Australia, except from Townsville north, had an idea that the war was going to be down there pretty soon anyhow. We would lose New Guinea and the Japs would then be invading Australia, so they weren't sending any supplies up to New Guinea. . . . Bombers were up there with no tail wheels, no props, and needing new engines, and fighters with tail feathers gone and shot up and nothing to replace them, tanks leaking. It was a hell of a mess.

This was changed. Too much was being done from the rear, without knowledge of combat conditions.

As for equipment, he needed more fighters, bombers, and transports, a large infusion of 150-gallon droppable fuel tanks, and racks for the parachute fragmentation bombs that he had ordered. He directed Maj. Paul I. "Pappy" Gunn, a real find, to design and install them on the A–20s. Gunn had already developed a package of four .50-caliber machineguns (500 rounds per gun) for the nose of the A–20. Subsequently, Kenney ordered Gunn to do the same for the B–25.

*   *   *   *   *

In 1942, overall command in the Pacific was fragmented. Basically, it was to remain that way throughout the war. Coordination had broken down over roles and missions and, as General Brett had emphasized, over personalities. At this point, the Pacific war was a holding operation. The Joint Chiefs of Staff, first convened in 1942, and the theater commanders agreed that in the Pacific, forces had to be built up prior to any counteroffensive. The battle of Midway was a turning point in that the Japanese had lost the ability to mount a sustained offensive. Japan's lengthy "oil line," extending from the home islands southwest to the Netherlands East Indies, was vulnerable to attack.

There was disagreement within the American military high command as to the proper strategy to adopt. General MacArthur, Commander of the Southwest Pacific Area, advocated the southern Pacific strategy, a series of thrusts from New Guinea through the Bismarck Islands, to the Philippines. Forces would be built up in Australia, and would use Port Moresby as an advance base. This would be primarily an Army operation with MacArthur in control.

Adm. Chester W. Nimitz, heading the Pacific Ocean Area command, and Adm. Ernest J. King, Chief of Naval Operations in Washington, argued that the Army plan would be too expensive in terms of men. They wanted a movement across the Central Pacific, through the Marshall Islands to the Marianas, and then to the Philippines. The Joint Chiefs compromised by adopting both strategies. With fast carrier task forces, amphibious assault groups, and air power, the United States could employ an "island-hopping" strategy, bypassing Japanese strong points. This kind of attack could be used in the Central Pacific and also along the northern coast of New Guinea. But in 1942, the buildup of American forces in the Pacific was held back by the "Europe-first" strategy and the impending November 1942 invasion of North Africa.

In Europe, the mission of strategic bombers was to destroy Germany's war economy. In the Southwest Pacific there were no typical strategic targets

Left to right: Adm. Chester W. Nimitz, Adm. Ernest J. King, and Adm. Raymond A. Spruance on board USS *Indianapolis*.

other than a few oil refineries. Thus, in the Pacific the air mission was to interdict Japan's sea supply lanes and enable the ground forces to conduct an island-hopping strategy.

Kenney realized he first must gain control of the air. He had to strike Japanese airdromes, defeat the enemy's air force on the ground and in the air. He also had to support Allied troops in pushing back the Japanese forces, strike enemy shipping supply lines, and hit enemy concentrations wherever found. In the New Guinea campaigns of late 1942 and early 1943, culminating in the capture of Buna, the Fifth Air Force began to confront and cut down the Japanese air strength. And in March 1943, the Japanese suffered a terrific thrashing in the Battle of the Bismarck Sea, losing large numbers of warships and merchant vessels as well as planes.

Kenney's bombers and fighters were supporting the Allied push along the northern New Guinea coast, driving the enemy out of Lae and Salamaua. In November 1943, B–25s and B–24s struck the big Japanese base at Rabaul, New Britain, sunk warships and merchant vessels, and destroyed many planes on the ground and in the air. Kenney also moved early to convince MacArthur of the advantages of airlift. In late 1942, General Kenney's transports airlifted thousands of troops from Australia to Port Moresby and from Port Moresby over the Owen Stanley mountains to Buna, New Guinea. Trucks could not be loaded through the cargo doors of a C–47 transport, so the inventive Kenney had the trucks cut in half with acetylene torches, flown over the mountains, and then welded together again. In September 1943, Kenney's C–47s dropped some 1,700 paratroops into Nadzab, cutting off the Japanese in the Lae-Salamaua area, thus providing an air base at Nadzab and securing Allied control of the Markham River Valley. This was the first large-scale troop airlift of the war.

Kenney, the consummate tactician, had directed that his bombers use instantaneous fuse setting for attacks on shipping. He knew that a target as small as a ship was extremely difficult to hit and believed that in a near miss a surface burst was more effective than an explosion several feet under water. Brig. Gen. Kenneth Walker, head of 5th Bomber Command, wanted to return to one-tenth second delay fusing. Kenney told Walker to have one of his crews drop a few instantaneously fused bombs on an old wreck lying on a reef outside Port Moresby. Kenney then had a corporal row him and Walker out to inspect the damage. "The evidence was there," Kenney related.

> The bombs had missed the vessel by twenty-five to seventy-five yards and yet fragments tore holes all through it. Some of them were two to four square feet in area. . . . Ken finally said, "Okay, you win, I am convinced." I turned to the corporal and said, "Corporal, come back here and sit in the stern with me. General Walker is rowing us back."

Ken Walker was one of Kenney's favorite lieutenants. Walker had been one of the originators of the Air Corps' strategic bombing doctrine while on the faculty of the Tactical School (see chapter on Harold George) and was one who believed in leadership by example. A few weeks after the Port Moresby bomb test, Walker was killed while leading an attack on Japanese shipping at Rabaul. He was awarded the Medal of Honor posthumously.

General MacArthur's confidence in Kenney grew in direct relation to these impressive operations. MacArthur was clearly delighted with the results his airman was wringing out of "shoe-string" forces. "I am having an interesting time," Kenney observed, "inventing new ways to win a war on a shoe-string. We are doing things nearly every day that were never done in the books. It really is remarkable what you can do with an airplane if you really try. Any time I can't think of something screwy enough, I have a flock of people out here to help me."

General Kenney spent as much time as he could visiting his people—his kids, as he called them—"out there." He looked after his troops from the mess hall to the flight line. His was a very personal kind of leadership. The troops responded to his informality, his rough-cut sense of humor, his knowledge of operations, and his genuine concern for their well-being. Also, Kenney's Distinguished Service Medal and Silver Star told them that he had been there and knew what they were going through.

Kenney badgered Arnold in Washington for more resources. If the AAF in Europe did not like the B-24, P-38, and P-47, then Kenney would gladly have them. During these exchanges of correspondence, or occasionally a visit to Washington, Kenney usually managed to squeeze a few more groups out of Arnold. It was touch and go. Arnold reminded Kenney that the Pacific

Lt. Gen. George Kenney (left) with Gen. Hap Arnold

Boeing's long-range B-29, a bomber Kenney pressed Gen. Arnold to send
to his Fifth Air Force.

could not be considered "from an offensive viewpoint." The major strategy
thrust there was still defensive. MacArthur strongly backed Kenney in these
matters. Arnold and MacArthur never got along famously. "MacArthur
resented what he considered Hap's interference," Kenney recalled. "The old
man treated Arnold like he was still a cadet. . . . He made his own plans and
ran his own war and did a goddam good job of it, too. There was that underlying antagonism."

In addition to the question of resources, primarily replacement crews
and planes (Kenney kept trying to spring more P-38s from Arnold), another
important issue evolved during 1943–44 between Kenney and Arnold. In the
summer of 1943, Kenney began to press General Arnold for a commitment
to send B-29s to the Southwest Pacific. Kenney planned to have airfields built
in northwest Australia with an air depot in the Darwin area, and to use the
very long-range B-29s to strike the great oil refineries at Palembang, Sumatra,
and Balikpapan, Borneo. Kenney saw oil as "the one essential commodity"
Japan needed to stay in the war. "If you want the B-29 used efficiently and
effectively where it will do the most good in the shortest time," Kenney
emphasized to Arnold, "the Southwest Pacific Area is the place and the Fifth
Air Force can do the job. . . . Japan may easily collapse back to her original
empire by . . .[1944], due to her oil shortage alone."

In Washington, AAF planning groups worked during the summer and
fall of 1943 to create a comprehensive B-29 employment plan. Brig. Gen.
Kenneth B. Wolfe, chief of the B-29 special project, and Brig. Gen. Laurence

S. Kuter, Assistant Chief of Air Staff, Plans, favored using the B–29s directly against the Japanese home islands, rather than as Kenney wanted to use them. Arnold himself had not wavered in his belief that employment directly against Japan would be the most effective use of these long-range bombers. Early plans called for basing the B–29s in India and staging them through China to strike Japan. President Roosevelt, in principle, had approved this plan, code-named Matterhorn. At the end of 1943, during the Cairo Conference, Roosevelt put his stamp of approval on basing B–29s in India and China by May 1944, and beginning B–29 operations from the Marianas by the close of that year.

In Washington, there had not been unanimous approval of this plan. The Navy had opposed it in the Joint Chiefs' War Plans Committee, preferring bases in Australia. The Army Air Forces, represented on the committee by Brig. Gen. Haywood S. Hansell, Jr., argued for the China plan. Hansell had based his rationale on a comprehensive targeting report furnished by Arnold's Committee of Operations Analysts, at work since the spring of 1943 on target selection in Japan. There was essentially no opposition to eventually sending B–29s to the Marianas. The argument centered on where to operate from in the interim. Ironically, Kenney and the Navy favored Southwest Pacific basing, and Arnold and his planners stuck to the China plan. Striking Japanese shipping and oil would help the Navy's thrust through the Central Pacific. This employment strategy for the B–29 was basically the same as Kenney's, which envisioned the denial of oil as the crucial soft spot in Japan's armor.

General Arnold viewed it differently. The B–29 was to be the ultimate expression of the AAF's strategic bombing doctrine—high-altitude, precision bombing against the enemy's industrial structure. In early 1944, this could be done only from China. Eventually, heavy attacks from the Marianas might knock Japan out of the war prior to an invasion of the Japanese home islands. This was the way Arnold and his AAF planners saw the issue. Moreover, Roosevelt himself had all along insisted that sustained bombing of the home islands be done as soon as possible.

Kuter informed Kenney in March 1944 that B–29s would first be sent to India and China, then to the Marianas by October. Also, it was planned to stage the India-based bombers through Ceylon to strike oil refineries at Palembang. Overall, the JCS decided on twin drives: through the Central Pacific, bypassing Truk to take the Marianas; then through the Carolines and Palaus to join MacArthur's forces in November for an attack on Mindanao in the Philippines. Kenney felt betrayed. MacArthur and Admiral Nimitz had lost out to the views of Arnold and Admiral King, Chief of Naval Operations. Indeed, Kenney thought that long-range B–29 attacks from the Marianas against Japan actually would accomplish little and be no more than "nuisance raids."

Another matter that concerned Arnold was that of control. He was determined to keep direct control of the B-29s rather than assign them to a theater commander. Kenney, in retrospect, acknowledged this point: "Every once in a while Arnold would get sore at me about something or other. He thought I was still working for him, but I wasn't. I was working for MacArthur." The Joint Chiefs, in April 1944, approved formation of the Twentieth Air Force, directly under Arnold as executive agent of the JCS. Headquarters, Twentieth Air Force, would be located with Arnold in Washington.

In June 1944, Kenney brought the Thirteenth Air Force under his command, joining it together with the Fifth as the Far East Air Forces (FEAF). Subsequently, the Seventh Air Force would also come under FEAF. MacArthur's forces, supported by Kenney's Far East Air Forces, continued north and west to push the Japanese back towards the Philippines. In September 1944, General Kenney moved his headquarters from Brisbane to Hollandia, the former Japanese base on the north coast of New Guinea. The Marianas had been taken and the first B-29s arrived there in October 1944.

In the fall of 1944, MacArthur and Nimitz converged on the Philippines. Avoiding the large Japanese concentration on Luzon, the two major U.S. forces headed towards Leyte, between Mindanao and Luzon. The Japanese Combined Fleet attempted to defeat this invasion but failed. Two of their three forces were decimated, and the third fled. The Japanese suffered heavy losses in battleships, carriers, cruisers, and destroyers. The landing succeeded. The Japanese Combined Fleet was finished as a fighting force. Aircraft of Kenney's Far East Air Forces supported the Leyte landings, and over Mindoro and Luzon they flew missions in support of both the Navy and the ground forces. Finally, with the Philippines and then Iwo Jima and Okinawa in Allied hands, the Japanese had been driven back to their home islands.

In the spring and summer of 1945, Maj. Gen. Curtis E. Lemay's B-29s of the XXI Bomber Command (Twentieth Air Force), abandoning the AAF doctrine of high-altitude, precision bombing because of weather conditions and dispersed industrial targets, struck Japan's major urban and industrial centers, reducing large areas of these cities to ashes. All of this, combined with the Navy's effective blockade, drove the Japanese to the ropes.

On August 6, 1945, the first atomic bomb was dropped on Hiroshima. On the 9th, the Soviet Union declared war on Japan. Also on the 9th, a second atomic bomb was dropped, on Nagasaki. Japan sued for peace the next day. The surrender document was signed aboard the U.S. battleship *Missouri* in Tokyo Bay on September 2, 1945. Kenney, Commander of the Allied Air Forces in the Southwest Pacific, and Commanding General, Far East Air Forces, was on the deck of the *Missouri* to watch General MacArthur accept the Japanese surrender. Among those also present were Gen. Carl A. Spaatz, who had come from Europe to command the U.S. Strategic Air Forces

(USSTAF) in the Pacific after the European war ended; Maj. Gen. Curtis E. LeMay, USSTAF Chief of Staff; and Lt. Gen. Barney M. Giles, Spaatz's deputy. The Pacific war was over.

General Arnold wrote Kenney:

> The brilliant offensive of the Far East Air Forces under your inspiring leadership was an outstanding factor in Japan's defeat. Looking back to the heroic operation of the early war in which, gravely outnumbered and undersupplied, you rose from the dust of the Port Moresby strips to stop the Australia-bound Japs in their tracks, it may be truthfully said that no air commander ever did so much with so little. All that you have done since has made air history. The Army Air Forces honor your fighting spirit, to which we so largely owe today's splendid triumph.

MacArthur subsequently said: "Of all the commanders of our major Air Forces engaged in World War II, none surpassed General Kenney in those three great essentials of successful combat leadership: aggressive vision, mastery over air strategy and tactics, and the ability to exact the maximum in fighting qualities from both men and equipment."

Kenney and his kids had won a great victory over the Japanese. He and the airmen under his command had fought an air war that demanded constant tactical and technical innovations and had written a stirring and important chapter in air history. In so doing, the Far East Air Forces produced more than its share of the highest scoring air aces—Richard I. Bong, Thomas B. McGuire, Jr., Charles H. MacDonald, Gerald R. Johnson, and Neel E. Kearby, among others.

*　*　*　*　*

With the war over, Arnold appointed Kenney Commander of the Pacific Air Forces. Then, at Arnold's direction, General Kenney returned to the United States in October 1945 to testify in support of the drive to establish an independent air force. To the Senate Military Affairs Committee, Kenney emphasized the need for a single Department of National Defense, with coequal Army, Navy, and Air Force. Unity of command, he said, was just as essential in Washington as in the field: "The committee type of command exemplified by the Joint Chiefs in World War II was a poor compromise for a single authority capable of decision. The most that can be said for it is that it did not prevent us from winning the war."

Kenney returned to the Pacific, and MacArthur announced in December that the Pacific Air Forces had been joined into the Pacific Air Command United States Army (PACUSA)—an amalgam of the Far East Air Forces and the U.S. Strategic Air Forces—to be headed by Kenney. Immediately, Kenney named Lt. Gen. Ennis C. Whitehead as his Deputy Commander, Maj. Gen. Clements McMullen ("the best supply man in the business") as Chief of Staff, and Maj. Gen. Kenneth B. Wolfe, Commander of both Fifth Air Force and PACUSA Headquarters.

Then, unexpectedly, the War Department announced that General Kenney had been named the senior American member of the United Nations Military Staff Committee, and concomitantly, AAF representative to the Joint Chiefs of Staff. Kenney left for London, where the UN committee convened, during the first week of January 1946. The Military Staff Committee of the United Nations Security Council consisted of representatives of the military chiefs of staff (Army, Navy, and Air Force) of the United States, the Soviet Union, Britain, France, and China. The committee had been created to advise and assist the Security Council on all military matters, to implement plans for the use of a UN armed forces contingent whenever such a force might be established, and to supervise the strategic direction of this force. Kenney—as always—was articulate, sometimes unpredictable, and quick on his feet. For example, on a University of Chicago "Roundtable" discussion of the UN with a law professor and a professor of modern history, Kenney became the statesman and struck an idealistic note:

> I wonder if we cannot afford some idealism. . . . The small-minded cynics of the world may sneer at idealism, but we must keep to our ideals, those same ideals that we fought for in World War I and World War II. So long as we keep them, we are a thinking, living, progressive, and driving force toward a better world—a better world for ourselves and a better world for all mankind.
>
> I believe that too often when we are afraid of progress, we take refuge behind such stock phrases as "Let's be realistic"; and "Let's keep our feet on the ground"; and "Let's stick to the old tried and true methods. " What we must realize is that world survival is at the crossroads. We do not want World War III.

In this fast-moving, eventful postwar period, Kenney, in March 1946, was suddenly named as the first Commanding General of the Strategic Air Command. General Spaatz, who succeeded Arnold as Commanding General, AAF, in March had directed formation of the Strategic Air Command, Tactical Air Command, and the Air Defense Command. Kenney's appointment was logical in the sense that after the war the AAF had only four full generals: Arnold, Spaatz, Kenney, and Joseph T. McNarney. Arnold had retired and McNarney had been named acting Supreme Allied Commander, Mediterranean. Thus, Kenney's rank and his impressive accomplishments in the Pacific weighed greatly in his favor. He had directed heavy bomber units—B–17s and B–24s— but not the very long-range B–29s, which operated directly under Arnold and the Twentieth Air Force.

Kenney returned from London in March, but continued to work in New York where the Military Staff Committee had been relocated. Maj. Gen. St. Clair Streett became his deputy at Strategic Air Command and, with the

Air Chief Sir Guy Garrod, (center), Chief, British Military Staff to the UN Military Staff Committee, being welcomed by Gen. Carl Spaatz, (left), Commanding General, AAF, and Gen. Kenney, Commanding General, SAC.

former Continental Air Forces staff, ran the daily operations of SAC. Kenney had wanted Whitehead as his SAC deputy, but Whitehead demurred and had recommended McMullen, the supply and maintenance man whom Kenney had known for many years. As the summer passed and Kenney continued in New York, Streett ran the command. Whitehead suggested to Kenney that the time had come for him to take active command of SAC.

Kenney failed to make SAC his top priority until the end of the year. In December 1946 he appointed McMullen, his associate of long standing, as deputy commander. Kenney and McMullen had entered the Signal Corps in 1917, and McMullen had served under Kenney in the Pacific. When McMullen took over as deputy in January 1947, Kenney gave him responsibility for day-to-day operations. This was a period of austerity, the Army Air Forces having quickly demobilized after the war. The Strategic Air Command suffered from a shortage of personnel, and McMullen was determined to have the command become more efficient. He also was aware that the command needed the ability to quickly move its units to forward bases. McMullen was widely recognized in the AAF as extraordinarily competent in matters of organization and supply. In retrospect, the problem with McMullen's approach was that he neglected the training of combat crews.

With the unification struggle approaching a climax in early 1947, General Kenney continued to speak throughout the country in favor of a separate air force. Assistant Secretary of War for Air Stuart Symington and Spaatz encouraged these forays. They considered Kenney, who was a good and willing speaker, to be especially adept at this kind of activity, and Kenney himself was convinced that he was making a vital contribution. McMullen, he reasoned, was well able to run SAC. But by late 1947 and early 1948, SAC unit commanders believed that in a period of growing international tension the first priority should be given to building a combat-ready force.

In February 1948, the Soviet coup in Czechoslovakia took place; in March, President Harry S. Truman labeled the Soviet Union the number-one enemy of peace; and in that summer the Berlin blockade occurred. Under these circumstances the leadership of the newly independent United States Air Force decided it must reassess combat capability. Gen. Hoyt S. Vandenberg, who succeeded Spaatz as Chief of Staff of the Air Force in April 1948, called in Charles Lindbergh to conduct an assessment of SAC's combat readiness. Lindbergh's report, submitted in September 1948, concluded that SAC, suffering from serious personnel and training difficulties, was in a low state of readiness. In October 1948, General LeMay, Commander of United States Air Forces in Europe, who had directed the B–29 offensive against Japan, was named to replace Kenney as Commander of SAC. LeMay's attention would not be divided among United Nations duties, speaking assignments, and running the Strategic Air Command.

George Kenney was assigned as Commander of the Air University at Maxwell AFB, Alabama. He remained there until his retirement in August 1951. As the Air University Commander, General Kenney was energetic and uncompromising with the truth as he saw it. He enjoyed challenging conventional views:

> I don't think an airplane should be considered a tactical airplane or a strategic airplane. I think it is an airplane. It may drop its eggs on targets ten miles away . . . and the next day you may be working 5,000 miles away, and to say that one is tactical and the other strategic really doesn't tell the story and it uses these two ground terms which we should keep out.

Kenney continued to speak throughout the country, stressing that the United States should have "the Number One Air Power," the ability to take a severe first blow, and then retaliate upon the enemy. "No nation or combination of nations," he said, "will even consider attacking us if faced with certain destruction." Kenney emphasized that air power must be in being: "Airplanes on order, in the blueprint stage, and airplanes that we may hope to get some day, will be of no use when the bombs begin to fall. If war comes we will have to meet it with what we have at that time."

It was perhaps fitting that General Kenney should have closed his Air Force career as head of the USAF's premier educational complex. For a good part of his career Kenney had been a teacher, instructing others in how to fix airplanes, fly them, and defeat an enemy in war. He was a talented strategist and tactician, but above all, an inspiring leader who knew operations—how to run an air force in combat.

In 1949, Kenney published *General Kenney Reports: A Personal History of the Pacific War*, to favorable reviews. In the 1950s, after retirement, he wrote books about General MacArthur, Major Pappy Gunn, and the air ace, Richard I. Bong. Kenney was a good writer, characteristically straightforward, and he could turn a phrase.

After his retirement, Kenney kept in close touch with "the old gang," the men with whom he had served in peacetime and in two wars. He served as President of the Air Force Association (AFA) in 1953-54, as its board chairman the following year, and as a member of the AFA Board until his death. For ten years he also was President of the Arthritis and Rheumatism Foundation.

General Kenney died at Bay Harbor, Florida, in 1977. His career spanned two world wars and the history of air power from the Wright brothers era to the atomic Air Force. A determined and eloquent champion of air independence and peace through strength, he played an important role in the fight to establish a United States Air Force. Through all the years since he made his first flight with Claude Graham White, he remained true to himself. He had courage, and he had character.

Sources

The two basic sources for General George C. Kenney's military career are his World War II notebooks and the Kenney papers, both on file in the Office of Air Force History, Washington, D.C., and at the USAF Historical Research Center, Maxwell AFB, Alabama.

The eleven Kenney notebooks contain documents, notes, and diary material, and are the primary source that General Kenney used for his book, *General Kenney Reports: A Personal History of the Pacific War* (Duell, Sloan and Pearce, 1949). The notebooks are indispensable not only for Kenney's career, but to anyone interested in research on the air war in the Pacific. The Kenney papers are especially good on the post-World War II period. They include drafts of Kenney's speeches and books from the immediate postwar period and through the 1950s and 1960s.

For the generalist, the best book on Kenney as MacArthur's airman is, of course, *General Kenney Reports*, cited above. Also see the official history, *The Army Air Forces in World War II*, Wesley F. Craven and James L. Cate (University of Chicago Press, 1951; Reprint, Office of Air Force History, 1983) especially Vols. I, IV, and V.

Histories of the units that flew in the Pacific are on file in the Office of Air Force History and at the Research Center. There also are a number of official monographs on specialized aspects of the air war in the Pacific. For General Arnold's view, see Henry H. Arnold, *Global Mission* (Harper, 1949).

For a perceptive discussion of the B–29 issue between Kenney and Arnold, consult Stanley L. Falk, "General Kenney, the Indirect Approach, and the B–29s," *Aerospace Historian*, Fall 1981.

General Kenney's career is traced in a number of official interviews as part of the Air Force Oral History Program, at the Research Center and the Office of Air Force History. The most comprehensive and illuminating is an interview with Kenney by James C. Hasdorff, conducted in August 1974 at Bay Harbor Islands, Florida. It is especially rich in material on the interwar years and on World War II, and particularly good on Kenney's relations with his commanders and colleagues. Also see interviews with Lt. Gens. Ennis C. Whitehead and Barney M. Giles.

For the official summary report on air operations in the Pacific, consult the United States Strategic Bombing Survey's *Summary Report (Pacific War)* (Government Printing Office, 1946). Also see Louis Morton, *Strategy and Command: The First Two Years* (Office of the Chief of Military History, 1962). Other books of interest to the general reader include Steve Birdsall, *Flying Buccaneers: The Illustrated Story of Kenney's Fifth Air Force* (Doubleday, 1977), and Vern Haugland, *The AAF Against Japan* (Harper, 1948).

For the interwar period, the best book is DeWitt S. Copp, *A Few Great Captains* (Doubleday, 1980). Copp is perceptive in evoking the flavor of the period.

For General Kenney's postwar career, especially as Commander of the Strategic Air Command, 1946–48, consult Harry R. Borowski, *A Hollow Threat: Strategic Air Power and Containment Before Korea* (Greenwood Press, 1982).

7

William E. Kepner:
All the Way To Berlin

Paul F. Henry

William Ellsworth Kepner was always a scrapper. He was the kind of American military man *Time* magazine's World War II reporters loved to write about. He was a general who, at the age of fifty, flew fighter missions over German-occupied territory—a tough, laconic veteran who led by example. But Bill Kepner was more than that. He had been a pioneer in the Air Corps' brief flirtation with balloons and airships, an early explorer of the stratosphere, and a defender of fighter aviation in the years when the bomber was king. His tactical innovations as head of VIII Fighter Command during World War II were a lasting contribution to the development of air warfare. They played a major part in defeating the Luftwaffe and assuring success of the Combined Bomber Offensive that destroyed the military infrastructure of Nazi Germany.

George Harvey Kepner and his wife Julia Ann had given their son William, born in predominantly rural Miami, Indiana, in 1893, a solid foundation of Midwestern values. Young Bill demonstrated old-fashioned stubbornness and a fierce streak of independence by leaving Kokomo High School one marrow-chilling November day in 1909 to enlist in the United States Marine Corps. Thus a promising Kokomo sophomore began a relationship with the armed forces that was to occupy nearly forty-one years of his life.

Marine Corps ways agreed with the athletic sixteen-year-old Kepner who, thirty years later, reflected that the Corps "isn't a particularly easy way to live, but it is a very satisfactory way. " Convinced, nevertheless, that he needed to complete his education, Kepner accepted an honorable discharge and Marine Corps Good Conduct Medal in November 1913, and returned to school

151

with plans for a medical career. This dream was short-lived, however. In 1916, Indiana National Guard units were being called up for service on the Mexican border; Bill Kepner applied for and received an officer's commission. He accompanied his unit to Mexico, was augmented into the Regular Army and promoted to first lieutenant on June 14, 1917.

Kepner, by summer's end a captain, went overseas with the 4th Infantry, 3d Division of the American Expeditionary Force. As "I" Company commander, he saw action in the Chateau-Thierry and St. Mihiel offensives and was decorated for individual heroism in hand-to-hand fighting. Combat brought out the natural aggressiveness and determination that grew out of Bill Kepner's Marine training and flinty personality. "The only time you can quit with any self-respect," he said, "is when you are dead."

By 1918, Kepner had developed a passionate interest in flying. That interest grew, he wrote, "especially after using my Infantry Company's ground fire to drive off three German fighter planes who forced a French pilot to land in our Company area across the Marne River at Chateau-Thierry." His article, "Reminiscences of an LTA Pilot," which appeared in the September 1978 issue of *Air Force Magazine*, recalled an early try at transferring to flying duty:

> After Chateau-Thierry and St. Mihiel, I asked, at an officer's meeting, to transfer to the Air Service for airplane pilot training. Colonel Halsted Dorey replied "Yes, if

Maj. William E. Kepner

you want to be a frill. You have a man's job where you are. " When the meeting was over, he put his arm around my shoulder and promised me a battalion. . . .

Kepner was given the 3d Battalion for the Meuse-Argonne campaign. Under his command the unit captured enemy strong points at Farm de Madelaine and Mt. Faucon. These were key German positions which, once lost, helped accelerate the final surrender. This battle also brought Kepner's World War I combat to a close; he was seriously wounded and spent months recuperating in a French hospital.

Some fourteen months after the Armistice, Captain Kepner was back in the States, assigned to the 61st Infantry at Fort Gordon, Georgia. He immediately applied for pilot training, preferably at Arcadia, Florida, an airplane station. He got Arcadia, all right, but it was in California where all the U.S. balloon schools had been combined at Ross Field.

Most Army officers considered balloons to be in somewhat the same category as pack mules—cantankerous and unpredictable beasts of limited utility. Besides, Kepner had observed that during the recent war, "It seemed as though, sooner or later, every balloon was shot down. " He wired an urgent message to the Army's Adjutant General pleading that a mistake had been made in his assignment. The sharp reply from headquarters read: "There is no mistake. Go to Arcadia, California, and no more direct contacts out of channels. " He reported to the school in November 1920 and graduated with the rating of Balloon Observer the following May. Another student who completed the course that year was Oscar "Tubby" Westover, who later became Chief of the Air Corps.

Kepner's reluctant acceptance of his professional fate did not obscure the more positive aspects of a lighter-than-air career. Some of the Air Service's best-known pilots, like Frank Lahm and Benjamin Foulois, had begun their flying careers in balloons. Sport ballooning in the 1920s was an international pastime, and the Army had traditionally participated in racing events with teams selected from among its crack balloon crews. Though Kepner could not have anticipated it, the Air Service was to embark in the 1920s on a short-lived airship program. It was as a sport balloonist and airship pilot that Bill Kepner achieved recognition and began earning his place as an aviation pioneer.

Ballooning was by its very nature a demanding activity. Floating about under a creaky fabric bag of highly flammable gas, at the mercy of fitful winds, and standing in the 1,500-pound basket, which acted like a berserk pendulum in the slightest turbulence, required at the least a strong constitution. Balloonists of the day acted as their own meteorologists, logisticians, navigators, repairmen, and general all-around roustabouts. These hardy aviators required thorough preparation in all the basic skills because, Kepner reasoned, "only then can they expect to have any idea where they are apt to go" once that first bag of ballast goes overboard.

Following graduation from the balloon school, Captain Kepner was named Commander of the 32d Balloon Company, but his military experience in balloons was destined to be short. These floating observation posts were being replaced by large, engine-driven airships. The Army was systematically deactivating all balloon units. So, after only seven months in command positions with two different balloon companies, Kepner was sent to the Army Airship School at Langley Field, Virginia. Though a student, he also was named Commander of the Airship School Detachment. There was a lot going on in lighter-than-air. The Army and Navy were vigorously exploring the military utility of airships, and young pilots enjoyed the pleasant prospect of flying nonrigid, semirigid, rigid, and pressure rigid airship types. To fledgling airship pilots like Bill Kepner, "military lighter-than-air (LTA) looked like a serious business that was well started."

To Kepner fell the additional privilege, while still a student, of serving aboard the huge semirigid airship *Roma* during its initial familiarization flights. The *Roma*, acquired from the Italian government, crashed during a test flight in February 1922, and all but eleven of the forty-five crew members aboard were killed. Kepner had been ordered at the last moment to move a small airship out of *Roma's* way so she could be taken from the hangar. Minutes later, *Roma* crashed in flames as Kepner watched, stunned, from his own airship.

Kepner graduated from the Airship School in June 1922 and left Langley in the heat of the summer to command the 18th Airship Company at Aberdeen, Maryland. His new station was home of the Ordnance Proving Ground, and it was there that his flight-test experience began with bombing tests and long-range navigation sorties in Army C–2-class airships.

*   *   *   *   *

Bigger things were in store for Kepner as spring returned to Maryland in 1923. In March, he was selected to attend rigid airship training with the Navy at Lakehurst, New Jersey. In exchange for supplies of helium gas, the Navy offered to provide Air Service crews with rigid airship training. This was a unique chance for Army people to master the largest active airships in the world, and to prepare for possible joint operations with the Navy. Kepner graduated as a Naval Aviator, Zeppelin Pilot, and served as assistant navigator on the *Los Angeles*, a rigid airship.

By 1926, when Bill Kepner finished his tour of duty at Lakehurst, Scott Field near St. Louis had become the Air Service's airship training center. The

Airship School also flight tested new airship designs. In April, about three months before the Air Service became the Air Corps, Captain Kepner reported for duty at Scott. With some 340 hours of flying experience at Lakehurst, he was the logical choice to test-fly the RS-1, newest and largest semirigid airship in existence. This mammoth vehicle had a 700,000-cubic-foot gas capacity, two engines with 17-foot propellers, and a top speed of 75 miles an hour. The RS-1 made a number of cross-country flights and participated in Army combat maneuvers near San Antonio, Texas. Kepner, now chief of the RS-1 test program and assistant commandant of the Scott airship training center, personally assayed the durability of the craft while flying through towering midcontinental thunderheads between Vicksburg and Memphis on the return trip to Scott Field. "Several times the airship was sucked up into the clouds then forced down to tree-top level," Kepner remembered. "The nose frame was crushed and the helium gas containers developed leaks." Using blankets and hastily improvised patching materials to stop the leaks, Kepner and crew brought the RS-1 home from what turned out to be its last long voyage. This proud but scarred airship was dismantled in the winter of 1928.

Kepner also found time in 1927 for some "outside activities." He and Lt. William Eareackson joined two other Air Corps teams in the National Balloon Race at Akron, Ohio. They earned a third place after drifting all the way to the Maine coast and landing at night in a fog-enshrouded graveyard. A short distance further and they would have been out to sea. This showing earned Kepner and Eareackson a spot on the U.S. balloon team and a chance at the 1927 International Balloon Race. They finished in the middle of a field of fifteen contestants after a harrowing experience. Plagued by bad weather from the start, Kepner and his crewman were swept up in a thunderstorm to an altitude of 27,000 feet without benefit of oxygen.

In the 1928 National Race, Kepner and Eareackson led the entire field, though not without cost. Once again they were trapped within the black folds of a thunderstorm. Even after the balloon at last cleared the clouds, the wild ride was far from over. Years later General Kepner still vividly remembered that ride:

> We went at great speed down a valley, took out three 20,000 volt electric lines, and crashed into a six-line assembly. Our wet drag rope crossed two of the lines and put out all electricity in the area. We then hit a two-arm railway telegraph pole and hung there until we could push off and go on throughout the night to win the race, landing the next morning at Weems, Virginia, just before going out to sea.

During the storm, the two airmen had attached their parachute release handles to the balloon's rope rigging and sat on the edge of the basket awaiting their fate. Three other pilots taking part in the race were either burned or killed by lightning.

Their victory earned Kepner and Eareackson the right to represent the United States in the 1928 Gordon Bennett International Balloon Race. This time they had relatively clear sailing compared to the drama of the National Race. They took first place by a wide margin and brought home the King Albert of Belgium Trophy—the first Air Corps team to win it since Lt. Frank Lahm in 1906.

In March 1929, Captain Kepner became Chief of the Lighter-Than-Air Branch, Experimental Engineering Section, at Wright Field, Ohio. He spent over three months during the summer test-flying a metalclad airship, the ZMC–2. Kepner believed this new design "was the strongest-type airship ever built," and "offered to fly it through a line squall to prove it." It was becoming increasingly clear, however, that the Air Corps did not share his confidence. Many airships were being "retired" or passed off to the Navy. Kepner himself began casting about for a way to realize his earlier dream of being an airplane pilot. He had done just about all there was to do in lighter-than-air. His balloon-race victories and experimental airship testing invested him with a well-deserved reputation. The King Albert of Belgium Trophy, with Kepner's name prominently displayed, decorated the Air Corps Chief's office. It was a good time to move on.

While on detached duty for flight tests at his naval airship alma mater at Lakehurst, Kepner learned of his assignment to the Air Corps Primary Flying School at March Field, California. He completed training there in October 1931, the same month he was promoted to major, and graduated from

Moving ZMC–2 out of the hangar for its first flight in 1929.

The Kepner Collection

the advanced course at Kelly Field, Texas, in February 1932—a little more than a month after his thirty-ninth birthday. At last, he pinned on the coveted airplane pilot wings that had eluded him for some twelve years. His balloon, airship, and aircraft ratings—six in all—put him in a class of experience few airmen had achieved.

The vagaries of the service being what they were, the Air Corps (with no little irony in Kepner's view) promptly returned him to Wright Field for more airship duty. This time, the craft was Goodyear's TC–13. After two months of flight test, Kepner *finally* bade experimental airships farewell forever, and, in March 1932, was installed in the Air Corps Materiel Division at Wright Field as Chief of the Purchase Branch. He had not seen the last of lighter-than-air piloting, however. Bill Kepner said a final good-bye to balloons with characteristic dash—in a stratospheric balloon flight for the National Geographic Society.

*   *   *   *   *

This flight was a national event that captured public attention in the summer of 1934. It grew out of earlier ascents by Capt. Hawthorne C. Gray in which Kepner had assisted, both in laboratory experiments and as a ground crew team member. On the second of Gray's flights in his open-basket balloon he reached 42,470 feet but died in the attempt when he inadvertently dropped a full oxygen bottle as ballast instead of an empty one.

Kepner's 1934 mission, under the joint auspices of the National Geographic Society and the Army Air Corps, was far more sophisticated than Gray's fatal 1927 try. The enclosed gondola, which contained more than a ton of scientific equipment and 7,000 pounds of ballast, was constructed of a lightweight magnesium alloy. Christened *Explorer I*, it was attached to a balloon more than 300 feet high with a three-million-cubic-foot gas capacity. Two other crew members, Capt. Albert W. Stevens and Lt. Orvil A. Anderson, accompanied Kepner to perform scientific experiments and help control the balloon in flight. The purpose of this exploration, as the *National Geographic* rather dramatically put it, was in part to investigate ". . . the mysterious ozone layer of the upper air. " More specifically, the scientific objectives were to analyze cosmic radiation, define the ozone layer's position, check air composition, and record accurate pressure-temperature-altitude data.

In specifying a launch site, Kepner laid on some exacting criteria. "I need, " he said, "a hole 400 feet deep with vertical walls; a 500-foot-square grassy meadow at the bottom, with a 20,000 volt electrical line; a railroad

157

Left: *Explorer I* before flight; *center:* with fabric torn, *Explorer I* falls to earth; *below:* crew members of the flight from left to right: Maj. Kepner, Lt. Orvil Anderson, and Capt. Albert W. Stevens.

Air Force Magazine

and a first-class truck highway running through it; and, if possible, I would like a good trout stream running through it." As luck would have it, the Chamber of Commerce in Rapid City, South Dakota, provided just such a place—trout stream and all. Kepner and his crew dubbed it the "Stratobowl" and made preparations for a late July launch.

The lift-off occurred on July 27, 1934, in something of a circus atmosphere. Some 120 cavalry troops, watched by Sioux Indians in full ceremonial regalia, nervously displayed their lack of experience as balloon handlers, while hundreds of local residents cheered and felt-hatted newsmen spoke busily into large microphones. The ascent was uneventful until about 57,000 feet. There, a large hole appeared in the balloon bag and the crew was forced to check the ascent. They reached 60,613 feet before Kepner was able to arrest the climb and begin a controlled descent. On the way down, the balloon fabric deteriorated increasingly and, after depressurizing the gondola at 20,000 feet, the three men put on parachutes in case they had to abandon ship. In the meantime, a national radio audience (and the Air Corps Assistant Chief, fellow balloonist Oscar Westover) listened in on the drama. At about 4,000 feet, the balloon, now full of oxygen-contaminated hydrogen, exploded and the crew bailed out, Kepner going last at about 500 feet.

All three members of the expedition landed safely in freshly tilled soil near Loomis, Nebraska, and despite the gondola's destruction, Kepner estimated that the flight had been 60 to 70 percent successful. With this rather wooly adventure, Bill Kepner ended his lighter-than-air career. It had been a fitting glorious culmination of air achievements that began for him at the Army Balloon School in 1920. The *Explorer I* mission was a ground-breaker for later stratospheric experiments crucial to the modern Air Force. Ironically, it occurred the same year that the Air Corps officially washed its hands of lighter-than-air aviation. Kepner, too, had new interests. The balloon and the airship were now twin anachronisms, bulbous dinosaurs of aviation. Bill Kepner and the Air Corps left them behind at the same time.

* * * * *

Major Kepner's partners in the flight of *Explorer I*, Captain Stevens and Lieutenant Anderson, had urged him to join them in a second stratospheric mission scheduled for the summer of 1935. The prospect of breaking the 1934 Russian altitude record, which still stood following the aborted *Explorer I* attempt, strongly appealed to Kepner, but he felt compelled to say no. He had postponed attending the Air Corps Tactical School in order to pilot

Explorer I. Now Maj. Gen. Douglas MacArthur, the Army Chief of Staff, paid Kepner the compliment of asking the Air Corps Chief to inquire whether Kepner would prefer to command the second stratosphere flight or go to school. Kepner chose the latter and reported to the Tactical School, Maxwell Field, Alabama, in the summer of 1935. He was in good company: class members included Ira Eaker, Benjamin Chidlaw, and Nathan Twining, among other future Air Force giants.

Kepner, by virtue of seniority, was class president. He and his seventy fellow students faced an intensive nine-month course designed not merely to teach air strategy and tactics, but to prepare career officers for staff responsibilities. Among the Tactical School faculty members were some of the Air Corps' best thinkers. Men like Harold George, Haywood Hansell, Laurence Kuter, and Claire Chennault debated the issues of air power in what was a vigorous, sometimes acrimonious, academic forum. The curriculum was strongly influenced by the War Department General Staff; only about half of it was allocated to air subjects, but school authorities allowed lecturers and students to discuss their ideas on the use of air power, free of restraint. The willingness of Tactical School theorists to hear opposing views regarding air power employment may have been genuine, but there is little doubt that in the mid-thirties, bomber advocates, who believed that strategic bombing alone could win the next war, held sway over a small band of pursuit enthusiasts led by Claire Chennault.

Maj. William E. Kepner

Kepner was urged privately by Captain Chennault to champion pursuit, yet his interest in the argument seems to have been in practical hardware rather than theoretical doctrine. But the conflict between Tactical School bomber and pursuit advocates was fundamentally doctrinal and consequently all the more extreme. The bomber theorists believed fervently that heavy bombers flying in formation could penetrate enemy defenses during daylight hours in order to bomb with precision, and do so at an acceptable cost. That error in judgment extracted an extremely high price in bomber losses during the early months of U.S. participation in World War II. It presaged the long-range fighter escort problem which lay in Kepner's future, waiting to challenge him in the European theater, long after he had left the theorists at Maxwell to their heady dispute.

Before leaving Alabama, "Kill" Kepner became part of another pioneering venture. His friend and classmate, Ira Eaker, had conceived the idea of making a flight from coast to coast guided only by aircraft instruments. Its purpose was to demonstrate the effectiveness of extended navigation using radio and instrument aids. Eaker asked Kepner to pilot an observation aircraft flying alongside to reduce the hazard for Eaker of flying "blind" under an instrument hood. No stranger to experiments, Kepner readily agreed. Toward the end of the Tactical School course, the two aviators tried the idea out on the Commandant, Col. John F. Curry. He encouraged Eaker to seek permission from the Air Corps. In May, the flight was approved and on June 2, 1936, Eaker and Kepner took off from Mitchel Field, Long Island.

They made the journey in two Boeing P-12s, an aircraft of proven reliability that had been a first-line pursuit plane since its addition to the Air Corps inventory in 1928. The trip, made in hops because of the P-12's limited range, took four days, with Eaker going under the hood as soon as his P-12 was airborne and remaining there until they were over the next landing field. Bad weather along part of the route forced Kepner to fly close formation on Eaker, relying solely on the "blind" P-12 for flight attitude and navigation.

Kepner was promoted to lieutenant colonel on June 16 and assigned as a student at the Command and General Staff School, Fort Leavenworth, Kansas. The years between 1937, when he graduated from the Staff School, and 1941 found Kepner in a variety of positions. As the nation moved somnolently but inevitably down the road to another world war, he was getting himself and the air arm ready to fight. Following the course at Leavenworth, he spent a year on the General Headquarters Air Force staff at Langley Field, Virginia, before assuming command of the 8th Pursuit Group at the same field. This organization and its sister pursuit group (the 1st at Selfridge Field, Michigan), were equipped with a mix of P-12s, Boeing P-26s, Seversky P-35s, and Curtiss P-36s. The P-26, an open-cockpit aircraft with fixed landing gear, was ancient technology by aviation standards, while the P-35 had proven hopelessly underpowered at altitude. Although the P-36 was vastly superior in performance to other first-line pursuit aircraft, it was available in only limited numbers. In the fall of 1938, Kepner was selected to command all defense aviation during the Fort Bragg maneuvers. This comprehensive joint exercise pitting pursuits against the new B-17 bomber was used with great success by Maj. Gen. Frank Andrews, the GHQ Air Force Commander, to assess fighter and bomber capabilities for the Chief of the Air Corps.

Kepner's tour at Langley concluded with his promotion to colonel and assignment to Mitchel Field as executive officer of the 2d Wing in February 1940. He shortly moved up to executive officer for the Air Defense Command, and when the First Air Force was organized in January 1941, Kepner became its first chief of staff. The following August, he organized and commanded the First Air Support Command and during the Carolina maneuvers that fall, commanded all aviation under First Army. The Air Corps, as in the Fort Bragg exercises of 1938, was again flexing its muscles in preparation for the war many felt was just around the corner. Indeed, the Carolina maneuvers were to be the last "practice." After December 7, 1941, the game was for real.

*   *   *   *   *

Christmas 1941 was a dismal holiday for the American people. Customary good cheer had vanished in the aftershock of our sudden embroilment in the war. We clearly had been caught unprepared at Pearl Harbor. Our feeble resistance on Oahu seemed a sign of military weakness. During the years since Colonel Kepner had commanded the 8th Pursuit Group in 1938, however, a great deal of progress had been made in strengthening American air power. Since mid-October of that year, President Roosevelt had been emphasizing the need to increase U.S. air defenses. In 1939, Charles Lindbergh toured Air Corps bases examining equipment and visited most of the country's major aircraft producers. He reported his findings to an Air Corps board whose purpose was to devise a plan for aircraft and weapons development. Though it would be difficult to substantiate direct benefits of the so-called "Kilner Board," the period 1939-41 did become a time of frantic aircraft industry activity, much of it to support Great Britain and France, which was not exceeded until the months after Pearl Harbor.

The first B-17s had been delivered to Langley Field in March 1937, and the Air Corps, despite the usual fiscal and political obstacles, continued to buy them in slowly growing numbers. Pursuit aviation also had seen some changes, as Kepner discovered when he took over the IV Interceptor Command two months after the war started. The Bell P-39, Republic P-47, and Lockheed P-38 had replaced the older, slower, and less capable machines of Kepner's Langley Field days. Ironically, the Air Corps Tactical School arguments of the 1930s about pursuit versus bomber employment had persisted, and now (in 1942) the bomber people still were very much in the doctrinal driver's seat. Bomber preeminence had not been materially affected even by the air lessons of Spain's civil war and the Battle of Britain, which clearly showed the limited effect of strategic bombing on civilian morale and the essentiality of fighter escort to keep bomber losses at an acceptable level.

Kepner, a spanking new brigadier general in February 1942, tackled his duties at IV Interceptor Command (later IV Fighter Command) with characteristic verve and optimism. As he once said of himself, "I am much happier when the going is difficult than I would be if it were all calm and rosy." Faced with a contingent of inexperienced flyers and new, untried equipment, Kepner laid out a course of intensive training. He radiated confidence in America's ability to wage and win the war.

Kepner's deep belief in tactical flexibility found its natural expression in the fast-maneuvering, powerful fighter planes under his command. He was eager to join the units already in combat. "How I wish I could be with them," he had written to Larry Bell, president of Bell Aircraft. But nearly a year passed before General Arnold, in the spring of 1943, selected him to run the VIII Fighter Command, European Theater of Operations. Kepner had done a superb job organizing and training the IV Fighter Command; Arnold had a problem that needed solving, and Kepner was the right man to solve it.

The bomber commanders of Eighth Air Force, despite early optimism about autonomous bomber operations, were beginning to feel the need for improved fighter escort in their raids over Europe. General Arnold himself was subjected to public pressure as a result of heavy bomber losses. In 1942, Maj. Gen. Carl "Tooey" Spaatz, Eighth Air Force Commander, believed that the bomber forces' firepower and formation tactics negated a requirement for fighter escort under virtually all conditions. His successor, Ira Eaker, also was confident initially that the bombers could operate successfully beyond the range of fighter escort. In the fall of 1942, he had written to General Arnold that "three hundred heavy bombers can attack any target in Germany by daylight with less than four percent losses." But bomber losses rose sharply in December and January, prompting General Eaker to press Arnold for help in fixing the escort problem. Kepner's selection to command VIII Fighter Command was, at least in part, a response to Eaker's plea.

By April 1943, Kepner had a clear set of marching orders from the Commanding General of the Army Air Forces. As he recalled during an interview in the summer of 1944:

Looking at flying range from l. to r.: Col. Stewart Towle, VIII Fighter Command Chief of Staff; Maj. Gen. William Kepner; Col. Francis Griswold, Ass't. Chief of Staff; and Col. Robert Burns, A–3.

[the bombers] needed protection, needed it well organized, and a long way in, and *right now.* . . . General Arnold sent me over here; said he wanted it set up and he was going to leave me to do it. How it was done was up to me, but there was no doubt in my mind that he wanted this escort.

Kepner's natural impatience, a trait hardly dimmed by his promotion to major general on April 27, drove him to see how much progress could be made on the escort problem even *before* he shipped overseas. He thought it possible that the P–38 could accompany bombers all the way to Berlin and that the P–51 had the same potential. On his own initiative he visited the companies that built the P–38, P–51, and P–47, and told the company presidents that they had to increase the range of their fighters. "I told them that I wanted to get to Berlin and had to have more gas in these planes." His insistence on range extension had results, but they were slow in coming.

In August 1943, Kepner arrived in England, proceeding to Watford and his new headquarters, a converted hotel called Bushey Hall. Here at the "front office" (known to the flying crews as "Ajax") he found the situation worse than he had expected. In the first place, the North African campaign (Operation Torch) had drawn off the bulk of American fighter resources in England. Kepner's predecessor, Brig. Gen. Frank O'D. "Monk" Hunter had consequently husbanded his resources. Despite increasing pressure, Hunter was reluctant to use his small force except to protect the bombers during their initial penetration and withdrawal. The few American pursuit craft available were P–47 Thunderbolts. Known as "Jugs" because of their unusually shaped fuselage, the eight-ton P–47s had a maximum combat radius of approximately 175 miles. Still, General Hunter had not pushed for the longer range P–38s, preferring first to give the P–47 a complete trial in combat. To Kepner's feisty nature, this showed a decided lack of aggressive thinking.

At the time, VIII Fighter Command had only six groups of P–47s divided into two wings. Three of the groups were for training while the remainder were combat operational. These units had been providing limited penetration and withdrawal support close to the French coast since their first escort mission in May 1943. Ninth Air Force fighters also were called upon to fly escort beginning in late 1943, and continued to support VIII Fighter Command until shortly before D-day in June 1944. Kepner acknowledged that short escort missions had some value: they provided combat experience for "green" pilots and demonstrated tactical ideas that would prove useful once long-range escort was begun. But short missions were not good enough, and no one knew this better than the bomber people themselves. In an appeal to VIII Fighter Command for more and deeper escort, Bomber Command's Maj. Gen. Fred Anderson had written, "It is obvious that the ideal fighter

Formation of P–47 Thunderbolts.

165

protection is that which can accompany the bombers from enemy territory to [the] target. Failing that, the greater the escorted penetration the better." To the new fighter boss, the urgency of this message and Fighter Command's failure so far to deal effectively with the problem were equally apparent.

Kepner picked his whole organization up like a rug and gave it a shake. He put combat-experienced people into staff positions; thus, there was never "the combat pilot's viewpoint" and "the headquarters viewpoint." They were one and the same. In the ever-shifting tactical environment of the European theater, this closeness of staff and line people turned out to be crucial in disseminating the "latest word" to all aircrews.

The Air Technical Section that Kepner established had been feverishly at work since January 1943 trying to provide a British source of external auxiliary fuel tanks for the P–47s. They tried a number of tanks that winter, but leaks, pressurization problems, and the British steel shortage frustrated their efforts. By summer, however, Air Technical Section began having some success, providing 75-gallon, 108-gallon (for which Kepner personally interceded with the British), and 150-gallon tanks through the remainder of 1943.

The new centerline tanks were thought by the pilots to look rather ungainly. They called these extra fuel tanks "babies." Skepticism of the flyers notwithstanding, the babies did the job. P–47 escort range increased dramatically. With no tanks, combat radius had been 175 miles; with a single 75-gallon tank it jumped to 280 miles; with one 108-gallon tank it reached 325 miles, and with two external tanks 450 miles. Soon these tanks, General Kepner exulted, " . . . [permitted Thunderbolt operations] within sight of Berlin, and that is a long step from the 175 miles, with the same damn airplane and the same boys flying it." The problems of pressurization, material shortages, and initial lack of support from U.S. suppliers had been overcome by persistence of Kepner and his staff.

Air Technical Section complemented the auxiliary tank program with other P–47 range and performance refinements. They replaced the Pratt and Whitney R–2800–21 engines with the –59 and –63 water-injected versions; they perfected fuel tank jettison systems, and installed a highly efficient paddle-bladed propeller.

While General Kepner applauded these technical improvements, he was keeping the pressure on in other areas to lick the long-range escort problem. Fearful bomber losses suffered in the August and October 1943 Schweinfurt-Regensburg raids, due primarily to the lack of long-range fighter escort, had lent heightened urgency to the task. These combined raids had resulted in 95 of 441 aircraft lost on the August strike, and 82 of 257 on October's mission. Kepner urged his fighter groups to protect the bombers at all costs. A sign he posted in every briefing room read, "We have two scores we are aiming at—first the number of bombers we bring back safely, and second, the number of German fighters we destroy."

Under Kepner, air commanders were encouraged to experiment with new tactics. He insisted on "skull sessions" between pilots and planners. One early product of this procedure was refinement of the relay escort system that had been started under Monk Hunter. By late 1943, one group of fighters was escorting the bombers in their initial penetration of enemy territory, then a second group picked up the bomber stream and escorted it to the target where a third group would take over. Successive groups of fighters accompanied the bombers on their withdrawal. These tactics required thorough coordination and navigational skill, but they permitted the fighters to proceed straight to the rendezvous, thus extending range and minimizing the time spent weaving across-course above the much slower bombers. After October 1943, flight leaders also could get radar vectors to rendezvous points, courtesy of the new British "Y" Service.

Satisfied that substantial improvement in P–47 capability was under way early in the fall, Kepner turned his attention to bringing the longer range P–38 Lightning and P–51 Mustang into the theater. At the end of September, he gave first priority to assembling P–38s that had arrived in England by surface transport. By October 15, some of these aircraft were already in action. Initially, the few P–38s available to accompany bombers all the way to the target were greatly outnumbered, but as their numbers increased during November and December, the P–38s were holding bomber losses in the target area to a supportable level for the first time since deep penetrations had been halted in the wake of the October Schweinfurt mission. With the arrival of

P–51 Mustang

167

Lightnings, General Kepner later recalled, "We began to think . . . that we were in the long-range escort business." Like the P-47s, the P-38s were out-fitted with external tanks that improved their already superior range from an untanked combat radius of 260 miles to 520 miles with two 75-gallon wing tanks, and then to nearly 600 miles with two 150-gallon tanks.

The P-51 Mustang was slower arriving in the theater. It was early December 1943, before the P-51 became operational in Europe. General Kepner had insisted that Mustangs would be the only satisfactory answer to truly long-range escort. General Arnold had asked the RAF's Air Chief Marshal Portal to put his P-51s at the disposal of VIII Fighter Command for long-range escort. In January 1944, the RAF did provide four Mustang units. Meanwhile, Kepner was angry that P-51s coming from the States were slated for Ninth Air Force. The Eighth and Ninth Air Force Commanders reached a compromise: the 354th Fighter Group, first ETO American unit before 1944 to get the Mustang, was operationally assigned to VIII Fighter Command even though it belonged on paper to Ninth Air Force.

Originally built by North American Aviation for the British, the Mustang did its job extremely well. Incredibly, it had gone from design to first flight in less than 100 days. Pilots who flew the Rolls Royce Merlin-powered version agreed that the Mustang was the world's finest fighter plane. Its awesome basic fighting radius of nearly 500 miles could be augmented by external fuel to 850 miles. This once unheard of endurance for a pursuit aircraft was a quality referred to by crews as "seven-league boots," and it signaled the final push to develop an indomitable long-range fighter capability.

By any standard, this rapid rise in fortune for long-range escort during General Kepner's first four months of command was remarkable. In September the P-47s had been limited to 175 miles, and by November they ranged some 450 miles from England. The advent of P-38s in October and P-51s by December heralded a turnaround in the air war. The combined offensive punch of Eighth Air Force, Ninth Air Force, and the RAF fighter arms had indeed done the trick, changing the momentum of the entire war. At VIII Fighter Command, Kepner had driven his people—staff, engineers, flyers—to get the most out of the weapons available in the theater at any given time. According to General Kepner, "if it can be said that the P-38s struck the Luftwaffe in its vitals and the P-51s are giving it the coup de grace, it was the Thunderbolt that broke its back."

*   *   *   *   *

A lot had changed since the departure of most VIII Fighter Command aircraft to North Africa in early 1943, and since the peak bomber losses of that fall. Allied statistics echoed the transformation. As bomber claims of enemy aircraft destroyed dropped steadily after October, fighter claims mounted. Enemy fighters were not getting through the fighter screen to hit the bombers.

This shift had taken place during a period in which orders from General Eaker at Eighth Air Force were to "stick with the bombers" and not to wander off challenging the German fighters. But General Kepner had always wanted his fighters to seek out the Germans. Colonel Zemke's 56th Fighter Group had, in fact, been doing just that despite the official ban on leaving the bombers in order to forage for Germans. According to Zemke, his people pioneered a roving tactic in which ". . . the attempt was made to disrupt the enemy before he could launch an attack. The immediate results were apparent on the score card—a sudden spurt of air victories for the 56th." The idea was to split the escort into a "seeking" unit that swept the skies ahead of penetrating bombers or behind withdrawing bombers while the rest of the escort provided continuous close flank cover. Finally, said Zemke, "the tactic leaked and I was invited to a dinner at General Doolittle's—with Kepner and a number of others in attendance." They pressed the young group commander for details, and a new aggressive escort policy was born. Doolittle, General Eaker's successor at Eighth Air Force, cleared the fighters to range away from the bomber formations and seek out the enemy.

Lt. Gen. Hap Arnold (left) with Brig. Gen. James Doolittle

Doolittle's decision also reflected the offensive spirit of General Arnold's New Year (1944) message to his commanders: "Destroy the enemy Air Force wherever you find them, in the air, on the ground and in the factories." Kepner was quick to see that new opportunities to exploit fighter flexibility were on the horizon. On January 17, 1944, he issued a prophetic message to the pilots of his command:

> A fighter pilot must be able to use his versatile weapon in whatever way will do the greatest damage to the enemy . . . high or low, near or far, protecting bombers, destroying enemy fighters, preparing the way for our advancing ground troops, cutting the supply lines, strafing airdromes and other necessary missions. . . . Be ready. Today we are flying high altitude escort for heavy bombers. Tomorrow . . . ?

That offensive philosophy suited the fighter-pilot temperament. And, as the message had forecast, VIII Fighter Command's turn to the offensive did not stop with bomber escort.

Col. Glen Duncan, Commander of the 353d Fighter Group, started something new early in 1944. He led his flight in a strafing attack on a German airfield as they were returning from what had been an uneventful escort mission. One pilot described this armed buzzing as "roaring down at terrific speeds on a chosen object, zooming over it with inches to spare—and the closer the better—add the hazards of flak and ground fire and you have a sport that is practically irresistible." Duncan's experiment soon grew to be a major (and unauthorized) tactic in VIII Fighter Command.

In his own way, Kepner kept his superiors informed:

> Once when my VIII Fighter Command was "tearing into anything" in Germany en route to or from the bomb target, I was riding in an auto with Spaatz. I said, "General, my Fighter Command is doing some screwy things en route and returning, but I think they pay dividends." Tooey Spaatz laid his hand on my knee and replied, "Yes Bill you are right, and so long as they pay dividends you will have a job." I got the point.

Kepner decided this "unorganized guerrilla warfare" needed a dash of method. In late March 1944, he organized a unit that became known as "Bill's Buzz Boys." Volunteers from groups throughout the command gathered at Metfield for training by Colonel Duncan. The unit's mission was to develop airdrome strafing tactics that would be used throughout VIII Fighter Command.

Its mission completed, the unit was dissolved on April 12, 1944. Shortly thereafter, Kepner and his planners came up with the "Chattanooga Choo-Choo" and "Jackpot" strike missions against railroads and airfields respectively. On a single mission, as many as 1,000 fighters might be assigned. Each fighter group was given one of fifteen geographical sectors in Germany consistent with the range of aircraft assigned to the group. By the late spring of 1944, Ninth Air Force units also were doing armed reconnaissance on a large scale.

The effects on Germany of this concentrated strafing were devastating. In April alone, VIII Fighter Command strafers claimed 1,791 German aircraft destroyed and over 1,000 others damaged. Enemy ground movements in daylight were all but halted in many areas, and the enemy had to resort to special camouflage, dispersal, and night techniques. Captured German documents attested to the effectiveness of strafing by Kepner's pilots and their Ninth Air Force colleagues, reporting that even motorcycles and isolated soldiers were attacked. After the war, Germany's fighter commander, Adolph Galland, said: "Nowhere were we safe from them; we had to skulk on our own bases. . . . [It was] a logical extension of tactics, permitting fighters to leave bomber formations to seek out the enemy."

Long-range escort, which made possible the first daylight raids on Berlin in March 1944, had been so effective against the Luftwaffe that in April Allied fighters were routinely leaving the bombers to destroy German planes on the ground. On May 20, three weeks before D-day, Kepner's fighters were cleared to fly strafing missions against enemy transportation in occupied France. Because General Kepner had had the foresight to organize and disseminate new tactics developed by his best pilots, the VIII Fighter Command was ready for a wide range of tasks to support the landings at Normandy in June 1944.

Kepner's fighters were even prepared to drop bombs on D-day. According to Col. Hubert Zemke, Commander of the 56th Fighter Group, as early as November 1943, his P–47 pilots were dropping bombs in level flight behind formations of B–24s flying at medium altitude. They later practiced rudimentary dive and skip bombing too. As in the strafing experiment, each unit sent a representative to learn these techniques and bring them back to his outfit. Fighter bombing was used to some extent by VIII Fighter Command, but it never became a major activity as it did for Ninth Air Force fighter bombers.

In each extension of its combat function, VIII Fighter Command reflected its commander's belief in tactical flexibility as the key to fighter effectiveness. Each venture paid off because it was thought out in terms of the enemy threat and was tirelessly followed up to see if it was working. Kepner hounded logisticians and suppliers, but granted combat tacticians free reign to experiment and innovate. Ideas were not judged on who thought them up; if they were good, they were used until they no longer worked. It was this trait of tactical open-mindedness that helped make VIII Fighter Command an effective combat organization. Wing Commander Nigel Tangye of the RAF claimed some three weeks after the Normandy invasion that in his opinion one of the most remarkable achievements of the American air forces was the flexibility of Eighth Fighter Command. "No other command—RAF or USAAF," he said, "has ever been asked to mix the strategic with the tactical in such precise terms."

D-day itself had seen VIII Fighter Command fly a prodigious number and variety of sorties. Its P–38s provided a large measure of the cover given the nearly 6,500 vessels transporting the assault force. The P–47s and P–51s, together with Ninth Air Force fighters, provided a solid curtain of air superiority. Kepner put it this way:

> We formed a screen across the English Channel to the east of the surface vessel traffic that went clear down around 50 miles south of the beachhead, across the Cherbourg peninsula, and back across the Channel to the English coast—a half circle, and we maintained that thing from five minutes before first light on D-day until after 11 o'clock that day, solid, so that not a single damn German airplane came through there to go to the beach.

In a ground strike role, too, General Kepner's men helped bottle up German road and rail activity within fifty miles of the front, sharing the interdiction task with the Ninth Air Force. Hermann Goering declared that "the Allies owe the success of the invasion to the air forces. They prepared the invasion; they made it possible; they carried it through."

For the airmen, the invasion itself was almost anticlimactic: "If you see fighter aircraft over you, they will be ours," General Eisenhower told his invasion forces. And that is the way it was. Some observers believe the air war was won in March and April 1944, during the peak escort and fighter ground-attack effort. Regardless of when the actual victory occurred, General Bill Kepner's versatile VIII Fighter Command played an important role in defeating the Luftwaffe. Following the invasion, Eighth Air Force bombers continued their deep thrusts into Germany, and VIII Fighter Command, with nearly half its strength now in P-51s, provided increasingly effective cover for the bombers.

*   *   *   *   *

Early in August 1945, Kepner turned his office at Bushey Hall over to Brig. Gen. Francis "Butch" Griswold and took command of the Eighth's 2d Bombardment Division. The VIII Fighter Command in its brief ETO existence had flown more than 137,000 sorties and lost almost 1,300 pilots and planes, but it had destroyed or probably destroyed some 4,500 German aircraft and damaged 2,400 more. Bill Kepner could feel content about the job his once frustrated and struggling command had done. It had played a dominant role in what he himself knew was ". . . the greatest offensive fighter battle ever fought."

Hitler's Luftwaffe chief, Hermann Goering, said after the war that without long-range fighter escort, the Allied air offensive never would have succeeded. General Kepner remembered hearing Goering's opinion long before it became part of the official record of interrogations:

> When Germany surrendered at Rheims, France . . . General Cannon, General Vandenberg, and I were waiting in the adjacent room for orders, and in case Germany

refused our terms, we would start air operations immediately. When everything ended okay, General Spaatz came out laughing and said to me, "Bill, I asked Reich Marshal Goering, 'When did you know the jig was up?' Goering replied, 'When I saw the American fighter planes knocking down our German fighter planes over Berlin, I knew you could protect your American bombers and would bomb us out of the war.' " General Spaatz continued, "I understand you had some problems getting our fighter planes over Berlin, so I pass the compliment to you."

When Kepner assumed command of the 2d Bombardment Division in mid-August, he did not say farewell to VIII Fighter Command units. In September, Eighth Air Force Commander General Doolittle distributed Fighter Command's units among the Eighth's three bombardment divisions. Doolittle's objective was to more closely integrate fighter and bomber control, and to that end, Kepner's 2d Bombardment Division got five of the VIII Fighter Command's fifteen P–47 and P–51 groups. After the reorganization, General Kepner's new command consisted of some 900 B–24 bombers and more than 500 fighters. It operated in much the same fashion as a "numbered" air force and conducted bombing operations against Germany until V-E Day in May 1945. Under Kepner's leadership, the 2d Bombardment Division radically improved its visual bombing accuracy and experimented with a number of radar bombing techniques. The fighters continued to provide both escort for the bombers and offensive and harassing operations.

As the war approached its end, General Kepner was given command of Eighth Air Force, a job whose earlier distinguished incumbents were Generals Spaatz, Eaker, and Doolittle. Kepner's main concern following the surrender was management of Eighth Air Force withdrawal from the European theater. As that air force passed from the scene in August 1945, he took over the reins of Ninth Air Force, in whose care all duties of the Occupational Air Forces were left—aerial policing, photomapping, organizing air bases, and supporting the military government. By December, the process of demobilization was sufficiently advanced that all Ninth Air Force duties were transferred to the XII Tactical Air Command, with General Kepner as its new boss.

In January 1946, Bill Kepner finally returned to the United States. Nearly two and a half years had passed since General Arnold sent him to the European Theater. It had been a long war. But typical of Kepner's service history, he did not stay put for long. Within the month, he was named Deputy Commander for Army and Navy Aviation, Joint Task Force 1. Operating directly under the Joint Chiefs of Staff, this organization was responsible for "Operation Crossroads," America's nuclear testing in the Pacific.

Nine months later, Kepner traded the middle of the ocean for the middle of the American continent, arriving at Scott Field, Illinois, to head up Air Technical Training Command. There he remained until October 1947 when he was assigned to the office of the Deputy Chief of Staff for Research and Development at Air Force Headquarters. Within the deputate, Kepner held several positions, all directly responsible for Air Force nuclear weapons and

The Kepner Collection

Maj. Gen. Kepner aboard the flagship *McKinley* during the 1946 Bikini
atoll atomic bomb tests.

programs. In August 1948, he left Washington to take command of the Air
Proving Ground at Eglin Air Force Base, Florida.

There was one last operational command in store for Bill Kepner. He
was promoted to lieutenant general in June 1950, and named Commander
in Chief of the unified Alaskan Command, succeeding his old Air Corps Tactical School classmate, Nathan Twining. Kepner's early years with the Army
and Marine Corps made him remarkably well fitted to lead a triservice command. Since 1947, when the Joint Chiefs had put Alaska's defense in the hands
of a senior Air Force officer, F-80, F-82, and F-94 jet interceptors had stood
watch against possible Russian air attack. Kepner's Army and Navy units in
Alaska had similar defensive duties for their own special provinces of land

and sea. Conditions in Alaska's muddy summers and devastating winters were primitive, but "if the enemy invades," said Kepner, "we'll hand him quite a jolt."

In December 1952, about three weeks before his sixtieth birthday, General Kepner relinquished his post to Maj. Gen. Joseph Atkinson and returned to Washington for a retirement ceremony on February 28, 1953, at Bolling Air Force Base. His more than forty years of military service spanned the period from America's tentative first steps in military aviation to the creation of nuclear weapons. He died at Orlando, Florida, in 1982 at the age of eighty-nine.

General Kepner's career as a member of three military services—and his work as a lighter-than-air pioneer, stratosphere explorer, and fighter commander—is unique in the annals of Air Force history. His technical and tactical skills and his willingness to experiment in both areas earned him a place among the leaders in the development of air warfare.

Sources

The core source for this biographical sketch is the Kepner Document Collection, housed at the USAF Historical Research Center, Maxwell AFB, Alabama. The collection contains hundreds of personal and official documents along with a number of tapes, manuscripts, photographs, and other memorabilia given to the Center by General Kepner. These are invaluable in gaining a sense of the man and of the impact he made on his surroundings. Several telephone interviews with the General and a series of letters to the author written between January 1981 and July 1982 were instrumental in clarifying material in the collection and in gathering personal anecdotes.

A few general works provide background information pertinent to the various periods of Kepner's career. Most useful among these is the *Army Air Forces in World War II*, edited by W. F. Craven and J. L. Cates (University of Chicago Press, 1951; Reprint, Office of Air Force History, 1983). Volume II, *Torch to Pointblank* (1949) and Volume III, *Europe, Argument to V-E Day* (1951) are especially valuable. Other general sources include DeWitt S. Copp's *A Few Great Captains* (Doubleday, 1980); and *The Mighty Eighth* by Roger A. Freeman. Copp s *Forged in Fire* (Doubleday, 1982) examines WW II Air Force operations with considerable detail on the Combined Bomber Offensive and the long-range escort problem.

By far the best source of "atmosphere" from the fighter operations standpoint is Grover C. Hall's *1000 Destroyed: The Life and Times of the 4th Fighter Group* (Aero Publishers, 1978). In several letters to the author, Colonel Hubert "Hub" Zemke provided first-person operational accounts that also help capture the flavor of VIII Fighter Command.

Several 1930s' issues of *Scientific Monthly* and *The National Geographic* aid in reconstructing the "Explorer I" stratospheric expedition, but the major source on this topic is an oral history interview from the Kepner Document Collection. *Air Force Magazine* (September 1978) and *Aerospace Historian* (September 1971) contain lengthy articles that survey Kepner's balloon career. His manuscript entitled "Riding the Storm in a National Balloon Race" also contributes details on ballooning experiences. *Life, Time,* and *Army, Navy and Air Force Journal* yielded a number of human interest items from General Kepner's service in VIII Fighter Command, the nuclear test program, and Alaskan Air Command.

Among many pertinent official documents several merit mention. The first of these, a very thorough unit history indeed, is *Achtung Indianer!: The History of the United States VIII Fighter Command* (East Anglia, U.K., 1944) by Lt. Col. Waldo Heinrichs. Other significant sources include *The Long Reach: Deep Fighter Escort Tactics* (VIII Fighter Command, 1944), and *Eighth Air Force Tactical Development: August 42–May 45* (Army Air Forces Evaluation Board, 1945).

8

Elwood R. Quesada: Tac Air Comes of Age

John Schlight

Only a few times in the history of military affairs have technological breakthroughs occurred that truly can be called revolutionary. The introduction of the stirrup in the fourth century, the longbow in the thirteenth, gunpowder in the fourteenth, and the airplane in our time qualify for that distinction. Each new invention, however, challenged comfortable ideas and forced a rethinking of accepted practices and doctrines.

Although among the first of the world's nations to purchase military aircraft, the United States after 1909 fell behind several other countries in taking advantage of the new weapon. Arriving late to World War I and buffeted afterwards by the twin obstacles of conservative military thinking and national economic plight, the airplane was not fully assimilated into America's military mainstream until the eve of World War II. Even then its role remained a matter of dispute, and it took that world conflagration to illustrate what military aircraft could do.

Through all of these fluctuations a relatively small group of men in the Army's aviation branch worked to discover and publicize the airplane's potential. These flyers shared some traits: a genuine enjoyment of the excitement and challenges posed by this new vehicle, a conviction that the airplane's potential was being stifled by institutional constraints, and a willingness—indeed an eagerness—to question standard solutions to problems. At the same time this group was far from monolithic. Often its members differed among themselves as to how airplanes should best be used. Bomber advocates believed fervently that not only their planes, but also their arguments in support of them, could bowl over any opposition. Others favored fighter planes, but not

177

all for the same reasons. Some advanced the escort role of pursuit planes, others the interdiction capability of attack aircraft. But virtually all looked with disdain upon using airplanes to directly support ground forces.

Some of these early aviators fought principally with their pens, while others let their actions and personalities speak for them. Among the latter was Elwood R. "Pete" Quesada, who, in his twenty-six-year career, dealt in one way or another with most of the major issues associated with the growth of American air power.

The son of a Spanish businessman and an Irish-American mother, Quesada was born in 1904 in Washington, D.C., rather than in his parents' home in Spain. His mother preferred American doctors to deliver her children. He was, by his own characterization, "basically an immigrant." His entrance into the small aviation brotherhood in 1924 was as unorthodox as the way he achieved many of his later accomplishments. Quesada was quarterbacking the small University of Maryland football team that year when a moonlighting Air Service lieutenant who often refereed games recruited him to play for the team at the Army's flying school at Brooks Field in Texas in the fall. Enrolled there as a primary cadet with 150 other students, he took quickly to the World War I-vintage Jennies that were used as trainers. By contrast, the Brook Field football team lost every game, and Quesada missed six weeks of flight training after he broke his leg on the gridiron. His strongly competitive nature led him to forego his Christmas leave to catch up under the tutelage of Lt. Nathan Twining, one of the school's instructors. The next spring he entered the advanced flying training school at nearby Kelly Field with the fourteen other successful primary graduates, including Thomas White, Earle Partridge and, for a while, Charles Lindbergh. At Kelly, Quesada learned to fly pursuit planes—the Sopwith SE–5 and the MB–3—and received his wings and a reserve commission as a second lieutenant.

In 1925 the Air Service was at its nadir. Still part of the Army, the fledgling aviation unit had to compete with the other Army branches for funds and resources. It had only 880 officers and an equal number of planes, most of them obsolete. Flying officers were either recent West Point graduates or came from the other branches of the Army. Quesada was neither and returned to civilian life. While at Kelly he had played for the San Antonio Army Baseball Team in several exhibition games against the St. Louis Cardinals. Upon graduation he accepted an offer of $1,000 to sign on with the major league club. Quesada notes, with a scarcely concealed smile of irony, that the Army team's pitcher, Dizzy Dean, accepted $500 for the same offer. Quesada's stint with the team lasted only a week. Aware of his vulnerability to certain pitches, he returned the money to the club's manager, Branch Rickey, and ended his baseball career.

The outlook for the Air Service brightened the following year with congressional passage of the Army Air Corps Act. In addition to changing its

Lt. Elwood R. Quesada

name, the Army's air arm embarked, in 1927, on a five-year program to increase its numbers of officers and planes. A few inactive reserve officers, Quesada among them, were brought on active duty and given regular commissions. Working at the time as a criminal investigator for the Treasury Department in Detroit, he had felt the lure of the Army during his frequent visits to former classmates and familiar airplanes at nearby Selfridge Field.

His first assignment, to Bolling Field in Washington, provided important contacts and opened new vistas for the young lieutenant. Bolling at the time had a dozen different types of planes used by the Air Corps Chief, Maj. Gen. James E. Fechet, and members of his staff, including Maj. Carl A. Spaatz and Capt. Ira C. Eaker. Quesada's job as engineering officer was to keep the planes in good condition. He learned to fly all of them and quickly gained a reputation as a superb pilot and mechanic and as an energetic officer.

One Sunday in March 1928, while Quesada was riding a horse in Rock Creek Park, the Bolling commander drove up and informed him that Fechet wanted to see him immediately. A German plane, trying to be the first to fly the Atlantic from east to west, had gone down in Labrador, and the American government wanted the Air Corps to fly parts to the stricken plane. Two Loening amphibians, with Quesada at the controls of one and Eaker piloting the other, took off from Bolling. At the end of the first leg Quesada, with Fechet aboard, set the plane down on the Bay of Fundy only to have it stranded on the bay's sandy bottom when the tide went out. After digging

179

holes in the sand under the plane's wheels to let down the landing gear, Quesada taxied up the beach and took off from land though he had come in as a flying boat. The mission succeeded, and in July, Fechet, impressed with Quesada's flying skill and ingenuity, made him his flying aide.

The planned five-year buildup of the Air Corps was slowed by the country's economic travails in the late twenties and early thirties. Air Corps officers still formed a relatively small and exclusive group, most of whom knew each other from their flying training days or subsequent assignments. Personal relationships played a large role in determining assignments and jobs. Much of the Air Corps' energy during these years was devoted to gaining public acceptance of the airplane as a versatile instrument for America's expanding society. This push for publicity had been behind the Air Corps' participation in the balloon expositions and speed races of the twenties and in Eaker's assignment as a pilot on a goodwill trip through Central and South America in 1927. It also partially explains the decision, in 1928, to see how long an airplane could stay aloft by refueling in the air. Quesada's close

Participants in *Question Mark* refueling, from l. to r.: Capt. Ross G. Hoyt (pilot of refueling plane); Capt. Ira C. Eaker; Maj. Gen. James E. Fechet (Chief of the Air Corps, not a crew member); Maj. Carl Spaatz; Lt. Elwood Quesada; and MSgt. R. W. Hooe

association with Fechet won him a berth as a pilot on the historical experiment. For nearly seven days in January 1929, along with Spaatz and Eaker, he helped fly a three-engined Fokker, called the *Question Mark*, as it orbited between San Diego and Los Angeles. Two modified Douglas C-1 transports, led by Capt. Ross Hoyt, served as "refuelers." Fuel was transferred through a hose, usually handled at the receiving end by Spaatz. Since there were no radios aboard, messages were written on blackboards, in whitewash on the fuselage of a plane that flew alongside, or attached to the end of the hose and supply line. Communication between a refueling crew member and his pilot was by means of a string tied to the pilot's arm. After eleven thousand miles, the *Question Mark* landed only because one of its engines began to falter. A generation later, while on an official visit to Vietnam years after his retirement, Quesada marveled at what this early flight had wrought as he witnessed wave after wave of American fighters and bombers refueling in mid-air for strikes against the North Vietnamese.

Following a two-year tour as an assistant military attaché in Cuba, Quesada returned to Washington as executive officer and flying aide to F. Trubee Davison, the Assistant Secretary of War for Air. In the summer of 1933, after Davison had left his post and became president of New York's Museum of Natural History, he and Quesada undertook a flying safari through Africa to gather animals for the museum.

The Air Corps' desire to gain a place in the sun was partially responsible for its unsuccessful experiment with carrying the mail the next winter. When in February President Roosevelt canceled as fraudulent the government's contracts with the commercial airlines, Quesada asked the Air Corps Chief, Maj. Gen. Benjamin Foulois, if Army flyers could handle the job. Foulois, according to Quesada, never one to say no, agreed. Between February and June 1934, Army pilots flew their transports, bombers, pursuits, and observation planes on missions for which neither they nor their equipment were prepared. Seat-of-the-pants flying, characteristic of much of Army aviation up until then, was unequal to the task. Most of the tactical planes lacked radios, gyros, artificial horizons, night-flying equipment, and even such rudimentary items as thermometers for detecting icing or cockpit lights for reading the instruments.

Quesada, by then a first lieutenant, was dispatched as chief pilot at Newark Airport in New Jersey, from where he flew round trips every other night to Cleveland. Piloting a Curtiss Condor, one of the Army's newest planes with navigational equipment aboard, he had little trouble. On half of his westward flights, however, headwinds forced him to land at the same small, private airfield in western Pennsylvania to refuel. After several weeks the field's manager, weary of rising at two in the morning to pump gasoline in subzero and snowy weather, left the key in a prearranged hiding place so that Quesada could help himself. The return runs, with the wind at his back, required no stops. One of them he flew in the record time of one hour and twenty-seven minutes. Pilots on the eighteen other runs were not so fortunate. Before the airlines resumed carrying the mail in June, sixty-six Air Corps planes had crashed and twelve pilots had died.

Quesada's spreading reputation as a diplomat and superior pilot netted him several more assignments as flying aide and executive officer to important government figures. After the airmail experience, in the summer of 1934, he was assigned to Hugh Johnson, the administrator of Roosevelt's National Recovery Administration (NRA). In addition to flying Johnson to all parts of the country, Quesada acted as a research assistant, helping him with congressional testimony and checking the accuracy of his speeches. With the demise of the NRA, Quesada became, briefly, an assistant to Secretary of War George Dern. For a short time after that he was an aide to Brig. Gen. George Marshall at Fort Benning, Georgia.

Quesada later acknowledged the value to him of these years as executive to the mighty. While the contacts he made were important, even more valuable in later years were the useful skills he developed in understanding the mind-set of military and civilian leaders, in sharpening a keen negotiating ability, and in being able to plan from a perspective that placed the Air Corps against a larger background. This latter trait, in particular, set him aside from many of his contemporaries. Continued service as an aide also prompted Quesada to the belief that his career was taking on a lopsided appearance, and he welcomed a fresh assignment.

Early in 1935, Quesada joined Col. Frank M. Andrews as the new GHQ Air Force was getting underway. Billy Mitchell's vitriolic campaign in the twenties for an air force separate from the Army had alienated many Army officials. Successive Air Corps Chiefs, Fechet and Foulois, through patience and diplomacy, had calmed the fears of many among the opposition, and by 1934 some Army leaders were beginning to see merit in a separate branch of bombers, pursuit, and attack planes which, still part of the Army, would provide a semblance of independence. The result was a new task force, the GHQ Air Force, whose creation, it was hoped, would deflate the Air Corps' resurgent move toward divorce.

On the first day of 1935, Andrews was appointed Commander of the GHQ Air Force with the job of organizing the force and activating it by March. At first, with only Quesada at his elbow in the State, War, and Navy Building in Washington, Andrews organized the GHQ Air Force and selected the people he wanted on his staff while Quesada handled the paperwork. When the outfit moved to Langley Field, Virginia, several months later, Quesada went with it as commander of the headquarters squadron which involved, among other things, "kicking people out of barracks so the GHQ could come in."

The move to Virginia went smoothly, and Andrews, now a brigadier general, rewarded Quesada with an assignment he wanted, to the Air Corps Tactical School at Maxwell Field, Alabama. At that time the school was a center of ferment. In contrast to the War Department's defensive view of aviation, the Tactical School taught that the offensive mission of strategic bombing was more decisive than supporting ground forces or defending the coastline. Corollary to this notion, and possibly partially responsible for it, was the view widely held among aviators that an independent bombing mission would never be accepted as long as the Air Corps remained under the thumb of the Army. Quesada came to share these views with what he later called the "agitators," noting that "agitation is how you get things done very often."

His year at Maxwell was followed by a year at the Army's Command and General Staff School at Fort Leavenworth, Kansas, and then to his first operational assignment as a flight commander in a bombardment squadron at Mitchel Field, Long Island. In this job less than a year, he was sent, in the summer of 1938, to Argentina as a technical advisor to the military. The Argentinian Air Force, which at the time had 150 American bombers and fighters, was trying to pattern itself after the American Air Corps. Chosen for his mechanical and organizational ability, Quesada was assigned to help them. He and four other American aviators assisted in installing maintenance and supply systems and a method of instruction for blind flying. The Argentinians had received a license to build their own aircraft engines and had opened a factory at Cordoba to produce them. Their lack of organizational skill, however, was making it costly for the government, both economically and politically. Being the only bachelor among the Americans, Quesada was sent to Cordoba, "where there was nothing but a wonderful climate," to install a system of quality control and inspection.

The night before Quesada left Buenos Aires for the States in September 1940, some American naval officers threw a party for him. At the height of the festivities he promised to relieve them of an unwanted Grumman amphibian plane by flying it home. With only a few five-gallon tins of gasoline, a screwdriver, a pair of diagonals, and some safety wire on board, he took off the next morning, flew over the Andes to the Pacific, and up the coast to Panama. His unannounced landing at the tightly guarded American naval air station there caused an uproar. As he climbed from his plane the airdrome officer asked who he was. Unable to locate a Captain Quesada in the Navy's register of officers, the AO summoned the station's commanding admiral. It took some time for the impish Quesada to clear up the suspicious phenomenon of an Army officer with a Spanish name flying a U.S. Navy plane from Argentina. Several days later he completed the flight to Norfolk, Virginia, becoming the first aviator to fly that route solo.

* * * * *

By the time Quesada returned from Argentina, the nations of Europe had been warring for a year, England was successfully weathering Hitler's bid to cow it from the air, and Maj. Gen. Henry H. Arnold was Chief of the Air Corps. As a result of his overseas experience, Quesada became Arnold's foreign liaison chief, working closely with the British embassy to supply them with information about Air Corps planes and equipment. When Arnold went to England in April 1941, Quesada accompanied him. The Lend-Lease Act was only a month old, and one of Arnold's purposes was to make arrangements with the British for flying American planes to England. As the Chief's aide, Quesada did the spadework for the trip, negotiating the itinerary, preparing the issue books, and memorizing scores of facts for the discussions. While in London the two witnessed the German bombing of the city. In visits to Royal Air Force bomber and fighter bases Quesada was impressed with the courage and determination, less so with the quantity of equipment, of the British flyers. Agreements were reached on Air Corps-RAF cooperation. Out of this visit was born the Ferrying Command, predecessor of the Air Force's later worldwide military airlift organizations.

Once back in Washington it fell to Quesada to set in motion many of the programs that flowed from the agreement—arranging for people to administer the Air Corps' portion of the Lend-Lease plan, transferring aluminum to England, and training British pilots in Air Corps schools. For his trouble, Arnold, now Commanding General of the newly designated Army Air Forces, rewarded the major with a promotion and his much-sought-after command of the 33d Fighter Group of P-40s at Mitchel Field.

When the United States entered the war in December, the Army created the Eastern Theater of Operations under Gen. Hugh Drum to defend the east coast against German submarines and, although not seriously expected, German air attacks or landings. The First Air Force became part of this defense force. In August 1942 Quesada, by now a temporary colonel, turned over the 33d to one of his squadron commanders, William Momyer, and took charge of the I Fighter Command. His job, in coordination with the Army's antiaircraft artillery, was to train P-40 pilots to intercept enemy planes, particularly at night. No sooner had he settled in his Philadelphia office than he landed in a jurisdictional dispute with the Army's artillery commander, Brig. Gen. Sanderford Jarman, over who was responsible for identifying planes flying in the area. It was the Army's practice to identify airborne planes at night by playing searchlights on them. After one of his pilots, blinded by the lights, crashed while trying to land, Quesada issued a written order banning the searchlights. He included in the order an *obiter dictum* that, since German

Chief of the Air Corps Maj. Gen. Hap Arnold (left) with Army Chief of
Staff George Marshall

planes could not much more than cross the twenty-two mile English Channel
from their home bases, it was to be assumed that there were none within a
thousand miles of the United States. All planes flying over the U.S., therefore,
were friendly. A sharp verbal exchange ensued between the colonel and the
general, after which Jarman preferred charges and sought to court-martial
Quesada. The Army Chief of Staff, General Marshall, sent his inspector
general and General Arnold to look into the matter. Both reported that, while
Quesada had been impulsive, the Army practice was wrong and the court-
martial should be dropped. Marshall, more than any of the top Army leaders,
appreciated air power's potential and the need to bring bright, young, energetic
officers into the general officer ranks. The lights were turned off, the charges
dropped, and Quesada was promoted to brigadier general and returned to
Mitchel Field to activate the 1st Air Defense Wing.

Early in 1943 Quesada took his defense wing to North Africa, where
it joined the XII Fighter Command in defending the Allied forces against
air and submarine attacks, and in protecting friendly shipping and attacking
enemy convoys in the Mediterranean. Within a month he was commanding
the XII Fighter Command.

Shortly before he arrived in Africa, at the Casablanca Conference in
January 1943, the decision was made to unite British and American forces
into functional, combined commands—all bombers in one command, fighters
in another, air defense planes and equipment in a third, and training in a

fourth. It was hoped, correctly, that this would help stop bickering among the Allies and, more importantly, end the piecemeal dissipation of air resources that had been taking place. Quesada was present at a meeting in Tripoli, attended by Spaatz and the other American and British air leaders, to decide who would head each of the four new combined air forces. He remained uncharacteristically silent for a long time as the British argued forcefully for control of all the commands since they had had more experience in the war. Finally, unable to contain himself longer, Quesada reminded the airmen that this experience they claimed included Dunkirk, Singapore, Crete, Greece, and a host of other British Army losses. Spaatz leaned over, tapped Quesada on the knee, and said, "Take it easy, Pete." The British airmen, principally Air Vice Marshal Sir Arthur Coningham, who harbored an undisguised dislike for some of the early leaders of the British Army, got the point and agreed to Quesada's suggestion that they choose commanders according to the predominance of force in each command. The British were given control of the tactical and air defense air forces, while Brig. Gens. Jimmy Doolittle and John K. Cannon took over the bomber and training commands. Quesada, whose XII Fighter Command was absorbed into the new Northwest Africa Coastal Defense Force under Sir Hugh Pugh Lloyd, donned a second hat as deputy commander of that defense force.

One of the more important results of this meeting was the friendship that sprung up between Quesada and Coningham. The air marshal had led the British tactical air forces at El Alamein the preceding winter. By force of personality he had convinced Gen. Bernard Montgomery that he could get the most out of his planes, not by using them as artillery, but by letting them wrest the air from the Luftwaffe and attack German airfields and lines of communication behind the front. Quesada and the other American tactical flyers had been advocating such independent use of tactical air power but had been unable to win their point as convincingly as the air marshal. Through his acquaintanceship with Coningham, Quesada would become one of the major conduits through which tactical air doctrine and practice would flow from Africa to continental Europe and eventually to the United States Air Force.

With the Germans cleared from Africa and the Allied invasion of Sicily and Italy well established, most of the major leaders of the African campaign moved to England in October to prepare for the invasion of the continent. Quesada went along with Eisenhower, Tedder, Bradley, Patton, Coningham, and, later, Doolittle, in transferring the African system of combined organizations to England. Lacking a long American tradition of tactical air power, Quesada and the other tactical planners fell back on what they had learned from both British and German air operations so far in the war, much of it formalized in Field Manual 100–20, which had been written and approved during the North African campaign. They borrowed their organization from the British, inspired by Coningham's insistence that tactical aircraft cooperate with the ground forces as an independent force. The American IX Fighter Command was set up as a coequal of the numbered American army, to work closely with it. An analysis of the Luftwaffe campaigns over Poland, France, England, and Africa led them to conclude that, while the German Air Force had achieved some dramatic local successes, its failure to gain control of the air at the outset doomed it to eventual defeat. Furthermore, by being tied too closely to the German armies, the Luftwaffe lacked the flexibility it needed for ultimate success.

Allied preparation for the invasion was divided into two phases. At first, Allied planes would gain control of the air over France and the Low Countries and destroy enough of Germany's industrial base to make a landing possible. In the forefront of this phase were the heavy bombers of the Eighth Air Force and British Bomber Command, supplemented, as they became operational, by the medium bombers and fighters of the newly created Ninth Air Force. Immediately prior to the invasion, tactical air units would participate in isolating the landing areas by knocking out roads, bridges, and rail lines. In the second phase, during and after the landings, the Ninth Air Force and the British Tactical Air Force would back up the ground assault.

Lt. Gen. Lewis H. Brereton (left) and Maj. Gen. Elwood Quesada (center) talk with officers on a visit to an airfield in France.

The Ninth Air Force, commanded by Maj. Gen. Lewis H. Brereton, was being built from a few remnants of the old Ninth from Africa, the medium bombers transferred from the Eighth in England, new units arriving from the States, and unattached airmen already on the island. Units for Quesada's IX Fighter Command began arriving from the States in November 1943 at the rate of one or two a week. Thanks to prior planning and Quesada's energy, most of these fighters were flying missions within three days of their arrival. By December he had built his command to two wings, each with four eighty-plane groups of P–38s, P–47s, and the newly introduced P–51 Mustangs. One of these outfits was a reconnaissance group. At the end of February, the command had grown to four wings of nine groups. To get ready to support the two American armies, the First and the Third, after the landings, Quesada's fighter command, swollen to eighteen groups by May, was split into two tactical air commands, the IX Tactical Air Command (TAC), which Quesada commanded directly, and the XIX TAC, led by Brig. Gen. O. P. Weyland. Quesada was dual-hatted, commanding both the parent IX Fighter Command and one of its two tactical air commands. All told he was responsible for more than 1,500 fighter planes.

Brig. Gen. O. P. Weyland, (left) XIX TAC Commander, discusses plans with IX TAC Commander Maj. Gen. Elwood Quesada

Integrating and training the new fighter groups was hectic. Months of training were compressed into weeks as the fighter command prepared for the invasion. Quesada was determined to indoctrinate his incoming flyers with the interdiction techniques he had witnessed in Africa. He brought generals and other specialists who had flown in the African campaign to lecture to the aviators. He sent officers to Italy to observe the methods of cooperating with the ground forces being used by the tactical planes of the AAF's Twelfth Air Force, and then brought them back to assist his training program. Reflecting his understanding of human nature, and to stimulate his flyers' interest, Quesada labeled these activities "combat drill," rather than the unpopular "training." He set up bombing courses and ran the pilots through drills in dive and glide bombing, low-level attacks, night flying, low-level navigation, patrol convoys, and smoke laying. As part of his program to convert fighters into fighter-bombers, he directed his pilots on practice missions against bridges, locomotives, trucks, and tanks at the British Millfield School training center. He even devised a means of hanging a pair of 1,000-pound bombs on his P–47s. Unhappy with the second-class status accorded reconnaissance in Africa, and deeming his one reconnaissance group insufficient for such a large command, he insisted that his fighter pilots become proficient in reconnaissance. Little joint training with the ground forces took place, however. The prewar attitude that close air support of ground forces was not a priority air mission still prevailed among flyers at all levels.

Improvisation abounded. Quesada, sensitive from his African experience to the critical importance of communications for such a wide-ranging operation, helped to devise a telephone system that was to prove invaluable after the invasion. One day a young draftee who had been an AT&T technician before the war demonstrated for him an FM transmitter and receiver he had bought in a surplus store in New York City. America's conversion from AM to FM had been halted at the outset of the war, and much of the unused equipment had been sold as surplus. Quesada checked out the equipment by setting up the transmitter at his headquarters at Middle Wallop and the receiver at Land's End, the same distance from his headquarters as was Normandy. The excellent static-free reception convinced him to take some sets with him to the continent. Producing $600 from his pocket, he sent the technician back to New York to find as many sets as he could and bring them back to England. The equipment was loaded on a landing craft and used on D-day.

While touring an early-warning radar site in southern England, Quesada put his air defense experience to good use. The radar sets were being used defensively to detect enemy planes. As he was looking at the screen at one of the sites, a series of blips appeared over Brest. Since the normal flight path of returning American bombers was over Dover, it had been assumed that the radar blips were German planes. At the same time conversations could be heard from a radio receiver elsewhere in the room between the crews of an American bomber force that was lost. Quesada had the operators install the right crystals to talk to the Americans. When he told the pilots to turn right, the images on the screen followed his instructions. He realized immediately that this defensive equipment could serve an offensive purpose. By connecting a Norden bombsight, upside down and backwards, to the radar, he helped create a ground control system his fighters later used to great advantage on the continent during bad weather. This same principle was later used by the Strategic Air Command to score practice bombing missions, and in Vietnam to control fighter and bomber strikes.

These "combat drills" were sandwiched in between operational missions. The fighters of the Ninth flew their first missions early in December 1943, escorting the bombers of the Eighth and Ninth Air Forces over France and the Low Countries. In midmonth, P–51s, with Quesada flying one of them, set a distance record escorting B–17s to Kiel, a round-trip distance of almost a thousand miles. On many of these missions, however, the Mustangs developed firing problems. The planes' guns started jamming after sharp turns, leaving the pilots at a disadvantage against German fighters. Quesada knew instinctively that these hundreds of young, untested aviators would fly better if they trusted their leaders to solve their problems. After examining the post-strike photography, he drove over to Brereton's headquarters where he complained vociferously about the malfunctioning guns "his kids" had to use. Brereton's response was to put in a call to General Arnold. When the chief came on the phone, Brereton handed the instrument to Quesada saying, "Alright, Pete, tell him what you told me." Never one to back away from a challenge, Quesada told Arnold about the mess and how his pilots deserved better. Arnold promised over the phone that he would have it cleared up. That night a group of technicians was on its way from Wright Field, and within days the problem was solved.

Attacking problems head-on became a Quesada hallmark. When the Mustangs experienced a rash of problems with fouled spark plugs on return trips from escort missions, many pilots were forced to ditch in the North Sea. Some were lost because, in the excitement of their preflight check, they had failed to hook their dinghies onto their flight suits. While setting technicians to solve the spark plug problem, Quesada also took immediate steps to make the crew chiefs responsible, through written statements, to see that the dinghies were attached to the pilots' harnesses before takeoffs.

In December 1943, Quesada's fighters became part of the combined British-American tactical air force, the Allied Expeditionary Air Force, commanded by Air Marshal Sir Trafford Leigh-Mallory. Originally Quesada was supposed to get all the Mustangs while Eighth Air Force got the P–38s and P–47s. When the longer-range Mustangs proved to be better air-to-air fighters,

Eaker, then commanding the Eighth, implored Brereton to let some of them come to his command. Quesada, knowing that the Thunderbolts and Lightnings were better for interdiction and close air support missions, persuaded Brereton to let some of them go.

The primary mission of Quesada's planes was to help gain control of the air over France before the invasion by defeating the German Air Force. Until April 1944 they did this, in between training, by escorting the bombers, and by tempting German fighters into the air and destroying them. As a second priority the fighters hit installations along the French coast that the Germans were building to launch their buzz bombs. Direct attacks on airfields and industrial complexes were last on the list. By March, many of the pilots were becoming impatient with escorting bombers and anxious to fly more interdiction missions. The following month, for the first time, the number of dive-bomber missions outnumbered escort flights.

During these preinvasion months, Quesada flew along with his pilots. While no law prevented a general from flying, it was frowned upon. But Quesada insisted that he had to know what was going on and that he could make better decisions based on experience than on operational reports. He adopted the attitude that if others could go he should be allowed to, especially since he was "just as expendable and damn near as young" as his pilots. Also, he conceded, he "didn't want those little jerks to think I couldn't fly as well as they could." His only hesitation stemmed from concern that the other pilots would feel they might have to devote a lot of attention to protecting "the old man."

Maj. Gen. Quesada seated in the cockpit of a Lockheed P-38.

By April the Ninth began to move away from escorting bombers to the priority missions of tactical aircraft—gaining control of the air and isolating the battlefield. Units moved into Hampshire along the southern coast, and Quesada shifted his headquarters to the western edge of London at Uxbridge. Hundreds of daily flights, in concert with the bombers, wiped out the German airfields in France and bombed railway centers, marshaling yards, bridges, rolling stock, and coastal batteries. This phase of the campaign was aimed at weakening the enemy to the point where he would be unable to match the Allied rate of buildup around the beachhead once the invasion took place. To mask the landing site, the Ninth Air Force divided its efforts between the Cherbourg Peninsula and the Pas-de-Calais area, 160 miles to the north, where the enemy was expecting the invasion.

At a meeting of the top Allied military commanders several days before D-day, all eyes turned toward Quesada when he predicted that the landing would go unopposed by the German Air Force. "How can you be sure?" asked Churchill, who was presiding. The uninhibited general responded confidently that Allied fighters had met decreasing resistance from German planes over the past six weeks, that control of the air was an established fact, and that it would stay that way.

This intuition proved correct when only 750 German planes took to the air on D-day, most of them far from the beachhead. The landing went smoothly with Quesada's fighters covering the beaches, escorting sea and air convoys, and hitting coastal batteries, enemy troops, and bridges behind the landing sites. Only on Omaha Beach was the landing stalled. By shifting several of his groups from air-to-air missions to a full day of strikes against German artillery, he helped to remove the obstacle.

Leaving his XIX Tactical Air Command behind in England to prepare under Weyland for its later action with Patton's Third Army, Quesada flew his P-38 to France the following day, landing "with one wing over a cliff." Near the beachhead he set up his command post alongside that of Gen. Omar Bradley, with whose First Army he would be working.

Communication equipment and control radars were quickly installed, and the engineers began building a dozen airfields so the fighters could move over from England. By the end of June, nine of the fields were in use, and seven groups of fighters had moved over permanently from the island. Several days after the landing, General Eisenhower arrived at the command post for a visit. When he was ready to return to England he asked Bradley to radio ahead his arrival time. Quesada offered instead to call by radio telephone, and within minutes the supreme commander was talking to his headquarters in England over Quesada's static-free hook-up. Eisenhower was surprised to learn of Quesada's superb communications which surpassed those of the ground forces.

Right: Maj. Gen. Quesada (center) and Col. Ray J. Stecker, (right) commander of first fighter-bomber group based in Germany, attend ceremony in which aviation engineers complete first allied airstrip in Germany; *below*: Maj. Gen. Quesada talks to Thunderbolt pilots of the Ninth Air Force.

Several weeks later, during a subsequent visit, Eisenhower expressed interest in accompanying Quesada on a fighter mission he was planning to fly over Paris. The Germans had moved a large number of airplanes into ten fields around the French capital, and Quesada agreed to take the commander along to have a look. At the short, unfinished airfield, which had steel planking for a runway, Eisenhower climbed into a makeshift back seat of a P-51 from which the 70-gallon fuel tank had been removed. With Quesada at the controls, they took off and linked up with the other planes of the flight. Quesada prudently decided against going to Paris, and they flew instead over the battlefield about fifty miles south of the field. Eisenhower was full of questions and impressed with the formation flying, breakaways, and the communications. Landing back at the field, they were spattered with mud, evoking from Eisenhower the comment that his friends had misinformed him by telling him that airmen lived in hotels. Although this excursion brought down on Eisenhower a strong rebuke from Marshall, and Spaatz slapped Quesada's wrist, the IX TAC Commander felt it was worthwhile in cementing relations and giving Eisenhower firsthand experience with the air forces.

Except during the capture of the city of Cherbourg late in June, Quesada's fighters concentrated until late July on interdiction missions. Close air support was not entirely absent, however. The Normandy countryside proved a surprise for both Bradley and Quesada. High hedges that separated the numerous fields provided a natural defense for the Germans, making it more necessary than anticipated for the fighters to strike close to the American lines. But basically the American infantry fought its way down the peninsula while the fighters struck targets outside their view. One job for the fighters was to make it as difficult as possible for the German divisions, which had been poised around Calais, to move westward when they realized that the only landing was to be in Normandy. Quesada's planes, along with the Royal Air Force, hit these troops day after day, and they arrived in Normandy not as unified divisions but as disorganized mobs of tanks. On one occasion, learning of a possible meeting between Rommel and some high German officials, Quesada led a flight of P-38s and destroyed a number of vehicles and buildings at the suspected site. The results were never learned.

When the fighting reached the base of the Cherbourg peninsula and the Allied troops encountered stiff German resistance around St. Lô, this situation began to change. Flying back to England, Quesada and Bradley conferred with Spaatz, Leigh-Mallory, and Doolittle in planning a carpet bombing strike against the enemy to soften them up for the American attack. Back in Normandy a few days before the attack, Quesada suggested to Bradley that the tanks could best exploit the paralysis caused by the bombing if they concentrated their attack into several columns rather than across a broad front. Bradley agreed, and Quesada promised to keep a continuous cover of fighters

194

over the head of each column to warn the tank commanders of hidden enemy forces and to respond to their calls for assistance. He also told Bradley that if the Army would send a tank over to his headquarters he would install Air Force radios in it and, if the experiment worked, would assign pilots to the lead tanks to operate the radios and advise the ground commander what the airmen saw. In this way the pilots, trained to spot and describe targets as they would appear from the air, could talk in airmen's terms to their counterparts flying above. Bradley agreed and ordered his ordnance people to send a tank to IX TAC Headquarters. The soldiers thought the general had made a mistake and sent it, instead, to the 9th Infantry Division. Quesada, becoming impatient, called Bradley, who then had it sent to the correct place. When it arrived the Air Force guards would not let it in, seeing no need for a tank. The situation was cleared up, the radio installed, and the experiment worked. Quesada was in on the creation of an element of air control parties that would form the nerve center for later tactical air efforts in Korea and Vietnam.

The subsequent breakthrough at St. Lô was in many ways a turning point not only for tactical air doctrine but for Quesada as well. Having shared until then the flyer's almost universal aversion to working too closely with ground

Top-ranking officers touring American installations in Europe, l. to r.: Lt. Gen. Omar Bradley, Gen. Hap Arnold, Gen. Dwight Eisenhower, and Gen. George Marshall

troops, he underwent what was almost a battlefield conversion in coming to appreciate at close range the necessity of cooperation.

A large part of Quesada's success arose from the mutual understanding and confidence that had developed between him and Bradley. Suspicion between other ground and air commanders had not entirely evaporated and was kindled by inevitable mistakes on both sides: antiaircraft artillery occasionally shooting down American planes and the fighters at times inadvertently bombing friendly troops. The two generals worked together to dispel these antagonisms and to make their own commanders appreciate the conditions under which the others worked. At breakfast one morning, for instance, Bradley showed Quesada a message from V Corps complaining that a planned major offensive had been canceled the day before because of a heavy unintercepted German air attack. Enraged that he had not heard of it, Quesada checked with his operations officer only to learn that two German planes had flown over a regimental headquarters destroying one truck and injuring one man. Knowing that actions spoke louder than words with Bradley, Quesada persuaded him that the two of them should investigate the incident personally. Picking up the corps and division commanders on the way, the four generals confronted the regimental commander, who pointed to the charred remains of a truck and introduced them to the regimental cook who limped up with a shrapnel wound in his rump. Quesada then pulled from his pocket a list he had compiled earlier and read off the Allied air action of the previous day—1,000 bombers had dumped 4,000 tons on Germany, and on the way home 600 fighters had straffed everything in sight. "But our whole army," he concluded, "was stopped by two planes that dropped no bombs, set a half-track on fire, and shot a cook in the ass! If air power is as effective on the Germans as it seems to be on us, why aren't we in Berlin?" Bradley and Quesada rode home in silence. The following day the Army commander sent a strongly worded letter to all his commanders outlining the incident and telling them that they must be prepared for an occasional air attack. Bradley was aware that Quesada had staged the inspection, and Quesada knew that what he had done was a better way of getting his point across than simply telling his counterpart.

Quesada's intimate working relationship with the Army, however, was not without its price. He was criticized by some airmen who felt that his support of the infantry was abetting those who thought the Army should have its own air force. Quesada waved such objections aside. He was where the fighting was, and his job was to help in any way he could. He couldn't "just sit there and say 'Hell, no!' "

On the march to Avranches, which fell near the end of July, tanks and planes cooperated in numerous ways. On one occasion a Sherman tank, surrounded by thirteen Tigers, was saved when a squadron of P-47s scattered the enemy's vehicles. Often the Thunderbolts, in response to Army appeals, cleared roads of enemy tanks lying in ambush. Once, when the radios went dead, the tanks shelled a railway station as a signal for the dive-bombers to attack the station. At another time the tanks used their tracer bullets to mark targets for Quesada's fighters.

The airplanes of IX TAC were tied to the fast-moving army by Quesada's fighter control radar. Set up in tents and constantly moved eastward to keep pace with the ground forces, the radar scanned the entire battlefield and directed the fighters as they flew between 1,300 and 1,800 sorties each day. When the planes flew cover for the tanks, the control tent turned direction of them over to the pilot in the lead tank of each column.

It was the First Army, now under the command of Gen. Courtney Hodges, that received the initial jolt of the German counteroffensive in the Ardennes shortly before Christmas. From his headquarters at Verviers, just north of this Battle of the Bulge, Quesada directed his fighters, and those of the British 2d Tactical Air Force which Coningham had turned over to him, against the advancing German tank columns. Bad weather hampered operations at first. On the 18th, as the Germans moved through a total ground fog, Quesada asked for volunteers from the reconnaissance group to fly through the mist and check on the German advance. Two Mustangs, flying through the fog a hundred feet off the ground, discovered sixty tanks and armored vehicles moving toward Stavelot. Ninth fighter bombers spent the rest of the day destroying most of them. After the weather cleared on the 23d, Quesada's fighters, along with those of Weyland's XIX TAC, helped to halt the Germans by cratering and cutting rail and road lines, blocking choke-points and narrow passes, and destroying many tanks and vehicles.

None of Quesada's bases were overrun during the German counterof-fensive, although at one point ground attacks against some of them appeared imminent. To prepare for the expected assault Quesada ordered the antiair-craft artillery moved out onto the nearby roads and pointed horizontally down the route along which the enemy was expected. The tanks never appeared. The Germans seldom hit the fields from the air. One exception occurred, however, on the first day of 1945. As a companion to their ground attack, the Germans planned a massive strike against Allied airfields by an armada of Luftwaffe planes. Alerted to the enemy's intention by the Ultra system, which was reading German code traffic, Quesada ordered pilots stationed at the antiaircraft positions to identify the planes for the gunners. When the attacks came, not one Allied plane was lost.

Quesada's converted radar sets came into their own during the Battle of the Bulge. Pilots flying over the snow-covered terrain were having trouble distinguishing enemy tanks and vehicles from friendly ones. Quesada moved two of the radars close to the action, and the radar operators, who knew where the front line was, advised the pilots when to strike and when to hold their fire. The radar operators knew better than the pilots whether they were or were not on the German side of the line. At the same time the Ninth's long-range radars were instrumental in guiding dozens of stricken B–17s, returning from bombing runs over Germany, safely onto local airfields.

Having eliminated the German salient, the Allied armies pushed on to the Rhine at Cologne. The biggest obstacle in their way, the city of Duren, was heavily bombed by RAF and Eighth Air Force bombers and Quesada's fighter bombers. When the advance ground units discovered the bridge at Remagen intact, Quesada assigned his fighters to fly patrols over it for four days to ward off any German attempts to destroy it as Allied soldiers streamed across. He stationed one of his ground controllers high up on the bridge to direct the air battle if one developed over the structure. Neither of these actions, however, proved necessary.

Once across the Rhine, Quesada's planes assisted the American armies in trapping more than 100,000 German soldiers around Paderborn. Discovering a hornet's nest of German airfields there, his fighters destroyed hundreds of Nazi planes, including jets. For all practical purposes the German Army was defeated, and the Allies met little further resistance during their subsequent march to the Elbe.

Throughout the sweep across France, the Low Countries, and Germany, Quesada earned a reputation for dash, imagination, and above all, leadership. Sensitive to the concerns of his men and of their parents, relatives, and well-wishers back home and in England, he kept up a voluminous correspondence with them, allaying their fears and keeping them abreast of the war's progress. In a letter to Quesada's mother, his aide noted that the general had become a "star" and a hero to many concerned with America's success. "Quesada was a peach to work with," wrote Bradley to Arnold in September, "because he was not only willing to try everything that would help us, but he inspired his whole command with this desire."

*   *   *   *   *

With the surrender of Germany accomplished and the defeat of Japan assured, AAF leaders resumed their prewar campaign for a separate air force. Newly elected President Harry Truman was known to favor a reorganization of the military structure. In an attempt to gain direct access to him, Spaatz and Arnold tried to have Quesada assigned as his military aide. The general returned to the States in April, shortly after Roosevelt's death, but Truman bluntly refused.* Quesada, instead, became the chief intelligence officer of the Army Air Forces, "an administrative job that just bored the hell out of me. " After Japan capitulated later in the year, Quesada, still in the new Pentagon, became part of an informal group including Spaatz, Eaker, Fred Anderson, Lauris Norstad, and Hoyt Vandenberg, which set out to sell the idea of a separate air force. While negotiations with the Navy took place at the Secretary's level, this group worked to persuade senators and the Army of the soundness of the plan. Quesada's role was to convince the Army, specifically Eisenhower and Bradley, and Senator Leverett Saltonstall, the Chairman of the Armed Services Committee, that the Army did not need its own tactical air force. Principally through his wartime relationship with them, Quesada persuaded the Army generals that the air force knew better how to use its airplanes and that the flexibility air power had demonstrated so successfully in the war would be maintained by a separate air force. At one point, with Quesada present, Spaatz promised Eisenhower that if Eisenhower supported separation, the Air Force would always meet its commitment to the Army by providing permanent and strong tactical air forces. In part as a result of this promise, Eisenhower and Bradley were won over.

When it appeared that separation was assured the following March, Quesada took over the Third Air Force in Tampa, Florida. At the same time the postwar Army Air Forces was divided into three separate but unequal branches: Strategic Air Command, Air Defense Command, and Tactical Air Command. Two months later, Quesada started building the Tactical Air Command combining his Third Air Force, the old Ninth and Twelfth Air Forces, and the wartime IX Troop Carrier Command. The wartime arrangement whereby numbered air forces were made up of commands was reversed, and commands were now composed of numbered air forces. The new Tactical Air Command's mission was to be prepared to participate in joint operations with the Army and Navy and to perform interdiction operations on its own.

Quesada approached his new job with the conviction that the best way to keep the tactical air mission from falling back under the Army was to provide such outstanding support that the Army would be totally satisfied and forget about having its own air force. In this he was fully supported by his Plans and Operations officer, Col. William Momyer. In May, Quesada transferred his headquarters to Langley Field and in October was joined next door at Fort Monroe by Gen. Jacob L. Devers and his Army Ground Forces Headquarters. At that time Quesada received his third star. The two commanders set about to institutionalize their wartime experiences in air-ground cooperation.

---

*He had a military aide—an Army ground officer.

Quesada's attempt to build a combat arm was hampered at first by the need to offset the rapid postwar demobilization with a vigorous recruiting program. On top of this, Truman embarked on a severe budget-cutting program that forced the AAF to lower its plans for expansion from seventy to fifty-five groups of airplanes. By year's end TAC manpower had dwindled drastically. Its three numbered Air Forces were cut to two with inactivation of the Third Air Force. The number of troop carrier wings that had been planned was reduced and several airfields closed. In a country weary of war, the AAF was experiencing difficulty attracting good people into the aviation cadet program.

Undaunted, Quesada pressed on with establishing the command. In November 1946, he introduced the first jet plane, the P-80, as a successful fighter-bomber for close air support. By August 1948, he had integrated the first F–84s into Tactical Air Command. Throughout 1947 and 1948, he and Devers experimented with joint training. The Army wanted to split the planes up into small groups to work directly with individual ground units. Quesada, ever mindful of the flexibility that had served him so well during the war, convinced first Devers and then Spaatz that the tactical airplanes should remain centrally managed by him. Late in 1947, the Twelfth Air Force practiced supporting amphibious landings off the coast of Florida and trained

Lockheed F-80 (redesignated from P-80)

Newsbureau, Lockheed-California Company

Republic F–84 Thunderstreak (formerly P–84)

with the 2d Infantry Division in Alaska. At the same time, the Ninth Air Force dropped airborne soldiers of the 82d Airborne Division in New York State. The following March, the Twelfth Air Force worked with Army ski troops in the mountains of Colorado, and during May provided column cover to the tanks of the 2d Armored Division in Texas. Quesada's wartime experiences were finally being translated into doctrine and practice.

The starkest illustration of Quesada's theories of air-ground cooperation was a week-long exercise, called Operation Combine, in which all fighter, reconnaissance, and troop carrier squadrons, several units of the Strategic Air Command, and elements of the 82d Airborne Division demonstrated the awesome power of combined arms. The Ninth Air Force put on this demonstration each year at each of the eight Army Ground Forces schools. Along with this training in close air support, the Ninth Air Force practiced interdiction by repelling a hypothetical invasion of the Carolina coast. By means of these exercises Quesada was honing not only the airmen but also tactical air doctrine that had flowed from World War II. By 1948 the command had 300 fighters, half of them jets; 63 medium bombers; 100 reconnaissance planes, also half jets; 237 airlift planes; and 80 liaison aircraft. During the summer Quesada sent several thousand traffic controllers and maintenance specialists to Europe to help break the Soviet ground blockade of Berlin.

Commanding General of the Ninth Air Force, Maj. Gen. William D. Old (left), with Lt. Gen. Quesada at Operation Combine III

While Quesada battled with elements in both the newly created Air Force, and the Army, which wanted to create its own tactical air arm, worldwide developments were conspiring against his efforts. Since he took over the command in May 1947, the Cold War had set in. That very month Hungary had installed a Communist government, followed in June by the announcement of the Marshall Plan. Early in 1948, Czechoslovakia followed Hungary, and in the summer the Soviets tried to cut off Berlin from the Allies. In June, Hoyt Vandenberg replaced Spaatz as Air Force Chief of Staff. The emphasis on strategic preparedness and deterrence, which had been instrumental in creating the separate Air Force, assumed even greater significance. In the fall of 1948, Quesada was called to Washington and informed by Vandenberg that he was going to reorganize the Air Force's operational commands. The Strategic Air Command would be strengthened while the Tactical Air and Air Defense Commands would be reduced to headquarters and placed under a new Continental Air Command. Quesada objected, reminding the chief of the promise to Eisenhower that there would always be a tactical force to support the Army. Vandenberg, disagreeing with Quesada's philosophy that the best way to keep tactical air out of Army hands was to make it indispensable while under the Air Force, and viewing Quesada's attempts at cooperation as a pathway to Army domination, went ahead with the plan. Spaatz, now retired, was furious. Quesada, "personally offended" at what he considered a violation of trust, turned down an offer to head the new Continental Air Command. Instead, he went to the Pentagon to help draft legislation aimed at nationalizing the Air National Guard, an assignment he later characterized as "very unpleasant, disagreeable, and unsuccessful."

In 1949, Quesada's diplomatic skill was again called upon as he headed the nation's first hydrogen bomb test at Eniwetok Atoll in the Pacific.

Working for both the Atomic Energy Commission and the Defense Department, he first weeded out from amidst hundreds of supplicants the experiments to be included. He then commanded the test, which involved building the site, installing the equipment, negotiating with scientists from Robert Oppenheimer to Edward Teller, and seeing to the smooth running of the project. The test was a success in large part due to Quesada's skill in organizing and mollifying.

Amidst a swirl of media reports that he was "resigning in protest" over the treatment of tactical air power, Quesada retired in 1951. If disillusionment and disappointment over the broken promise to Eisenhower did not cause this decision, they at least accompanied it. Having been married four years earlier to Kate Davis Pulitzer, daughter of St. Louis publisher Joseph Pulitzer, and by then the father of a young son, he felt impelled to embark on a civilian career. His technical and managerial abilities resulted in successful stints as a manager at Olin Industries, organizer and director of Lockheed's Missile System Division, special assistant to President Eisenhower, administrator of the Federal Aviation Administration, part owner of the Washington Senators baseball team, and president of L'Enfant Properties in his native Washington, D.C.

Quesada continued his crusade for stronger interservice cooperation after his retirement. In an article in *Colliers* magazine in 1956, he became the first in a line of critics, including one later Chairman of the Joint Chiefs of Staff, to recommend publicly stronger unification of the services and reorganization of the Joint Chiefs. In particular he proposed, as have others since, that the Joint Chiefs no longer remain heads of their individual services when entering the joint arena.

The Tactical Air Command was revived during the Korean conflict and strengthened during the 1960s as the nation shifted to a military strategy of flexible response and fought the war in Vietnam. Both the doctrine and tactics of America's reborn strong tactical air arm mirrored Quesada's accomplishments in World War II and in his postwar creation of the command. The Air Force acknowledges the debt it owes to this pioneer. Its pantheon of "senior statesmen" who meet each year with the Air Force Chief of Staff is composed basically of retired four-star generals—Ira Eaker, Jimmy Doolittle, and Elwood "Pete" Quesada.

Sources

General Quesada's papers reside principally at two locations: the Manuscripts Division of the Library of Congress in Washington D.C., and the Dwight D. Eisenhower Library in Abilene, Kansas. The former collection contains correspondence and official records relating to World War II. The majority of the papers at the Eisenhower Library deal with Quesada's post-military career in civilian aviation. A relatively small number of military papers there consist of the general's wartime correspondence with the families of airmen and of documents concerning his tenure as Commander of the Tactical Air Command. A limited number of speeches and interviews can be found at the USAF Historical Research Center at Maxwell AFB, Alabama.

Four oral history interviews with the general are extant. One done in 1960 for the *American Heritage* journal and another with the Office of Air Force History in 1975 include many details of both his military and civilian careers. A third interview, with the author in 1982, confines itself to his military years. Finally, the Office of Air Force History has published a group interview, *Air Superiority in World War II and Korea* (Office of Air Force History/GPO, 1983), in which Quesada discusses the question of air superiority with three former colleagues in the Tactical Air Command, Generals William W. Momyer, Robert M. Lee, and James Ferguson.

Quesada's views on air-ground and interservice cooperation are summarized in several presentations he made to a group of Air Force and Army officers in 1947 and 1948 and in a *Colliers* magazine article published in 1956 titled "Peace at the Pentagon."

Several official histories of the Ninth Air Force's operations in Europe in 1944 exist at Maxwell AFB and in the Office of Air Force History in Washington, D.C. These repositories also contain histories of the Tactical Air Command and of many of the fighter groups which Quesada led in World War II.

General Quesada makes cameo appearances in many of the memoirs by American military leaders of World War II, including Eisenhower, Bradley, and Arnold. He is also treated briefly in such secondary works as Kenn C. Rust's *The 9th Air Force in World War II* (Aero Publishers, 1967); Kent Roberts Greenfield's *American Strategy in World War II: A Reconsideration* (John Hopkins Press, 1963); Russell F. Weigley's *Eisenhower's Lieutenants* (University of Indiana Press, 1981); and DeWitt S. Copp's *A Few Great Captains* and *Forged in Fire* (Doubleday, 1980 and 1982).

9

Hoyt S. Vandenberg:
Building the New Air Force

Noel F. Parrish

When he reached the summit of his career, Hoyt Sanford Vandenberg, Sr. was considered by some to be young and inexperienced. His youthful appearance and athletic manner shadowed his middle-aged status through the early 1950s. A Washington newspaper described the new Air Force Chief of Staff as "the most impossibly handsome man on the entire Washington scene."

Vandenberg was born in Milwaukee, Wisconsin, on January 24, 1899, a descendent of early Dutch settlers in New York. His father, William Collins Vandenberg, was a successful businessman. Hoyt was educated in the best schools, where he developed his interest in sports, including golf, tennis, and polo. He also had an opportunity to observe the workings of politics and statesmanship in the busy life of his famous and influential uncle, Senator Arthur H. Vandenberg of Michigan.

Young Vandenberg developed his talents as an Eagle Scout, at military prep school, and in the highly competitive life of a cadet at the U.S. Military Academy. His grades at West Point were very low, but he gained what he had most wanted all along—assignment to the Air Service. At that time, the ability of West Point graduates to complete flying training was disappointing. This was especially true of those who had high grades at the Academy. At least, there was some comfort for frustrated aspirants to pilotry in their belief that foot soldiers are more intelligent than airmen.

General Parrish was special assistant to General Vandenberg during his subject's tour as Chief of Staff of the Air Force from April 1948 to June 1953.

205

Graduating in 1923 in the bottom tenth of his West Point class "did not indicate brilliance," but his record in the Advanced Flying School at Kelly Field, Texas, which had its own ground school, disclosed latent talents both in the air and in the classroom. In the same year he earned wings, 1925, Vandenberg married Gladys Rose of Tuxedo, New York, whom he had met at a West Point dance. Their family included a daughter, Gloria Rose, and a son, Hoyt Sanford Vandenberg, Jr., who became a distinguished Air Force major general.

Ironically, Gen. Carl Spaatz, whose West Point grades were highest among several Air Force chiefs, was the principal sponsor for Vandenberg, whose grades were the lowest. General Spaatz did not consider scholastic achievement a major indicator of future performance, even though the *Newsweek* column he wrote after retirement established him as the most successful author among all the Air Force chiefs.

After earning his pilot wings, Vandenberg moved upward not only in responsible assignments, but also through the Army's most advanced schools. Following three years with the 3d Attack Group at Kelly Field, the young lieutenant was selected to instruct at March Field, California. The Air Service had recently become the Air Corps, and there was a slight expansion. Two years of training other young pilots led to his assignment in 1929 to the 6th Pursuit Squadron at Schofield Barracks, Hawaii. Within six months he became squadron commander.

Back in the States in September 1931, the thirty-two-year-old first lieutenant arrived at the brand new school for Air Corps Flying Cadets at Randolph Field, Texas, where he became a flight commander. (The author arrived at Randolph at the same time, but as an inexperienced Flying Cadet, otherwise known as a "dodo.") In 1934, Vandenberg completed a total of five years as an instructor in all types of Air Corps planes, an experience he valued highly as a study of combined human, aerial, and mechanical behavior.

By 1934, Vandenberg was more than ready for studies on the uses of aircraft in war. On graduation from the small Air Corps Tactical School at Maxwell Field, Alabama, he entered the Command and General Staff School at Fort Leavenworth, Kansas, graduating in June 1936. Now a captain, his work at Leavenworth was followed by two years on the Air Corps Tactical School faculty. After years of argument between the Air Corps and the other combat arms, there now was a growing disagreement on the proper use of air power within the Air Corps itself. A few intellectually inclined airmen tried at Maxwell Field to reach an agreement on air doctrine and strategy.

The low-profile role of Vandenberg at the Tactical School is well explained by Brig. Gen. Jon Reynolds in his thorough account of Vandenberg's life before the onset of World World II. Vandenberg was able to serve as a much-needed moderator between those who demanded more big bombers and others who

Gen. Hoyt S. Vandenberg

preferred many more little pursuit planes. He avoided becoming emotional while discussing theories. For this, and perhaps other reasons, he was selected to attend the Army's most advanced school, the Army War College. Thus, when he graduated from the War College in 1939, he had completed almost a decade of steadily advancing military studies.

During the next three years, Vandenberg was moved through increasingly important staffs. From Gen. Henry H. Arnold's Office of the Chief of Air Corps, he was assigned to Air Staff Plans when the Air Corps became the Army Air Forces (AAF) in June 1941, and was authorized its own staff. Then, as Air Staff A–3 (Operations and Training), he supervised the AAF's expansion program in the months after Pearl Harbor. In mid–1942, he was assigned to Gen. Dwight D. Eisenhower's staff in England, to develop air plans for the North African operation. This early war planning earned him the Distinguished Service Medal for "exceptional ability, energy, judgment and brilliant professional knowledge."

Later in the same year, the fast-moving Colonel Vandenberg became Chief of Staff of the Twelfth Air Force under Brig. Gen. James H. Doolittle and was responsible for organizing that complex command. The North Africa-based Twelfth included fighters, bombers, air support units under ground commanders, a troop carrier wing, and service commands. It was an evolutionary step toward a European command with its own air forces to fight its own air war. Vandenberg again was decorated, and soon entered the war in person.

In November 1942, the bomber and fighter planes began their struggle against a far more experienced Luftwaffe, at considerable cost to both sides and especially to German bases. Vandenberg was said to "sneak off on combat missions" more often than Doolittle felt his irreplaceable chief of staff should. But he always returned with proposals to change techniques, air discipline, and tactics, all of which improved results immeasurably.

After sorties over Pantelleria, Sicily, and Italy, Vandenberg had become a brigadier general and chief of strategic forces under Lt. Gen. Carl Spaatz, Commander of the Northwest African Air Forces. At the close of this campaign, Vandenberg was credited with planning and supervising the interdiction operations intercepting German men and supplies coming to Tunisia, operations that caused the sudden German retreat across the Mediterranean. In August 1943, he was brought back to AAF Headquarters in Washington, spent four months in Moscow as head of the Air Mission to Russia under Ambassador W. Averell Harriman, then was sent to General Eisenhower's Supreme Headquarters in London as Deputy Commander of the Allied Expeditionary Air Forces. He was praised by the British as "outstanding in his tactical planning."

*   *   *   *   *

In August 1944, two months after the Allied landings in Normandy, General Eisenhower selected Vandenberg, who had been Vice Commander of the tactical Ninth Air Force, to replace Lt. Gen. Lewis Brereton as its Commander. The functions of the Ninth were almost unlimited as the Allied armies moved across France into Germany. The Ninth's task, along with the Royal Air Force 2d Tactical Air Force, was to soften the enemy's defenses, destroy his vehicles and supplies, and block or weaken all his efforts.

While the more famous Eighth Air Force suffered heavy losses from enemy planes and high-altitude flak, the fighter planes and pilots of the Ninth were under constant fire as they dive-bombed and strafed enemy forces and equipment, and occasionally met German fighters in the air. At medium and low altitudes, the Ninth's bombers and more numerous fighters were always in range of enemy antiaircraft artillery and often of machineguns, rifles, and even pistols. Their direct support and interdiction operations saved many thousands of our fighting men on the ground. *Newsweek* reported in December 1944 that some groups of the Ninth had suffered almost fifty

Lt. Gen. Carl Spaatz (center) confers with other generals of his command in England, from l. to r.: Maj. Gen. Ralph Royce, Maj. Gen. Hoyt Vandenberg, and Maj. Gen. Hugh Knerr

percent casualties. Sometimes a squadron of twenty-five planes could operate only a third of that number, but this was not uncommon for low-altitude bombing and strafing.

Some critics, including a few top airmen, felt that the Ninth's forces, in English terms, "had got to working too closely with ground force commanders," giving them extra support at the expense of more important, and less costly, missions far behind the enemy front. That may have been true in principle, but not in the current situation. The Allies' advance into Germany was threatened with delay or failure because of the heavy losses of our fighting men on the ground. The Army's most prestigious planner, Gen. George C. Marshall, had to rely on our tactical air forces and the toll of German force taken on the Eastern Front by seemingly inexhaustible Russian infantry. Most Allied military leaders approved enthusiastically when Vandenberg's Ninth covered the drive of Gen. George Patton's Third Army, especially when reduced losses on the ground more than repaid increased losses in the air. Patton said, "I make the German armies move so fast they have to use the roads, and the Ninth bombs and strafes them off the roads."

In April 1945 Vandenberg earned his third star. In May the war in Europe

209

was over. The Ninth had launched almost 400,000 sorties in 19 months. About 5,000 of its men were killed, wounded, or missing; they claimed more than 4,000 German planes destroyed in the air and on the ground, plus more than 3,000 "probables." The Ninth had lost fewer than 3,000 planes, mostly fighters, largely to German antiaircraft fire. Other destruction imposed upon the enemy included nearly 100,000 motor and horse-drawn vehicles, some 65,000 railroad cars and engines plus uncounted thousands in railroad yards, more than 6,000 tanks and armored vehicles, and 17,000 gun positions. Reporters from Eastern Europe wrote after the German surrender: "The Ninth's Commander, a brilliant but little-known flier and planner, was Lt. Gen. Hoyt S. Vandenberg. He is called 'one of the chief architects of the system of air and ground cooperation.' "

*   *   *   *   *

Immediately after the German surrender, Vandenberg was ordered to the Pentagon again. In July, he became Assistant Chief of Staff for Operations of the Army Air Forces. Permanent military rank became very important in the postwar period, and in October 1945, President Truman nominated three relatively young air officers for permanent brigadier generalcies. Legislation was required because they lacked the years of service that the law specified. The three officers were Lt. Gen. Vandenberg and Maj. Gens. Curtis E. LeMay and Lauris Norstad. The two major generals were colleagues of Vandenberg before, during, and after the heavy action in both Europe and the Pacific. In less than three years, Vandenberg would appoint Norstad to be his deputy for operations, and LeMay to command the Strategic Air Command. It was typical of Vandenberg's leadership style for him to select as his most important assistants two men of almost opposite characteristics, one a positive activist and the other a brilliant intellectual, for very different responsibilities. He could understand both.

After six months of service as deputy for operations, Vandenberg served for six months as chief of the intelligence division of the War Department General Staff. Next, he was named director of the Central Intelligence Group, which later became the Central Intelligence Agency. After fifteen months he returned to the Pentagon and rejoined Gen. Carl Spaatz, Commander of the Army Air Forces, as that general's deputy commander and chief of staff. When the Navy gave way to compromise and the Air Force became a separate service in September 1947, General Spaatz became the first Air Force Chief of Staff. Vandenberg immediately became Vice Chief of Staff and succeeded

General Spaatz as Chief when Spaatz retired in April 1948. Thus began a unique tenure as Air Force Chief of Staff for five full years, through the threatening Russian blockade of Berlin, the rapid Russian development of nuclear weaponry in addition to their huge army, and a three-year war in defense of South Korea.

After assuming his last office, Vandenberg was questioned by a congressional committee on the necessity of having so many officers in a much smaller postwar Air Force. He answered that in World War II, Air Force officer losses in Europe exceeded Infantry officer losses in that theater. The committee did not believe him until he produced statistics and reminded the committee that the air war over Europe began many months before our ground forces could become heavily involved. Such ignorance of Air Force history on Capitol Hill neither surprised nor irritated Vandenberg. He knew that several years would have to pass before Air Force veterans or associates would begin to populate congressional committees. He knew also that he would have to speak to the public in general, and to all military men in uniform, until they began to understand the unusual and often unique characteristics of an effective air force.

Even more important was the requirement for cooperation among the services. It was fortunate for all concerned that General "Tooey" Spaatz was willing to remain on duty as the first Chief of Staff of the new Air Force for seven months, despite his declining health. His compromises and cooperation with Army leaders and with President Truman had given him high prestige. Vandenberg appreciated his continuing advice and assistance, especially since General Arnold's illness had practically removed him from the scene. Although he was the first full-term Chief of Staff of the new Air Force, Vandenberg knew very well that he was not its founder. But he was destined to be the new service's basic builder.

The first task for the new Chief of Staff was to reorganize an Air Force that still was only partially detached from the Army. The Army had retained many support functions such as hospitals and chaplains "in order to save money." General Eisenhower, as Army Chief of Staff, had made some concessions, but his successor, Gen. Omar Bradley, held his ground. A new organization, applicable to an Air Force, would have to be approved by a Congress that was generally controlled by Army and Navy sympathizers, when those services seemed reduced in importance by the new and popular service. But this was only one of the problems.

The first dangerous Communist threat was the Berlin Blockade of 1948, countered by the airlift that stripped the Air Force of its transport capability elsewhere. This nightmare was followed soon by the Russian-supported attack against South Korea that may have been inspired by severe reductions of all American military forces. In just five disturbed years, Vandenberg had to

211

Chief Justice Fred Vinson administers oath of office to Gen. Hoyt S. Vandenberg, the new Air Force Chief of Staff as he replaces outgoing Chief Gen. Spaatz (center) in April 1948. Also present are Sec. of Defense James Forrestal (left) and Sec. of the Air Force Stuart Symington (far right).

establish a new internal organization, regulations, principles, and traditions, a process that had preoccupied Army, Navy, and Marine commanders periodically for a century and a half.

With his vice chiefs, first Gen. Muir Fairchild and then Gen. Nathan Twining, Vandenberg was responsible for balancing the efforts of five deputies and half a dozen major commanders. During a very rare comment on his own abilities, Vandenberg told the author, who was his special assistant, writer, and confidant, that he considered himself less intelligent than some of his accomplished subordinates. He explained that he was well satisfied just to keep their brilliance focused in the right direction. He had no desire to outshine any one of them.

In addition to a well-equipped and well-organized Air Force, Vandenberg was most concerned that it be well-educated and well-trained. While he had earned no distinction for himself as a West Point cadet, he recognized the value of his years at the Military Academy and determined to win an academy for the Air Force. It was not easy. The country was in the antimilitary period

that usually follows a war, and tax burdens remained heavy. The long fight
to establish an independent Air Force had been won by agreeing to forego
several institutions possessed by the Army and Navy, such as general hospitals
and academies. General Eisenhower, along with President Truman and other
influential citizens, declared that the Air Force should be satisfied with volun-
tary transfers of graduates from the Army and Navy academies. To
Vandenberg, this was gross discrimination that denied the Air Force the
benefits of education, training, and fellowship such as the other services had
long enjoyed. His first step was to win over his fellow West Point alumni,
which he accomplished by carefully worded and sincerely delivered arguments,
public and private. Among the alumni who finally supported an Air Force
academy was, of course, President Eisenhower.

Vandenberg's talent for negotiation and persuasion was severely tested
from the beginning of his long tenure as Air Force Chief. When originally
established as a so-called "independent" Air Force, some of the necessary
parts were lacking. The Air Force was basically an independent flying corps,
with the Army providing such supporting services as engineering, medicine,
and law. This was awkward for the Air Force, but Vandenberg wisely did not
press the issue.

After several months, Eisenhower's successor as Army Chief of Staff,
Gen. "Lightning Joe" Collins, changed his mind, advocating that future
budgets be divided more or less equally among the Army, Navy, and Air Force.
Collins wanted to apply more of his budget to his deficient combat forces.
There followed considerable negotiation as Army support organizations
yielded some personnel authorizations to the Air Force. The Army Medical
Corps Commander refused to sign his part of the agreement, so General Collins furloughed him until a deputy signed. All this was done without another
interservice squabble, because Vandenberg waited patiently while he prepared
for the new responsibilities.

Much more difficult and almost impossible to compromise was the
establishment of a legal organizational charter for the Air Force after it had
been operating without one for many months. Vandenberg wanted to follow
the plan of Generals Spaatz, Arnold, and others, to avoid a separate corps
within the Air Force, and thus escape internal frictions that had existed inside
the Army and Navy. This was not to be, at least in certain professional
specialities. Congressman Carl Vinson of Georgia, sometimes called "Mr.
Navy," supported the Army view and avoided legislation giving the Air Force
the organization it wanted. The Army corps organization was forcibly applied
to the Air Force; it was more difficult to recruit doctors, engineers, and such,
unless their professional prerogatives were established by a separate internal
organization. Vandenberg was reasonable on this matter, and was persuaded by his son-in-law, an Army veterinarian, that the Air Force needed

a veterinary corps for purposes much more important than treating pet poodles.

A more fundamental but equally forlorn hope was Vandenberg's effort to rid the Air Force from the arbitrary separation of its combat units into "tactical" and "strategic" forces. The distinction between the two was never clear, since at that time the strategic and tactical air forces both had bombers and fighters. Did it mean large and small planes, or long- and short-range planes and missiles, or weapons set aside for separate functions only? Actually, it meant one, more than one, or none of the above, depending on one's point of view.

Army spokesmen often had yet another view, which was that tactical air units should be set aside for use on call by the Army. This view, more or less, was accepted by Congressman Vinson and his committee, and the burdensome labels remained. Intermittent discussions as to whether the Army should annex tactical air entirely continued into the Vietnam War. In both Korea and Vietnam, strategic bombers on tactical missions delivered the heaviest final blows. No wonder Vandenberg agreed heartily with British Air Chief Marshal Lord Tedder, that the two titles should never have been imposed upon air forces.

*   *   *   *   *

Always in demand for public appearances, Vandenberg had to ration his time on platforms, and all subject matter was carefully selected. The present and future security of the country came first, based on the conviction that the Congress and the public should know as much as our enemies obviously knew. He was determined to speak simply, directly, and, above all, accurately. Statements to the other service chiefs, to his civilian superiors, to the Congress, and to the public had to be the same in basic content. This required careful wording and complete consistency.

Despite the variety of Vandenberg's views and decisions during nearly five years as Air Force Chief of Staff, there were no contradictions, reversals, or retractions of any statements. Such a record was made possible by the unwavering simplicity of his purpose and his unmistakable sincerity. His first and only admonition to me on the writing of his statements was perfectly clear: "Never . . . say anything that is not completely factual or will not stand up under close examination. Never stretch the facts, or beg a question, or exaggerate one bit."

Friendly as he was toward his busy staff and carefully chosen commanders, Vandenberg did not hesitate to move people who failed to focus on the prescribed goals. The postwar Air Force was so crippled by wholesale demobilization and budget cuts that only the small Strategic Air Command was manned and equipped for combat. When he learned that the crew training was being concentrated on flying proficiency rather than combat readiness, he relieved the commander and replaced him with General LeMay. The list of college professors available for consulting was drastically shortened to fit the need, but the list of friendly newsmen was lengthened. Columnist Walter Lippman, journalists Joe and Stewart Alsop, editors C.J.V. Murphy of *Fortune*, and James Shepley of *Time-Life*, and a few congressmen and senators— despite the shortage of Air Force veterans on the Hill—were personal friends of the Air Force Chief. It was important to maintain such contacts with men of influence in the Washington area, for Vandenberg was repeatedly under attack by past and present members of the elder services.

The first organized public attack came in his second year as Air Force Chief, and it came from the Navy in the form of the "revolt of the Admirals," sometimes called the "flat-top mutiny." This unique phenomenon was triggered by Secretary of Defense Louis Johnson's canceling the Navy's plans for the first super carrier. Led by Adm. Arthur Radford, a group of recalcitrant Navy officers openly defied regulations and precipitated their well-planned congressional hearing. Radford and others testified that the new long-range

National Archives

Adm. Arthur Radford

B–36 was worse than worthless, that nuclear weapons were immoral, and that the most dangerous enemy of the United States soon would be China rather than Russia. To climax the show, a Navy civilian anonymously accused Vandenberg of accepting a bribe to buy the controversial B–36 bomber. A now-forgotten senator delivered a bitter speech accusing Vandenberg of numerous blunders and evil doings. Air Force Secretary Stuart Symington, together with the Chairman of the Joint Chiefs, Gen. Omar Bradley, successfully defended and explained all Air Force actions. The Chief of Naval Operations, Adm. Louis Denfeld, who at first had tried to check the "mutineers," then joined them, and finally resigned to run unsuccessfully for senator in Massachusetts. Denfeld was replaced by the more intellectual Adm. Forrest Sherman, who became one of Vandenberg's closest friends.

While Vandenberg did not enjoy this disrupting circus, it was clear that both the Navy and the Air Force had profited from the encounter, and that his responses to the investigation increased his rapport with the Congress and the public. His new relationship with the very rational Admiral Sherman was a relief, and his long-established ties with General Bradley were renewed. This was fortunate, for the new budget crisis affecting all the services brought open reactions from the chiefs, and Vandenberg stood alone. He maintained his determination to speak the truth as he saw it when called upon, and if necessary, when not called upon.

In a special meeting intended to mollify worried congressmen who had questioned the wisdom of a deep military budget cut, Vandenberg refused

Secretaries of Defense and Armed Services at a press conference in 1949, l. to r.: Secretary of the Air Force Stuart Symington, Secretary of the Army Kenneth Royall, Secretary of Defense Louis Johnson, and Secretary of the Navy John Sullivan

to serve as an echo for statements he knew to be evasive and unjustified. When Secretary of Defense Louis Johnson, who took office in March 1949, compounded the scars of demobilization and the lapse of the draft by a drastic budget cut, he called upon military leaders to justify his sudden action. The meeting was almost, temporarily, a success. The senior Navy and Marine officers present were obviously unhappy, but noncommittal. The Army representative, while admitting weakness, argued that all was well because the Communists were even weaker. "We military men," he said, "are never satisfied. We would like to fortify the moon if you gave us the money." A professor who worked for the CIA was introduced to give further assurance that the Communist governments would always try to expand by subversion rather than military action. Some were not fooled, but it was especially unfortunate for Secretary Johnson that Vandenberg had lead the CIA's predecessor organization and knew better.

At the conclusion of the briefings, a small but brave congressman, Clarence Cannon of Missouri, rose to say bluntly that he was not impressed by the evasions offered, and especially not by the "learned professor's dubious claims." Everyone knew, Congressman Cannon insisted, that our armed forces were being dangerously weakened, and that the professor's story of the Communist love of peace was so much tommyrot. "Everybody knows," said Cannon, "they are getting ready to fight, and there is going to be a war." The trouble is, he explained, that people do not want to believe it. They want more roads, bridges, and government spending at home. "We congressmen," he said, "have to provide the people with what they want. If we don't, we will be replaced by somebody who does. We will all just have to rely on our fine military men to do the best they can, with what they have, when the showdown comes."

After a short silence and general bewilderment, the quiet Vandenberg rose to say: "I want to stand up and be counted as one who admits there will be a war—and it will be soon." No one spoke further, not even as the sober group slowly dispersed.

In May 1950, our ambassador in Seoul warned us of impending trouble in Korea, as had the U.S. Military Assistance Group in Korea some two months earlier, but the warnings were ignored. To act upon them would have interfered with domestic political plans. Within a few weeks came the well-prepared Communist invasion of South Korea, for which we were pitifully unprepared, and which ultimately would cost the lives of more than 33,000 of our "fine military men" who had to do "the best they could with what they had." As the attack had become more imminent, Vandenberg warned in ever stronger public statements against the danger of reducing our strength in the face of a rising threat. The Air Force Chief got little help in his crusade. Surprisingly there was more open agreement with him among politicians than among his Army and Navy colleagues.

*   *   *   *   *

Political leaders neither awed nor frightened Vandenberg, but he respected all who deserved respect, and worked well with them. His well-known uncle had long been both minority and majority party leader in the Senate. Arthur Vandenberg was called "the Republican architect of bipartisan foreign policy," and his nephew had observed in wartime the value of political-military cooperation. The Air Force Chief of Staff was especially proud of having influenced his normally isolationist uncle to support the Marshall Plan and U.S. membership in NATO, thus making these policies possible. Air power, the Chief had argued, would soon make the globe too small for isolation. The possibility of single-nation security would be just a memory, perhaps even for Russia.

A bipartisan military policy as well as a bipartisan foreign policy was Vandenberg's plan. Air Force Secretary Stuart Symington was his most cooperative official partner. As Secretary, Symington absorbed most of President Truman's disfavor resulting from Air Force transpolar and global nonstop flights. These demonstrations of aeronautical advance were branded by spokesmen of the Army and Navy as publicity stunts designed to usurp the attention and funds their services had received previously. A widely quoted speech by Symington suggested what one B–36 could do to Stalingrad, as compared with what an invading army might hope to do. This resulted in a protest by General Bradley to the President. Truman, a World War I captain of artillery who depended considerably upon the advice of Generals Marshall and Bradley, approved a ruling that a military service member must not speak critically of another service. Quite consistently, the President appeared before a Marine Corps veterans' convention to apologize for having aired an ancient joke that a Marine squad contained seven riflemen and a press agent.

Symington was not forgiven by the President and soon resigned in April 1950, later to run successfully for the Senate. His departure from the Air Force was a serious loss. To Vandenberg, it was almost a tragedy. Symington had provided liaison between the political world, which contained the constitutional Commander in Chief of military forces, and the military world, which held the only people capable of implementing the President's military orders. Most important in the Symington-Vandenberg harmony was the Secretary's opinion that political appointees should speak freely on economic, legislative, and political matters, while military leaders should express themselves openly and honestly on military matters, and disregard partisan political pressures.

Secretary Symington was succeeded by a strong-minded lawyer-politician, Thomas K. Finletter, who initially was regarded as promising because his name was attached to the Finletter Report of 1948, which emphasized the importance

Above: Secretary of the Air Force Stuart Symington (left) and Gen. Carl Spaatz announce setup for the Dept. of the Air Force in Oct. 1947; *right*: Symington's successor as Secretary of the Air Force, Thomas K. Finletter, climbs into a T–33 jet trainer fighter.

219

of military aviation. Secretary Finletter soon developed a confessed jealousy of respected men in uniform. In hearings before the House and Senate committees, Finletter displayed an obvious desire to silence military leaders who had earned attention, especially Generals Bradley and Vandenberg. He soon usurped the position of his Air Force Chief as the authority on military tactics, strategy, and weapons, much to the annoyance of committee members as well as Vandenberg. Vandenberg finally avoided such meetings, rather than sit and listen to long and questionable lectures by his civilian superior. The Secretary's icy attitude continued until there was a *faux pas* in the seating of his wife at an Air Force dinner; despite Vandenberg's formal apology, that was the end of oral communication between the two. Important messages were delivered by courier from one office to the other. Later, Finletter tried to dispense with Vandenberg entirely, just a few months before the Chief would qualify for full retirement. The Secretary's plan to move General LeMay from the Strategic Air Command into the Chief's position was leaked, as a *fait accompli*, to the *Washington Post*. It was defended on the ground that LeMay was a quiet and dutiful soldier, but it was a move that nobody, including LeMay, really wanted. Washington *Fortune* editor Charles Murphy immediately notified retired chief Tooey Spaatz who persuaded his old friend Harry Truman to overrule the restless Air Force Secretary and keep Vandenberg on the job until his approaching retirement date.

National Archives

President Harry Truman

Repeated worries about war during the spring of 1950 and the United States' declining ability to meet conventional attacks around the world bothered many in the administration. Vandenberg's influence in defense affairs was increasing, though he disagreed with the Army's military spokesmen and the chorus of political appointees on what needed to be done. The Congress voted funds to reduce the military decline, but the added appropriations were not spent by the Truman administration. Before his retirement on April 24, Secretary Symington was prepared to challenge this new practice, but he was restrained from doing so. Vandenberg also practiced reasonable restraint. He did not enter the economic debates, did not criticize his colleagues or his superiors as individuals, nor did he mention that the Department of Defense was surprised by the early explosion of the first Russian atomic weapon in September 1949, shortly after the department had rejected an accurate prediction by Air Force intelligence.

These and other circumstances help explain why President Truman did not threaten to dismiss Vandenberg but instead extended his appointment to record length. After the Korean War began, the President dismissed the bombastic Secretary of Defense Louis Johnson, who had boasted that in case of war in Korea, we would win a complete victory in an hour.

*   *   *   *   *

North Korea invaded the Republic of Korea on Sunday, June 25, 1950. Vandenberg wasted no time in recriminations, but rather worked wholeheartedly with everyone engaged in the common effort. After many months, he admitted privately that the famous summons to meet with the President and Secretary of State on that Sunday afternoon was scarcely fair to the Joint Chiefs. They had received little warning of the decision to enter combat and had no time to study, or even to consider, the problem. The Secretary of State had fooled the Pentagon as well as the Kremlin when during a speech at the Washington Press Club on January 12, 1950, he drew a map illustrating the new plan to withdraw forces from Taiwan and South Korea. Even General MacArthur, in Tokyo, had been persuaded to approve the withdrawal of our meager contingents from South Korea, because of the increasing depth of our military decline. Yet Vandenberg and Admiral Sherman were told to move their still unmobilized forces into action immediately. Our first shot was fired on June 27 by an F-82 pilot herding North Korean interceptors away from transport planes that were evacuating American personnel from the U.S. embassy in Seoul.

As Vandenberg explained, there was no argument or discussion of the decisions or the difficult military problems involved in that Sunday meeting with President Truman. There was, in fact, no discussion of anything other than the possibilities of intervention by Russia and China, and that was merely spontaneous speculation. After the Chinese did intervene in late October 1950, only the continuing skills of our best World War II fighter pilots defeated swarms of Russian-built MiGs with a few F–86s, and prevented our Air Force there from being overwhelmed as were our ground forces. From that time on, Vandenberg was deeply involved in trying to provide a ceiling over the heads of our Army and its vulnerable but vital bases. The Joint Chiefs had been unable to communicate effectively with United Nations (UN) Commander Gen. Douglas MacArthur, so Army Chief Joe Collins and Vandenberg were sent to discuss what to do next, following the debacle caused by the intervention of China. After their return, Vandenberg revealed in confidence that General MacArthur was found in a tragic mood. MacArthur demanded that he be ordered to abandon the Korean peninsula or "stand and die" on the ground he still held. Instead, the two visitors agreed with MacArthur's new field commander, Lt. Gen. Matthew Ridgway, that it would be possible to stand without the annihilation of our forces there. Most of our retreat from North Korea after China entered the war had been completely motorized. General Ridgway was confident that the Chinese, pursuing on foot, could not catch up in winter before he regrouped his forces, replenished his supplies, and prepared to meet them.

As he had done so often, and at such risk, during World War II, Vandenberg determined to see for himself the situation behind enemy lines. He flew at low altitude in a small transport plane over much of the area occupied by the Chinese forces. There was little evidence that they were present, despite their numbers. Their ability to disperse and to hide, with their equipment, even in the rough terrain, was impressive. Even their tracks in the snow were concealed.

To the south, our own forces were exposed, necessarily, in open areas. Our few ports and supply routes were crowded with vehicles, supplies, fuel, and ammunition. They were highly visible and vulnerable to air attack. Because our troops and materials had to be funneled in from overseas, there was no acceptable solution other than avoidance of a bombing contest. Chinese forces and Russian bombers with Chinese insignia were widely deployed across Manchuria. The United States was forbidden to bomb there. They offered no easy and vital targets, such as our close and narrow supply channels. In this circumstance, Vandenberg could justifiably support the administration's policy of restraint.

Also, Vandenberg joined the other chiefs in supporting President Truman and General Bradley in the awkward but necessary order that brought General

Attending a briefing in Korea, 1951, from left to right: Chairman of the
Joint Chiefs Gen. Omar Bradley; Fifth Air Force Commander Maj. Gen.
Frank Everest; and Commander-in-Chief, Far East, Gen. Matthew Ridgway

MacArthur home in 1951. The frustrated United Nations commander had
resisted, and sometimes ignored, the newly organized Joint Chiefs of Staff
in the first exercise of their authority in war, and this created extreme problems. In September 1950 the President had replaced Secretary of Defense Louis
Johnson with the sensible and trusted Gen. George Marshall. Marshall alone
had sufficient prestige and style to stand against MacArthur's opinions during the congressional hearings that followed the eloquent oration of the "old
soldier" who would "just fade away" because the war would not be fought
his way. Vandenberg was next in importance for his testimony, and he was
faced with a serious dilemma. MacArthur had argued that a more aggressive
use of air power could have been decisive, and this was a possibility if we
could have developed the necessary forces.

Only five of us were present at a private discussion of how Vandenberg
should answer the penetrating questions that would be asked, mostly by
Republicans. Distinguished lawyer-professor Barton Leach of Harvard was
a principal counsel. "What is your attitude toward MacArthur?" Leach asked.
Vandenberg replied that he admired the brilliant strategist and commander,

but thought he was now seriously in the wrong because he refused to consider the problem of defending Europe against a possible Soviet attack in retaliation for our presence in Korea. Leach admonished him to keep perfectly cool in testimony, never reveal the slightest irritation at MacArthur's attitude, and speak clearly for the record. General Bradley had taught him, said Vandenberg, to speak deliberately and never hurry an answer. "The record," said Bradley, "will not show how much time you took to answer, but it will record permanently everything you say." Certainly Vandenberg could not denigrate the power of nuclear weapons or preach their nonuse unless he wished to destroy "deterrence" and encourage the Kremlin to risk other advances.

As usual, Vandenberg's numerous answers were direct, simple, and accurate. He testified that MacArthur's demand for bombing China would be dangerously impractical even with the most effective weapons, since our "shoestring air force" would be unable at the same time to destroy both China and Russia if the latter entered the war. This was an unpopular truth, but inescapable; the Strategic Air Command had just begun expanding. Vandenberg's testimony, though attacked by the opponents of air power, was well supported by classified information revealed to the committees. Vandenberg's experience in gathering intelligence gave him an understanding of the necessity of keeping collection methods secret. He did not reveal that we often penetrated China for photographs, or that the Chinese were frantically digging ditches in their large cities to help protect against bombing, or that the Taiwanese were helping us in every way possible. But in a press conference, he admitted we had heard Russian spoken among the MiG pilots attacking us, despite the State Department's unsuccessful efforts to cover up Russian participation in the war. There were public debates, pro and con, on the question of using atomic bombs, even after the Army made a survey of several months that found no "appropriate targets" in Red China. Vandenberg was opposed to the nuclear gamble for the more cogent reason that we were unprepared for any follow-up after such use, and there could be retaliation against Europe.

At the same time, he was urged, mostly by Air Force members, to suspend close air support for our battlelines until we destroyed enemy supply lines. Participants and students of the successful Normandy interdiction of World War II claimed that a similar effort in Korea could render the Chinese ground forces helpless from lack of supplies, and thus win the war. The Air Force Chief knew better, from extensive experience. "We used to bomb and close the Brenner Pass every day, and the Germans opened it every night," he said. Furthermore, he was aware that the success of interdiction depended upon heavy ground attacks to force the enemy to consume his supplies faster than they could be delivered. Such attacks were not pressed by our forces after the deliberate stalemate began in late 1951.

High-speed, high-altitude F–86 Sabrejets, which were critical aircraft to the air war in Korea.

Despite the numerous restrictions on bombing in North Korea, interdiction of supply routes remained important, and North Korean air bases were attacked repeatedly. Losses to ground fire and MiGs remained serious. Vandenberg called upon the heavy bombers to do tactical work at night, and he raised the level of pull-outs for the dive bombers. At last, electronic gunsights for the F–86s were provided and Vandenberg himself talked some reluctant aces into changing their tactics. There was a shortage of F–86s, the only planes in existence capable of challenging the Russian MiGs, and every effort was made to keep them in action.

Air Force sorties rose from less than a 100 a day early in the war, to nearly 1,000 a day 2 years later. The Chief was finally in charge of an effective force, though it was scarcely comparable to the largest air force ever on the continent of Europe, the Ninth Air Force he had commanded in World War II.

*   *   *   *   *

When he became Air Force Chief of Staff, Vandenberg had only one unit ready to deliver atomic bombs in the entire Air Force. Frantic demobilization after World War II, followed by drastic budget cuts, had made our national defense dependent almost entirely on the employment of nuclear weapons. Vandenberg's concern with the Truman Administration policy of building a cheap national defense on our monopoly of the atomic bomb had begun before the first Russian nuclear explosion. That 1949 surprise for all but Air Force Intelligence and some civilian scientists caused him to foresee an aggressive move by the now-confident Communist community. But Defense Secretary Louis Johnson ordered military leaders to say nothing other than to boast with him that the Russian breakthrough was no surprise, and steps had already been taken to counter its consequences. Vandenberg remained silent on the subject. He would not support that preposterous assertion.

By the time General Eisenhower was inaugurated as President in January 1953, the nation as a whole had agreed there would be "no more Koreas," which meant that resistance to Communist aggression must be provided principally by long-range weaponry. This was something of a gamble, but Vandenberg hoped that our resolve to maintain an unmistakably superior long-range force, and a respectable short-range delaying force, would together with our allies, provide at least minimum security. Funds and designs for this force were prepared during the Korean War, but the postwar euphoria and demand for a rise in the standard of living restricted all military plans, beginning with the Air Force.

Newly appointed Secretary of Defense Charles "Engine Charley" Wilson, who took office in January 1953, declared publicly that Vandenberg had agreed with him that drastic cuts in Air Force strength would not seriously weaken its power. Since he had made no such statement, Vandenberg corrected the record. Secretary Wilson, who had boasted that he would "bang brass heads together," insisted otherwise and declared that his cuts would only eliminate Air Force "fat." This led to a congressional investigation, and a public debate.

By the summer of 1953, Vandenberg's strength was failing rapidly because of advanced terminal cancer. As we briefed him for this appearance before the investigating committee, he tried to rest by stretching his still athletic form across chairs in his office, and he warned us that this would have to be his last public appearance.

On a Sunday afternoon, Vandenberg met at his home with his old friend Senator Symington, James Shepley of *Time-Life*, and four other advisors. The conference, to discuss his forthcoming testimony before the committee, lasted most of the afternoon. Weak, exhausted, and in constant pain, Vandenberg was leaning forward against his arms on the table. After a pause, he rested his forehead on his arms for a few moments, then raised his head to say: "It is not as easy as you think. I have always been a team man, and not a troublemaker, but here I am disturbing a President I admire." The advisors insisted it was too late to withdraw from the debate and declared he was doing the President a favor by calling attention to a serious blunder by his Secretary of Defense.

As the meeting dispersed, Vandenberg rose, then motioned me aside to say: "Don't try to agree with what you have been hearing. . . . Just write my statement the way *you* think it ought to be." There was no criticism of the

226

President or of Secretary Wilson. They were praised as sincere and dedicated men who had been misinformed by new and inexperienced advisors. The advisors had seriously miscalculated the effects of drastic deletions from the Air Force program, Vandenberg told the committee, and he stated precisely what the effects would be.

President Eisenhower was irritated by this exposé of his neophyte Defense Secretary. Yet the President was a true gentleman. He exerted no pressures against those who spoke in opposition, waived all censorship of Vandenberg's public statements, and punished no one who was involved in the debate.

After his retirement in mid-1953, Vandenberg lived through several months of drugged pain as his body wasted away. President Eisenhower and Secretary Wilson visited the slowly dying man and left with tears in their eyes. The funeral at the National Cathedral was awesome, with almost everyone of importance in Washington filling the great Gothic church. As one of the several colonels serving as ushers, I noticed a dignified and solitary man standing near a pillar. It was Dean Acheson, the former Secretary of State, whom many had blamed for the Korean War. He seemed to have been forgotten in the few months since John Foster Dulles had replaced him.

Within two decades, Dean Acheson would write in his memoirs that the public statement of "massive retaliation" as a policy revealed increased dependence on nuclear war. Acheson wrote that neither Dulles, Vandenberg, nor military leaders in general were to blame. Acheson said that "drastic cuts" of the military budget "rather than foreign policy or military strategy" led to "rationalization of necessity." Massive retaliation, a policy whereby acts of Soviet aggression would be met with unlimited retaliation, was a policy that Vandenberg struggled to restrain during the last months of his life.

Acheson failed to note, at the conclusion of his important recognition of generally avoided truth, that the Truman administration had followed the same policy of nuclear dependence into 1950, thus inspiring the blitz in Korea. Vandenberg had spoken against increasing reliance on nuclear delivery, for he was bold enough to face the fast-arriving future in which the United States might receive as well as deliver a nuclear attack. Acheson condemned the Kennedy-McNamara and Johnson policies of "mutually assured destruction (MAD)" as being, from the simple Dulles beginning, "unworkable, outmoded when uttered, and profoundly disturbing to our allies." Vandenberg had spoken clearly and authoritatively on the same subject many years earlier. He knew well the cost of conventional unpreparedness and dreaded the trend toward nuclear forces adequate only for attacking cities.

Often Vandenberg said that our strategic forces existed for the purpose of striking back against enemy long-range forces that attack or actively threaten us. He said our most important reaction is "to insure that air attacks against us must not be repeated. This is more important than mere retaliation.

Our principal aim is not to destroy *another* nation, but to save *this* nation. We cannot waste our forces on mere revenge. "

Vandenberg's death was a loss to the nation because of his rare abilities, steadiness, and persuasive influence that extended beyond his military responsibilities. The Air Force in its present and future form is a monument to him. He organized its basic structure and selected many of the leaders who followed him.

For all of us who worked closely with him, Vandenberg's indomitable spirit has remained alive and influential through the ups and downs of our nation's efforts to remain the world's best hope for at least a few more generations. Vandenberg's early successors, Nathan Twining, Thomas White, and Curtis LeMay, continued to build on his principle of honest recognition for even the most unpleasant truths. Thus Vandenberg and the Air Force leaders who followed him have created and kept alive a tradition of readiness to sacrifice temporary ease and comfort rather than endanger the survival of nations determined to be free.

Sources

There is no biography of Hoyt Vandenberg, the most spirited and determined of the Air Force Chiefs of Staff, and he did not live long enough to consider writing his memoirs. Much of the information in this essay is from the author's close association with Vandenberg during his years as Chief of Staff (April 1948–June 1953). The pre-World War II period of Vandenberg's career is covered adequately in a doctoral dissertation by Brig. Gen. Jon F. Reynolds (Duke University). There are frequent references to Vandenberg's role in World War II and as Chief of Staff in *A History of the United States Air Force 1907–1957*, Alfred Goldberg (ed.). D. Van Nostrand Company (New York, 1957) and references to the former period in *Forged in Fire*, DeWitt S. Copp, Doubleday (New York, 1982). After his retirement in 1948, General Carl Spaatz wrote a weekly column for *Newsweek* magazine in which Vandenberg's decisions and policies were discussed frequently. The four volume *History of the Joint Chiefs of Staff*, edited by Terrence Gough, includes much recently declassified information and is indispensable to an understanding of the environment in which Vandenberg operated during his last years. There are many references to Hoyt Vandenberg in a USAF Oral History interview of Noel F. Parrish on file at the U.S. Air Force Historical Research Center, Maxwell Air Force Base, Alabama.

10

Benjamin O. Davis, Jr.: History on Two Fronts

Alan L. Gropman

By 1948, the newly independent United States Air Force had been reduced through the demobilization of the postwar years to the threshold of impotence. There were plenty of airplanes to equip fifty-five groups, but not enough hands with the right skills to man them. Some units that were short of pilots possessed too many navigators and maintenance men, while others had spare pilots but not enough airmen with support skills to keep their airplanes flying and combat ready.

The obvious solution was to transfer people among units. That solution was blocked by a self-imposed policy of racial segregation that had been a traditional United States Army practice since the founding of the country. But now the Air Force was no longer part of the Army. It no longer need be hampered by outmoded tradition. Lt. Gen. Idwal Edwards, USAF's Deputy Chief of Staff for Personnel, argued that the "efficient utilization of personnel is an essential element . . . of effective air power." Air Force Chief of Staff Gen. Hoyt S. Vandenberg agreed. Assigning people by race rather than by ability was antithetical to effectiveness, and operational effectiveness was becoming crucial. Three years after V-E Day, it was clear that our still heavily armed wartime ally, the USSR, was emerging as a threat to the demobilized West, and the weakened USAF was still laboring under a personnel fetish that went back to the days of the smooth-bore musket.

In April 1948, three months before President Harry S. Truman's Executive Order 9981 directed desegregation in the armed forces, the Air Force announced its intention to integrate racially. Slowly and hesitantly the other services followed the Air Force lead, watching the results of what was to them a radical departure from tradition.

229

It was not until 1951 that the Army, embroiled in the Korean War, agreed that segregation was undermining combat effectiveness, and accepted integration, having observed the smooth implementation of Air Force desegregation. The Navy, which had inaugurated token integration in 1945, only to keep its entire mess corps black well into the next decade, was the slowest to realize the reform. The country, with its Air Force in the vanguard of the military services, quickened its march toward racial equality—an issue that had been opposed for more than two centuries.

Edwards's and Vandenberg's landmark decision was heavily influenced by the achievements of a man of uncommon judgment and moral courage. That man was Benjamin O. Davis, Jr., the first black to graduate from the U.S. Military Academy in the twentieth century, leader of the only black combat air group during World War II, and the first black general officer in the United States Air Force.

Segregation eventually would have been banned in the armed forces had there not been a Ben Davis. It is a reasonable assumption, however, that racial integration in the military would have followed a different and probably much slower course toward equal opportunity had it not been for him. The fighter units Davis trained and led in combat demonstrated that not just one, but hundreds of blacks could perform creditably on the ground and in the air

Cadet Benjamin O. Davis, Jr.

in the most technically demanding of the armed services. His innate dignity, intelligence, and measured judgment saved from early disaster a politically-inspired experiment that ultimately led to greater efficiency in the military services and moved the nation a major step forward toward racial equality.

Benjamin O. Davis, Jr., was born on December 18, 1912, in Washington, D.C., the son of the officer who became the first black general in the United States Army. Davis's mother died when he was three years old. Young Ben's stepmother became a major influence on his life. She had a master's degree in English, encouraged him to read good literature, and, after the Davises were transferred from Washington, pushed him to graduate from the racially integrated Central High School in Cleveland, Ohio, at the age of sixteen. She also encouraged him to run, successfully, for president of his senior class. Ben's father insisted on good manners, integrity, responsibility, and punctuality—virtues that were to be especially useful in a military career. The senior Davis taught his son to play chess, at which Ben became exceptionally proficient, and bridge, which became a life-long hobby.

After high school, Ben Davis attended college at Western Reserve University, Ohio State University, and the University of Chicago before receiving an appointment to the United States Military Academy at West Point from Congressman Oscar Depriest of Chicago. Davis was the ninth black to enroll at West Point since its founding in 1802, and the fourth to graduate.

The Army he joined in July 1932 was a reflection of American society of the time. If anything, it was more tightly segregated on racial lines than was society at large, and West Point was no exception to the general Army practice. From the time he entered the Academy to graduation in June 1936, Davis had no roommate. Upperclassmen directed that he be "silenced"—that no cadet speak to him—hoping to drive him from West Point. With one brief interlude at the "recognition ceremony" marking the end of Plebe, or freshman year, the silencing continued throughout his four years at the Academy.

Despite this extreme social pressure, Davis graduated thirty-fifth in a class of 276. *Howitzer*, the Academy year book, said of him: "The courage, tenacity and intelligence with which he conquered a problem . . . more difficult than Plebe year won for him the sincere admiration of his classmates, and his single-minded determination to continue in his chosen career cannot fail to inspire respect wherever fortune may lead him. " Soon after graduation, Lieutenant Davis married the vivacious and strikingly beautiful Agatha Scott, whom he had met while he was a cadet and she was attending college in Connecticut. She and Davis's parents were pillars of strength that helped him survive his ordeal at West Point.

Davis had been smitten by flying from his barnstorming ride as a lad of fourteen, and applied for flight training with the recommendation of Academy Superintendent Maj. Gen. William D. Connor; but the segregated

Air Corps took no blacks in any capacity, service or flying. He was assigned to the Infantry as commander of a black service company at Fort Benning, Georgia, and in a year was enrolled as a student in the Infantry School at that post. This assignment came earlier than normal for Davis, largely through the intercession of General Connor, who had taken a great interest in Davis's career.

Upon graduation from the year-long course, Davis became an ROTC instructor at the all-black Tuskegee Institute of Alabama. Agatha Davis, more gregarious than her reserved husband, soon had the two of them at the center of Tuskegee's social life, built mainly around the Institute's faculty. Among other things, she organized a ballroom dancing class; and the Davises have been members of dancing clubs in many places ever since. After nearly three years at Tuskegee, Davis was assigned to Fort Riley, Kansas, as an aide to his father, Brig. Gen. Benjamin O. Davis, Sr., and soon thereafter to the newly formed black flying school near the town of Tuskegee. Tuskegee Army Air Field was established by the Air Corps (which became the Army Air Forces on June 20, 1941) because of pressure from President Franklin D. Roosevelt, who was campaigning for an unprecedented third term. Roosevelt was responding to an intense campaign by the black press and the National Association for the Advancement of Colored People to open flying training to blacks. In December 1940, the Air Corps, at Roosevelt's order, reluctantly submitted a plan to the Secretary of War for creating a single, segregated pursuit squadron with a complement of 47 officers and 429 enlisted men. The 99th Pursuit Squadron was activated at Chanute Army Air Field, Illinois, on March 22, 1941, with ground-crew training only. Tuskegee Army Air Field was officially established on July 23, 1941, to train pilots.

The AAF's leaders had grown up in a segregated society and believed that blacks could be used only in limited roles within segregated units. Like many in civilian life, air leaders were convinced that blacks were neither mentally nor physically capable of mastering flying, and that in war they could not compete successfully against white American or enemy pilots. It was widely believed, furthermore, that blacks had no capacity for leadership and that even blacks themselves did not want to be commanded by other blacks. But the pressures on Roosevelt dictated a black commander for the experimental combat unit. Since it was totally accepted that whites would never take orders from blacks, the 99th Pursuit Squadron would have to be black, from the newest enlisted man up, and a black commander found to hold the unit together.

Captain Davis, because he was a Military Academy graduate and had the physical and mental capabilities to fly, was chosen to be leader of the first class of thirteen that entered flight training in August 1941. There was, however, a short delay in Davis's movement from Fort Riley to Tuskegee

Tuskegee Army Air Field graduates from left to right: George "Spanky" Roberts, Benjamin O. Davis, Jr., Charles H. Debow, Lt. R. M. Long (instructor), Mac Ross, and Lemuel R. Custis

because word of the change in AAF policy had not been broadcast widely. Before proceeding to Tuskegee, Davis was required to pass a flight physical. He appeared before the post physician at Fort Riley only to be failed for epilepsy, a disease he has never had. This matter had to be corrected by another flight physical, this time performed by a doctor who was aware that flying training had been opened to blacks.

Of the initial group of thirteen that was led by Davis, the young captain and four cadets graduated as fighter pilots in the United States Army Air Forces on March 7, 1942. The five original Tuskegee Army Air Field graduates formed the nucleus of the 99th Pursuit Squadron. In time Tuskegee Army Air Field graduated almost 1,000 black Americans. These men have been known ever since as the Tuskegee Airmen.

When the 99th Pursuit Squadron completed its combat training, the AAF could find no commander in a combat zone who would accept the units. For a year, successive deployment dates passed while the 99th continued to fly training missions. Davis worked tirelessly to keep his unit's morale high. He knew that discrimination was keeping his men out of combat, and he knew that the longer the 99th stayed out of the fighting the harder it would be to achieve success. He also knew the dangers of protest, for black aviators had too many enemies waiting to pounce on them.

With a dignity and bearing none of his men ever will forget, Davis led the 99th through interminable training sorties waiting with a well-disguised impatience for the opportunity to fly and fight. When finally ordered to North Africa in the spring of 1943, Davis and his men carried the knowledge that upon their performance rested the future of blacks in military flying. This, on top of the weight of combat flying, was a heavy burden for the men, but they bore it willingly for the opportunity to prove themselves. When asked to single out his greatest achievements from the time he entered West Point until he retired from government service, Davis responded immediately that it was keeping the men of the 99th and later the 332d Group flying and fighting to prove that they were the equal of whites, instead of wasting energy and endangering their future by protesting racial discrimination. "God knows," he said, "they had enough to protest about."

The 99th sailed to Africa in April 1943, with 26 pilots and more than 300 enlisted men aboard a ship with several thousand American fighting men, most of whom were white. Davis was made executive officer of the troop ship, one of the first times a black had been given a position of authority over whites. After training near Fez, Morocco, with the 27th Fighter Bomber Group and receiving a tutorial from the lengendary Philip Cochrane, the 99th was attached to the 33d Fighter Group at Fordjouna, Tunisia, for operations. Before the first combat mission of the 99th, Davis called the men together and told them that they were now to receive their baptism of fire and with it their great opportunity for themselves and for all black Americans. "We are here to do a job, and by God, we're going to do it well, so let's get on with it."

On June 2, 1943, the 99th, led by Lt. Col. Davis, flew its first mission in obsolescent P-40s, strafing enemy targets on Pantelleria Island. For the next seven days the squadron did not sight an enemy aircraft. Finally, on the morning of June 9, a flight of six P-40s was jumped by twelve enemy fighters, and a disorganized melee ensued with neither side scoring a kill. Two days later Pantelleria surrendered to U.S. forces without an invasion, the first island to so fall in World War II.

On July 2, 1943, the 99th scored its first victory when Lt. Charles B. Hall, on his eighth mission and first sighting, shot down a FW-190, one of the Luftwaffe's most effective fighters. (Hall shot down three enemy aircraft before the end of his combat tour.) That day also marked the 99th's first losses as Lts. Sherman White and James McCullin were killed. Later in the month, the 99th, flying ground support strafing missions, took part in the successful invasion of Sicily, Operation Husky. The unit, however, was not to shoot down another enemy aircraft until the new year.

Lt. Col. Davis in cockpit of a P-51.

In September 1943, three months after its first combat sorties, it was reported that the 99th had unsatisfactory air discipline, and that the unit disintegrated when attacked by enemy fighters. The 99th also was accused of not being properly aggressive, the pilots showing their timidity by attacking undefended secondary targets when their primary target was covered by antiaircraft fire. The men were accused of simply not having the same desire for combat as whites, and yet, contradictorily, were criticized elsewhere in the same report for engaging in a dogfight with Me–109s escorting Ju–88 medium bombers instead of pressing home an attack on the bombers. The Me–109 was a much more dangerous aircraft to attack than the relatively sluggish, less maneuverable, and lightly armed Ju–88. While the Tuskegee Airmen were properly criticized for diverting from their main mission (which was to attack bombers threatening ground troops), they were displaying a marked—if misplaced—desire for combat. It also was said by one of the general officers endorsing the report that "the Negro type has not the proper reflexes to make a first-class fighter pilot."

Commanders in the theater recommended that the 99th Squadron be withdrawn from combat flying. The Tuskegee Airmen's dream almost ended. The proposal was approved at all levels, including the Commander of the Army Air Forces, Gen. Henry H. Arnold. General Arnold not only recommended that the 99th be withdrawn from active combat flying, but also that the 332d Fighter Group, then being formed, not be assigned to a combat theater once it completed its training, and that plans for creating an all-black medium bomber group be abandoned. Recognizing the political implications of such a move, however, Arnold recommended that his proposed actions be taken only after they were approved by President Roosevelt. The Air Staff prepared a draft letter to Roosevelt from Army Chief of Staff Gen. George C. Marshall that would effectively end the black aviation experiment.

The report of deficiencies in the 99th came under review by the War Department's standing Advisory Committee on Negro Troop Policies, which was led by John J. McCloy and included General Benjamin O. Davis, Sr., in its membership. McCloy, knowing that Colonel Davis was back in the United States to assume command of the 332d Group, insisted that the younger Davis be brought before the committee to explain the negative reports.

Davis noted that the 99th went into combat with handicaps that were overlooked by the unit's detractors. Because no one in the 99th had any combat experience, there was bound to be a lack of self-confidence and tactical errors in the unit's initial encounters. Davis acknowledged that the 99th lost its formation integrity the first time it was attacked by enemy fighters on June 9, but asserted that this attack was by first-rate German fighters against his less-capable P-40s, that the Tuskegee Airmen were outnumbered two-to-one, and that the enemy had suprised his unit from above. But even in this single instance of losing cohesion, the pilots fought it out with the Germans man-to-man, losing no one to the Luftwaffe. And no one fled the battle scene.

White units, Davis pointed out, also did poorly on arrival in a combat zone, but were usually leavened by experienced white pilots as formation and element leaders on their early combat missions. The 99th had no such luxury. The commander of the group to which Davis's 99th Squadron was attached believed that segregation and the experimental nature of the 99th required the squadron fly into combat alone, even in its initial tests.

Davis insisted his men showed no lack of desire for combat; in fact, because the 99th was twenty to thirty percent smaller than a typical white fighter squadron, and received no replacements during its first two months of combat, his men often flew more often than typical white pilots, sometimes as many as six sorties a day. He and his men encountered enemy fighters on eighty percent of their missions and always stayed in the contest. No superior, he said, had intimated otherwise. He also flatly denied that his men ever failed to attack an assigned target because of enemy defenses.

Davis's articulate defense helped convince the committee, and through it the highest U.S. Army leadership, that the Tuskegee Airmen deserved more time to prove themselves. General Marshall agreed that the 99th should not be removed from combat on the little evidence presented by the Army Air Forces. He also recognized the political implications of not giving blacks a fair chance.

In January 1944, the Air Forces' recommendation that the 99th be sidelined was permanently shelved, in large measure because the squadron, under Maj. George S. "Spanky" Roberts (whom Davis had personally groomed for command), began to prove itself to objective evaluators. During the nine months the outfit flew under Roberts's leadership (while Davis was completing the 332d Group's training and moving it to Italy), the 99th was attached to the 79th Fighter Group. Here the men were treated fairly, but remained segregated. Morale was high, and many 99th pilots asked to remain in combat at the end of their normal tours.

On the morning of January 27, after more than three weeks of arduous close air support for Allied infantry at Anzio, fifteen pilots of the 99th, still flying obsolescent P-40s, met a larger number of German FW–190s. Six German aircraft were destroyed and four others damaged. Considering the mismatch in aircraft, it was a remarkable performance. That afternoon three more German aircraft were shot down and a fourth was listed as probably destroyed. The next day the Tuskegee Airmen shot down four enemy aircraft, and between February 5 and 10, another four were downed. The dry spell was over.

In the same months that the 99th scored so well over Anzio, the 332d Fighter Group under Davis's command began to arrive in the theater. At first the 332d's three squadrons—the 100th, 301st, and 302d—flew low-performance P–39 ground attack fighters. In June 1944, they were joined by the 99th, while the group was transitioning to the rugged, higher-performance P–47. The next month the group transitioned once again to the P–51 Mustang, the best fighter developed by the United States during World War II. In its first six months in Italy, furthermore, the 332d changed bases three times.

Needless to say, it took precious time to change aircraft this often. In addition to familiarizing pilots with a new airplane in a combat theater, the enlisted ground crews had to be trained to maintain and arm the new equipment. It is a testimony to Davis's leadership and managerial ability that these tasks were accomplished smoothly and that his unit performed admirably despite constant changes. Considering, furthermore, the experimental nature of the Tuskegee Airmen units and the close scrutiny under which they operated, it is significant that the discipline rates for Davis's squadrons were comparable to those of white flying units and much superior to those of black service units commanded by whites. Davis was a severe disciplinarian who operated "by the book," and he expected no less from his subordinate commanders. He was aided, no doubt, by the fact that his men had a professional fighting mission to perform, while black service unit morale suffered from the lack of a comparable mission.

Davis's men flew more than 1,500 missions and some 15,000 sorties. A look at a few of their missions in first-line fighters will illustrate the diversity of their combat assignments and the breadth of combat leadership Davis had developed in his group.

On June 9, the 332d scored its first kills on the first of a series of 200 bomber-escort missions that earned the 332d "Redtails" the unique record of never having lost a friendly bomber to an enemy fighter. That day, with Colonel Davis leading, thirty-nine P–47s took off from the 332d's base at Ramatelli Airdrome on the east coast of central Italy escorting B–24s to targets at Munich, Germany. As the escort approached Udine, Italy, a formation of Me–109s made a diving attack on the American bombers with a flight of Tuskegee Airmen in pursuit. Lt. Wendell Pruitt closed on the tail of a German Me–109, scoring the first of many kills for the newly equipped fighter group.

In one segment of the battle, Davis led a flight of eight P–47s in an attack on eighteen German Me–109s, with the Tuskegee Airmen scoring several victories. The thirty-nine members of the 332d took on more than one hundred German fighters, destroying five Me–109s and damaging another. They lost one of their team, and another had his aircraft badly damaged by flak. Davis earned the Distinguished Flying Cross for his leadership and bravery during this mission.

Davis, now commander of a four-squadron group and a base with thousands of men, could not fly as often as he wished. While no single individual led as many missions as did Davis himself, he called on the lieutenants he had so carefully trained to lead the majority of the missions. He believed it crucially important that as many black officers as possible have an opportunity to prove themselves as combat leaders.

One such mission on June 25, 1944, was uniquely successful: fighter pilots of the 332d, led by Capt. Joseph Elsberry (later to shoot down three German fighters on a single mission), sank a German destroyer in the Gulf of Venezia. This was the only sinking of a major naval combatant during the war solely by fighters using machineguns.

On July 18, the 332d had its best day to date. Capt. Lee Rayford led sixty-six P–51s on a bomber escort mission to southern Germany. The Tuskegee Airmen were to join the bombers immediately prior to their run over the target and escort them through bombs-away and recovery. The bomber formation was late, but the men of the 332d waited in the area. They knew if they departed, the bombers would have no escort on the most dangerous phase of the mission. Although the men of the 332d were outnumbered, they shot down eleven German fighters—nine Me–109s and two FW–190s—without losing a fighter. One B–24 was destroyed by flak.

On July 24, Davis led fifty-three P–51s escorting bombers to southern Germany with the added mission of conducting a fighter sweep of the area after the bombers had hit their target. Again the 332d fought outnumbered, and this time destroyed four enemy aircraft without losing any of the B–24s to the German fighters. After the bombers were well on their way home, Davis led his men in a strafing attack on ground targets. Two days later the 332d, under the command of Capt. Melvin Jackson, escorted bombers to Marken-dorf, Austria, shooting down five Me–109s, with two more probably destroyed and another severely damaged.

On July 27, fifty-two P–51s from all four squadrons of the group, led by Captain Rayford, flew cover for B–24s. Once more the 332d was out-numbered by German fighters in the area, but pressed in with the bombers, and eight enemy fighters were shot down.

A senior commander, under whom the 332d served, testified in 1945 before a group of general officers that the success of the 332d should be credited to Davis, for "unless he led a mission, there was doubt that it would be completed. His officers lacked leadership, initiative, aggressiveness, and dependability." The accomplishment of the 332d when Davis was not leading refute those charges. Davis could lead, no doubt, but so could the men he prepared for leadership.

Formation of P–51 Mustangs, fighters which Davis and the men of the 332d Fighter Group would use for bomber escort missions to Germany.

*   *   *   *   *

The year 1945 was to bring many significant missions, including the 332d's greatest air-to-air combat triumph—thirteen kills on March 31, 1945. A week earlier the 332d had been the first Italy-based fighter group to escort bombers to Berlin and return—a distance of 1,600 miles. On that March 24 mission, Colonel Davis led fifty-four P-51s escorting B-17s in their strike on the Daimler-Benz tank assembly plant. The Tuskegee Airmen had to fight their way in and out against the best aircraft the Luftwaffe had, including at least thirty of the newest jet and rocket fighter aircraft.

As Davis and his men approached Berlin, the bombers were attacked by a formation of twenty-five Me–262 jets that screamed into the middle of the American formation. The Tuskegee Airmen fought off waves of these jets. Davis and his men were supposed to be relieved by another fighter group just short of the target, but the relieving unit failed to make the rendezvous. Despite low fuel and ammunition, Davis ordered the 332d to press on to the target with the bombers. Over Berlin, Davis's P-51 developed severe engine trouble, making him a liability to the bombers he was supposed to escort and to the rest of the aircraft in his unit. Reluctantly he turned the formation over to Lt. Armour McDaniel, one of his most trusted leaders, and turned south toward Italy.

It was Davis's policy that when one of his fighters had to drop out of formation, it would proceed home escorted by another fighter. That way if the disabled fighter was forced to crash-land or ditch, or if the pilot had to bail out, another pilot would know the location of the downed man. In this case, because of the gravity of the escort mission, Davis set out alone for Italy, nursing a sick Mustang for 800 miles to his home base.

Meanwhile, the 332d fought off German fighters, never losing a bomber to the attacks of Germany's fastest and most sophisticated aircraft. At the end of the day the Tuskegee Airmen could claim three Me–262s shot down and another six damaged, with the loss of only one of their P-51s. Prior to that day only two of the Luftwaffe jets had been destroyed by American fighters. The 332d was awarded the Distinguished Unit Citation for this mission. Pilots were cited by Fifteenth Air Force for their "enthusiasm" and "esprit de corps," as well as "conspicuous gallantry, professional skill and devotion to duty."

Three weeks later, on April 15, Davis led thirty-six P-51s through low clouds and mountainous terrain to strafe a railroad near Munich, Germany, and Salzburg, Austria. The targets were extremely well defended by ground fire. Davis and his men made repeated passes, and he was credited with destroying or damaging six locomotives. Davis remained in the area at perilously low altitude and only reformed his squadron, now dangerously low on fuel, when there were no more targets available. For pressing the attack in bad weather and difficult terrain and against intense ground fire, Davis was awarded the Silver Star.

On April 26, the men of the 332d had the distinction of destroying the last 4 enemy aircraft destroyed in the Mediterranean Theater of Operations during the war. Eleven days later the war in Europe ended. By a large margin Davis's men had destroyed more aircraft than they had lost. They had shot down 111 enemy aircraft, nearly all fighters, and destroyed 150 on the ground. More than 600 boxcars and other rolling stock were destroyed or disabled. One destroyer and 40 boats and barges had been sunk.

Not one friendly bomber had been lost to enemy airplanes during 200 escort missions. This unique success was a testimony to more than the skill of the Tuskegee Airmen; it also highlighted the discipline drilled into them by Davis. By the time the unit had begun flying P–47s in the late spring of 1944, air superiority over Italy and Germany was in Allied hands. Davis insisted, therefore, that his men keep uppermost in their minds that their objective on escort missions was to defend bombers successfully and not to score victories. When German fighters were sighted near friendly formations, Davis ordered his men not to chase the Luftwaffe but to stay close to the bombers, even when the bombers flew into flak-laden skies. His tactical approach to escorting was conservative and probably would have been out of place at an earlier time or in a different part of the combat theater, but in the case of the 332d it worked brilliantly.

One must remember, furthermore, that Davis and his men had fought on two fronts: against the enemy abroad and against the discrimination they had suffered from birth and which did not end when they donned their country's uniform and laid their lives on the line. While the men were under Davis's command they answered insults his way, with articulate silence and the demonstrated ability to fly and fight. Davis saw to it that his Tuskegee Airmen swallowed their pride and hurt, fought their battles in the air, and gave the lie to their detractors.

Another great handicap is little known. With notable exceptions, 99th and 332d pilots had little aptitude for flying as measured by the standard aptitude tests used at that time. At the outset of training the AAF tried to maintain the same standards for black aviators as for whites. To qualify for flying training a white had to score a seven on the "Stanine" aptitude test's nine-point scale. This did not mean that those who scored lower could not learn to fly; it meant that the Air Forces expected to pay too high a price in training time and effort to produce pilots of lesser ability from those scoring below the standard. The aptitude test, which was periodically checked, was found to be valid.

It was discovered early, however, that there was no way to fully man the 332d at the seven level. The entrance standard was reduced steadily until at times the AAF was forced to ignore the score, although the test was still given. Some of the pilots in the 332d had scores of two, and the vast majority stood below seven. The 99th and 332d, therefore, were flying outfits made up of men with an average aptitude about half that of white units. That was an indictment of the segregated school systems of America—*de facto* in the North and *de jure* in the South—and in no way reflected on the men's native ability. The extent of this problem seemed only to magnify Davis's achievements, which continued into his next assignment at Godman Army Air Field, Kentucky.

*   *   *   *   *

In May 1945, Davis was rushed back to the United States to take command of the 477th Medium Bombardment Group, an organization whose morale had been destroyed by a white commander so insensitive in his dealings with blacks that General Arnold was forced to fire him and his entire white staff. This unhappy organization labored under multiple disadvantages from the time it was created in January 1944 until Davis assumed command seventeen months later. It had four disruptive unit moves—from Selfridge Field, Michigan, to Godman Field at Fort Knox, Kentucky, to Freeman Field, Indiana, and back to Godman Field. Race problems with neighboring communities and within the organization were a major factor in several of these dislocations.

The 477th's white commander had reserved all command positions for white officers, although some of the blacks were combat veterans and senior in rank to many of the whites. He and all his white subordinates also refused to associate socially with the black officers, who were relegated, against Army regulations, to a segregated officers' club. This led to a mutiny of black officers at Freeman Field in April 1945, during which more than 160 were arrested, almost all of them pilots and navigators. These arrests precipitated an uprising of virtually all black officers on the base, which resulted in the group's being moved back to marginally adequate Godman Field. The white commander who demoralized the 477th Group acted with the approval of the First Air Force Commander and most of the senior officers at Army Air Forces Headquarters.

In its first year of training, when the 477th had a reasonable expectation of reaching combat, the group logged nearly 18,000 flying hours with only

Col. Benjamin Davis, Jr.

2 minor accidents, neither attributable to crew error. In the first 3 months after the officers' club mutiny and the move back to Godman Field the unit suffered 5 accidents with 11 fatalities, all attributable to crew error. The men were demoralized, for they had witnessed the AAF's willingness to subordinate combat crew training to the issue of who could enter an officers' club. This was the unit Davis inherited.

Lt. Gen. Ira Eaker, Deputy Commanding General of the AAF and formerly Commander of Mediterranean Allied Air Forces in 1944, chose Davis for command because he was confident of Davis's leadership capabilities. The 477th was directed to prepare for combat in the Pacific, although the theater air commander did not want blacks. To hasten the unit's preparation, two of the four B–25 squadrons were disbanded and two of Davis's fighter squadrons from Italy were added, making the 477th a composite group.

Davis was known to most of the men, for all of the fighter pilots and many of the bomber pilots had served under him previously. They knew that he stood for professionalism, rigid discipline, flying and playing by the rules, and the outward ignoring of prejudice in order to undermine it by demonstrating the ability to fly. Davis was respected by the men; most important, they now expected to be treated like men and were on their way to fight the Japanese. Morale soared. Accidents disappeared, and the First Air Force Inspector General declared that the 477th would be ready to deploy to the

Pacific on schedule. However, Japan surrendered before the group completed its training. Davis's raising of morale and effectiveness was in no way connected to a change in the military's treatment of blacks, for discrimination did not end; only the bigotry within the group stopped when Davis took command.

Soon after the Japanese surrender, the military began to discharge men and dissolve units with abandon, but the 477th was retained and reduced to one B–25 bomber and one P–47 fighter squadron. Early the next year the unit was moved from Godman to Lockbourne Army Air Field, Ohio, where the leading Columbus, Ohio, newspaper editorialized that America was "still a white man's country" and objected to America's "servants" fighting for the country.

Davis did his best in the uphill fight to win the confidence of Columbus and central Ohio by staging frequent air shows, firepower demonstrations, and static displays. By the spring of 1949, he had succeeded in convincing the local civilians that his outfit was just another Air Force unit. However, relations with the communities were never as friendly as those enjoyed by most other Air Force units.

In addition to commanding the flying group, Davis, as base commander, was responsible for supporting the 55th Fighter Wing (a National Guard unit), the 82d Troop Carrier Squadron, Army Air Forces Reserve ground support units, and several other AAF organizations. All of these "tenant" units on the base were white. The record shows nothing other than clearly professional support by Davis and his men, and proper relations between the white tenants and their black hosts. It is probably worth noting, however, that none of the white officers or NCOs from these tenant units ever joined the Lockbourne officers' or NCO clubs, although they were invited.

The blacks, moreover, continued to suffer under segregation, most notably in terms of promotion. There was only one black unit in the Army Air Forces, and, therefore, room for only one colonel and a handful of lieutenant colonels. Had the combat veterans of the 477th been white, all of them would have held higher ranks in 1946.

In mid-1947, the 477th was redesignated the 332d Group, later Wing, and soon thereafter the B–25 squadron was deactivated. The 332d received no special favors and was called on to perform like any other wing. A highly proficient unit with motivated aircrews, it won an Air Force gunnery meet in 1949, and passed all major inspections that determined its fitness for war.

Despite the 332d's achievements, segregation posed numerous, serious problems for the wing. As noted earlier, personnel shortages could not be filled from units that had surplusses, and the 332d had numerous shortages. There were fifty-five flying wings in the Air Force, some of which had extra pilots, a critical shortage for the 332d, but none of the fifty-four white wings could assign a man to the 332d. Similarly, the 332d, once it had dropped the B-25s, had surplus navigators and bombardiers, but they could not be used in the Strategic Air Command, which was short of navigators, because that command was all white.

By the autumn of 1946, the 332d had fallen to only 22 of its authorized 75 pilots. The gap was narrowed very slowly but never completely closed. The AAF was no longer willing to train blacks with significantly lower aptitude than the standard, and there were too few blacks with the aptitude to fly who were willing to join the segregated military in peacetime. In 1949, the wing was up to 242 of its authorized 260 officers, but had on board only 1,381 of its authorized 1,931 enlisted men.

The familiar social indignities, furthermore, continued to plague the 332d. Whenever they flew away from their own field the men were socially segregated. During training maneuvers they generally ate and slept in segregated facilities and attended separated officers' and airmen's clubs, if there were separate clubs to attend. But Davis's men conducted themselves with cool dignity under these degrading conditions, for that was his policy.

It was not that Davis favored segregation; rather he believed that protest was not the way to undermine it. He, like his father, had always opposed segregation. When both Davises were called upon to testify before a board of general officers that met in 1945 to determine the best use of blacks in the United States military, both attacked racial segregation directly. The younger Davis based his condemnation of the policy on its inefficiency. He asserted the men of his units and blacks in general could have made a far greater contribution to the war effort had they been assigned according to ability and not race. He told the board that blacks had not been given a square deal by the Army, and that lowering standards, as had been done with the 332d and 477th, was unwise. He argued that blacks of aptitude equal to whites would be successful in white flying schools and advocated nonsegregated training. He believed strongly that white officers would accept competent blacks as long as the senior officers were willing to judge people irrespective of race. Davis said the War Department had to take the lead in promoting equal opportunity, and then make sure that senior officers supported that policy.

Davis's stand was courageous, for segregation was the policy, and the War Department showed no signs of wanting to abandon it. He recognized the personal risks in criticizing the top command. The senior black civilian in the War Department, Truman Gibson, refused to recommend integration when his turn came to testify before the same board, although in his heart he favored it. Yet Davis continued to speak out to the press and to black and white military and civilian audiences.

But it was not primarily Davis's testimony and public statements that helped to end segregation. It was his performance. The outfits he trained and led during and after World War II served as capably as other line Air Force organizations. The men of the 332d could be used in white units. When by 1948 Air Force leaders, perplexed by the difficulties of dealing with the under-manned 332d, accepted that fact, integration became an obvious answer. It was then that Lt. Gen. Idwal Edwards recommended, and Chief of Staff Gen. Hoyt Vandenberg agreed, that segregation in the Air Force be ended. In May 1949, the 332d Wing was disbanded. More than ninety percent of its officers and enlisted men were reassigned according to their specialties to white Air Force units that needed proven professional people. Henceforth blacks coming into the Air Force were to be assigned based upon their abilities and nothing else. No one was to be "either helped or hindered because of the color" of his skin. Such a policy could not have been adopted in 1941 when few in the War Department or the Army Air Forces believed that blacks could do the job of whites.

In 1949, there was a very powerful minority in the Air Force that continued to oppose integration. Even the top leaders who ordered an end to segregation were generally insensitive to the effects of segregation on blacks. If they had believed that racial segregation made a more efficient fighting machine than integration, they never would have abandoned segregation willingly. In fact, General Vandenberg and his Chief of Personnel, General Edwards, were on record after World War II as favoring segregation, but both of them gradually came to the same conclusion: segregation was preventing efficient operations—and they would not tolerate inefficiency.

It took months of arguing with stubborn Air Force generals who refused to recognize either the achievements of Davis and his men or the costs to the Air Force of segregation. Finally, Edwards and Vandenberg told these men that there would be no room in the Air Force of the future for people who opposed integration. Both men had the wholehearted support and encouragement of Air Force Secretary Stuart Symington and Assistant Secretary Eugene Zuckert, and the powerful weapon of President Truman's election campaign-motivated Executive Order 9981, which directed equal opportunity in the services. But it was Col. Benjamin O. Davis, Jr., and the Tuskegee Airmen he led, who provided living proof that the moral imperative of racial integration was attainable.

On the eve of the breakup of the 332d Davis assembled his unit for a final commander's call. He told his people of the new policy and explained that it meant equality of opportunity not only for them but for all blacks coming into the Air Force. He expected that soon the other services would adopt similar policies. Davis wanted his men and women to be justly proud of moving the Air Force to such a reform, for it was their performance that had accomplished this dream. He also insisted, moreover, that they had nothing to fear from integration, because they were not just "colored troops," but were, rather, fully qualified members of the United States Air Force, as accomplished and ready to perform the mission as any whites. That fact had been demonstrated over the war-torn skies of Europe and repeatedly in the post-World War II period. He said: "I have faith in you. I have the fullest confidence in you. I know you and what you can achieve and I know that you will succeed."

Even after integration took place, Benjamin O. Davis, Jr.'s career was still shaped by race, for no one would expect that all prejudice stopped when the Air Force formally ended segregation. The official sanctions and discriminations ended, but the Air Force was composed of thousands of people whose attitudes had been conditioned by prejudice, and although institutional bigotry ended, personal prejudice was much harder to uproot. Davis was mindful in the years ahead that the Air Force, as well as the Defense Department and many hostile individuals, were wary of the new racial policy, and many watched for signs of problems and failure. He was particularly aware of his own conduct and was determined never to give anyone reason to challenge or complain about his performance. This meant choosing not to favor those blacks who had served him and his units so well. He believed that had he chosen to build the careers of blacks by placing them in key staff or command positions, he would have had to intervene improperly in the personnel system, and would have violated his own principle of never choosing subordinates on the basis of race.

Davis's first assignment immediately after the 332d completed desegregation in the summer of 1949 was as a student at the Air War College at Maxwell Air Force Base in Montgomery, Alabama. A War College assignment was overdue for Davis, and he was one of the more senior students attending the course. The challenge here was reminiscent of those he had faced years earlier at West Point and Fort Benning. Only a few of his classmates were eager to demonstrate the workability of the new policy of integration, which was barely four months old. Instructor and peer ratings found Davis to be "outstanding," "extremely capable," "sound, intelligent," and "a good leader," but he and Mrs. Davis were socially isolated during most of that academic year.

With many of his classmates, Davis moved from the Air War College to Air Force Headquarters at the Pentagon in Washington, D.C. In 1951, he became Chief of the Air Defense Branch of Air Force Operations and later Chief of the Fighter Branch. Following his Pentagon tour, Davis was sent to Advanced Jet Fighter Gunnery School at Nellis AFB, Nevada, in preparation for command of a jet fighter wing. Upon graduation in November 1953, he was given command of the 51st Fighter Interceptor Wing at Suwon Air Base in Korea.

While in the Pentagon, Davis supervised whites, the first black to do so at Air Force Headquarters, but they were few in number. In Korea, however,

Col. Davis with two of his men of the 51st Fighter Interceptor Wing at Suwon Air Base in Korea where he served as Wing Commander.

Davis commanded a wing made up of three fighter squadrons and supporting units, manned almost entirely by whites. Davis was treated with the respect that his rank and position demanded. Because the people in the unit were overseas, they were much more cordial to Davis than had been the majority of his Air War College classmates. The wing performed well under his leadership.

In July 1954, Davis was named Director of Operations and Training in Far East Air Forces Headquarters, located in Tokyo and commanded by Gen. Earle Partridge. Three months later he was promoted to brigadier general. Mrs. Davis, for her part, used their foreign travels to learn about the cultures they lived in and near. While in Tokyo, she organized an American-Japanese club to help promote mutual understanding.

The following summer, General Davis was appointed Vice Commander of Thirteenth Air Force, headquartered at Clark Air Base in the Philippines, and Commander of Air Task Force Thirteen (Provisional) at Taipei, Taiwan, a delicate post that combined diplomacy with the need for military command ability. His mission in Taiwan was to build an organization from scratch that would demonstrate the resolve of the Eisenhower administration to defend the Republic of China. Air Task Force Thirteen was to maintain assigned or attached forces in a state of readiness for immediate offensive or defensive air operations in defense of Taiwan and the Pescadores. Davis would command all Air Force strike aircraft when they were moved from other bases to Taiwan. If hostilities arose, he would be the air task force commander in combined operations involving both the Nationalist Chinese and United States Air Forces. He, therefore, was involved in training the Republic's air force so that it could work with his own.

Davis was sent to Taiwan with 5 enlisted men—a cadre that grew to more than 430 officers and men. He was given no buildings or transportation facilities—a problem that had to be solved while he was establishing command relationships with Air Force strike and air defense squadrons and creating a 24-hour-a-day operations center. On top of all this he had to deal with proud Chinese political and military leaders who needed American support but resented it at the same time. Davis established excellent relations with President Chiang Kai-shek, his son, Chiang Ching-kuo (the present President of the Republic), and with the entire senior Chinese military leadership.

When Davis completed this assignment in April 1957, he left a fully operational command and control facility that had been built from nothing. Gen. Laurence S. Kuter, Commander of Pacific Air Forces, noted that Davis had the ability to "tactfully criticize at the right time and places," and to say "no" to the Chinese when they were asking for something that could not be given them. Yet he maintained their complete cooperation.

Many years later, a Republic of China officer told Air Force Gen. Bryce Poe that sending Ben Davis to Taiwan was the smartest thing the United States could have done. The communists in mainland China, North Korea, and elsewhere kept telling the Nationalist Chinese that "the little brown man"

Chinese Nationalist Minister of National Defense discusses agenda to visiting U.S. officers from l. to r.: Brig. Gen. Edwin Walker, Maj. Gen. Harold W. Grant, and Brig. Gen. Ben Davis

does not have a chance in America, and here the senior American military representative on Taiwan was "a man of color." General Davis's work on Taiwan, this officer believed, had an enormous impact on U.S. relations in the Far East—probably more than even the State Department realized.

Davis was reassigned from Taiwan to Europe, where he served first as Chief of Staff of Twelfth Air Force, then as the Deputy Chief of Staff for Operations in Headquarters, United States Air Forces in Europe, at Wiesbaden, Germany. He held the latter position—normally a two-year assignment—for more than three years and was promoted to major general. While at Wiesbaden, General Davis played tournament bridge with Gen. Gabriel P. Disosway, the Commander of U.S. Air Forces in Europe, as his partner. They were undefeated over a period of several years. General Davis also found time for an occasional round of golf. A better-than-average golfer, he still shoots in the eighties.

From Wiesbaden, Davis was assigned to the Air Staff in the Pentagon as Director of Manpower and Organization. There he directed a staff of almost 160 officers and senior civilians who established manpower policies for the Air Force and justified the $6 billion Air Force personnel budget to the

Gen. Gabriel Disosway pins second star on Maj. Gen. Davis, which he receives while serving as Deputy Chief of Staff for Operations, USAFE.

Department of Defense, the Bureau of the Budget, and Congress. He was selected for promotion to lieutenant general while in that assignment.

Next, Davis was assigned once more to Korea as Chief of Staff of the United Nations Command, and Deputy Commander of United States Forces, a position he held from April 1965 to July 1967. There he was responsible for coordinating all combat preparations for both American and Korean forces. His position had considerable diplomatic prestige, but Davis wanted a command.

After Korea, he was given command of Thirteenth Air Force at Clark Air Base in the Philippines, but it was not, as he hoped, a combat command. During the Vietnam War, Seventh Air Force in Saigon was the focus of Air Force combat activity. Davis was responsible for the air defense of the Philippines, and had under his command more than 55,000 people; however, his most important function was to provide logistical support and fighting forces for Seventh Air Force. When his units went into combat in Vietnam they were put under the operational command of Seventh Air Force, as were all groups provided by Tactical Air Command and most other Air Force sources, with the exception of the Strategic Air Command.

Lt. Gen. Davis with 2d Infantry Division in Korea in 1966.

Left: Maj. Gen. Davis as USAF Director of Manpower and Organization visits Eielson AFB, Alaska in 1961 and is greeted by the base commander, Col. Stephen Henry; *below*: Davis with President Ford in August 1974.

Davis longed for another combat command but was given instead the position of Deputy Commander in Chief of U.S. Strike Command at Mac-Dill Air Force Base, Florida, with additional duty as Deputy Commander in Chief, Middle East, Southern Asia and Africa. He believed this might be a holding assignment while he awaited a fourth star and a major air command, but that never materialized. He retired from active Air Force service in 1970.

Unquestionably race played a role in General Davis's post-integration career. Both he and Mrs. Davis enjoyed overseas assignments where they met less racial discrimination than in the States. But it was overseas, most importantly, that the Air Force was willing to use Davis as a commander. All of his commands after Air Force integration were overseas, despite his outstanding record as a commander. The Air Force apparently believed that the time was right for senior black commanders, but not in the United States.

Soon after his retirement from the Air Force, Davis served briefly as Safety Director for Cleveland, Ohio, where he commanded the city's police and fire departments, and reduced a crime rate that had been surging before his arrival. Shortly thereafter he was appointed Director of Civil Aviation Security, responsible for the Department of Transportation's anti-hijacking measures. Later, he was named by President Richard Nixon as Assistant Secretary of Transportation (Environment, Safety and Consumer Affairs). In these positions he helped cut the number of hijackings in the United States from thirty-four to zero in less than two years.

Upon retirement from the Department of Transportation in August 1975, General Davis received a letter from President Gerald Ford:

> Throughout an exceptional career in the Air Force, marked by both heavy responsibility and great achievement, you demonstrated a capacity for making the tough as well as the right decisions. It was this ability, as well as your broad experience and qualities of leadership, which were needed at the beginning of this decade to counter the acts of air piracy then threatening aviation travel at both the national and international levels. Under your direction . . . security of the American airways has been restored with an absolute minimum of disruption to the freedom of movement of travelers. You can take pride in this accomplishment and a large measure of personal satisfaction in the physical and emotional well-being the program brought to millions of American travelers.

The letter was signed simply, "Jerry Ford."

Davis's contribution to the safety of American air travel was significant, but it paled by comparison to his role in Air Force racial integration, a reform of incalculable benefit. Davis set out in 1941 to help achieve integration in the military forces by disproving the core argument for segregation: the widespread belief that blacks could not perform as well as whites. He succeeded. The integrated Air Force unquestionably became more efficient than a segregated force had been. In 1941, the armed services were depriving themselves of the effective services of ten percent of the American population; today that no longer is true. Equally significant, segregation provoked endless disturbances that often crippled military effectiveness, because unequal opportunity definitely undermined morale. The Air Force (like the other services and civilian enterprises in America) has had to relearn that fact several times. Today it faces the last two decades of the twentieth century as the service with the most harmonious race relations and as the most thoroughly racially integrated major institution in American society.

When Davis joined the Army Air Forces, he was its only black officer; when the Air Force integrated in 1949, there were fewer than 375, or about 0.6 percent of the officer corps. By 1983, the more than 5,000 black officers in the USAF comprised about 5 percent of the officer force. While Davis was the first and only black general from 1954 into the 1970s, in 1983 the active-duty Air Force had 10 black generals and more than 100 black colonels. There has been similar growth in the Reserve Forces. In 1949, blacks made up less than 2 percent of the master sergeant supervisory rank, contrasted to more than 14 percent in 1983. Today, 17 percent of Air Force enlisted people are black, compared to 6 percent in 1949.

General Benjamin O. Davis, Jr., can claim a larger measure of credit for inaugurating this critical reform than can any other person. None of his many achievements holds for him the satisfaction of moving the United States Air Force to racial integration. For that pioneering accomplishment, America stands in his debt.

Sources

There are no book-length or chapter-length biographies of Benjamin O. Davis, Jr. His was a largely untold story before the publication of the present volume, and he is deserving of much deeper treatment. One can find information on Davis scattered in several popular histories. For example, Charles Francis, *The Tuskegee Airmen* (Bruce Humphries, 1955) is a useful, if generous, account of black aviators in World War II, that makes up in enthusiasm what it lacks in scholarship. Similarly, Davis appears often in Robert A. Rose, *Lonely Eagles: The Story of America's Black Air Force in World War II* (Tuskegee Airmen, Inc., Western Region) which was privately published, but is available through the Tuskegee Airmen Association. Rose's book is less reliable than Francis's. Davis is also treated in Alan M. Osur,

Blacks in the Army Air Forces During World War II (Office of Air Force History, 1977), which is scholarly. While the first two volumes mentioned are too oriented toward the combat accomplishments of the black aviators, the last underemphasizes these achievements. Finally, one can find many scattered references to Davis in Ulysses Lee, *The Employment of Negro Troops* (Office of the Chief of Military History, 1966). Lee's is an exceptionally fine history, and his writing on the treatment and achievements of American blacks during World War II has not been surpassed.

For Davis's contribution to integration in the Air Force, the armed forces, and the nation, see Alan L. Gropman, *The Air Force Integrates, 1945–1964* (Office of Air Force History, 1978). Davis also is treated in Morris J. MacGregor Jr., *Integration of the Armed Forces, 1940–1965* (Center of Military History, 1981). Gropman and MacGregor give much less prominence to the role played by President Harry S. Truman in armed forces integration than does Richard M. Dalfiume, *Desegregation of the U.S. Armed Forces: Fighting on Two Fronts* (University of Missouri Press, 1969), and readers may wish to delve into Dalfiume for another point of view.

Official histories of the units Davis commanded during and after the war are available at the Office of Air Force History, Bolling AFB, Washington, D.C., and at the U.S. Air Force Historical Research Center at Maxwell AFB, Alabama.

Davis's contribution to America is worthy of a full-length biography. Unfortunately he has retained few private or personal papers, but he is in exceptionally fine health, has an outstanding memory, and is warmly approachable. A professional historian with solid experience in oral history should begin to mine this source now. Most of Davis's subordinates, furthermore, are alive, and many are eager to talk about him.

11

Nathan F. Twining:
New Dimensions, a New Look

Donald J. Mrozek

Nathan Farragut Twining was the first Air Force officer appointed to the nation's highest military post—Chairman of the Joint Chiefs of Staff (JCS). He was a direct and seemingly uncomplicated man who said what he believed to be true, made no impossible promises, and fulfilled all of his commitments. He inspired confidence in those who served under him and in those whom he served.

During World War II, Nate Twining commanded air forces in the Pacific and the Mediterranean. As a field commander, he was regarded more as a tactician than a strategist. When President Eisenhower appointed him Chief of Staff of the Air Force, and then Chairman of the JCS, Twining was thrown into a highly charged military-political environment where policy and strategy took precedence over tactics. He made the difficult transition without abandoning either directness or candor. Eisenhower characterized his leading airman as "a man of integrity and great common sense."

In his personal life, Twining was an accomplished outdoorsman who hunted wild turkeys with a rifle and whose collection included many big game trophies. His marksmanship was to stand him in good stead during the war, when his plane was forced to ditch in the Pacific. An ardent golfer, he numbered Arnold Palmer among his friends.

General Twining rose to the top of his profession while the Air Force was in a period of technological, tactical, and strategic transition from the equipment and ideas of World War II to those of the nuclear era. He was fortunate to serve under a President whose defense policies fit to a remarkable degree with the ideas and aspirations of the Air Force. That good fortune, coupled with Twining's experience, integrity, and sound judgment, marked him as one of the more successful Air Force Chiefs and among the most respected Chairmen of the Joint Chiefs of Staff.

Although the ultimate course of his career was affected by chance and fortune, Nathan Twining was born into a family that was positively disposed toward the military. One of his brothers became a captain in the Navy, while his younger brother, Merrill Barber Twining, rose to lieutenant general in the Marine Corps and served as commandant of its school at Quantico, Virginia. Nathan was born in Monroe, Wisconsin, on October 11, 1897, the son of Clarence Walker Twining and the former Maize Barber. He attended public school there until the family moved to Portland, Oregon.

Twining joined Company H of the Third Infantry, Oregon Army National Guard in June 1916, held its military leaders in high regard, and enjoyed his duties. His father strongly approved of his taking the examination for appointment to West Point, as Twining's forebears had fought in America's earlier wars. His grandfather had been dismissed from the Quakers for fighting in the Civil War (and had two brothers who were killed at Vicksburg). The wording on the tombstone of another of Twining's ancestors summarized the patriotic dedication to which Nathan felt himself heir: "If anybody ever asked why I went to war, please tell them that I loved my country." This sense of family tradition, dating back to his ancestors' arrival at Plymouth in 1635, bolstered the military interests and patriotic sentiment that grew from Twining's own experience.

After service along the Mexican border in 1916 in pursuit of Pancho Villa, Twining returned to Oregon as a first sergeant and was soon called up again when the Guard was ordered to protect Portland against violence feared from the International Workers of the World, or "Wobblies," who were believed to be plotting to overthrow the government.

Soon after, Twining received word that he had been appointed to West Point. His first inclination was to turn down the appointment. It looked as though the United States would become involved in World War I, and he wanted to be a part of the action. His regimental colonel dressed him down properly, explaining that he could do far more as a lieutenant and do so much more quickly. Nathan reconsidered, entered the Academy in June 1917, and completed the abbreviated wartime course in November 1918. Ten days after graduation, the war was over. Twining's West Point class was recalled in December 1918 for further study, officially ending their work in June of the next year.

After advanced training at Fort Benning, Georgia, and in preference to a promising assignment with the infantry demonstration platoon there, he went to Arcadia, Florida, for primary flight training. He then served as an

Maj. Gen. Nathan F. Twining

aide to Brig. Gen. B.A. Poore at Camp Travis in San Antonio. Eventually, Twining arranged for his release to complete pilot training at Brooks and Kelly Fields, Texas.

After earning his wings in 1924, Twining, who was an excellent pilot, served as a flight instructor at Brooks and then at March Field, California, where he became a check pilot. While stationed at March, a friend in Los Angeles who owned a yacht wanted to enter a sailing race to Honolulu. He asked Twining, who knew nothing about sailing, to go along as a crew member. The yacht, which was not designed for open ocean racing, lost its mast and radio antenna in a storm. They finally made it to Honolulu seven days after the last of the other contestants.

Nate Twining's prewar flying experience was in pursuit and attack aviation. After three years at March, he was assigned to the 18th Pursuit Group at Schofield Barracks, Hawaii. While there, he married Maude McKeever, the daughter of a plantation owner. The couple had two sons—Richard Grant and Nathan Alexander—and a daughter, Olivia, who later married the son of Air Force Maj. Gen. Haywood S. Hansell.

After the Twinings returned to the States in July 1932, most of the next three years was spent with the 3d Attack Group at Fort Crockett, Texas, with a brief interlude as engineering officer for the Central Zone at Chicago when the Air Corps flew the mail in early 1934. In March 1935, Twining was named assistant operations officer of the GHQ Air Force's 3d Wing at Barksdale Field, Louisiana. While at Barksdale, he was promoted to captain, after seventeen years as a lieutenant.

From August 1935 to June 1937, Twining attended two of the more interesting service schools of the interwar years—the Air Corps Tactical School at Maxwell Field, Alabama, and the Command and General Staff School at Fort Leavenworth, Kansas. There followed three years in which he gained valuable experience in maintenance and logistics as Air Corps technical supervisor at the San Antonio Air Depot.

*　　*　　*　　*　　*

With the outbreak of the war in Europe, the long-sought Air Corps expansion got underway. In August 1940, Major Twining was assigned to the Office of the Chief of the Air Corps in Washington, where he served successively as Chief of Technical Inspection in the Operations Division, as an assistant executive to Lt. Gen. Henry H. Arnold, and as Director of War Organization and Movements. In June 1942, he was promoted to brigadier general.

In July 1942, Twining went to the South Pacific as Chief of Staff for Maj. Gen. Millard F. Harmon, Jr., who had served as Chief of the Air Staff from January 1942 until becoming Commander of U.S. Army Forces in the South Pacific under Rear Adm. R.L. Ghormley. Twining thought Ghormley a stuffed shirt. The admiral would not allow his officers to take off their ties in that tropical climate, and fought the war without ever leaving his headquarters ship. Ghormley was soon replaced by Adm. William "Bull" Halsey.

In January 1943, Twining became Commander of the Thirteenth Air Force. Shortly after his promotion to major general the following month, Twining's B-17 was forced to ditch at sea. He and his crew tossed about on a life raft in the blazing sun without food, save for one albatross that was shot soon after ditching. The weakening crew was confident that General Twining could bring down another albatross with the last cartridge in their pistol. Twining shot the circling bird so perfectly that it fell near the raft. Although the albatross provided meager fare, it did revive their spirits. After six days, just before the search was abandoned, they were picked up by a Navy patrol bomber. Twining was so badly burned by the sun that he required skin treatment for several months.

In mid-1943, Admiral Halsey gave Twining tactical control of all AAF, Navy, Marine, and Allied air forces in the South Pacific. As COMAIRSOU, Twining supported landings on the Treasury Islands and Bougainville. Then, after seventeen months of combat operations in the theater, General Harmon decided that Twining needed a short rest in the States. Back in Washington, he paid a courtesy call on General Arnold and mentioned that General Harmon expected him back on duty in a couple of weeks. Arnold said, "You're not going back. I'm giving you a week to take over the Fifteenth Air Force."

In Italy, Twining succeeded Maj. Gen. James H. Doolittle, who was transferred to command the Eighth Air Force in England. As Commander of the Fifteenth from November 1943 to July 1945, Twining oversaw the 1944 bombing of Romanian oil fields at Ploesti, and his units participated in attacks on the Messerschmitt factory at Regensberg, both costly in aircraft and crews but crucial to the strategic bombing campaign. Early in 1944, he was given an additional assignment as Commander of the Mediterranean Allied Strategic Air Forces.

Twining's experience in the Mediterranean seemed to confirm what he had learned at the Air Corps Tactical School and what had become standard fare on the Air Staff. His concern over losses was genuine and profound, but he believed the decisiveness of a full-scale strategic attack justified the sacrifice. Years later, reflecting on the risks of continuing the costly bombing of synthetic oil plants in Germany when foul weather precluded poststrike reconnaissance, Twining underscored the persistence with which strategic bombing was to be carried out in World War II: " . . . if you're going to be successful in your air attacks, you must go out day after day, day after day, and not give the enemy a chance to rebuild; just keep it knocked down." This lesson stayed with him the rest of his life.

Twining also learned some lessons about dealing with the Russians. As Soviet forces advanced to the west, a bomb line was established beyond which American planes were not to go. Several times, the Russians shot down crippled American bombers that were attempting to make emergency landings in Soviet-held territory. Crews that managed to land safely to the east of the bomb line were interned by the Soviets.

Once, late in the war, the shoe was on the other foot, though accidentally. Fifteenth Air Force sent a formation of fighters to strafe a German column moving along a valley in Yugoslavia near advancing Soviet units. The formation leader went one valley too far and attacked a Soviet column, killing several Russians, reportedly including at least one general. Soviet Yak fighters attacked the Americans, and Twining's pilots shot down all of them. Twining expected to be relieved of his command for this error, but instead, the Soviets sent a message thanking Twining for the fine support he had given them, and saying that they understood the navigation error that had caused

261

Above: Maj. Gen. Twining (left), Fifteenth Air Force Commander, with Lt. Gen. Ira Eaker, Commander-in-Chief, Mediterranean Allied Air Forces, in Bari, Italy, 1944; *below*: Twining attends Italian troop review.

the incident. According to Twining, the Russian liaison officer at his head-quarters told him not to apologize further. They had, he said, plenty of generals.

With the war over in Europe, General Twining returned to Washington in July 1945. His stay was brief. The following month, General Arnold sent him back once more to the Pacific to take over command of the Twentieth Air Force, headquartered at Guam, from Maj. Gen. Curtis LeMay. LeMay's first question was, "What in the hell are you doing here, Nate?" to which Twining, replied, "If you don't know, Curt, it's too late." Twining, essentially a kind and considerate man, never understood Arnold's way of doing business.

Twining had not been told about the atomic bomb and its impending use against a Japanese city. He was skeptical of the strange orders from Gen. Carl Spaatz, Commander of the U.S. Strategic Air Forces in the Pacific. The bomb had to be dropped visually and could not be brought home if weather prevented visual bombing. Spaatz himself was less than enthusiastic about the untried weapon. Believing, as General Arnold did, that Japan was on the verge of surrender and that the bomb need not be used, he insisted on a writ-ten order for its first use. Twining, for his part, refused to order the Hiroshima mission until he was briefed on the bomb. Years later he recalled: "I was led inside the fence and they told me what it would do. Of course, I did not believe them. It was an awful looking thing . . . warts all over it . . . terrible."

The atomic bomb left the doctrinal issue of precision strategic bombing moot, but it clearly showed that truly massive firepower had become available. Twining later mused that dropping the weapon might have served as "a good lesson for the world," thinking that it was better for everyone to understand what the weapon could do. He may also have thought that it contributed to deterrence by reducing doubt about the willingness of the United States to use its nuclear arsenal.

In December 1945, Twining was named head of the Air Materiel Com-mand (AMC) at Wright Field, Dayton, Ohio. Although never an expert in science and technology, he came to know capable scientists in and out of the military and developed a greater awareness of the effects of surges and cuts in budgets for personnel and research. His good working relationship with Assistant Secretary of War for Air Stuart Symington helped Twining press successfully for test facilities in the Mojave Desert and at Cape Canaveral, Florida, which were crucial to future jet and rocket testing.

Similarly broadening was his service as Commander in Chief of the Alaskan Command, starting in October 1947. In that assignment, Twining commanded Air Force units charged with patrolling airspace close to the Soviet Union as a part of the nation's deterrent effort. It also gave him authority over the smaller Navy and Army contingents based at Kodiak and Anchorage, respectively. From a personal point of view, Twining's love of nature and the

Commanding generals of the reorganized Air Forces, Mar. 1946, standing, l. to r.: Lt. Gen. Nathan Twining Maj. Gen. Donald Wilson, Maj. Gen. Muir Fairchild; seated from l. to r.: Lt. Gen. John Cannon, Gen. George Kenney, Gen. Carl Spaatz, Lt. Gen. Harold George, Lt. Gen. George Stratemeyer and Maj. Gen. Elwood Quesada.

outdoors made his stay enjoyable. Friends recalled a sense of nostalgia that Twining showed when talking of his aerial exploration of that expansive, unspoiled land. To airmen, however, Alaska was important because of its proximity to the only potential adversary of the United States, the belief that any surprise attack on the United States would come over the north polar area, and the emphasis placed on air strategy as the key to national defense.

*　　*　　*　　*　　*

In July 1950, Twining returned to Washington to serve briefly as head of Air Force personnel, then as USAF Vice Chief of Staff under Gen. Hoyt S. Vandenberg, with whom Twining had taken flight training at Brooks and Kelly Fields. Vandenberg was respected as a leader and aviator, gifted as an athlete, and by no means harmed politically as nephew of the influential Senator Arthur Vandenberg of the Senate Committee on Foreign Relations.

General Vandenberg brought Twining into a solid working relationship that established a measure of continuity in the Air Force's contacts in Congress and with the Office of the Secretary of Defense. This proved especially important as General Vandenberg's health worsened, requiring Twining to sit in as substitute on the Joint Chiefs more frequently than was customary and adding to his routine responsibilities as Vice Chief of Staff.

Twining's stint as Vice Chief was no picnic. Essentially, the Vice Chief manages the day-to-day affairs of the Air Force, but during Twining's tenure there were the additional pressures of the Korean conflict and of General Vandenberg's declining health. Apart from the demands of the war itself, the Korean crisis and the increasing truculence of the Soviet Union persuaded the Truman administration to strengthen U.S. and Allied forces elsewhere as well. The change of political administrations in January 1953 caused some anxiety, if only because of the uncertainties that it automatically fostered.

Despite his personal admiration for Eisenhower, Twining worried over his prospects as a politician and national leader. After Eisenhower's first campaign speech, Twining observed that it sounded little like the old Ike. "Already they are telling him what to say," Twining remarked. "Shades of Ulysses Grant!" While these concerns dissipated after Eisenhower came into office and after Twining saw him in action, relations with some officials in the new administration often proved difficult. General Vandenberg defended the Air Force's budget and program requests against Secretary of Defense Charles Wilson's assertions that many millions could be cut safely. Twining took on the formidable task of effecting some working compromise. Meanwhile, General Vandenberg's health continued to fail despite his brave efforts to carry on the public side of his duties. Twining often had to substitute for him as a strong advocate of the Air Force program, while he, at the same time, was seeking an acceptable compromise with Secretary Wilson's staff.

As Vice Chief, Twining had disagreements with some officials of the Eisenhower administration, even when there was broad agreement on policy goals. But these disagreements did not damage Twining's career or reputation. President Eisenhower appointed him to succeed Vandenberg as Air Force Chief of Staff on June 30, 1953. Under both Truman and Eisenhower, first as Vice Chief and later as Chief, Twining worked vigorously to realize the expansion of the Air Force, which Secretary Symington had been able to initiate with congressional approval of what was widely termed the "70-group program" that provided the basis for U.S. strategic air power in the 1950s. Twining later judged that the service had gotten nearly all it really wanted.

Twining also thought that Congress displayed considerable cooperation, especially in recognizing the importance of modernizing the force structure. An important case was conversion to jet aircraft, including the B–52; another was commitment to the ballistic missile programs. Leavened by men experienced in defense such as Symington (who had been elected to the Senate after he resigned as Secretary of the Air Force) and strengthened by such well-placed Democrats as Mendel Rivers, Carl Vinson, and Richard Russell, the group in Congress favoring a relatively high and consistent level in defense spending worked closely with Twining and other officers. Since the Air Force played an especially important role in the defense strategy developed during Truman's and Eisenhower's administrations, Twining thus enjoyed good relations with those in positions of power whose agreement was essential to building a strong force.

For all his personal ability, much of Twining's success on behalf of Air Force interests in the early and middle 1950s depended on the fact that Congress and two successive Presidents generally were favorably disposed toward an expansion of air power. Moreover, Twining's success was enhanced by an underlying political consensus—the bipartisan agreement that political rivalries over domestic concerns would not be allowed to generate antagonisms over foreign policy. That consensus had been strengthened by the participation of Senator Arthur Vandenberg, until his death in 1951. His conversion to international involvement during the years immediately after World War II and his work in favor of a combat-capable military force had made Air Force interests much more acceptable.

Communism was clearly regarded as a global and potentially lethal threat to the United States, particularly through what was seen as Soviet domination

Gen. Twining at a 1956 press conference.

of radical-leftist politics around the world and Soviet sponsorship of wars and revolutions. This view lacked some sense of the complexities within the Communist sphere and missed the interplay between the internationalist political pretensions of Communism and the parallel but different drives of anticolonialist nationalism. Nonetheless, this view of the Soviet Union did much to create a political climate favorable to a sustained defense buildup by providing a highly visible and truly ominous threat. The strategy that emerged under President Eisenhower, which placed the Air Force in an especially important role, made far more sense in the context of a global threat than such a strategy could possibly have made without that stimulus.

*   *   *   *   *

Twining's effectiveness as Air Force Chief of Staff was enhanced by other political circumstances, both national and international, that affected the limits of growth for the American military. On the national scene, the change of leadership that occurred in the U.S. armed forces at the outset of the Eisenhower administration was wholesale. In his memoirs, President Eisenhower denied that the appointment of four new service chiefs in rapid succession had any special motivation—a disavowal perhaps necessitated by the somewhat tumultuous relationship between President Truman and some of his military subordinates, as well as the convenience to Eisenhower's broader purposes of the rapid turnover of military leadership.

Eisenhower called it mere coincidence that General Bradley's term as Chairman of the Joint Chiefs and General Collins's term as Army Chief of Staff ended in late August 1953, closely following General Vandenberg's retirement for disability on May 7, 1953. The President feared, however, that useless speculation as to the successors of the retiring senior officers would develop, and so announced well in advance that Adm. Arthur C. Radford would succeed General Bradley and that Gen. Matthew B. Ridgway would be appointed Army Chief of Staff. On June 2, Adm. Robert B. Carney was named to succeed Chief of Naval Operations Adm. William M. Fechteler, whose two-year term was ending. Only Gen. Lemuel C. Shepard, Commandant of the Marine Corps, continued, since his term did not expire until January 1, 1956. Thus, General Twining assumed leadership of the Air Force and membership on the Joint Chiefs of Staff at an unusual moment of parity with the heads of the other services. In a sense, as a highly experienced staff officer well versed in the ways of Washington, Twining was an unusually rich beneficiary of what was partly an accident of timing.

On the international scene, the war in Korea came to an end. As President Eisenhower later acknowledged, the removal of this nagging problem permitted more serious attention to the nation's long-range military needs and challenges. Indeed, at least for Eisenhower, the novelty of the new look at defense policy that he ordered the Joint Chiefs to take lay largely in its avoidance of quick fixes, impulsive responses to crises, and sudden fluctuations in spending and procurement. The "normalcy" which Eisenhower wanted to develop in the defense area required the comparative calm of the postwar environment. It also meant that whatever program emerged early in the Eisenhower years was likely to receive enduring support from the President once he had accepted it. This proved to be the case.

For all its dislocations, the quadrupling of defense spending during the Korean War did not bring economic disaster as some had predicted. After the truce, far higher levels of spending were sustained than ever before in peacetime—well over twice what had been spent under Truman before the war.

Since the emphasis on strategic forces in the Eisenhower administration's New Look weighted funding heavily in favor of the Air Force, it was easy for Twining not only to act as an advocate of his own service, but also to stand strongly for the administration's policy. This helped to win him White House support throughout the eight years of the Eisenhower administration. Unlike a growing group of Army officers that included General Maxwell Taylor, Eisenhower and key Air Force leaders tended to view regional and even many local problems as ultimately instigated by "the head of the Communist power." Eisenhower thus believed that a firm commitment to escalate a conflict—usually described as answering a challenge in a manner of our own choosing under a policy of "Massive Retaliation"—would probably deter conflict in the first place. The way to minimize the problem of "brushfire wars," apart from preserving limited conventional forces to engage in one or possibly two of them at a time, was to strengthen the nuclear-armed Strategic Air Command. Ultimately, this policy rested as much on psychology as it did on the specifics of the nation's force structure. To a degree, the policy fit with Twining's own experience.

Moreover, the President firmly believed that the United States could not afford by any criterion—humanitarian, economic, political—to attempt to govern world affairs or to meet global military problems by providing the bulk of the manpower needed to defend our allies and friends. The structure of the U.S. armed forces thus was shaped, in part, by a division of military responsibilities between this country and its allies, and the United States was better off to play its long suit. In essence, this meant concentrating on its strategic nuclear capability, guaranteeing a massive retaliation in the event of attack on an ally or other external interests. Meanwhile, the United States would also continue to support scientific research and technological development. In the context of the late 1940s and 1950s, this assured the Air Force of the most crucial military role.

Circumstances may have favored Twining, but it is also true that he took advantage of them with skill and enthusiasm. Moreover, Twining apparently felt free to provide advice to the President through the chiefs, unhindered by other administration officials. He later recalled, for example, that the New Look had been given its broad contours in meetings of the Joint Chiefs, unaffected by precise guidance from the President and without the involvement of Secretary of State John Foster Dulles. In Twining's view, this demonstrated the confidence Eisenhower placed in his military advisors. It also may have indicated the degree to which Eisenhower expected cooperation with the broad drift of his own thinking. Twining thought that Admiral Carney's departure from his post as Chief of Naval Operations stemmed from disagreements with administration policy and Eisenhower's desire to have only "good chiefs" working out the defense issues. "Good" evidently meant broad conformity to the administration's emphasis on strategic capability and on the Air Force, making Carney's periodic "tirades" on defense questions, as Twining called them, especially irritating.

President Eisenhower and Secretary of State John Foster Dulles (far right) meeting with President Diem of South Vietnam.

Twining also had his disagreements with Eisenhower and did not hesitate to air them before the President. He deeply objected to having American military advisors, who were sent to Vietnam when the French left after the Geneva Accords of 1954, wearing civilian clothing and being addressed without ranks. Although this complaint suggested the limits of Twining's concern over the political subtleties of the Southeast Asian problem, it also reflected his burning desire for clarity, order, and forthrightness in any military effort.

More significant as an expression of his commitment to deterrence was his advocacy of the use of nuclear weapons to relieve the French garrison at Dien Bien Phu in 1954 before the French withdrew from the war, despite his reluctance to have U.S. forces engaged in Southeast Asia. From one to three bombs would have done the job, he later said, lifting the Viet Minh siege without endangering the French. Tests on tactical use of nuclear weapons had been conducted in the Nevada desert, so Twining's view depended on more than guesswork. Using the bomb would have eliminated any doubt that the United States would employ atomic weapons tactically, thus strengthening conviction among friend and foe about the reliability of U.S. deterrent power. Twining and others were overridden in the Dien Bien Phu debate, but his strong advocacy of a nuclear strike did not cost him future advancement or the confidence of the President—perhaps a tribute to both men.

A key duty of the chief of a military service—possibly the single most important one in a practical sense—is to win approval of a budget satisfactory to his service. Here, Twining had at least a leg up on his brother chiefs. Since the defense program devised for the New Look heavily favored the Air Force, Twining could afford to be relatively less aggressive as an advocate or dissenter. Eisenhower persistently fought what he viewed as unwarranted special interest lobbying by the individual services. He often told the chiefs to put the common interest of a truly national defense above the services' parochial interests in cutting the budgetary pie.

To his long-time friend E.E. "Swede" Hazlett, Eisenhower wrote on August 20, 1956: "I have made little or no progress in developing real corporate thinking" among the services as a whole and the chiefs in particular. He considered the "kindest interpretation" he could put on this sad state of affairs was that "each service is so utterly confident that it alone can assure the nation's security, that it feels justified in going before the Congress or the public and urging fantastic programs. " He wanted the chiefs to appreciate the balance between what America could afford to spend on defense and what was required to keep the economy healthy. He was continually frustrated by having the chiefs seem to respond favorably to his injunctions yet continue to propose "minimum requirements" for their services' budgets that "mount at a fantastic rate. "

Eisenhower predicted both ominously and presciently: "Some day there is going to be a man sitting in my present chair who has not been raised in the military services and will have little understanding of where slashes in their estimates can be made with little or no damage." Then, according to the President, the most serious effects of interservice rivalry would reveal themselves, and the military would lose influence over the entire budgetary process and hence over the entire range of military capabilities that it supported. Meanwhile, Eisenhower could only rely on finding men with "the breadth of understanding and devotion to their country" that permitted them to identify with a national defense policy over the interests of their respective services. Despite Twining's deep commitment to the Air Force program, the symmetry of his views with those of Eisenhower cast him in a favorable light.

Twining himself occasionally reflected on the deeply imbedded problems of military special interest, not only among, but also within the services. Brig. Gen. Noel Parrish remembers that Twining once warned against the parochialism of commanders: "You may be satisfied with the way they do their jobs, but their jobs will be limited in time and they are not likely to worry about what will happen in the future to their commands, and the Air Force, and the country." It was not a matter for blame, since the key responsibility of the commanders was to be ready in the present. "I have to think of that, too," he added, "but I have to get ready for the future. . . ."

With plenty of solvable, or apparently solvable, problems to deal with, General Twining refused to waste energy worrying about situations over which he had no control. During the peak of the "flying saucer" sightings that swept the country, he held a brief press conference following a speech in Amarillo, Texas. After a few questions about the world military balance, which Twining had discussed in his speech, the newsmen zeroed in on the flying saucer scare and if the Air Force was doing anything about it. "I don't worry about these stories," Twining replied. "If such things really arrive from outer space, they are so far ahead of us that we could not possibly defend ourselves." That ended the discussion.

During the 1950s, the Air Force received enough budgetary support to expand and modernize its strategic aviation units and its tactical forces (the latter at least up to 1956) and to move decisively in the field of intercontinental ballistic missiles (ICBMs). Twining approved what he considered an Air Force version of the Manhattan Project, which was directed by Maj. Gen. Bernard Schriever and aimed at rapid development of an accurate missile that would carry a thermonuclear warhead. Recent scientific reports had persuaded Twining that building a relatively light but high-yield fusion weapon that could be carried by an ICBM was technically feasible. He later claimed that even Secretary of Defense Wilson did not know about the Air Force's crash program, although the results counted for more with Wilson than did the fact that Twining had exercised an extraordinary degree of independence by using

271

resources for a program that had not won universal agreement either among the chiefs or in the Defense Department.

*   *   *   *   *

In 1954 and 1955, a crisis developed over Quemoy and Matsu, two of the Tachen Islands held by the Nationalist Chinese on Taiwan but claimed by the People's Republic of China. At that time, the announced U.S. policy for confronting aggression was Massive Retaliation, perhaps with nuclear weapons. That crisis illustrates how a President and his military advisors might have different views on using strategic forces to implement Massive Retaliation without transforming a regional confrontation into global war.

When mainland China's artillery assault against Quemoy began on September 3, 1954, intelligence officials forecast the possibility of a Communist invasion within days. General Twining participated in a meeting at Eisenhower's temporary White House in Denver on September 12. He joined JCS Chairman Admiral Radford and Admiral Carney in advocating outright commitment to defend the offshore islands claimed by the Nationalists, meanwhile preparing against the contingency of a strong Chinese Communist attack. The predominant view among the chiefs was that U.S. measures could be kept confined to the region and that U.S. military advantages, such as the continuing ability to block Communist coastal communications, made the risks involved in holding the islands worth taking. Eisenhower disagreed, warning that any attack he likely would authorize against China might not share the limits imposed on U.S forces during the Korean War. Thus, in his view, the course recommended by the chiefs, which they intended as a limited commitment, might become something larger than a brushfire war or a narrowly confined conflict. Eisenhower believed the "logical enemy" was the Soviet Union rather than China, and thus even a lesser engagement held a substantial risk of becoming a prelude to World War III.

Twining and others did not accept the idea of yielding territory or evacuating U.S. and Nationalist personnel from the islands, apparently because they did not fully accept the logic behind Eisenhower's approach. Twining saw no reason to assume that a strike against China would trigger a world war, particularly in the context of the immediate problem. Hence, limited-force employment remained a possible and reasonable option, even if the ultimate goal was comprehensive deterrence of conflict across the whole spectrum by building an overwhelming striking force.

Despite such differences, Eisenhower appears to have maintained confidence in Twining, in part because of the latter's candor. At the same time that he might advocate a particular course, Twining often cautioned the President about its possible pitfalls. His balanced assessments and avoidance of an unthinking "can do" attitude were revealed during the crisis over Lebanon in July 1958, when that country's strongly pro-Western political leader called for U.S. military support against Communist-inspired attacks on the government. Twining warned the President that distance and time made it inevitable that the first Marine battalion deployed in Lebanon would be ashore alone for at least twelve hours before reinforcements could be brought in. Meanwhile, arrangements were made to airlift the Army's 187th and 503d Airborne Battle Groups from Germany. Twining transmitted to the President the recommendation of the Joint Chiefs that Air Force tankers be moved to forward positions and that SAC go on "an increased level of alertness," but he cautioned Eisenhower that there might be adverse political effects, especially if these actions were misinterpreted by the Soviets. Such sensitivity to matters that were not narrowly military seems to have contributed to Eisenhower's favorable opinion of Twining and to the general's ability to gain an attentive hearing for his recommendations.

The administration hoped to limit its Middle East losses following the murder of Iraq's King Faisal in 1958 and the overthrow of his pro-Western regime. The administration relied heavily on providing support to friendly Middle East nations through airlift as well as by creating an enhanced military presence closer to the region. Eisenhower ordered Twining to prepare to use, subject to the President's approval, whatever force was needed to prevent a move by the new and presumably unfriendly Iraqi government against Kuwait. Eisenhower's determination that the gravity of such a move should be widely perceived removed the nicer political calculations from the process of contingency planning. Stationing a Marine regimental combat team in the Persian Gulf thus did not strike Eisenhower as either provocative or controversial but rather as a necessary move that "would probably bring us no closer to general war than we were already."

Twining showed a cautious approach in 1959 in discussing the Allied ability to defend West Berlin when the Soviet Union announced its intention to turn access to the city over to the East Germans. He warned the President not to rely on the same sort of airlift that Truman had used a decade earlier if the ground routes to Berlin were again sealed off. Berlin's Tempelhof Airport could not accommodate the largest civilian jet-powered cargo aircraft that would be called into service.

Matching Twining's stability in times of crisis and adding to his effectiveness in coordinating overall defense was his persistence in fighting through the administrative and bureaucratic morass that constantly threatened to bog down military readiness. Although no one has fought that battle to total victory, Twining showed more skill at it than did most others. Illustrative was his service with the special advisory group on the Defense Department's implementation of the 1958 Reorganization Act. Secretary of Defense Neil McElroy appointed, as members of the group, JCS Chairman General Twining, Gen. Alfred Gruenther, and former Chairmen of the JCS Arthur Radford and Omar Bradley. Nelson Rockefeller and former Secretary of Defense Robert Lovett also joined the special panel. Participation did not depend on the offices currently held by its members but apparently on their personal suitability to developing a more streamlined and responsive military. Twining thus had a chance to advance his own interest in genuinely unified combat commands and in substantial centralization of research and development.

The administration's firm call for unity at least helped to channel cases of parochialism and reduce some of their effects. A case in point was the development in 1959 of the Integrated Field Operations Center with a joint staff to devise and maintain comprehensive targeting and planning for a possible strategic war. The issue behind this Center and the planning it would undertake were complicated. On the one hand, the forces to be used in strategic war were managed by the separate services. On the other hand, they would have to be used in a way that would optimize their effect and eliminate duplication, waste, and inefficiency. Institutional interests of the services and their relative roles in defense were involved. After the development of the submarine-launched Polaris missile, Secretary of Defense (and former Secretary of the Navy) Thomas Gates strongly advocated establishing a jointly staffed Center. Gates believed operational effectiveness now demanded that the Navy, in effect, move in with SAC for purposes of joint target selection and operational planning. Despite some objections from military professionals (including some in the Air Force) and partly because of his desire to advance genuine economies and close cooperation of the services on functional or "horizontal" lines, Eisenhower approved the measure. The backing of a Chairman of the JCS who was an Air Force officer and the backing of a Secretary of Defense who had been intimately associated with the Navy provided an auspicious context for the move.

Throughout the 1950s, Twining and Eisenhower remained steadfast in their shared vision of America's best defense, seeking protection against encroachments from special interest groups in and out of the services that sought to increase funding for programs not favored under the New Look. In the end, their position proved to be somewhat double-edged. On the positive side, the national defense program enjoyed a significant measure of coherence. Strategic offensive systems provided an assurance of retaliation in the event of an attack against the United States or its critical interests. Continental defense, including interceptors and warning systems, lent credibility to the threat of retaliation by lowering the impact of an enemy's first strike.

Meanwhile, alliances promised to provide a degree of balance between ground forces, air power, and naval forces. The negative side was that the tactical capabilities of U.S. forces were slighted by comparison.

If the general political vision that guided Eisenhower was not to be shared by his successors, then the system of defense he had favored would seem dubious. Some observers, including Air Force officers, thought that close air support and tactical bombing had become virtual orphans and that conventional ordnance was frozen at World War II levels of technology. Meanwhile, the Army leadership, especially under General Maxwell Taylor, pressed for funds to prepare for small wars. Twining believed that Taylor's proposals could be countered, at least as long as Eisenhower was President. Both Twining and Eisenhower may have underestimated the rapidity with which strategic assumptions would change as missiles accumulated in the arsenals of both superpowers. An increasingly vocal and persuasive group of analysts concluded that the risks of escalation to the nuclear level exceeded the risk in actually fighting smaller wars.

Twining's lack of enthusiasm for General Taylor stemmed in part from their occupying opposing ends of the spectrum on strategic ideas. But it also grew out of differences in temperament and in the manner in which Taylor

Gen. Maxwell Taylor (left) at a White House meeting with President Kennedy, 1962.

John F. Kennedy Library

seemed to cultivate his views. Twining thought that Taylor should have come "on board" rather than continue to press Eisenhower for a change in strategic outlook and force structure. In a meeting with Twining on July 27, 1958, the President allowed that Army and Navy leaders believed too much emphasis had gone to the strategic nuclear side under the New Look, but added that he remained opposed to increasing funds for conventional and counterinsurgency forces. Taylor meanwhile directed some of his efforts to explaining his ideas to Democratic political figures, notably the Kennedys, some of whom shared tennis and other activities with the Army chief. Taylor and other Army officers also were reported to be visiting the Kennedys on weekends at Cape Cod. There was nothing technically wrong with such meetings, but Twining and others, including some Army officers, thought them less than completely proper. Although the long-term fate of his strategic views thus became clouded, Eisenhower had made sure that the three Secretaries of Defense who served him continued in the spirit set early in his first term. Such consistency on the part of a President has been rare in American public life, and it was a superb match for the first airman to serve as Chairman of the JCS.

*   *   *   *   *

As the Eisenhower administration entered its waning months, Twining faced the prospect of the end of his effectiveness as Chairman of the JCS. Later he commented that he could not have served President Kennedy well because of the disjunction of their views and what he considered a reluctance on Kennedy's part to consider unwelcome advice. Eisenhower attributed Twining's departure to ill health (not inconsistent with the President's custom of playing down possible controversy). There seems to have been a measure of truth in both claims. Twining was hospitalized in 1959, and there was some concern about his ability to continue with the rigors of his office. Twining also regarded Nixon's defeat in the 1960 elections as probable. After just over three years as Chairman of the JCS, Twining retired on September 30, 1960, making way for Eisenhower to appoint Army Chief of Staff Gen. Lyman Lemnitzer as his successor.

Immediately after his retirement, Twining was named Vice-Chairman of the Board of Holt, Rinehart and Winston, although he claimed no knowledge of the publishing business. He retained that association through 1967. He also became a director of United Technologies—an activity closer to his special interests while in military service. Yet Twining stayed close to the public arena more because of his enduring interest in national defense issues, especially at the strategic level, than because of his business connections.

At a reception given in his honor at Andrews AFB, Maryland, departing Chief of Staff Gen. Twining greets Adm. Arthur Radford. Shown in receiving line, from *l. to r.*: Mrs. Twining, Gen. Twining, Mrs. James Douglas, and Sec. of the Air Force James Douglas.

Twining devoted considerable time and energy to outlining his views on the development of postwar defense in his book *Neither Liberty Nor Safety*, published in 1966. The book explained both Twining's sense of the historical context that encouraged Americans to move along certain strategic lines and his appraisal of how well those lines had been pursued. He provided a balanced, noninflammatory judgment of interservice rivalry, seeing it as very much the child of technological changes that had so altered time and space in the use of weapons as to eliminate traditional land-sea-air divisions. He approved of the emphasis on offensive capability in the years after World War II, particularly when coupled with continental defense, seeing no alternative if enough power were to be maintained to deter a potential aggressor. He also reaffirmed his dissent from those who had erroneously predicted that the defense would prove dominant over the offense in the 1950s and who had foreseen no early capability in the ICBMs.

Twining avoided sharp criticism of political leaders of the 1940s and 1950s. He defended Dean Acheson's remarks concerning a U.S. defense perimeter that excluded Korea and Taiwan as delicate diplomatic language for a firm and decisive statement of what the U.S. would defend unilaterally and the areas it would help defend in conjunction with other members of the United Nations. As to the Korean conflict itself, Twining objected only to what he viewed as indecision after Chinese combat units entered the war. The speculation over "limits" to war rubbed him the wrong way and found no place in his conception either of the principles of war or of common sense. The conduct of the Korean conflict from late 1950 on clearly distressed Twining. He saw in it the roots of a serious concession to the Soviet Union—namely, that it could fight proxy wars with impunity and that the United States was a paper tiger.

Twining revealed the underlying difference between himself and some other defense observers and analysts when he named as America's key error in the 1950s its "determination to accept the status quo and initiate no action which would increase world tensions." From his point of view, it was imperative to expand the free world and to defend it by putting the Communist world on the defensive. As part of this approach, he saw no reason to shy away from integrating tactical nuclear weapons into U.S. plans for defending its own interests or those of its allies. To do otherwise seemed to Twining merely an encouragement of aggression. He did not deny that risks existed, but he distinguished among different kinds of risks. The worst was to imperil liberty by a false resort to merely temporary safety. Thus, in order to avoid an all-out nuclear war, the United States should be willing to consider using nuclear weapons to end quickly a lower level conflict. This would tend to reduce the likelihood of such conflicts or proxy wars in the future when it became apparent that the United States would choose the weapons least costly in terms of manpower, money, and time.

Meanwhile, limiting strategic forces struck Twining as similarly counterproductive, for the certainty of deterrence seemed to him to depend on preserving clear superiority. His reasoning derived not from emotion but from a professional observation: although military plans and programs were aimed at affecting enemy intentions and thus achieving deterrence, they had as their immediate concrete objective the ability to fight a war and cope with the enemy's actual capabilities irrespective of intent. Lasting deterrence could not be predicated upon transitory intentions, especially since intentions could shift with changes in the balance of forces.

Twining espoused these views in his support of the American Security Council, a lobbying group on defense issues, notably in advocating deployment of an antiballistic missile system (ABM). As cochairman of the council's special National Strategy Committee, Twining participated in its 1969 report on "The ABM and the Changed Strategic Military Balance, U.S.A. vs. U.S.S.R." The report was concerned as much with Soviet intentions as with capabilities, and insisted that America's security demanded military superiority to overcome both enemy capabilities and the intentions they might spawn.

Given Twining's sense of the primacy of strategic security to the full range of defense and other national concerns, it is hardly surprising that he was sharply critical of the pattern of American involvement in Vietnam, a position doubtless deepened by his lack of confidence in some of its key designers.

Although he had disagreed with President Eisenhower's decision to observe a moratorium on atmospheric testing of nuclear weapons, Twining saw this measure as an error of calculation rather than of spirit—of the head rather than the heart. However, he objected both to the substance of the Test Ban Treaty executed by the Kennedy administration in 1963 and particularly to the pressure that was exerted to make the Joint Chiefs publicly support the measure while harboring serious professional objections to it. Corruption of the whole system of defense policymaking and program execution seemed in the offing as Secretary of Defense Robert McNamara appeared intent on concentrating authority in his office and on ignoring the experience and advice of the military, from the Joint Chiefs on down. Although he had seen centralization as a likely trend while chairing the JCS, Twining was greatly concerned about the implication with someone such as McNamara in charge. By ignoring professional military advice, the Kennedy administration pursued a policy that Twining believed maximized the disadvantages faced by the United States in actual combat, while damaging the system fostered by Truman and Eisenhower. Although less critical of Lyndon Johnson, Twining nonetheless saw his policy as mired in half measures and tainted by a sickening attrition in Vietnam that would eat away at the American commitment.

When Twining died at Lackland Air Force Base, Texas, on March 29, 1982, he left behind a legacy of accomplishment that was enviable. He had shared in building the modern bomber force that was the backbone of early postwar deterrence, supported strong and technologically advanced tactical air and airlift forces, called the cards right on the important ICBM program, and contributed to the evolution of the system of military administration at the Pentagon.

Throughout his career and in his years of active retirement, Twining staunchly represented a particular vision of national security and a distinct approach toward defense—one not best described in political terms such as "conservative" but better styled as "professional. " If his profession was peace, as the SAC motto put it, his tools were the hardware of deterrence. The philosopher William James believed that life became more valuable to those who lived for something beyond themselves. Nathan Twining unstintingly sought the higher goal of national security as the underpinning of American political liberty.

Sources

An invaluable resource for appreciating Twining's career and his views is his oral history interview, conducted in 1967 by John T. Mason, Jr., as part of the Columbia University Oral History Project. Most direct quotations of Twining in this essay come from that interview, available through the Oral History Research Office in Columbia's Butler Library. Several other direct quotations derive from recollections of Twining graciously shared by Brig. Gen. Noel Parrish. Also useful for an outline of Twining's career until retirement from the Air Force is Flint O. Dupre, *U.S. Air Force Biographical Dictionary* (Franklin Watts, 1965). Primary sources on the Air Force are available at the U.S. Air Force Historical Research Center at Maxwell Air Force Base, Alabama, but those interested in Twining's service in the 1950s should not neglect the papers of Dwight D. Eisenhower at the Eisenhower Library in Abilene, Kansas.

For comments on Twining as well as background concerning the broad range of national security issues, the two volumes of Dwight D. Eisenhower's memoirs are useful. See Eisenhower, *Mandate for Change, 1953–1956* (Doubleday, 1963) and *Waging Peace, 1956–1961* (Doubleday, 1965), in which direct quotations of the President used in this essay appear. Among other pertinent memoirs and commentaries are Thomas K. Finletter, *Power and Policy* (Harcourt, Brace, 1954), Vannevar Bush, *Modern Arms and Free Men* (Simon and Schuster, 1949), and Maxwell D. Taylor, *The Uncertain Trumpet* (Harper and Row, 1960).

The crucial background of Air Force thinking during Twining's career is studied in Robert Frank Futrell, *Ideas, Concepts, Doctrine* (Air University, 1971), and an important survey of defense reorganization in the years that included Twining's service in Washington is Paul Y. Hammond, *Organizing for Defense* (Princeton University Press, 1961). On the importance of the northern latitudes to strategic thinkers, see Melvin Conant, *The Long Polar Watch* (Harper and Row, 1962). Concerning the bipartisan consensus on foreign policy and its usefulness, see Ronald Steel, *Pax Americana* (Viking Press, 1967), and for Arthur Vandenberg's role in its development, see Lloyd C. Gardner, *Architects of Illusion* (Quadrangle, 1970). Donald J. Mrozek, "A New Look at 'Balanced Forces'" (*Military Affairs*, 38), explores symmetries between the policies of Truman and Eisenhower; but do not neglect Herman S. Wolk, "The New Look in Retrospect" (*Air Force Magazine*, March 1974).

For ideas reconsidered or formulated late in Twining's Air Force career or during retirement, see Twining, *Neither Liberty Nor Safety* (Holt, Rinehart and Winston, 1966), and Twining et al., "The ABM and the Changed Strategic Military Balance, U.S.A. vs. U.S.S.R." (American Security Council, 1969).

12

Bernard A. Schriever: Challenging the Unknown

Jacob Neufeld

World War II sparked an effusion of scientific and technical developments, among them radar, electronic warfare, jet engines, air-to-air and air-to-ground missiles, and data processing technology. But two innovations of unprecedented character were to affect the Air Force and the world balance of power the most: nuclear weapons and ballistic missiles.

Gen. Henry H. "Hap" Arnold, who led the Army Air Forces in World War II, believed correctly that the Air Forces' future lay in adapting scientific and engineering advances to air warfare. He was determined to continue in peacetime the cooperation between the Air Force, university scientists, and industry that had paid such handsome dividends during the war. One of the men selected to help fashion the technology of the postwar Air Force was a young colonel named Bernard Schriever, who combined some uncommon personal attributes with engineering training and combat experience. Schriever was to become the officer most closely associated with the development of ballistic missiles. Ultimately, he would be responsible for research, development, and acquisition of all new weapons used by the United States Air Force.

Bennie Schriever was recognized as an unusually intelligent man: a strong character with a precise, disciplined, but creative mind; a determination to master any task he undertook; and a willingness to make hard decisions. These characteristics were at least in part a result of an extraordinary background. He was born in Bremen, Germany, on September 14, 1910, the son of an engineer for the North German Lloyd Steamship Line. His earliest recollections are of German Zeppelins flying over his home on the way to bomb Great Britain in the First World War.

281

In 1916, the ship on which Bennie's father, Adolph, served was seized in New York and its crew interned. Early the following year, Elizabeth Schriever took her sons, Bernard and his younger brother Gerhard, to join their father in New York. When Adolph was released, the family settled in Texas, where they had relatives. Adolph was hired as a quality control engineer in a large engine plant in San Antonio. In September 1918, he was killed in an industrial accident, and Elizabeth Schriever, unskilled and not fluent in English, suddenly became the sole support of herself and two young sons.

There were some very difficult months when the boys had to be placed in a foster home until Mrs. Schriever found work as housekeeper for a wealthy San Antonio family. Her employers later built a small house for the Schrievers at the edge of the Breckinridge Park municipal golf course. The energetic Mrs. Schriever put up a small refreshment stand near the twelfth green and sold homemade sandwiches and cold drinks to the golfers. The Schriever boys contributed to the family finances by doing chores and caddying.

Even with the security of a home and steady employment, life was not easy for the boys, especially Bennie, who was expected to look after his younger brother. At a tender age, the boys had been cast from a stable, middle class North German environment into completely different geographic and social

Bernard A. Schriever

surroundings. Added to that was the strong current of anti-German feeling in this country during the 1920s. Bennie Schriever accepted it and in a true-life Horatio Alger story, determined to excel in everything he did. He graduated from San Antonio High School with honors, and as an outstanding golfer. Schriever then went to Texas A&M, graduating in 1931 with a degree in architectural engineering.

Engineering jobs were hard to find during the Great Depression. The six-foot-four-inch Schriever had two alternatives. He could become a professional golfer (he had been featured in Ripley's *Believe It or Not* for three times driving more than 300 yards to the same green and one-putting for an eagle), or, having been an ROTC cadet at A&M, he could accept a Reserve commission as a second lieutenant in the Field Artillery. The former alternative meant an easy and pleasant life; the latter, a chance to become an Army flyer, but with no guarantee of active duty for more than three years. At that time, Regular Army commissions were given only to West Point graduates. Schriever chose the Army and completed pilot training at the Army Air Corps Flying School, Kelly Field, Texas, in June 1933.

His first duty assignment was at March Field, California, where he served as a bomber pilot and engineering maintenance officer under Lt. Col. Hap Arnold. One of his most memorable experiences was flying the air mail when the Air Corps took on that job in early 1934. Schriever would remember the deaths of Army pilots who flew the mail in ill-equipped aircraft and with little training in instrument flying. He was determined to use his engineering skills to improve the flyers' lot.

Schriever's active duty ended in April 1935. He then applied unsuccessfully for a job with the airlines. In June 1935, the Civilian Conservation Corps (CCC), a New Deal agency that provided work for unemployed young men, hired Schriever as a camp commander in New Mexico. He remained there until October 1936, when he was able to return to active duty with the Air Corps. In December, he was assigned to Albrook Field in Panama, where he met and later married Dora Brett, the daughter of Brig. Gen. George H. Brett.

Schriever's industrious, efficient nature concealed a private, somewhat puckish, sense of humor. General George Brett's son, retired Lt. Gen. Devol Brett, tells how his father used to call on Schriever and another young lieutenant to fly formation with him in open cockpit P–12 fighters. General Brett insisted on a very tight formation. When they came in for a formation landing, however, the two young wingmen were supposed to drop back slightly to open up the formation. Instead, they would stick tight to the general's wing, then as they approached the end of the field, chop their throttles and land while General Brett had to go around for another landing.

In August 1937, Schriever was accepted as a pilot by Northwest Airlines, flying the route from Seattle, his new base, to Billings, Montana. The following January, he and Dora Brett were married in "Hap" Arnold's Washington, D.C., home. The Arnolds and the Bretts had been friends for many years, and since General and Mrs. Brett could not leave Panama for the wedding, the Arnolds volunteered to serve as *in loco parentis*.

On one of Hap Arnold's visits to the Boeing plant in Seattle, he and Schriever managed to get together for a golf game. Arnold told Schriever that some 200 Regular commissions were to be awarded. Schriever liked commercial flying, but military life appealed to him as offering broader opportunities than the airlines. It was a tough decision since he was about to become a Reserve captain and, if called to active duty, would be paid about $500 a month. If he won a Regular commission, it would be as a second lieutenant, with much lower active duty pay. Nevertheless, Schriever took the Air Corps examination and on October 1, 1938, was commissioned as a Regular second lieutenant and immediately assigned to the 7th Bombardment Group at Hamilton Field, California, as a B–18 instrument flying instructor.

After a year at Hamilton, Schriever was assigned to Wright Field, Ohio, as an engineering officer and test pilot. While there, he was selected as one of six officers to attend the Air Corps Engineering School—the forerunner of today's Air Force Institute of Technology. On completion of the one-year course, in July 1941, the Army Air Forces (which the Air Corps had become the previous month) sent Schriever to Stanford University to earn a master's degree in aeronautical engineering. By the time he graduated in June 1942, six months after Pearl Harbor, Schriever had been promoted to major and was assigned to the 19th Bombardment Group in the Southwest Pacific. He flew sixty-three combat missions in B–17s while serving as the group's chief of maintenance before he was taken off operations because of his experience and training as an aeronautical engineer.

By the war's end, Bennie Schriever had advanced in rank to colonel and in responsibility to Commander of the Advanced Headquarters, Far East Air Service Command. That organization was responsible for building and operating all maintenance, repair, and supply depots that supported the Far East Air Forces. He was one of the few air officers to witness the Japanese surrender aboard the USS *Missouri* in Tokyo Bay.

*   *   *   *   *

Col. Bernard Schriever's experience, educational background, and reputation as both a thinker and a doer destined him to remain on the technical side of Air Force activities. After the convulsive demobilization that followed World War II, the Air Forces had few officers with his qualifications. In January 1946, he was assigned to the Army Air Forces Headquarters in the Pentagon as Chief of the Scientific Liaison Branch in the office of the Deputy Chief of Staff for Materiel. He was fortunate to be working closely with Dr. Theodore von Karman, head of the Air Force Scientific Advisory Board (SAB). Von Karman took the young colonel under his wing and introduced him to many leading scientists, helping Schriever to reforge the connection between the scientific community and the Air Force that had existed during the war.

Schriever soon found himself at the center of a select group of young officers who believed that the Air Force had slighted scientific research and development since Arnold's retirement in February 1946. The group included Majs. Theodore Walkowicz, Peter Schenck, James Dempsey, Vincent Ford, and Ralph Nunziato. Maj. Gen. Donald L. Putt, Air Staff Director of Research and Development, was the senior member of this group, which campaigned for a separate research and development command and the establishment of a deputy chief of staff for development on the Air Staff. Aiding the group was retired Lt. Gen. James H. Doolittle, a close friend of Gen. Hoyt S. Vandenberg, who succeeded Gen. "Tooey" Spaatz as Air Force Chief of Staff in April 1948.

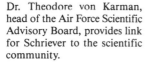

Dr. Theodore von Karman, head of the Air Force Scientific Advisory Board, provides link for Schriever to the scientific community.

This group prevailed upon the Air Force leadership to commission a SAB study of research and development. Dr. Louis Ridenour headed a committee of scientists that reviewed the status of R&D in the Air Force. The Ridenour Committee agreed with Schriever and his colleagues that Air Force R&D would be vastly improved by creating a research and development command. A parallel study conducted by a military committee led by Maj. Gen. Orvil Anderson of the Air University and completed in November 1949, concurred. The Anderson Committee also recommended that a deputy chief of staff for development be added to the Air Staff.

Following a one-year break from Pentagon duty to attend the National War College in Washington, Schriever was again assigned to the Air Staff. He wanted to become Vice Commander of the Air Proving Grounds, Eglin AFB, Florida, but instead was named Deputy Assistant for Evaluation under the newly created Deputy Chief of Staff for Development. In January 1951, Schriever's office, which performed or contracted for analytical work, was renamed the Development Planning Office. In addition to its planning function, the office oversaw the work of the Rand Corporation which had a contingent of eight to twelve people assigned to the Development Planning Office in the Pentagon.

As Assistant for Development Planning, Schriever devised a method of analysis called Development Planning Objectives, or DPOs. The purpose of the DPOs was to identify promising advances in technology and to coordinate them to meet future operational requirements of the Air Force. Separate DPOs were created for the major Air Force mission areas—strategic, tactical, airlift, air defense, and intelligence and reconnaissance. The intelligence and reconnaissance DPO was among Schriever's most important early achievements, but the highly classified nature of this field will prevent its public disclosure for many years to come.

The DPO methodology clashed with the Air Staff's traditional procedure for establishing weapons and equipment requirements. While Schriever sought to *push* technology forward to new advances, the traditionalists were content to merely *pull* it along as requirements demanded. As the new boy on the block, Schriever's approach produced some internal friction in the Air Staff. Although he did not always succeed, he enjoyed the confidence of the top Air Force leaders, Gen. Nathan Twining, who became Chief of Staff in June 1953, and Gen. Thomas White, Vice Chief of Staff.

Once convinced of the correctness of a position, Schriever never shrank from confronting such formidable opponents as the Commander in Chief of the Strategic Air Command (SAC), Gen. Curtis E. LeMay, who wanted, among other things, a nuclear-powered aircraft able to fly at supersonic speeds. Analysis showed that only a *subsonic* nuclear-powered bomber was feasible. Colonel Schriever, called to General LeMay's office to defend his position

Gen. Curtis E. LeMay, Commander-in-Chief, Strategic Air Command

against the SAC staff, held his ground. Expert scientific opinion supported Schriever's position, which ultimately prevailed.

LeMay and Schriever were destined to disagree frequently. Although the two men respected each other, their views often were quite far apart. LeMay, the operator, usually looked for solutions to near-term problems, while Schriever's vision was more attuned to the future. Among the major issues between the two were disagreements over the best method of inflight refueling, whether or not tactical aircraft should carry nuclear weapons, and whether strategic bombers should be designed as large aircraft attacking from high-altitude, or smaller aircraft with low-altitude attack capability. An advocate of the latter, Schriever was instrumental in developing the B–58 and pushing for the low-altitude attack.

Life in the Pentagon during the formative years of the postwar Air Force gave some foretaste of the pressure under which Schriever was to operate a few years later. It often was a seven-day work week with little opportunity for family life, let alone golf. By this time, the Schriever family included three children: a son, Brett, and two daughters, Dodie and Barbara. There was an occasional trip to Florida for a family gathering with General and Mrs. Brett, who were living in retirement in Orlando. While Bennie was at the Pentagon, Mrs. Schriever packed for the trip. At the end of the day he would load the family into the car and drive non-stop to Florida. Mental and physical stamina were trademarks of Schriever operations. Years later an officer who worked for Schriever said, "Anyone not in good physical condition, who doesn't have a trigger-quick mind, had better not work for this general."

*   *   *   *   *

Undoubtedly Bernard Schriever left his most prominent mark on the development of Air Force intercontinental ballistic missiles (ICBMs). When Schriever was selected to manage the ICBM program in mid–1954, it had suffered through a checkered history marked by stop-and-go development, unrealistic requirements, divided authority, low priorities, and indecision as to whether emphasis should be on ballistic or winged missiles, such as the Snark and Navaho, which essentially were unpiloted aircraft.

Research in the ballistic missile field had begun immediately after World War II, but soon fell victim to budgetary cuts that reduced it to dormancy. The program was resurrected in January 1951 as Project MX–1953, which led ultimately to the Atlas ICBM. In December 1952, a committee of the Air Force Scientific Advisory Board headed by Dr. Clark B. Millikan recommended a phased approach that would not produce an operational missile until 1965.

In March 1953, Schriever learned of a scientific breakthrough that appeared to make intercontinental missiles technically feasible much sooner than the Millikan Committee thought possible. At a meeting of the SAB, Dr. Edward Teller, one of the leading advocates of developing hydrogen weapons, reported on the successful test of a hydrogen bomb device in November 1952—the "Mike" shot. Dr. John von Neumann, head of the Institute for Advanced Study at Princeton, New Jersey, confirmed Teller's report and predicted that hydrogen warheads would be extremely light, with a high explosive yield. This news captured the attention of Schriever and Theodore Walkowicz, a retired Air Force officer. The two visited von Neumann and were convinced that the predicted new weapon, lighter and much more powerful than atomic warheads, promised to dispel one of the major obstacles in ICBM development. The missiles could be less powerful because of the lighter warhead and less accurate because of the warhead's greater destructive power. Von Neumann believed that a thermonuclear warhead could be built by 1960, weighing 1,500 pounds and with a one-megaton yield. Schriever urged the SAB to formalize these findings and prevailed upon von Neumann, Teller, and other leading scientists to issue a report in June 1953 which confirmed the feasibility of such a light-weight, high-yield warhead.

By this time Dwight Eisenhower had been inaugurated as President, and there were new faces at the helm of the Department of Defense. Harold Talbott was the new Secretary of the Air Force, and Trevor Gardner was his special assistant for research and development. Schriever and Gardner saw eye-to-eye on the significance of the thermonuclear warhead, or H-bomb, to ICBM development. In October 1953, Gardner formed a Strategic Missile Evaluation Committee, informally known as the Teapot Committee, made up of distinguished scientists and engineers under the chairmanship of Dr. von Neumann. Schriever's office provided Air Staff support for the committee.

In its report of February 1954, the Teapot Committee made several important recommendations. It confirmed the feasibility of building an operational ICBM by 1960, but believed that it would be possible only if a "radical reorganization" was effected, including the creation of a new agency that would be "relieved of excessive detailed regulation." The committee believed that missile accuracy could be reduced to three miles and warhead weight to 1,500 pounds. Intelligence reports that the Soviets were ahead of the U.S. in developing long-range ballistic missiles added urgency to the committee's recommendations.

At that time the Air Force used a single prime contractor to develop a new weapon system. Where relatively minor technological advances were involved, the single-prime approach worked reasonably well. However, when applied to major technological developments, it proved less effective because of constant changes in design, components, performance specifications, and inventory planning, with resultant program slippages and cost overruns. Clearly, if the ICBM program was to succeed, it required a new management philosophy.

Trevor Gardner, the principal architect of ICBM acceleration, believed that Soviet achievements in the missile field made development of the Atlas missile as urgent as had been the World War II atomic bomb project. He convinced Air Force Chief of Staff Nathan Twining and Secretary Talbott of the project's importance. In March 1954 the Air Research and Development Command (ARDC) was directed to establish a military-civilian group to "redirect, expand and accelerate" Atlas on a crash basis. In May the Air Force assigned Atlas top priority and directed that it be speeded up to the maximum extent technology would allow.

Although he had succeeded in gaining Air Force priority for ICBM development, Gardner believed it essential to dramatize the program so as to gain top *national* priority. Gardner asked Bernard Schriever, now a brigadier general, to manage the ICBM program. Schriever agreed, but only on condition that he be granted sweeping authority in order to get the job done.

The Western Development Division (WDD) was created as a new agency under Air Research and Development Command to manage the ICBM program outside the traditional Air Force bureaucracy. In August 1954 Schriever assumed command of the division, which was located at Inglewood, near Los Angeles. He also had the title of Assistant to the Commander of ARDC, which meant he could bypass much of the cumbersome bureaucracy.

General Schriever had two personal attributes that were invaluable in his new position. First was his calm, unflapable nature. The director of a top priority project is subject to extreme pressure from a number of directions. There is the inevitable competition for resources within the director's own service, exacerbated in this case by the desire of the Army and Navy to get a piece of the action, if not all of it. Some spectacular Soviet demonstrations of progress in the missile field were to raise the pressure to a level that would have been intolerable for a less disciplined person.

Another valuable attribute was Schriever's ability to persuade very senior and sometimes irascible officials to accept his views. Retired Gen. Bryce Poe, who served as Schriever's aide and assistant executive officer at Western Development Division, once went with the general and members of his staff to brief the redoubtable Gen. Thomas S. Power on a new organization plan. Power, who was head of the Air Research and Development Command, was in a particularly bellicose mood. He summarily rejected the proposal. As they left Power's office, Major Poe commented to Schriever that the rejection left them in a spot, since time was running out. "Don't worry," replied Schriever, "I'll go back and talk to him alone this afternoon." He did, and the organization plan was accepted.

General Power was an operator, interested in getting a job done more than in *how* it was done. That left Schriever considerable latitude in running the ballistic missile program. He rarely received directions on how to proceed. Most of the management innovations that characterized WDD and its successor organization were conceived by General Schriever and his staff.

Once the Western Development Division was established, a major unresolved question concerned the locus of responsibility for day-to-day management of missile development. Among the available choices were an aircraft manufacturer, a university laboratory, an Air Force organization with a technical staff, or a special independent contractor who, in effect, would become part of the organization. Schriever recommended the last option and proposed that Ramo-Wooldridge Corporation be given responsibility for systems engineering and technical direction. His recommendation was accepted. The Ramo-Wooldridge element at Inglewood was called the Guided Missiles Research Division, becoming Space Technology Laboratories in December 1957. Ramo-Wooldridge merged with Thompson Products in October 1958 to form TRW.

With a top priority, Schriever could ask for, and get, anyone he wanted for his own staff. He personally picked a small nucleus of men whom he knew well—people who could get things done even if they themselves were controversial. Such people were not always wanted by other commanders. "I wanted them," Schriever said, "because they were smart and would tell me not what I wanted to hear, but what they really thought." He also valued loyalty, not in the sense of agreeing with him, but the kind that inspired trust. And he believed that loyalty was a two-way street. At one point, General Power thought Officer Effectiveness Reports (OERs), the basis for promotion, were running too high. He directed all the commanders under him to lower those reports. Schriever had a study done which showed that the OERs of his people were lower than when they had been competing against a typical cross-section of officers in their previous assignments. He wrote General Power that he was not lowering, but raising OERs in his organization.

Among the first contingent of people selected by Schriever were Cols. Charles H. Terhune and Harold W. Norton; Lt. Cols. Benjamin P. Blasingame, Beryl L. Boatman, Philip C. Calhoun, Otto J. Glasser, Edward N. Hall, and John P. Hudson; Majs. Roger R. Hebner and Paul L. Maret; and Capts. David M. Fleming and Vernol L. Smith. Each was an expert in his field. For example, Ed Hall was an expert in propulsion systems. Without exception, those men rose to senior rank in the Air Force or to important civilian positions.

It was a matter of great personal pride to General Schriever that in many years of dealing with industry, not one official protest was lodged concerning irregularity in selecting contractors for the enormously costly ballistic missile programs. Schriever himself often was the target of lobbyists who sought favorable treatment for their clients. All of them failed. Schriever built a record of unquestioned integrity.

In July 1954 the Scientific Advisory Board had recommended developing an alternative missile to the Atlas. This recommendation was motivated by fear that Atlas's pressurized structure might collapse under stress—an unfounded fear, it turned out. The more conventional alternate missile, the XSM–68 Titan, offered greater prospects for "growth" and would create a secondary source for subsystems as a hedge against failure in the Atlas program. General Schriever recognized from the start that the ICBM program warranted an exceptional approach. He borrowed a page from the Manhattan Atom Bomb project of World War II by contracting with the ablest firms available for the major subsystems. There was a separate associate contractor for each major subsystem of both Atlas and Titan. This was insurance against failure of a single contractor. Major subsystems included guidance, propulsion, nose cone, and airframe.

Planning for the Titan appeared sound, although it intensified budgetary pressure on the Air Force. With the addition of still another missile, the intermediate range (IRBM) Thor, this pressure grew. Soon the 1,500-mile range

IRBM became a bone of contention between the Air Force and Army over roles and missions. At first the Air Force intended that Wright Air Development Center would develop the IRBM. However, General Schriever—fearing that this would drain scarce resources from the Atlas—proposed that the IRBM be built as "fall out" from the ICBM project. In May 1955 the Thor was assigned to Western Development Division.

Although Schriever's division amassed a variety of projects, ICBM development remained foremost in its plans. In October, separate teams were organized to develop the Atlas and Titan with instructions to maintain as much interchangeability as possible between subsystems. Comprising the Atlas team were Convair (airframe, assembly, and test); North American (propulsion); General Electric (nose cone); Sperry Rand (radio-inertial guidance); and AMF (accessory power). The Titan team was made up of the Martin Company (airframe); Aerojet-General (propulsion and accessory power); AVCO (nose cone); Bell Telephone (radio-inertial guidance); and American Bosch (all-inertial guidance). Schriever developed the computer capacity to automate management information on a nearly instantaneous basis. This permitted him and his managers to track progress in the various programs and concentrate on performance.

Meanwhile, Ramo-Wooldridge had formulated a novel test program for the Atlas. The original plan for building special test vehicles was abandoned in order to speed testing, using the basic Atlas itself. Initial tests were conducted on the simplest flyable missile, the Atlas A, which consisted of only the airframe, booster engine, and autopilot. Flight testing continued by building progressively more complex missiles that included incrementally the sustainer engine, missile staging, full guidance, and a separable nose cone. Finally, the refined operational version, the Atlas E, was tested.

Early in the test program General Schriever recognized that primary dependence on flight test was inadequate and very expensive. Since the time of flight was extremely short for missiles and they could be used only once, it would take a great number of flights to accumulate the necessary data. A ground, or static, program for testing components offered an alternative to flight testing. Western Development Division devised a test "pyramid" with emphasis on a thorough checkout at all levels prior to making a commitment for either static or flight testing. Although it appeared logicial, this test philosophy depended on the availability of specialized missile facilities. In fact, the ballistic missile programs created an entirely new class of support systems, including test facilities, launchers, training, and a host of other equipment that did not yet exist. It was essential that all the elements be ready on time if the system was to be completed quickly. Schriever's prescription—developing the various elements in such a sequence that they would be completed when needed—was called "concurrency." Needless to say, it involved considerable risk, but this was unavoidable if the United States hoped to win its race with the Soviets.

Schriever began to identify his facilities' needs in December 1954. Approval was deferred for some time because of an existing administration policy that forbade the concentration of missile facilities along the sea coasts. A master development plan was released in April 1955, but facilities and funding approval were not granted until July when Lt. Gen. Donald L. Putt, Deputy Chief of Staff for Development, approved the plan and reiterated the program's highest Air Force priority.

Trevor Gardner continued to campaign for top *national* priority for the ICBM program. However, the Air Force's sense of urgency was not completely shared within the Eisenhower administration. In February 1955, the President's Technological Capabilities Panel did, however, issue a report warning of progress in Soviet missile capabilities. Called the Killian Report after its chairman, Dr. James R. Killian, the report cited the vulnerability of North America to surprise attack. It recommended making the ICBM program "a nationally supported effort of the highest priority" and urged as an expedient measure the rapid development and deployment of the shorter range IRBMs. Gardner urged Congress, especially Senators Clinton P. Anderson of New Mexico and Henry M. Jackson of Washington, to emphasize the urgency of the ICBM program to the President. Throughout the summer Gardner, Schriever, and von Neumann briefed the various levels of government up through the National Security Council. In July the trio made a presentation to President Eisenhower. Finally, in September the President made the long awaited decision. ICBM development was to have top national priority and proceed at all possible speed.

Success depended, in large measure, on being free of unnecessary bureaucratic procedures. Schriever assigned an aide to chart the typical administrative chain of approval within the Departments of Defense and the Air Force. The resultant chart was said to resemble a bowl of spaghetti. Schriever and Gardner asked for simplified management procedures that would bypass many superfluous layers of review in the Office of the Secretary of Defense (OSD) and the Air Force. Hyde Gillette, Air Force Deputy Assistant Secretary for Budget and Program Management, headed a committee that recommended a streamlined chain of approval. The Gillette Procedures, issued in November 1955, established a single committee in the Air Force and another in OSD to serve as the ultimate review and decision authorities. These Ballistic Missile Committees were at the respective secretarial levels and were chaired initially by Air Force Secretary Donald A. Quarles and Defense Secretary Charles E. Wilson. Each committee was comprised of the assistant secretaries of the two departments, and had formal authority over the entire program. The committees delegated program approval and implementation to the lowest possible echelon and bypassed many of the regular reviewing agencies.

In February 1956 Trevor Gardner, who harbored serious doubts about the administration's commitment to research and development, resigned his position. He then launched a public campaign to warn the President and the people of the urgent need to overtake Soviet technological progress.

In July 1956 the ICBM operational plan underwent sharp scrutiny by the Air Force Ballistic Missile Committee when Secretary Quarles applied his "Poor Man's Approach" to missile development. This meant austerity and reductions in program objectives. More important, Quarles's decision changed the program's goal from achieving the earliest *possible* operational deployment, to achieving the earliest *practicable* one. His aim was to save money by stretching out the program. While the ICBM program did not suffer from serious funding shortages, the sense of urgency began to wane. Ironically, the funding crisis seems not to have caused any perceptible harm and may even have been beneficial, since it caused longer and more detailed facilities planning.

Secretary of the Air Force Harold E. Talbott (left) congratulates Assistant Secretary of Defense (R&D) Donald A. Quarles (right) after Quarles is named Talbott's successor as Secretary of the Air Force. Secretary of Defense Charles Wilson is also present.

In April 1957 the 1st Missile Division was activated at Camp Cooke, California (later Vandenberg AFB) to supervise the training and operational phases of the budding missile program. The following month work started on "soft," or above ground, missile sites at Vandenberg. By August the Air Force had selected the first Atlas and Titan operational bases, Warren AFB, Wyoming, and Lowry AFB, Colorado. The outline of an operational ICBM force began to emerge.

By January 1957, only thirteen months after Western Development Division had contracted with Douglas Aircraft for the Thor IRBM, that missile was ready for flight test—a record achievement. There were four failures before the Thor made its first successful flight from Cape Canaveral, Florida, on September 20. The Atlas met with two failures before its first successful flight on December 17, 1957—the fifty-fourth anniversary of the Wright brothers' flight.

Meanwhile, the Soviets had delivered a stunning blow to America's pride by launching the world's first artificial satellite, Sputnik, on October 4, 1957. Although the administration tried to minimize the military significance of the Soviet feat, Sputnik had been placed in orbit by a Soviet ballistic missile. The event produced an immediate impact on the Air Force ballistic missile programs. The so-called "Poor Man's Approach" and the recently imposed restrictions were quickly lifted, funding increased, plans revised, and the urgency of the program restored. In the months that followed Sputnik, the Ballistic Missile Division (WDD had changed its name in June 1957) undoubtedly experienced the most sustained high pressure in the history of Air Force weapons development.

During those hectic months, Schriever spent much time commuting between Inglewood and Washington. He would work all day on the west coast, spend most of the night flying to Washington (in those days it was a six to eight hour flight, depending on the weather), meet with Defense officials, and often fly back to Inglewood immediately.

Despite a seemingly impossible schedule and an undemonstrative nature, Schriever never abandoned his concern for the people under him. One trip to Washington was made when Bryce Poe and his wife were expecting their first child. While they were in Washington, Poe was notified that his wife had gone to the hospital. He told General Schriever that he would himself go back immediately by commercial air. "No," General Schriever said, "we'll both go." When they arrived at Bolling AFB, for the trip back, General Schriever who, unlike most VIPs, always walked out to his parked aircraft, told Poe to bring the plane up in front of Operations. While Poe was getting the airplane, Schriever called the hospital in California. As he climbed aboard he said to Poe in a matter-of-fact way, "Your wife just had a little girl." With that, he went to the back of the airplane and attacked the mountain of work that always awaited him.

Above: An Air Force Thor IRBM lifts off from launching pad at Air Force Missile Test Range, Cape Canaveral, Florida; *left*: lift off of an Atlas ICBM also from Cape Canaveral, Jan. 1958.

By the end of 1959 the first Thor IRBMs were already in the United Kingdom, and a token force of Atlas ICBMs became operational at Vandenberg AFB. Schriever's division could rightfully boast of having won the race against time. The Thor development, from program approval to the initial operational squadron, had taken only three and one-half years; Atlas's development time was a little more than five years, better than the six to eight years predicted by the Teapot Committee in 1954. By contrast, conventional aircraft and aerodynamic missiles were much longer in development. The B–47 took nearly eight years, the B–52 almost nine and one-half years, and the B–58 more than eleven years. Among the aerodynamic missiles, the Navaho was canceled in July 1957 after nine and one-half years of developmental work, the Rascal after eleven and one-half years, and it was nearly fourteen years before Snark became operational.

The alternate ICBM, the Titan, proceeded at a slower pace, taking almost six years to reach operational status. However, even as the first Titan lifted off from the Cape in February 1959, development of the more advanced Titan II was underway. The Titan II, a second generation ICBM, could be launched

Gen. Bernard A. Schriever

from an underground silo, was powered by storable liquid propellants, and had an all-inertial guidance system.

True to his reputation as a visionary, Bernard Schriever was not content merely to preside over development of the Atlas, Titan, and Thor. Important as these missiles were, he continued to search for new and better weapons. As early as 1955 the Western Development Division explored the feasibility of using a solid, rather than a liquid, propellant for ballistic missiles. The solids suffered from several technical problems related to burn rate, propulsive efficiency, and weight. If these problems could be solved, the solid-fueled missiles would be storable underground, quick reacting, easy to maintain, flexible, and cheaper to produce. When the Navy approached General Schriever for help in developing a shipboard IRBM, he encouraged them to experiment with solids. In the summer of 1955 the Air Force SAB convened a study group, chaired by Dr. von Karman, to address the problems that had to be solved to make solid-fueled rockets feasible. Schriever approached several industrial companies competent in this field to ask their cooperation.

By 1957 Ramo-Wooldridge began preliminary design work, convinced that solid fueled ICBMs were feasible. Schriever assigned Col. Edward Hall, the former director of the Thor program, to head the solid-fueled missile project. First known as Weapons System "Q," it evolved into the three-stage Minuteman. In February 1958 Schriever presented the Minuteman proposal to the Air Staff. Everyone, including Vice Chief of Staff Gen. Curtis E. LeMay, was enthusiastic. The Secretaries of the Air Force and Defense approved the Minuteman in a period of seventy-two hours and provided $50 million to start the program. Later, in 1959, when Gen. Thomas S. Power, then Commander in Chief of Strategic Air Command, asked that Minuteman be accelerated, Schriever accepted the challenge. In February 1961—only three years after program approval—Minuteman successfully completed its first flight from Cape Canaveral. Even more remarkable, the Minuteman was in an "all up" configuration: that is, all three stages, guidance system, and the nose cone separation were tested together, a first in missile development history. By the end of October 1962, at the time of the Cuban Missile Crisis, the first ten Minuteman were poised on combat alert inside their underground silos, just four years and eight months after program go-ahead.

General Schriever recognized that the ICBM program had put the United States on the threshold of space, and he had urged that Western Development Division assume responsibility for space R&D. He succeeded in having the office responsible for the development of a satellite system assigned to his division and in 1956 signed a contract for its development with Lockheed. The Eisenhower administration, however, was anxious to emphasize the peaceful nature of space exploration, concentrating space work on the International Geophysical Year (IGY) satellite and restricting its booster rocket

Right: Minuteman ICBM before launch at Cape Canaveral, Florida, 1961; *below*: view of Minuteman in silo prior to launch.

to non-military uses. In early 1957, Schriever, during a speech in San Diego, had called for a major space effort. He immediately heard from Washington that it was not appropriate to use the word "space" in future speeches.

Sputnik, of course, provided the impetus for the U.S. space program. The National Aeronautics and Space Administration (NASA), created in October 1958, depended heavily on the Air Force's Thor, Atlas, and Titan missiles as boosters for its space activities. On February 28, 1959, a Thor-Agena booster combination launched Discoverer I, an Air Force satellite, into polar orbit from Vandenberg AFB. Shortly after his success, Schriever was promoted to lieutenant general and in April 1959 assigned to head the Air Research and Development Command (ARDC). His achievements over a relatively brief span as head of the ballistic missile programs included the development of a new class of weapon systems, a second generation on the way, and the frontier of space well marked. His philosophy of central management was well enough defined to be emulated in other programs, and his development team in Inglewood was poised to assume new responsibilities.

*   *   *   *   *

Upon assuming command of ARDC, General Schriever introduced concurrency in weapon system development and acquisition—the concept that had worked so well in the Ballistic Missile Division for compressing acquisition time and getting operational systems into the hands of combat units more quickly. Under this management approach, Air Force Headquarters initiated the conceptual phase of a new weapon, systems centers provided the acquisition management, while the using commands refined systems during the operational phase. In December 1959 Dudley C. Sharp became Secretary of the Air Force and suggested expanding the concept to all weapon and support systems.

One of Schriever's major priorities in his new command was to have total responsibility for weapon system acquisition transferred to ARDC from the Air Material Command. This was not a new problem. When Schriever headed Western Development Division he possessed complete authority over all aspects of Atlas development, including engineering decisions, except for contracting and procurement. Air Material Command jealously guarded its right to those areas. However, Schriever worked out a solution in which AMC retained its authority through a field office collocated with WDD. This AMC office, called the Special Aircraft Projects Office and later renamed the Ballistic Missile Center, effectively came under Schriever's command. In April

1961 the Center was reassigned to ARDC's Ballistic Missile Division. Now, however, General Samuel E. Anderson, Schriever's predecessor at ARDC and the current commander at AMC, was adamantly opposed to a broader application of the idea. Anderson argued that ARDC and AMC should be merged under AMC, with integrated development, procurement, and production. A compromise solution offered by the Air Staff proposed improvements in management procedures and strengthening weapon system project offices, rather than a reorganization. The issue remained unsettled for two years, with Schriever and Anderson sticking to their guns.

With the advent of the Kennedy administration, space programs took on a new urgency. Roswell Gilpatric, the Deputy Secretary of Defense, had known Schriever when Gilpatric had been Under Secretary of the Air Force in the Truman administration and through his association with the Aerospace Corporation. Gilpatric proposed assigning the Air Force responsibility for research and development of all military space programs. However, the offer rested on the ability of the Air Force to resolve its split of research, development, and production between ARDC and AMC. Gen. Thomas D. White, the Air Force Chief of Staff, lost no time in deciding the issue in favor of Schriever's position. In April 1961 ARDC became the Air Force Systems Command (AFSC), and AMC the Air Force Logistics Command (AFLC). At last Schriever had reached the goal sought for more than a decade: to transform material development and acquisition from a functional to a systems approach.

Air Force Chief of Staff Gen. Thomas D. White

Schriever continued as Commander of AFSC and was rewarded with a fourth star.

On March 6, 1961, Secretary of Defense Robert S. McNamara issued directive 5160.32 assigning the responsibility for "research, development, test, and engineering of Department of Defense space development programs or projects which are approved hereafter," to the Department of the Air Force. In April Schriever established the AFSC Space Systems Division at Los Angeles.

Despite this promising start, many Kennedy administration officials, notably those around Secretary McNamara, believed that the Communist threat could be handled best through an accommodation with the Soviet Union. They believed that too much attention had been paid to strategies for deterring nuclear war that favored large missile and bomber forces. Instead, they adopted a policy of Mutual Assured Destruction (MAD) that required only enough weapons to survive an attack and destroy a high percentage of the Soviet population and industry. Consequently, Schriever saw many of his advanced missile programs, such as the railroad-based Minuteman and medium-range ballistic missiles, canceled. McNamara opposed spending too much on advanced technology, reasoning that it would build pressure to start

President Kennedy on way to attend a briefing in the Pentagon with Secretary of Defense Robert McNamara on his immediate right. Also with him are Deputy Secretary of Defense Roswell Gilpatric (scratching head) and Gen. Lyman Lemnitzer (forehead barely showing).

expensive new development programs. Consequently, the Secretary of Defense canceled many promising technology initiatives. Schriver favored pushing advanced technology ahead and believed that it was foolish to try to restrain the "technology clock." The United States would do so at its own peril since the Soviet Union certainly would not hold back. What irked Schriever most was that McNamara made many of these decisions, which were of a policy nature, with little or no discussion with Congress, much less public debate.

Another irritant was that the streamlined Gillette management practices, first instituted for the ICBM program, were discarded and replaced by new management procedures that effectively reestablished the former layers of review. These Schriever facetiously called "paralysis by analysis."

In 1963, at the suggestion of Air Force Secretary Eugene M. Zuckert, General Schriever established and directed a series of studies known collectively as Project Forecast. The purpose of these studies was to survey technology for the future needs of air warfare and to develop a long-range plan projecting five to fifteen years into the future. All of the functional missions, such as strategic, tactical, air defense, and logistics, were considered. Major technologies were divided into categories of interest to the Air Force, including materials, propulsion, electronic countermeasures, guidance, and navigation. Other panels studied general war, limited war, command and control, and political and economic conditions.

A summary report included recommendations relating to the programs that were needed to improve Air Force capabilities. Its central conclusion was that technology would remain the major determinant in achieving new capabilities. Improved weapons made possible by latent technology were considered more significant to national security than those attainable with existing technology—and of sufficient importance to warrant some delay in operational availability. Finally, it was demonstrated that reaching some policy goals depended on technological advances to counter the threat of continued Soviet progress. Project Forecast, completed in 1964, remains the most comprehensive survey ever conducted by a military service to assess the impact of advancing technology on its future capabilities to support national policy. It was one of General Schriever's most important contributions to national defense.

Under the Kennedy administration, emphasis shifted from strategic to tactical and airlift forces with the aim of deterring all wars, "general or limited, nuclear or conventional, large or small," as the President put it. Much of Air Force Systems Command's work under General Schriever thus was reoriented toward weapons and ordnance for limited conventional war, an area that had been slighted while this country was developing its strategic deterrent forces. Among limited war-related developments that had been advocated by Project Forecast were a long-range, high-capacity transport plane that emerged ultimately as the C–5A; a vertical/short takeoff transport for which conceptual studies were begun in August 1964; and very accurate guided "smart bombs" that were so effective in the later stages of the Vietnam War. Other developmental work focused on electronic countermeasures, a variety of air-to-air and air-to-ground missiles, navigation systems, communications, and conventional ordnance. In the last-named area, Schriever ran into some opposition from a still nuclear-oriented Air Force Headquarters. His fiscal year 1963 request for $40 million to develop nonnuclear munitions was cut to $15 million. He favored developing aircraft that were specialized for specific operational missions, and he considered Tactical Air Command's support of a single, multi-purpose aircraft to be a serious error.

President Kennedy and Secretary of Defense McNamara believed—mistakenly, as events have shown—that the Soviets would accept tacitly a strategy of Mutual Assured Destruction and that their missile buildup would level off at about the same strength as that of the United States. In keeping with that notion, the Air Force missile inventory was limited to 1,054 systems, and the bomber and air defense forces were reduced drastically in size. The search for new technology slackened markedly. This philosophy, and the autocratic manner in which defense policy was conducted, continued under President Johnson, with Robert McNamara remaining as his Secretary of Defense. General Schriever felt that he no longer could support the administration's defense policy. Although mandatory retirement was several years off, he retired voluntarily on August 31, 1966.

One of General Schriever's closest associates has said that of all of the generals he has known, none was as devoted to this country as Schriever. "Bennie, who came to this country as an immigrant, feels that everything he has achieved he owes to the United States." Since his retirement, General Schriever has been in great demand as a consultant to civilian organizations, but frequently he has served without fee as an advisor to the Air Force and the Department of Defense.

Shortly before his retirement, Schriever told a meeting of the Arnold Air Society in Dallas, Texas: "The world has an ample supply of people who can always come up with a dozen good reasons why a new idea will not work and should not be tried, but the people who produce progress are a breed apart. They have the imagination, the courage, and the persistence to find solutions. . . ."

No one typifies that breed better than Bernard Schriever himself.

Sources

The primary sources for General Bernard Schriever's military career are his personal papers on file at the USAF Historical Research Center, Maxwell AFB, Alabama. The papers detail his activities from 1954, when he assumed command of the Western Development Division (WDD) at Los Angeles, through his retirement as Commander of the Air Force Systems Command in September 1966. The Schriever papers contain official studies, minutes of meetings, letters, memoranda, and messages relating to ballistic missile and space activities. Another subdivision consists of congressional hearings and reports, and an extensive file of speeches.

General Schriever's early life was documented primarily through interviews. The most recent was a series of six interviews with Schriever conducted by the author from September through December 1982. The author also interviewed many associates of the general, including his executive assistant, Colonel Vincent T. Ford, and the WDD historian, Dr. Alfred Rockefeller. Finally, the Air Force Systems Command History Office has about a dozen relevant interviews with senior officers that were conducted by a former AFSC historian, Dr. Ernest G. Schwiebert.

There is no biography of General Schriever as yet; however, his work is discussed in numerous publications. One of the first books on ballistic missile development is Kenneth F. Gantz (Editor), *The United States Air Force Report on the Ballistic Missile* (Doubleday, 1958). Ernest G. Schwiebert's *A History of the U.S. Air Force Ballistic Missiles* appeared in a special issue of *Air Force Magazine* in May 1964.

A wealth of information is contained in congressional documents, most notably: Senate Subcommittee on the Air Force of the Committee on Armed Services, *Study of Airpower*, 84th Cong., 2d Sess., 1956; Senate Committee on Armed Services, Preparedness Investigating Subcommittee, *Hearings, Inquiry into Satellite and Missile Programs*, 85th Cong., 1st and 2d Sess., 1958; and House of Representatives Committee on Government Operations, Subcommittee on Military Operations, *Hearing, Organization and Management of Missile Programs*, 86th Cong., 1st Sess., 1959 and 2d Sess., 1960.

The most incisive and scholarly investigations of the ballistic missile programs were done by Robert L. Perry. Among his numerous writings are: "The Atlas, Thor, Titan, and Minuteman," in Eugene M. Emme (Editor), *The History of Rocket Technology* (Detroit, 1964); *The Ballistic Missile Decisions, P-3686* (The RAND Corporation, 1967); and *System Development Strategies, RM–4853–PR* (The RAND Corporation, 1966). Another important scholarly study that owes much to Perry's work is Edmund Beard's *Developing the ICBM: A Study in Bureaucratic Politics* (New York, 1976). A more general, but extremely insightful analysis is Robert Frank Futrell, *Ideas, Concepts, Doctrine: A History of Basic Thinking in the United States Air Force, 1907–1964* (Maxwell AFB, 1971), especially chapters 9 through 14.

As a visionary on the leading edge of technology, Schriever often was at the center of major controversies. Perhaps the best accounts of these controversies are: John B. Medaris and Arthur Gordon, *Countdown For Decision* (New York, 1960); Michael H. Armacost, *The Politics of Weapons Innovation: The Thor-Jupiter Controversy* (New York, 1969); and Edgar M. Bottome, *The Missile Gap: A Study of the Formulation of Military and Political Policy* (Teaneck, N.J., 1971). Also, of value is Eugene E. Evans, *Dispute Settlement and Hierarchy: The Military Guided Missile Controversy, 1955–1960* (unpublished Ph.D. dissertation, University of Illinois, 1963). General Schriever himself is an excellent and prolific writer. The most comprehensive guide to his writing is the annual *Air University Library Index to Military Periodicals*, Maxwell AFB, Alabama.

13

Robinson Risner:
The Indispensable Ingredient

T.R. Milton

In the spring of 1965, the United States air campaign against North Vietnam began in earnest, however imprecise its strategy and objectives or how remote the decisions on tactics. Bomb loads were dictated at the highest level, along with target selection and, sometimes, even the route to the target. The campaign was intended as a low-risk operation that would send signals of American power and resolve to those tough little men in Hanoi, who apparently were not listening.

The campaign, with its sonorous title of Rolling Thunder, was in fact an extremely high-risk proposition for the pilots involved. The targets soon became predictable, and since no one had told these professional Navy and Air Force airmen that they were merely giving signals, never mind the results, they pressed their attacks home. Almost instantly, the North Vietnamese began to collect prisoners of war. The problem was that we were not at war: no declaration, no mobilization, hardly any sacrifice for the vast majority of Americans. This undeclared war against North Vietnam was a private affair carried out by professional military pilots. Whether or not Hanoi would have behaved differently had the United States declared war is something we will never know. That question remains in the realm of useless speculation, as do so many questions about the Vietnam War. In any case, the captured pilots enjoyed none of the protection of the Geneva convention but were, instead, treated as no prisoners of war of civilized countries have been treated in this century.

The residents of Hanoi's filthy jails were randomly selected by the antiaircraft guns and missile sites in North Vietnam, which were in turn aided, as we have noted, by the predictability of the targets. Perhaps it is not entirely accurate to say the prisoners were randomly selected, for that leaves out the factors of courage and aggressiveness. The ones who pressed their attacks were subject to the highest risk. However fate decided who ended up in the Hanoi Hilton, it was a singularly heroic group that spent those years in Vietnamese captivity. Men like James Stockdale, Jeremiah Denton, Swede Larson, Dave Winn, John Flynn, and practically all the others came out with their self- and mutual respect intact. Only a handful failed the test. There are, in short, a great many stories worth telling about the people who spent those seven years in purgatory. This one is about Robbie Risner—James Robinson Risner—who comes as close to being an all-American hero as we are likely to find.

When Risner, his F-105 on fire, ejected over the rice paddies of North Vietnam, he was startled at the deafening sound of gunfire coming up from several hundred feet below. The usual impression a pilot has after the first wild seconds following an ejection seat bailout is one of unearthly quiet as he floats downward. This time it was different, and Robbie knew the game was over. There would be no rescue this time, as had been the case when he had been forced to bail out a few weeks earlier.

Like most men who excel in combat, Risner had a sustaining sense of invulnerability, the old silver-bullet syndrome. They might hit his airplane, as they had been doing with alarming frequency, but they were not going to hit him. They might even shoot him down, but Robbie Risner was not going to be anyone's prisoner. And then, that miserable September day in 1965, he was led down a North Vietnamese village street like a captured animal, the beginning of seven and a half years of torture, privation, and worst of all, the uncertainty that it would ever end.

A few months earlier, Risner had been on the cover of *Time* magazine, his newly won Air Force Cross on his chest. That *Time* cover had been a high point for the fellow from Mammoth Springs, Arkansas, whose adult life had been almost totally dedicated to achieving excellence as a fighter pilot.

The Air Force Cross—the first one ever—was awarded Risner in Washington after the April 1965 mission which saw him shot down for the first time, an early indication that worse things might lie ahead. He had led twelve F-105s on a strike against a radar site, and they had given the target a good hammering. Then, with the sort of aggressiveness that was to get him a reservation in the Hanoi Hilton a few months later, Risner made a low pass over the site to have a final look. A gun emplacement that had appeared to be out of action opened fire and hit him. He nursed his flaming airplane out over the Gulf of Tonkin, where he ejected. As he tells the tale, he scrambled into his dinghy so quickly he scarcely got wet. From his ringside seat in the raft, he watched the fun begin.

The North Vietnamese wasted no time in setting out from shore after their prize, and Risner's squadron mates sank the boats as soon as they reached open water. One particularly threatening vessel, a gunboat, was cut in two by F-105 cannon fire. The Vietnamese abandoned the venture in favor, presumably, of a short critique on the problem of boats against fighters.

Meanwhile, an SA-16, the faithful old Grumman amphibian that had seen yeoman service in the Korean War, arrived on the scene. The seas were heavy, and so was the SA-16 with a full load of fuel. It also developed that this was the crew's first rescue mission. After hauling Risner aboard, the excited rescue pilot began a takeoff run that almost ended in the old Duck-Butt's fatal swamping. Another try was equally harrowing, whereupon the pilot announced a plan to taxi out to the U.S. Navy some thirty miles away.

Risner was no rescue pilot, but a thirty-mile taxi over rough water did not strike him as a sound plan. One more wild run got the SA-16 into the air and back to Da Nang, everyone safe and sound. The SA-16, however, was sent to the boneyard, too badly damaged by the hammering it had taken to be repaired. The rescue was arguably the most exciting part of the day.

Capt. Robinson Risner

Risner was back in the cockpit flying missions against North Vietnam two days later. He had already seen more than enough combat to justify a comfortable billet on the staff back in Hawaii, but this was a fighting man who wanted nothing more than to be with his squadron.

*   *   *   *   *

It is fascinating to explore what makes the difference between a great fighter pilot and a competent pilot who flies fighters. A good place to start in the case of Robbie Risner, unquestionably a great fighter pilot, is with his formative flying years, for they had a lot to do with what happened later. Most important, it was during those early years that he learned how much he loved flying. He also began to gain the supreme self-confidence that is an essential trait of the truly gifted fighter pilot.

His education took place in the World War II backwater of Panama, a place that never heard a shot fired in anger, a peaceful little oasis between the European and Pacific wars. Some people in Panama relaxed and enjoyed the steamy tropical life with just enough flying to get by. In Risner's case, this was a chance to learn how to handle an airplane. There were few restrictions, little supervision, and always an available P-39 or P-38. The low-level flying skills learned during the war years in Panama at the expense of some native thatched roofs and apoplectic sailboat skippers were to be applied later on.

World War II, however, came and went without Robbie Risner making much of a mark. The mass demobilization following the war sent him back into civilian life in 1946, one of thousands with a set of pilot wings and no visible future in which they would ever be worn again. Risner went to Tulsa, where he opened an auto parts business along with a downtown parking garage, and married. At this point, having done all the customary things a young fellow did to start a postwar life, he joined the Oklahoma Air National Guard. There were to be no more wars in the euphoric world of 1946, so military service seemed a totally irrelevant career to Robbie Risner, as it did to most Americans. Flying, however, was something else. The Air National Guard was a way to remain in the air, this time in the P-51, every pilot's favorite fighter. It was a connection that gave Risner a fascinating experience, one that belongs in the script of a Hollywood thriller.

The Oklahoma Air Guard squadron had a party in mind with shrimp as the main course. The year was 1946, remember, and things were on the informal side. Risner was dispatched to Brownsville, Texas, in his P-51 to fetch the shrimp. Navigation gear had lagged well behind aircraft performance in World War II, especially in fighters, so cross-country flying in the P–51 had a certain element of adventure. Map reading, assisted by railway tracks, was still an important factor in getting from one point to another, just as it had been from the days of the SPAD. When Risner reached Texas that fall day, the hurricane season had begun, a fact which accounted for the heavy clouds covering his route. Since Robbie had no idea there was a hurricane lying in the Gulf of Mexico, he simply climbed above the clouds and began a little time-and-distance navigation. Then another phenomenon of nature took over, the jet stream—something of a mystery in those days when only military pilots ever flew above 20,000 feet.

When Risner's calculations told him the time had come to let down, he broke out of the clouds over an uninhabited bit of coastline, clearly not Brownsville. The jet stream had blown him far off course and into, as it turned out, Mexico, a lonesome stretch of Mexico, at that. With the P–51 nearly out of gas, he had either to put it down or bail out. He made a low pass on a sandy lake bed, rolling his wheels to test the surface. It seemed smooth enough, so he came around in a tight pattern and landed, the tanks now almost dry. As darkness fell, however, things got interesting.

Risner wrapped himself in his parachute against the swarms of mosquitoes and stretched out on the P–51's wing. Not long after, the hurricane came ashore. Risner rode out the storm in the cockpit of the airplane, where he watched the airspeed needle hit takeoff speed and the dry lake fill until water had covered the wing. All in all, it was a wild night.

The storm over, Risner had a series of adventures with knife fighters and pistol-toting outlaws, and almost too much even for Hollywood, a hand in the rescue of two beautiful Mexican damsels from their kidnappers. In short, he had one terrific story to tell the accident investigating board when he got back to Oklahoma.

*   *   *   *   *

Korea came along to end the happy little postwar era. Risner had kept up his flying with the Air Guard and was, by that time, a skilled fighter pilot, although one who had never seen combat. His squadron was called to active duty and switched to the F–80, the first Air Force operational jet. But, when it appeared the squadron was not going to Korea, Robbie had to look around for his own way to the war. There were, he discovered, openings in photo reconnaissance for pilots with a minimum of one hundred jet hours. Since he already had five hours in the F–80, he needed only ninety-five more. These he got in the next three weeks. While that may not seem much to a transport pilot, ninety-five jet fighter hours in three weeks is something for the *Guinness Book of Records.*

On his way to the port of embarkation, Risner managed to break his arm in a horse accident, a perfect reason to delay his departure—one, in fact, the authorities at the port would have invoked on their own—had Risner not concealed his injury. This was a fellow who was on his way to do a job.

The photo-recce business may have been a ticket to Korea, but it was not at all what Risner, the skilled though untested fighter pilot, had in mind. As it happened, an Oklahoma Air Guard friend was strategically placed to arrange a transfer to the famed 4th Fighter Wing, an outfit that had made its mark in England while young Robinson Risner was wiling away the war in Panama. With the transfer came a transition to the F–86, perhaps the finest pure fighter airplane ever produced. The F–86 Sabre was the vehicle in which the new aces of the jet age were achieving stardom, and MiG Alley was their stage. Even though the Korean War itself was viewed with distaste or apathy

Formation of F–86 Sabre jets, fighters which proved to be formidable combatants for MiG–15s in Korea.

Maj. Robinson Risner (right) receives the Air Medal from Col. James Johnson, Commanding Officer of the 4th Fighter Interceptor Wing, for meritorious achievement while participating in aerial combat, December 1952.

by an America largely unaffected by that conflict, the battles in MiG Alley had taken on the aura of an international sporting event. The race for top honors among Joe McConnell, Jim Jabara, and Pete Fernandez was front page news; it overshadowed the exploits of World War II aces like Frances Gabreski, John Meyer, and Robin Olds, who were proving jet combat was not exclusively a kid's game. The battle for leading MiG killer also obscured the lesser-known aces, Risner among them.

The transfer to the 4th Fighter Wing was not without its rough moments, brought on by the intensely competitive game in MiG Alley. Risner had shown from the first day that he was cut out for aerial combat. Thus, when the new guy from the recce outfit began to score victories, he had to face a bit of jealousy on the part of some of his seniors. It was nothing serious, but it did reflect the atmosphere of the time. The F-86 pilots were the glamour boys of an otherwise unpopular war, and glamour is not easily shared, one exception to the rule being the day little Pete Fernandez called out to Risner's flight that he had thirty MiGs cornered in case anyone wanted to help.

At any rate, the man from the Oklahoma Air National Guard, on his

313

way to eight victories, had quickly proved he belonged in the air combat major leagues. His wildest day resulted in a kill and one of the best war stories one is ever likely to hear.

Risner and his wingman were flying escort for a fighter-bomber mission against a chemical plant at the mouth of the Yalu. A wide screening turn took their two F–86s over a Chinese airfield near Antung, and Risner was soon engaged with a MiG. The ensuing dogfight, from 30,000 feet to the deck, was the real-life equivalent of the climactic scene in *Star Wars*. The MiG pilot rolled, half-rolled, stalled, did inverted turns, with Risner all the while in pursuit, firing his guns every time the MiG appeared in his pipper. Once, the two ended up in close formation, wingtip to wingtip, staring at one another. The end seemed near when the MiG pilot, leading a descending chase at close to the speed of sound, half-rolled and began a split-S at 1,500 feet. The split-S appeared to be a suicidal maneuver, but the MiG pilot pulled out along a dry river bed, blowing dust and small rocks in his wake. Once more the game was on as Risner, momentarily entranced by the enemy pilot's acrobatic show, took up the chase.

The MiG led them between the hangers of a Chinese airfield, then down the runway, Risner's wingman still hanging on and warning of heavy flak. Finally, the MiG crashed, taking with it the finest pilot Risner had ever seen. Then came the problem of getting home.

The wingman's fuel tank had been hit and was losing fuel rapidly. There was no chance he could make it back to base, but Cho Do Island did have a rescue unit. Acting with what had to be supreme self-confidence, Risner told his wingman to shut down his engine and stand by for a push.

Pushing a jet fighter with another jet fighter is not a maneuver pilots practice. In fact, it is doubtful anyone had ever tried it successfully before or since, but it worked that day. Despite the streaming hydraulic fluid that obscured his vision, Risner pushed the flamed-out F–86 to a point near Cho Do Island where the wingman bailed out. Unfortunately, although the bailout was successful, the pilot drowned when the wind caught his chute.

* * * * *

After 109 missions, Risner came home, this time determined to remain in the Air Force for a career he no longer viewed as irrelevant. The years after Korea began with a long tour at George Air Force Base near Apple Valley, California. Risner's squadron was equipped with F–100s, the first truly supersonic fighters, and had as a mission evaluating its very high-altitude air

Above: While assigned to George AFB, California, Maj. Risner evaluates high-altitude capabilties of the F-100 Super Sabre, the first truly supersonic fighter; *right*: Maj. Risner in F-100F "Spirit of St. Louis II," which he flies from New York to Paris, May 1957.

combat capabilities. It was a curious assignment in retrospect, for the F-100 was no great shakes above 30,000 feet, but the airplane was new in those days. On one of these missions, Risner zoom-climbed to 60,000 feet and simultaneously felt his jury-rigged pressure suit inflate to the limit. His face mask frosted over, he could not move his arms, and the constricting force of the pressure suit caused him to nearly lose consciousness. When he finally managed to regain control of the airplane, he was in intense pain. He was able to land, however, and an ambulance rushed him to the hospital, where the doctors discovered a slightly ruptured heart valve. In time the injury healed, and Risner was back on flying status again.

The following year he flew an F-100 from New York to Paris. This was the Charles Lindbergh Memorial Flight, and being chosen to make it was

315

a signal honor for the onetime pilot of the P–51 shrimp run to Brownville. At that point, with no wars in sight and lacking the college degree almost mandatory for high rank, Risner had reason to believe his career had reached its apex. There would be higher peaks to come, but only after some very low valleys.

A tour on the staff of the Commander in Chief, Pacific, was an instructional period for a man whose view of the military had been mainly through the windshield of a fighter airplane. The Pacific Command is headquartered at a Marine base—Camp H. M. Smith—on a green hill overlooking Pearl Harbor. While there is no law that stipulates the Commander in Chief, Pacific—or CINCPAC as he is called—will be an admiral, he has always been one, as surely as the Pope is chosen from the ranks of Catholic bishops. Other than the fact that they both wear a uniform in the service of Uncle Sam, there usually is little else in common between a junior fighter pilot and the admiral who serves as CINCPAC. This was particularly true in Risner's time, for CINCPAC was Adm. Harry D. Felt, a man who placed an extremely high value on the form, as well as the content, of wireless messages. Nothing reached the front office until it had been worked over and signed off by a long list of staff officers, the most senior coming last. The drafter of the message put his name at the bottom, next to the space reserved for the releasing officer. In Admiral Felt's time, the releasing officer was almost invariably himself.

In due course it became Risner's duty to draft a message of some importance. Since he had never written anything more involved than a squadron operations order, the assignment took on a certain significance, and he spent hours preparing his draft. As he trudged around the halls gathering the initials—the chops—of his endless superiors, he also saw his message heavily censored for extraneous language. When it finally reached CINCPAC, it was a marvel of brevity, all adjectives and conjunctions removed. The Admiral promptly sent the message back with a scrawled question and an order. "Who took out all the words? Put them back in." The feeling was not the same as the one he experienced when shooting down a MiG, but it gave Risner a pretty good glow nonetheless.

In the normal course of events, he escaped the CINCPAC staff with good marks from his Marine boss for a job well done. His orders read the 18th Fighter Wing at Kadena Air Base, Okinawa, and encompassed everything he could have hoped for: command of a squadron, F–105 airplanes to fly, and good living for his family, now grown to five boys.

Risner's squadron, on first acquaintance, was something of a disappointment—a mixed bag of pilots only a few of whom had much experience in the demanding business of fighter tactics. Since the F–105 was a big, demanding airplane itself, the new squadron commander faced a challenge. It is almost redundant to say the squadron came around in short order, a tightly knit, highly competitive outfit ready to take on anything and anyone.

The test came soon enough. Four years after the initiatives of President Kennedy to shore up the Diem regime in Saigon, the true nature of the war in Southeast Asia began to emerge. As the campaign against the ragtag Viet Cong began to succeed, the character of the opposition changed. Ho Chi Minh's regulars started down the trail through Laos in ever-increasing numbers. The war had clearly become one for Indochina, if not for all of Southeast Asia, rather than simply a counterinsurgency struggle in South Vietnam. In Ho's mind, it had been that kind of war all along.

An underlying factor had been the United States' position toward Laos. In the spring of 1961, President Kennedy had decided to try to neutralize Laos through compromise. Under this scheme, a cease-fire between the warring rightist and Communist factions was to be effected, and a coalition government, headed by a neutralist, Souvanna Phouma, was to keep Laos above the fray. The scheme was a failure from the beginning, although the United States clung to the fiction of a neutral Laos for most of the next four years.

F-105 Thunderchief diving on military target in North Vietnam.

During all this time, the North Vietnamese enjoyed a free, if rugged, journey to South Vietnam with troops and supplies. Finally, in 1964, the Communist Pathet Lao, abandoning the charade, withdrew from the coalition. Fighting resumed between the Lao factions, and it became plain to everyone, as it had been from the beginning to President Diem, that Laos was an integral part of South Vietnam's problem.

Nothing was simple in those days, least of all the Byzantine power structure through which American policy was administered. This was especially true in Laos, where the United States ambassador was not only the diplomatic chief of mission but the supreme factotum. In 1964, his name was William Sullivan—later to end his diplomatic career as our last ambassador to the court of the Shah of Iran—a bright, self-confident protégé of Averell Harriman who, in turn, had been the principal architect of the United States policy toward Laos. Sullivan decided that a bridge in the interior of Laos had become important to the Communist forces and, therefore, should be destroyed. He sent a message to the Commander in Chief Pacific, Adm. U.S.G. Sharp, requesting an air strike for that purpose.

Since bridges are hard things to hit with conventional bombs, the original estimates of airplanes needed for the job looked to an outraged Ambassador Sullivan like the start of World War III rather than the precise little operation he had in mind. The military then took a second look and decided a smaller effort might serve. Risner was ordered to lead eight airplanes to Da Nang in South Vietnam, with Ambassador Sullivan's bridge as the reason for the trip.

The air strike into the heretofore out-of-bounds Elephant Kingdom served as a lesson to Risner on the strange rules of this new war. When he and his flight reached the target, the bridge had already been destroyed. Risner spotted another bridge a few miles upstream, and not wishing to have wasted his time, he polished off that structure in two passes, firing Bullpup (GAM 83) missiles. On his return to base he discovered he had broken the rules. You struck only what the Ambassador to Laos said you would strike, and never mind the fact that it seemed illogical to leave the other bridge standing. So it was that a few weeks later, in February 1965, when he arrived with his squadron at Korat, Thailand, Risner understood the rules. It was war of a different sort.

*   *   *   *   *

Korat is located in central Thailand, a rural area north of Bangkok and thus out of the limelight. The Southeast Asia Treaty Organization had provided the United States with good reason to spend money for runways and other facilities at Korat; and Thailand, as a founding member of SEATO, had been more than willing to make Korat available for occasional USAF deployments. The arrival of the squadron from Okinawa, then, was more or less routine.

There was not much in the way of diversion at Korat. The nearby dusty town was a primitive place despite a sizable number of sleazy bars teeming with prostitutes with an awesome reputation for venereal disease. A more wholesome local attraction was the population of king cobras, perhaps the most dangerous and aggressive snake to be found anywhere in the world. The cool of the evening brought these creatures slithering out to bask on the taxiways. Together with scorpions, smaller cobras, various other tropical snakes, and the fearsome afternoon thunderstorms, life at Korat had a certain fascination. But for the pilots, the interest lay in the mission. Squadrons came to Korat to fly. This time, moreover, the flying would be different, real sorties instead of training missions within the borders of Thailand.

Risner's 67th Tactical Fighter Squadron, although high in esprit and confidence in their leader—after all, how many other squadrons had a jet fighter ace as a commander—was, nevertheless, low on experience. The first mission into North Vietnam was the baptism of fire for all but two or three of the 67th. As is always the case, the first missions in any war are dangerous ones: excitement, with accompanying breakdowns in air and radio discipline, invariably contribute to casualties that do not happen later on. This mission was no exception, and Risner saw three of his squadron go down. He came home after flying combat air patrol over his wingman until rescue arrived, low on fuel and with fourteen holes in his airplane, a pattern that was to continue.

As noted earlier, aggressiveness translates into risk, and risk means holes in one's airplane. The missions from Korat began to go routinely into North Vietnam, against an enemy now well prepared with flak guns and surface-to-air missiles, for the ever more predictable strikes of Rolling Thunder. At last the day came when Risner's luck ran out. His crippled F–105 just could not make the last two or three miles to the Bay of Tonkin and probable rescue. This time he was in the bag.

Low-altitude ejections are fast-moving affairs with little time left over for standard procedures like deploying survival gear. So, when Risner hit the ground, it was with forty-five pounds of equipment still tied on. He tumbled down the side of a dike, badly wrenching his knee in the process. When he had untangled himself and looked up, he was staring into the muzzle of a gun. For a moment, his own pistol in hand, he thought about a shoot-out,

319

something he had long ago decided upon if the unlikely happened and he found himself in the present fix. The North Vietnamese, a sensible man, motioned to Risner to look around. Guns were pointing at the downed pilot from every angle. The long night had begun.

His captors, on the whole, were reasonable enough, considering the fact that he was not only an enemy but one who had been terrifying the village only a few moments before while attacking the missile site. For the next hour Risner's squadron flew over the area, causing the villagers to tie him to a tree in a bamboo grove out of sight of the fighters. Offshore, he could hear the SA-16 circling, but this time rescue was plainly out of the question, and Risner wished his friends would go home.

In contrast to what was to come later, his treatment on the journey to Hanoi was surprisingly compassionate. A soldier, noting Risner's bare and bleeding feet, took off his sandals and gave them to the prisoner. A doctor came to treat his swollen knee, now exceedingly painful, and his guards fended off curious and occasionally hostile civilians. All things considered, it was not too discouraging an introduction to captivity.

The journey ended at Hoa Lo Prison, the infamous Hanoi Hilton, where he was dumped without ceremony into a filthy barred room and left to his thoughts. A few hours later the interrogation began, conducted by a man the POWs had already nicknamed "The Eagle." It was a reasonable sort of session, more or less in line with what Risner had learned in survival school. The next interrogator, however, "The Rabbit," gave a truer indication of what lay ahead. Risner, said The Rabbit, was not a prisoner of war but a criminal and would be treated as such. The Hanoi Hilton, it turned out, was not run according to the Geneva Convention.

Still, the first few days were not too bad. Risner made several tentative calls over the transom, established communication, and was able to find out who his companions were. News of the outside world was exchanged for news of prison life. At this point, the prospects were depressing but bearable. Besides, there was the shared feeling they would not be prisoners long. Mr. McNamara himself had predicted an end to the war by June 1966, and these men could tolerate anything for a year.

*   *   *   *   *

Rolling Thunder continued to send its signals, and with them, an increasing number of pilot hostages to North Vietnam. In addition to the Hanoi Hilton, now full, the Vietnamese had opened a series of makeshift prisons

320

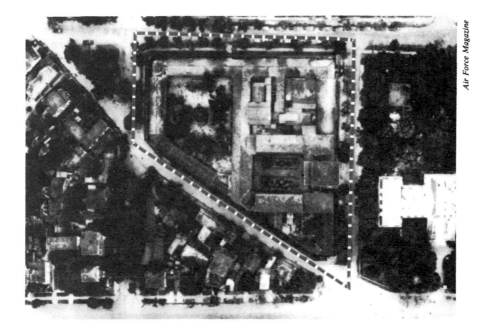

Air Force Magazine

The Hanoi Hilton, where Risner was imprisoned, shown here undamaged after bombing campaign of December 1972.

around the city. One, Briarpatch, in the hills west of Hanoi, was a primitive facility without lights or running water. The Zoo, in the center of town, had been a motel of sorts during the days of the French. In the Hanoi Hilton itself there were Heartbreak and New Guy Village, the latter becoming, in time, a dreaded place, for it was used principally for prisoners undergoing torture.

The effect of the increase in the number of prisons, together with the frequent transfer of prisoners from one location to another, was to make even more difficult the job the POWs had in creating a disciplined military organization. That they were able to do so remains one of the great tales of ingenuity and sheer guts.

Risner's reputation as a combat leader was secure the day he ejected over North Vietnam. His next challenge, however, that of leading his fellow prisoners, was to be the greatest test of his eventful life. He began by sending word through the covert communication system that he, Lt. Col. Risner, was now in charge. His next move was to tighten the communications net. Then he stepped out front by asking for a meeting with the North Vietnamese camp commander, up to this point, an unprecedented request. The purpose of the meeting was to demand better living conditions, to include more baths, better food, and outdoor exercise privileges. Having thus identified himself to the Vietnamese as the leader of the POWs, he was promptly marked a troublemaker and thus a candidate for persecution and harsh treatment.

Following this confrontation with his jailers, Risner circulated through the clandestine network a note in which he laid out a general policy for POW behavior. As luck would have it, a guard discovered the note and a thorough search of the cells turned up further evidence of the coalescing POW organization. A new and more brutal phase of Hanoi prison life began, one where any attempt to communicate risked severe punishment, and where solitary confinement in darkened cells, inedible food, and torture were to be the everyday rule.

Naturally enough, Risner, as the self-announced leader, was an early victim of this inquisition. When he refused to give any information beyond name, rank, and serial number, he was moved to the infamous section of the Hanoi Hilton known as New Guy Village and locked to a concrete slab. His diet for the next month was an occasional meal of bread and water. Still uncooperative, he was beaten and tortured with ropes, the Vietnamese version of the rack. Almost senseless with pain, he at last agreed to apologize, in writing, for bombing the Vietnamese people. The old dictum of name, rank, and serial number might have served well enough in the POW camps of World War II, but in Hanoi, it was just a way of getting your arms pulled out of their sockets. After that experience, Risner put out the word that it was possible to give a little now and then, but never without some sign that the statement on the tape had been made under duress.

It was during those years between 1965 and 1969—the truly bad ones—that the Vietnamese attempted to use the prisoners as tools in their psychological warfare campaign against the United States. There was the time, for instance, when Risner was selected to make a tape. If he refused, torture was to follow as a natural course. He chose, instead, to damage his voice, first by screaming and then, when that seemed futile, by gargling a mixture of water and lye-based soap. His voice thus altered, and his intonations curiously rearranged, he made the tape. Whatever the Vietnamese thought they had accomplished, it did not fool any of the prisoners.

There were, of course, other tapes of other kinds. One in particular, the tape of a speech against the war, made by George McGovern, was a favorite with the Vietnamese, who forced Risner to suffer through it, as he recalls, eight times. It was also difficult to bear the ceremonial visits to Hanoi by peace activists like Cora Weiss, Ramsey Clark, Jane Fonda, and Tom Hayden. These people came and went, to the great disillusionment of the men in prison.

During those terrible years the lot of the POWs grew steadily worse. Their constant companions were large and aggressive rats on the hunt for leftover scraps from the prisoners' scanty meals. Because of the filth in which they lived, the POWs were infected with worms, one more aggravation to men whose wounds and injuries had received little or no medical care. Conversation between prisoners was forbidden as a further step in the Vietnamese program of isolating the POWs from one another. Accordingly, they developed the tap code, an ingenious system in which letters of the alphabet were arranged in rows and identified by numbered taps. One way or another, with only the most fragmentary and clandestine instruction, they all learned the code. Tapping on the walls became the way of passing news, gossip, and above all, military orders, for the POW Wing took itself seriously. When security was at issue, they tapped out their messages in a more complicated code, even having one for Top Secret.

There were other ways of passing information: coughing in code, washing clothes in a tap rhythm, even walking with signaled foot stamps. This determination, and the developed ability to communicate, transformed the POWs from what could have become a bedraggled and self-pitying group of hostages into a disciplined military unit bearing up under a strain no similar group has experienced in modern history.

After 1969, the treatment of the POWs gradually improved, if only because of their increasing numbers. The U.S. raid on Son Tay had failed to release any prisoners, but it did have one immediate and welcome effect. Because the Vietnamese feared further raids, the POWs were concentrated in one section of the Hanoi prison. The morale of prisoners soared when they saw old friends, or met people they had known only through conversations tapped on the walls. With this new sense of unity and security came increased resistance to the Vietnamese. The POWs organized church services, entertainment, bridge tournaments—and retribution followed. One by one the ranking officers—John Flynn, Jim Stockdale, Dave Winn, Jerry Denton, Vern Liggon, Robbie Risner, George Coker, Harry Jenkins, Jim Mulligan, Herv Stockman, Jim Lamar, Jack Finley, Peter Schoffel—were pulled out and put in stocks or solitary confinement. At length, the senior officers were housed together in a separate section of the prison. It was all in vain, for the POWs had established themselves as a disciplined military unit.

Church services were a high point of the week, and Risner was a prime mover in those services. In the beginning, they were held more or less clandestinely, then, as time went on, openly. Without Bibles or any other religious supports, these tough men made up their own ecumenical services from the remembered bits of long ago.

At last, the end was in sight. There had been the B–52 "Christmas" bombings in December 1972 when the Paris negotiations broke down, a period of diversion for the POWs who saw their captors, for the first time, in obvious fear of American power. Then came the day of release. For Robbie Risner and his friends, it marked the end of a horrifying seven and a half years.

*   *   *   *   *

His return to civilization, after the first few weeks of euphoria, was not without its letdown. The nation's attitude toward the Vietnam War and the men who fought it was itself depressing. There were small celebrations here and there—the little Oklahoma town of Warr Acres gave Risner and his family a warm homecoming—and President Nixon had the POWs and their wives to dinner at the White House. But the country as a whole was indifferent to these heroes.

As was the case with many of these men who had been in virtual oblivion for so many years, there were other disquieting readjustments. Risner's marriage slowly failed in the year following his release. The break was an amicable one that allowed the couple to remain good friends who no longer shared the same interests. Later on, he remarried, this time to the widow of a USAF pilot who died in Vietnam.

After the excitement and turmoil of rejoining the world had died down, the Air Force put Risner back in the cockpit. At first, it was a tentative sort of thing, this retraining of a middle-aged pilot who had spent more than seven

Stepping off C–141 on return from Hanoi are Col. Robinson Risner (waving) and Navy Capt. James B. Stockdale (top right), both with military escorts.

years in the unhealthy environment of the Hanoi Hilton, but there was no need to worry. The old ace mastered the F-4 in short order and was soon leading his young classmates in all phases of fighter training. Next came command of an F-111 wing in New Mexico and a brigadier's star, and then, a last assignment at the Fighter Weapons' School in Nevada. The hero was finally home from the war, although, as it turned out, only to join in a new one, the war against drugs. Ross Perot, the computer magnate who had done so much for POW families, formed an organization called Texans' War Against Drugs, to combat the spread of drug use among the youth of Texas, and he asked Risner to head it. The former 67th Tactical Fighter Squadron Commander, former Senior Ranking Officer, 1st POW Wing, took the job in stride. It was a different sort of command, but the challenge was there, and that is all he had ever needed.

James Robinson Risner is, in retrospect, a peculiarly American hero, even to counting an American Indian among his ancestors. His beginnings were in the American tradition, for while log cabins had largely gone out of style when Risner came along, his family was almost archetypally Southwest United States, complete with a father who raised and traded horses. Risner is a product of small-town rural America, where basic virtues governed the way people lived. That early life gave him his sustaining belief in God. When things were at their worst, he recalled passages from the Bible, and prayer helped him through. When asked, it was with great satisfaction that he tapped the Twenty-Third Psalm through the wall to his neighbor.

Today, Risner looks back without bitterness on a war that cost him so much, secure in the feeling that he did his best. This feeling is common to the men who lived through the hell of that imprisonment, shot down in a conflict where there was no widespread public commitment to those who were called into service. The incentive to risk one's life under such circumstances was minimal in comparison to that of other wars when patriotism was in fashion. It is in this context that we must look on the collective behavior of those men in the Hanoi Hilton. They were well aware of the widespread national indifference and hostility to the war, and thus, to their part in it. New prisoners brought news of demonstrations back home, and worst of all, there were the visits of their own compatriots to Hanoi, as guests of their torturers. All the while, the brutal treatment went on: leg irons and solitary for minor infractions and far worse for such major crimes as attempted escape. It is strange, and something of a commentary on modern America, that the story of Air Force and Navy pilots in the Vietnam War has been largely hidden in the bathos of something called the Vietnam Syndrome.

No one has ever applied air power more accurately, and taken more risks in an attempt to make certain only military targets were hit, than did these airmen. Their skill and professionalism exceeded anything we have seen in

Col. Robinson Risner

the previous use of air power, with damage to Hanoi, for instance, slight if judged by World War II—or Beirut—standards. And then, when they were shot down, the dedication to country continued. The North Vietnamese were puzzled and somehow could not understand how these tough and disciplined men could have come from the same country as the antiwar activists.

Robbie Risner, as much as anyone, personifies these truly exceptional men. He was at the top of his fighter pilot profession with nothing more to prove, the first winner of the Air Force Cross. Given all he had been through, it would have been understandable if he had elected an honorable but less conspicuous role in prison. He chose, instead, to stick his neck out, just as he had always done.

Listening to him tell, in that calm, emotionless Western accent, the story of air combat in Korea, the hair-raising rescue in the Gulf of Tonkin, or the sad and painful Hanoi years, one is reminded of Gary Cooper or John Wayne. The difference, of course, is that this man really did all those things.

326

Sources

A major source is Robinson Risner's own book, *The Passing of the Night* (Random House, 1973). It was supplemented by interviews with Risner and other prisoners of war in North Vietnam, including Adm. James B. Stockdale, Brig. Gen. David Winn, and Col. Jon Reynolds.

The only comprehensive study of Air Force operations in the Korean War is Robert Frank Futrell, *The United States Air Force in Korea, 1950–1953* (Duell, Sloan and Pearce, 1961). Literature on the Vietnam War is voluminous. The best and most complete account of air operations is Gen. William W. Momyer, *Air Power in Three Wars* (Air University, Maxwell AFB, Alabama, 1978).

Observations on political aspects of the Southeast Asia conflict come largely from the author's personal experience as Commander of Thirteenth Air Force; member of Gen. Maxwell Taylor's group that surveyed the Vietnam situation for President Kennedy; Deputy Chief of Staff, Plans and Operations, Pacific Command; and U.S. Representative on NATO's Military Committee where the Vietnam War was under constant scrutiny, though the NATO allies were not participants.

Assessments of both military and political aspects of Vietnam and the POW tragedy appear in a number of articles by the author published in *Air Force Magazine* and other journals between 1973 and March 1983, as well as the annual Ira C. Eaker Distinguished Lecture on National Defense Policy, April 1982, published by the Air Force Academy.

Contributors

During World War II, DEWITT S. COPP served as an AAF Air Transport Command pilot in North Africa and the Middle East. Since the war, he has specialized as a book, film, and news writer, in military aviation and foreign affairs and has served as a correspondent in Europe, the Middle East, and Far East. Many of his eighteen books have been reprinted in Canada and Europe. He is winner of two book awards for Excellence and a Film Media Award. His two most recent books, *A Few Great Captains* and its sequel, *Forged in Fire*, were written under auspices of the Air Force Historical Foundation, published by Doubleday in 1980 and 1982, respectively, and received a Citation of Honor Award from the Air Force Association. After serving as Special Assistant to the Director of the federal agency, *Action*, he joined the staff of Voice of America as a writer-editor and subsequently tranferred to the United States Information Agency as Policy Officer on Soviet Disinformation.

JOHN L. FRISBEE is a retired Air Force colonel and command pilot whose assignments included head of the Air Force Academy History Department; Deputy Chief of Staff for Plans, 21st Air Force; and Special Assistant to the Air Force Vice Chief of Staff and to two Secretaries of the Air Force. From 1970 to 1980, he served successively as senior editor, executive editor, and editor of *Air Force Magazine*, published by the Air Force Association.

MURRAY GREEN served as a communications officer on an admiral's staff during World War II and participated in five major engagements in the Southwest Pacific theater. He transferred to the Air Force Reserve in 1950 and retired in 1976 as a colonel in intelligence. He also retired as an Air Force civilian employee after thirty-four years of service, including twenty-four in the Pentagon working for seven Secretaries of the Air Force, starting with Stuart Symington. He holds a doctorate in history from American University, has written frequently for military journals, and has contributed articles on air power to several encyclopedias and anthologies. In recent years, he has been working on a biography of General Henry H. Arnold.

COLONEL ALAN L. GROPMAN, USAF, Ret., is a principal analyst for the SYSCON Corporation of Washington, D.C. In his last active-duty assignment, he was Deputy Director of Air Force Plans for Planning Integration at Air Force Headquarters in Washington. He holds a doctorate in history from Tufts University and has been a member of the Air Force Academy history faculty, and Associate Dean of Faculty and Academic Programs at the National War College, Washington, D.C., where he also taught military history and strategy. Colonel Gropman was a master navigator with extensive combat experience in Southeast Asia. He is the author of many articles on military affairs and of two books: *The Air Force Integrates, 1945–1964*, and *Airpower and the Airlift Evacuation of Kham Duc*, published by The Office of Air Force History and Air University, respectively.

MAJOR GENERAL HAYWOOD S. HANSELL, JR., entered the Air Corps in 1928 after graduating from the Georgia Institute of Technology. Prior to World War II, he served as a bomber pilot; a member of the Pursuit Demonstration Team; instructor at the Air Corps Tactical School; Director of Strategic Air Intelligence in the Office of the Chief of the Air Corps; and Chief of the European Branch, Air War Plans Division, the Air Staff. During the war, General Hansell was Air Member of the Joint Strategic Committee, commanded Eighth Air Force bomber wings, served as Air Member of the Joint Plans Committee of the JCS, and commanded the XXI Bomber Command which launched the strategic air offensive against Japan from the Marianas Islands. He retired in 1946 but was recalled in 1951 to serve as Chief of the USAF Military Defense Assistance Program, then as Air Member of the Weapons Systems Evaluation Group's Review Board. Following his second retirement in 1955, he was a General Electric Company executive for twelve years. He is author of three books on strategic air warfare and of many articles on defense subjects.

LIEUTENANT COLONEL PAUL F. HENRY is Commander of the 335th Tactical Fighter Squadron, Seymour Johnson Air Force Base, North Carolina. The 335th "Chiefs" trace their history from RAF 121 Squadron, one of the three original American Eagle Squadrons of World War II. In 1967, he earned a Regular commission and a bachelor's degree in humanities from the U.S. Air Force Academy, where he won the Hall Nordhoff Trophy for achievement in English. Following pilot training, he flew 162 combat missions in Vietnam with the 315th Special Operations Wing. He earned a master's degree in English at the University of Connecticut and an M.Ed. from Auburn University, and has been a member of the Air Force Academy Department of English. His articles have appeared in several military and educational journals.

GENERAL T.R. MILTON is a 1940 graduate of the U.S. Military Academy. During World War II, he served as an Eighth Air Force B–17 pilot, Deputy Commander of the 91st Bomb Group, and Commander of the 384th Bomb Group. Postwar assignments included Chief of Staff of the Berlin Airlift task force; Executive Officer to the Secretary of the Air Force; Commander of Thirteenth Air Force; Deputy Chief of Staff for Plans, Pacific Command; Chief of Staff, Tactical Air Command; Comptroller of the Air Force; and U.S. Representative to the Military Committee of NATO. Since his retirement from the Air Force in 1974, he has been a regular contributor to *Air Force Magazine* and other defense-related journals, and a member of the Editorial Board of *Strategic Review.*

DONALD J. MROZEK is Professor of History at Kansas State University, and, from 1982 through 1984, Visiting Research Fellow at the Airpower Research Institute, Maxwell Air Force Base, Alabama. He received his doctorate in history at Rutgers University in 1972. Among his publications are articles on military history in several journals. He is coeditor of *A Guide to the Sources of U.S. Military History: Supplements I and II.* He also teaches and writes in the fields of American cultural history and the history of sport and leisure.

JACOB NEUFELD is Chief of the Air Staff History Branch of the Office of Air Force History. He holds bachelor's and master's degrees in history from New York University. From 1964 to 1966, he served in the Army Corps of Engineers as a company grade officer at Fort Campbell, Kentucky, and as an instructor at the Engineer School, Fort Belvoir, Virginia. Neufeld has been a historian with the Office of Air Force History since 1970 and served as Chief, Special Histories Branch, and the Editorial Branch. His official writing for the Air Force deals primarily with ballistic missile and space programs. He also has written monographs and special studies on jet engines and the development of the F–15 aircraft. In addition to contributing to many aerospace technical journals and reference volumes, he is co-author of *The Vietnam War, Air War Over Vietnam,* and *Life in the Rank and File.*

BRIGADIER GENERAL NOEL F. PARRISH retired from the Air Force in 1964. During World War II, he commanded Tuskegee Army Air Field, the only pilot training base for black cadets. After the war, he served as special assistant to two Air Force Chiefs of Staff, Generals Hoyt Vandenberg and Nathan Twining. Other assignments included Air Deputy of the NATO Defense College and Director of the Air University's Aerospace Studies Institute. After retiring from the Air Force, General Parrish earned a doctorate in history at Rice University and taught military history at Trinity

University, San Antonio, Texas, for ten years. He is the author of many articles on military affairs published in U.S. and foreign journals and of *Behind the Sheltering Bomb*, published by Arno Press in 1979. General Parrish died in April 1987.

Prior to his retirement from the Air Force in September 1983, COLONEL JOHN SCHLIGHT was Deputy Chief of the Office of Air Force History. A master navigator, Colonel Schlight flew in the Korean War and in Indochina during the French conflict with the Viet Minh in the early 1950s. Later assignments included a tour in Vietnam, duty as a member of the Air Force Academy Department of History, and Dean of Faculty and Academic Programs at the National War College. He holds a doctorate in medieval military history from Princeton University and is the author of two books on military history of the Middle Ages. He also has written extensively on Air Force operations in Vietnam. Colonel Schlight is presently Chief of the Southeast Asia Branch at the U.S. Army's Center of Military History.

COLONEL JOHN F. SHINER is a command pilot who holds a doctorate in military history from Ohio State University. After a tour of duty in Vietnam flying the C–123 in tactical airlift operati⁻ ıs, he served as a member of the Air Force Academy history faculty for ei₋ɴt years, and in 1981–82 was the acting department head. He next was assigned to the Directorate of Plans at Air Force Headquarters in Washington and is now Deputy Chief, Office of Air Force History. Colonel Shiner's articles on Air Force history have appeared in several journals. He was awarded the Moncado Prize for his 1978 article on the creation of the GHQ Air Force. His book, *Foulois and the Army Air Corps*, was published in 1983.

HERMAN S. WOLK is Chief, General Histories Branch, Office of Air Force History. He holds bachelor's and master's degrees from American International College, and studied at the Far Eastern and Russian Institute, University of Washington in 1958–59. He was a historian at Headquarters, Strategic Air Command from 1959 to 1966. He is the author of *Strategic Bombing: The American Experience*, and coauthor of *Evolution of the American Military Establishment Since World War II*. His book, *Planning and Organizing the Postwar Air Force, 1943–1947,* was published in 1984 by the Office of Air Force History. In 1974–75 Wolk was a member of the Office of the Secretary of Defense Special Project on the History of the Strategic Arms Competition.

Index

☆ U.S. GOVERNMENT PRINTING OFFICE: 2000-470-951

ISBN 0-16-048757-9